ROUTLEDGE LIBRARY EDITIONS:
DEVELOPMENT

THE ORIGINS OF ECONOMIC INEQUALITY BETWEEN NATIONS

THE ORIGINS OF ECONOMIC INEQUALITY BETWEEN NATIONS

A critique of Western theories on development and underdevelopment

CARLOS RAMIREZ-FARIA

Volume 110

Routledge
Taylor & Francis Group
LONDON AND NEW YORK

First published in 1991

This edition first published in 2011
by Routledge
2 Park Square, Milton Park, Abingdon, Oxon, OX14 4RN

Simultaneously published in the USA and Canada
by Routledge
605 Third Avenue, New York, NY 10017

Routledge is an imprint of the Taylor & Francis Group, an informa business

British Library Cataloguing in Publication Data
A catalogue record for this book is available from the British Library

ISBN 13: 978-0-415-58414-2 (hbk)(Set)
ISBN 13: 978-0-203-84035-1 (ebk)(Set)
ISBN 13: 978-0-415-60219-8 (hbk)(vol 110)
ISBN 13: 978-0-203-83533-3 (ebk)(vol 110)

Publisher's Note
The publisher has gone to great lengths to ensure the quality of this reprint but points out that some imperfections in the original copies may be apparent.

Disclaimer
The publisher has made every effort to trace copyright holders and welcomes correspondence from those they have been unable to contact.

The Origins of Economic Inequality between Nations

A critique of Western theories on development and underdevelopment

Carlos Ramirez-Faria

London
UNWIN HYMAN
Boston Sydney Wellington

Published by the Academic Division of
Unwin Hyman Ltd
15/17 Broadwick Street, London W1V 1FP, UK

Unwin Hyman Inc.
955 Massachusetts Avenue, Cambridge, MA 02139, USA

Allen & Unwin (Australia) Ltd
8 Napier Street, North Sydney, NSW 2060, Australia

Allen & Unwin (New Zealand) Ltd
in association with the Port Nicholson Press Ltd
Compusales Building, 75 Ghuznee Street, Wellington 1, New Zealand

First published in 1991

British Library Cataloguing in Publication Data

Ramirez-Faria, C.
Origins of economic inequality between nations : a critique of Western theories of development and underdevelopment
1. Economic development. Inequalities. Theories
I. Title
330.9001

ISBN 0-04-445842-8
ISBN 0-04-445843-6 pbk

Library of Congress Cataloging-in-Publication Data

Ramirez Faria, Carlos, 1936–
Origins of economic inequality between nations: a critique on Western theories of development and underdevelopment / Carlos Ramirez-Faria.
p. cm.
Includes bibliographical references and index.
ISBN 0-04-445842-8 : $49.95.
ISBN (invalid) 00444458436 (pbk.) : $18.95.
1. Economic development. 2. Income distribution.
3. Developing countries—Dependency on foreign countries.
I. Title.
HD75.R365 1990
338.9—dc20 90-12828
CIP

Typeset in 10 on 11 point Bembo

Contents

List of abbreviations

AMP	=	Asiatic mode of production
ECLA	=	Economic Commission for Latin America (CEPAL in Spanish)
GNP	=	Gross National Product
ILO	=	International Labour Organization
ISI	=	Import-substitution industrialization
LDC	=	Less developed country
MNC	=	Multinational corporation
MOP	=	Mode of production
NIC	=	Newly industrializing country
NIEO	=	New International Economic Order
OECD	=	Organization for Economic Cooperation and Development
OPEC	=	Organization of Petroleum Exporting Countries
UNO	=	United Nations Organization
UNCTAD	=	United Nations Conference for Trade and Development
US or USA	=	United States of America
USSR	=	Union of Soviet Socialist Republics

List of tables

Introduction

In different ways, the question most often asked today on contemporary events, usually admixed with deprecating mock-disbelief, seems to be: What is the world coming to? In this book, fortunately, we had only, or mainly, to deal with the past. However, the pace of change nowadays is such that the present, whatever that is, and indeed the past itself, are being continually subjected to scrutiny. What meaning – if any – can we still attach to previously proud Marxist theoretical and political structures? Is it even conceivable that it should be possible to rescue anything from the avalanche of change in Eastern Europe? And if the radical East–West divisions disappear, what is going to become of the apparently still subsisting 'Third World'?

Although we believe the wilder forecasts for the future contingent upon recent events will not be corroborated – Marxism, for instance, is probably far from dead – we feel on safer ground in simply expecting that, even if the future does seem to be having a signal influence today on the way people reason about current problems (think only of the high 'specific weight' of the debate on the greenhouse effect), the past will as usual have the final word on the way to approach most issues. One thing from the past that will not be easily expunged, is the disparity in economic development between nations. In other words, we still have many historical laps to go before the Third World, or the general bloc of the less developed countries (which is the only meaning we ascribe to 'Third World', and that mainly as a convenient designation), starts to crumble as a valid category, the way the Warsaw Pact or the Comecon are now unmistakably crumbling.

How important an issue the origins of international economic inequality is, or put in another way, how valid a case the theorists (and the politicians before and after them) of international economic inequality have made, is an altogether different question, and one we shall not consider at this point so as to preserve what little 'suspense' a work of this nature can have. However, we will not be revealing any secrets if we say at the start that the international *conditions* in which the problems of the economic inequality between nations are taken up, have changed drastically from what they were in the very recent past, when dependency theory, for example, was a matter of heated debate. In this respect, we have tried to relate scrupulously the evolution of ideas and their evolving historical context, and this tight relationship is what in the end validates the conclusion to which we arrive concerning the contemporary importance of the concept of interdependence.

In sum, the only unquestionable thing about change in the world today is change itself, which however is not deep or sweeping enough to begin to affect issues as significant as growing social inequities, environmental destruction, and stagnating or deteriorating underdevelopment; and all that we think we have a right to say about the future of the Third World in the present context is that, with the abatement of the passions that surrounded the clamour for redress and equality, it may now be time to get on with a realistic assessment of priorities for a world still sadly much too steeped in painful and often unnecessary inequalities.

The Origins of Economic Inequality between Nations

1 *Cultural relativism, Eurocentrism and Marx's Asiatic mode of production*

Perception of differences and Eurocentrism

Environment and despotism

During most of recorded history, humanity at any one time has been divided into a scattering of high cultures, which competed or warred on their frontiers or when probing the interstices between them by sea or by land, but which mostly kept to themselves in self-complacent if struggle-ridden isolation until the fifteenth century AD, when the overall pattern started to crack under the weight of European expansion. Nevertheless, up to the eighteenth century, Europe could not claim to be more than *primus inter pares* with a towering but subjective sense of its own superiority. This had changed dramatically by the middle of the nineteenth century: Europe by then could not only back its pretensions to superiority with a string of conquests stretching to the coast of China and the ramparts of Edo: it could and did arrogate to itself the condition of being the civilization *par excellence*. But for the ages before this happened, intercultural comparabilities seemed to overbear the relative advantages of any individual culture, and this led in the West to the relative prevalence of the perception of cultural differences and to a common general attitude of cultural relativism. It could be said then of *hochkulturen* in relation to each other that where there are no clear victors, there can hardly be loud boasting.

To explain the perceived differences, there arose in Classical Greece the environmental or climatic hypothesis, which obtained an ample predominance in the West until the advent of naked, self-justifying Eurocentrism, that is, the idea of the exceptionality and absolute superiority of Western civilization. The general environmental hypothesis traces social behaviour patterns and modes of thinking to the physical conditions in which people live, especially climate, soil and geography. A further, subordinate extension of this proposition contemplates the influence of the stars on human behaviour and constitutes the basic principle of astrology, which, however, is a mostly discredited branch of the theory. From this general point of view, the effects of the environment are pervasive: they extend to physical, intellectual and moral qualities, and, through this, affect politics, society and history. Environmental thinking of this sort is both materialistic and fatalistic, for it is grounded on the efficacy of the palpable: given one sort of climate, you obtain certain precise moral qualities, although there exists some ambiguity as to whether climate imprints them indelibly or coaxes them out from people circumstantially.

Again, no human community can escape the impact of its milieu and people are collectively determined by it, yet, for one thing, physical circumstances do not entirely cancel out individual free will, thus making moral judgement possible, and, for another, within the purview of this theory, it is often possible to modify that impact through wise choice in legislating. Although environmental theory stems from the historical occurrence of intercultural contacts and therefore is probably polygenetic, self-perpetuating and self-reinforcing, it is also true that the strands of the theory that classical Greece first spun and wove together have been influential, sometimes decisively, throughout the intellectual history of the West. In the writings of Montesquieu can be found both the most intricately deterministic statement of the environmental hypothesis, involving theorized effects of climate on human physiology (an idea that Montesquieu borrowed from the early eighteenth-century English writer J. Arbuthnot) and its most forthright limitation through the agency of human design, although it is not humanity freely shaping and modelling itself but observing and using the effects of the environment to its own ends. Human beings cannot, in his view, make themselves. They can, however, legislate for their own good against the vices that nature cossets in them.

Perception of differences, however, was in no way incompatible with what for lack of a better designation can be called 'normal ethnocentricity' – the collective self-esteem which is part and parcel of every culture – and if the Greeks, despite their vulnerability in face of their neighbouring rivals, never renounced their claims to superiority, it is hardly surprising that this was also a constant parallel theme to perception of differences in Western civilization. In fact, the Western perception of differences emerges over a background cacophony of blasting and blustering only because of the clarity of its timbre and the force of its logic. If the theory of environmental determinism can be said to be the ideal instantiation of pre-nineteenth century Western perceptions of cultural differences and cultural relativism, the concomitant and associated idea of political despotism probably best manifests the tendency towards forthright Western ethnocentricity. It was also Montesquieu who established the classical connection between the two with his speculations on the origins of despotism in the central Asian steppes, a concept so beguiling that the contemporary British economic historian E. L. Jones has made it the core of his own disquisitions on the origins of inter-cultural inequality, but environment and despotism are really independent intellectual strands. The influential testimony on Mughal India by the seventeenth-century French physician and traveller, F. Bernier, correlated despotism and the absence of legal property rights. In *The Wealth of Nations* (1776), Adam Smith emphasized instead the connection between Asiatic governments and the maintenance of public, specifically hydraulic, works for the benefit of agriculture. By then, all the elements were in place for an enquiry into the origins of the West's economic advance over all the other cultures, once the evidence for this happening had become manifest and indisputable (Table 1.1). But before any serious work on the subject could proceed, the West itself went through a prolonged intellectual phase of hubris and intense self-admiration.[1]

Table 1.1 Major Western historical sources for the definition of Oriental despotism.

State property of land	B3, M2
Lack of juridical restraint	B1, B3, M2
Religious substitution for law	M2
Absence of hereditary nobility	M1, B2, M2
Servile social equality	M2, H
Isolated village communities	H
Public hydraulic works	S, M2
Torrid climatic environment	M2, M3
Historical immutability	M2, H, M3

Key: B1 = J. Bodin; B2 = Francis Bacon; B3 = F. Bernier; H = Hegel; M1 = Machiavelli; M2 = Montesquieu; M3 = J. Mill; S = Adam Smith

Source: P. Anderson, *The Lineages of the Absolutist State*, London 1974 (p. 472).

Despite the often explicit but by no means unanimous pre-nineteenth-century Western denunciation of Oriental or Asian despotism as a form of governance, despotism itself did not necessarily connote weakness and, in reality, despotic empires such as the Ottoman were not up for easy grabs by Europe even at the start of the nineteenth century. By then, however, India had succumbed to British power and James Mill's notorious *History of British India* (1816), in which Indian backwardness is confidently related to the deficiencies of its legal practices, manifested an assertive tone of absolute contempt. The idea that India was afflicted by both lawlessness and despotic excess had been advanced already by Bernier, but in the pen of the British historian this perception is besmirched by vitriol and it stands as a monumental testimony not to its intrinsic scholarly significance but to the historical circumstances in which it was written. What can be said unequivocally is that when Mill wrote on India the world balance of strength had been altered radically in favour of Europe and the case for Eurocentrism was in the way of obtaining a plea of *nolo contendere* from any rival outlook in the West on non-Western cultures. It is not unfair to say that the change from perception of differences to outright Eurocentrism was gradual, determined by events that seemed to occur in slow motion, but that, if the kernel of Eurocentrism was embedded in the nebulous start of the process, the historical events that gave it definite sanction were probably lagging behind the European perception of its own superiority. By the time of the Opium Wars and probably long before them, the change to the unchallengeable Eurocentric vision had already been accomplished. In Goethe and Hegel, in whom Eurocentrism is perhaps less ordinary and less contemptuous than in Mill, this attitude has the disheartening plangency of a curtailment of reason and yet it was as unavoidable as doom. The eighteenth century consecrated the triumph of Eurocentrism with the accumulated evidence of centuries of European travels, commerce, exploitation and conquest. The nineteenth century added on the inflexion of self-righteousness and disdain. But what exactly is Eurocentrism?

Racism and social Darwinism

The combination of Western ethnocentricity and Western material advantages over other cultures – expressed in economic, military, and political terms – engendered the cultural attitude that is known as Eurocentrism. In one sense, Eurocentrism is a circular and self-justifying affirmation of absolute cultural superiority. It has no other foundation than strength and the 'rights' of conquest. In another sense, however, it is grounded on two signal intellectual manifestations of nineteenth-century Western thought: racism and social Darwinism, both again founded in part on the evidence of Western progress and Western expansionism, but with at least the semblance of rational justification. In this particular sense, Eurocentrism would qualify as a legitimate theory on the origins of intercultural and international inequalities, if it were not for its implicit proviso that inequality, or some relativistic cultural definition of equality, is simply inconceivable, and where there is nothing to explain there can hardly subsist the need to explain. Finally, and perhaps most significantly over the long-haul, Eurocentrism embodies the universal creed of modernization and material progress. But this perception is something that the world has come to accept as gradually the more invidious aspects of Eurocentrism have fallen by the wayside of history.

Racism offers at least two handholds for analysis, although the subject is admittedly too complex for facile summarization. There is racist thinking, which is a reflexive and patterned way of reacting to ordinary social relations, events and processes. It can be found in association with normal ethnocentricity, and it is probable that there has never existed a culture that has not indulged in racist thinking of one form or another. Western racial thinking, which derived a great deal of its strength and influence from slavery and slave trafficking, spread on the back of Western world hegemony and Western conquest, and thus became a force that far transcended the bounds of Western civilization. Racial thought and racial discrimination in the West – excluding, of course, certain notorious and isolated instances – no longer count with legal or overt social sanctions, and although by no stretch of the imagination can they be said to have disappeared, at least they are no longer as respectable as they once were. Doctrinaire racism, which for the sake of brevity can be identified with pseudo-scientific theories and world-historical interpretations that flourished in the nineteenth century and survived in etiolated or aberrant forms into the twentieth century, crumbled from the lack of solid scientific foundations and from the revulsion of humankind at the excesses that it nurtured and fostered.

Social Darwinism was perhaps marginally less intellectually inviable than racism, although the indefeasible symbiosis between them virtually assured that it could not prosper or even subsist without racism. To put it in a nutshell, and as G. Lichtheim expressed it, social Darwinism is the proposition that the weak deserve their fate. It is founded on the ideas of the pervasiveness of struggle and of the survival of the best and fittest. It was a going proposition before the irruption of Darwin's biological theories, but it gained considerable momentum from them, principally from their adaptation to social theory by Herbert Spencer although not insignificantly from Darwin's own speculations on the ancestry of humanity. Social Darwinism developed two distinct branches: a social branch, which had a conservative tinge and became very influential with the elaboration of the theory of eugenics by F. Galton and K. Pearson, and an international branch, which was almost spontaneously incorporated into imperialist theory and doctrine. In considering the relevance of racism and social Darwinism to Eurocentrism, it is not inaccurate or unreasonable to posit that if racism was the invariant motif throughout the nineteenth century in all manifestations involving intercultural and international relations, then social Darwinism provided the intellectual mechanics or dialectics whereby racism was employed to proclaim Western superiority. Unlike racism, which had a deep anchorage in cultural prejudice, not to speak of human psychology, social Darwinism died an almost instant death in the indecisive and self-destructive carnage of the First World War.[2]

As can be gathered from our reference to James Mill, the prevalence of Eurocentrism concurrent with Western world hegemony did not signal the demise of the theories that had been used in more relativistic times to explain cultural differences, but there were important changes. What in Montesquieu and many other authors had been a theory on environmental influence in a nineteenth-century writer and traveller such as E. W. Lane, had become an intellectual reflex to categorize backwardness. The consciousness of the inferiority of non-Western cultures was just as automatic a response, and it overshadowed the importance of environment as a cultural determinant. The superiority of Western civilization, which was considered to be the result of more than sheer materialism, stood out so clearly that mere climate could hardly explain it; and when the environment did come up as a significant part of theory, it had a very definite discriminatory rather than explanatory function.[3] Apart from its inherent inconsistencies and logical failures, which were there, of course, before the nineteenth century, climatic theory ultimately had reached the end of its useful life in a predominantly Eurocentric context. It sounded superfluous when speculations revolved around the loci of race and social Darwinism, *mission civilisatrice* and manifest destiny. However, the environmental hypothesis was too powerful to disappear altogether, and come back it did before long. It returned in a challenge/response version in a world historical context, rather than in the vague geographic mould it was cast into formerly owing to the limited scope of knowledge. And especially it returned in the developmentalist post-1945 awareness that unequal economic development had somehow to do with the differences between the torrid and the temperate latitudes.

The qualification of inferiority implied in the concept of Asiatic despotism did not necessarily indicate hopeless or eternal stagnation, and it was in this spirit that John Stuart Mill wrote in 1859 that despotism was a justifiable form of governance if in the end it dragged a society out of barbarism. This was consistent with the interpretation that his father, James Mill, put on Indian history and society, and it was part of the utilitarian programme for the reformation and progress of India. It was on a vision of despotism not unlike this one that Karl Marx and Friedrich Engels founded their theoretical explanation of non-Western economic backwardness, which was the most rational and fecund nineteenth-century elaboration of this type. Although imbued with an outspokenly Eurocentric outlook, Marx and Engels were also sincerely and passionately partisans of the idea of human equality. In less guarded moments, Marx occasionally indulged in racial and cultural slurs – and Engels once at least in print – but they were never guilty of the catalogues of insults and derogations that in their times apologists of colonialism were wont to prepare about non-European nations and peoples. Marx's Eurocentrism had strictly to do with the fact that the objects of his research and observation were European history and European society. On the other hand, Marx never lost an opportunity to castigate colonialism and to express his support and admiration for nations who resisted European encroachment. Despite his belief that Europe had achieved a superior stage of economic development, he had no patience with all the cant about its civilizing function and its moral and religious duties. And in the final balance of his work, he could even be ambiguous about the universal validity of the western European historical model of socio-economic development.[4]

The Asiatic mode of production

An asynchronous blending of disparate outlooks and ideas

Between Marx and Engels there arose in the 1850s the rudiments of a theory to explain why Asia never produced capitalism and why it seemed to lag so pathetically behind Europe in economic achievement. Marx, in particular, was influenced in his attitude towards India by Hegel's dour Eurocentrism. In a crucial interchange of letters, Marx suggested to Engels the idea, which he had culled from Bernier, that economic initiative in India had been stifled by the absence of legal private property, and Engels replied by suggesting that the right of private ownership might have been surrendered in exchange for the state's supreme role as builder and administrator of waterworks for agriculture, which were vital in climates of unreliable hydrography. With these notions, all of which pre-dated the nineteenth century, Marx outlined what he termed the Asiatic mode of production (AMP) and incorporated this concept into various versions of his theory on historical and socioeconomic stages.

There does not exist one consistent or canonical definition of the Marxist AMP, but in general it can be said that it is predicated on a blending of the ideas of environmental determinism and of Oriental depotism, and that it manifested itself ideally in the British colonialist perception of Indian society as composed principally of myriad self-sufficient and immutable village communities, in which the collective or communal ownership of land was paramount and over which all-powerful monarchs exercised absolute bureaucratic sway and appropriated by force the totality of potentially reproducible surplus, the *sine qua non* of economic progress. The AMP was thus a construct specifically devised to give a rational and materialist explanation for the lack of capitalist development in Asia, due to the absence of individual enterprise in the void created by precarious or non-existent private ownership. If from nowhere else, you could derive from this sequence of ideas that Marx and Engels considered that capitalism was an engine of historical progress and that its functioning depended on private initiative. Marx's and Engels' use of notions from the time of perception of differences in a rigorously and justifiably Eurocentric context resulted in the first objective, non-parochial, non-superioristic attempt to build a theory on the origins of economic inequality among cultures. The asynchronous blending of disparate outlook and concepts was not, however, the only potentially conflictual aspect of this elaboration, and the AMP was destined to become a notorious bone of contention among future Marxists. Its formulators themselves never felt totally comfortable with it and it is widely thought that they had a change of heart about it.[5]

The nub of the conflict had to do with the dynamic conception of history that Marx had taken from Hegel and modified to suit his materialist philosophy. Hegel believed that ideas ruled matter;

Marx, that material needs and conflicts determined events; both accepted that history was motion and change, and this was of the essence, even more so in Marx than in Hegel. In the realm of ideas, immobility was conceivable and, therefore, Hegel could claim that Asian societies were without history, without progress. The only negation of this proposition that he could have feared would have had to come from the facts, and the facts were amenable, docile, for they spelt out one thing and one thing alone: European progress and European supremacy in the face of Asiatic stagnation and irrationality. But a materialist, committed as he must be to equality of causes and laws, could hardly accept immobility as a valid universal historical principle, and that in effect was what Marx was doing in postulating, with Engels' connivance, an immutable, time-heavy and politically infantile AMP.[6]

I. Habib has countered *pour l'honneur* of Marxism one of the most controversial and damaging implications of the AMP: that the Indian economy before British colonial rule was immobile. His refutation is based on Marx's perceptions of Indian society and on his own researches into Mughal economic history. It also keeps strictly to Marxist methodological assumptions on socio-historical analysis. Habib does not pretend to demonstrate that pre-colonial Indian society was advancing towards capitalism, but he does try to show that it was dynamic rather than static in that it had experienced changes in its socio-economic organization before the imposition of British political supremacy. Elsewhere, he espoused the thesis, convincingly propounded also by other Marxists, that Marx evolved from his Eurocentric perspective of the 1850s towards a stance of anti-colonialism and of rejection of the unqualified idea that the capitalist destruction of pre-capitalist agrarian structures was necessary and inevitable. This last attitude belongs to a phase towards the end of Marx's life during which he was influenced by Russian Narodnist ideas, although it cannot be affirmed unreservedly that Marx accepted those ideas as being more than specifically applicable to social conditions in Russia.[7] There are, however, other bones to be picked in the theory of the AMP.

Modes of production and historical stages

In the corpus of Marxist theory, mode of production is a complex analytical tool built on the concepts of relations of production, means of production and forces of production. In any given socio-historical situation, the relations of production determine the ownership of the means of production, and consequently, who benefits from the surplus value produced by labour power: that is, the effort expended on production over and above the effort and time required to create the means necessary for the reproduction of the labour power. The forces of production refer to the organizational and technological means applied to the process of production and, as such, they serve both to characterize the process of production under any specific mode of production (MOP) and to create the conditions for change from one MOP to another. In the capitalist MOP, which is the Marxist paradigm for the definition of the general concept, a tiny minority of capitalists own the means of production – involving such forces of production as the concentration of workers in factories and the mechanization of the productive process – and thus appropriate surplus value from the labour power of workers, which, measured in time, is the final source of all the value incorporated into commodities for exchange. When we consider the theories on imperialism elaborated by R. Luxemburg and V. I. Lenin, we shall see more on how, in Marx's view, the capitalist MOP evolved within itself from the operation of the forces of production inside the rigid mould of capitalist relations of production, but our concern here is with the Marxist use of the concept of MOP in a historico-analytic context.

According to Marxist doctrine, capitalism is the last of the antagonistic MOPs in the sense that, from the contradictions inherent in its functioning, the only possible issue is the social ownership of the means of production, but capitalism itself had emerged, by the same process of change through the tug of economic contradictions, from another, less efficient MOP. In other words, the Marxist vision of history was informed by a succession of MOPs in time, each of which constituted a distinct historical stage. The concept of historical stages came to Marx via Hegel, though Hegel did not invent it himself. The first Marxist elaboration of the theory of stages appears in *The German Ideology*, co-authored by Marx and Engels in 1846, and it is almost identical to the prototypical Marxist historical model in Engels' *Anti-Duhring* (1878), a work renowned for the clarity of its exposition of the Marxist materialist philosophy, of which it is virtually the pontifical source as Engels claimed that Marx gave it his approbation and no one has so far seriously disputed Engels' assertion. The same general formulation also corresponds to the outline mentioned in the *Communist Manifesto* (1848) and, as it is not contradicted by any statement in the Marxist canon, it can rightfully be considered to be the basic scheme of history advanced by Marx and Engels. In it the stages in the evolution of society appear in this order: community, antiquity, feudalism, bourgeois society. The source both for the Marx/Engels theory on the origins of economic backwardness, i.e. the concept of the AMP, and for one of the most heatedly debated aspects of the theory of stages is that, between 1848 and 1876, and especially in Marx's *Grundrisse* (originally written in 1857/8) and in the *Preface to a Critique of Political Economy* (1859), Marx initiated the series of socio-historical stages with the category of the AMP. To complicate the issue even further, in the first volume of *Capital* (1867), although he emphasized the importance in India of autonomous village communities in lieu of the political despotism idea, he still retained by implication the concept of AMP. By the time of *Anti-Duhring*, Engels, under the influence of L. H. Morgan's evolutionary anthropological ideas and presumably with Marx's assent, had dropped the concept of AMP and had gone back to the more general idea of communal property, with the observation that this social form, for environmental or other causes, could prolong itself indefinitely in time (Table 1.2). Engels'

Table 1.2 The evolving Marx/Engels presentation of the stages in the evolution of human society.

	1845–1846[1]		1848[2]		1859[3]
1	Tribal Societies	1	Pre-history	1	AMP
2	Antiquity	2	Antiquity	2	Antiquity
3	Feudalism	3	Feudalism	3	Feudalism
4	Bourgeois society	4	Bourgeois society	4	Bourgeois society
	1878[4]		**1884[5]**		**Corresponding MOP for all outlines**
1	Community property	1	Savage state	1	Communal property
2	Antiquity	2	Civilization	2	Slavery
3	Feudalism	3	Civilization	3	Serfdom
4	Bourgeois society	4	Civilization	4	Wage labour

References: 1 *German Ideology* (Marx/Engels)
2 *Communist Manifesto* (Marx/Engels)
3 *Preface to a Critique of Political Economy* (Marx)
4 *Anti-Duhring* (Engels)
5 *Origins of the Family, Private Property and the State* (Engels)

Source: M. Molnar, *Marx et Engels et la politique internationale*, Paris, 1975, p. 233.

tardy rectification notwithstanding, there was enough combustible material in all of this to fuel the prolonged controversy that in time ensued.[8]

The different formulations by Marx and Engels of a materialist theory of historical stages has led to different contentious interpretations. A dogmatic unilinealist version of Marxism would have it that capitalism was preceded (and would always be preceded in pre-capitalist societies) by the feudal mode of production, and feudalism by an MOP based on slavery, and slavery by a still more primitive MOP characterized by the communal ownership of productive property. This is the orthogenetic view adopted quasi-officially by Soviet historians in a 1931 Leningrad ideological discussion that rejected the thesis of the AMP for what some see as reasons of political strategy, concretely, the Soviet pursuit of communist alliances with 'progressive' nationalist forces in less developed countries. At another extreme a multilineal reading of Marx (and in this case mainly of Marx) holds that it is not the order of succession of stages that matters as much as the formal sequence of a variety of possible MOPs in a dynamic historical context. This interpretation has been proposed by E. Hobsbawm, who, however, coincided with Soviet orthodoxy in the rejection of the AMP as a viable socio-historical category. In between these two extremes the consensual exegesis of the Marxist canon seems to be that since the Marxist theory of stages embodying successive MOPs was exclusively based on the interpretation of European economic history, it is principally, and barely not exclusively, valid for the socio-economic analysis of European history, and furthermore, that of all of the stages proposed by Marx and Engels, the only ones that can be placed in a necessary successive chronological order are feudalism and capitalism, and always in strict reference to the history of Western Europe. A general description of this interpretation can be found in P. Anderson, G. Lichtheim, and others. On the whole it seems to owe as much to contemporary historical research as to direct Marxist textual sources.[9]

Implications and critiques of the AMP

If the fundamental Marxist idea of a succession of different MOPs as the key to the interpretation of universal history has been whittled down to its bare bones, it was only to be expected that the concept of AMP, about which Marx and Engels had such strong latter-day misgivings, should have been cut to shreds by the same and other interpreters of Marx's thinking. The broadest possible refutation of the AMP is implicit in Hobsbawm's rejection of unilinearity on the colourable assumption that 'Marxism has always held the view that all peoples of whatever race or historical background, are equally capable of all the achievements of modern civilization once they are free to pursue them'. On this premiss, also shared by Lichtheim, who characterized Oriental despotism, erroneously it would seem, as 'theocratic monarchies', economic retardation had more to do with colonialism than with any endogenous feature of Asian societies. This is reinforced by Hobsbawm's categoric belief in the anti-colonialist Marx, a view which he expressed in this manner: 'It seems probable that Marx, who had earlier welcomed the impact of Western capitalism as an inhuman but historically progressive force on the stagnant pre-capitalist economies, found himself increasingly appalled by its inhumanity.' Admittedly, Hobsbawm's specific pronouncement could be subjected to a less radical, less anti-imperialist interpretation, but in the context of his wider historical views, in which colonialist exploitation contributed to the industrial breakthrough in England and the Industrial Revolution was the fulcrum of the division between the developed and the underdeveloped nations, it seems to discount the likelihood of Marx's belief in what Hobsbawm describes as a theory of 'Asiatic exceptionalism', although, strictly speaking, the AMP would seem to be 'exceptionalist' only in the absence of its basis on environmental determinism. Hobsbawm's fellow Marxist P. Anderson finds that the AMP, which he describes as a 'residual category', is not a sufficiently calibrated instrument of analysis, so that 'a very great deal of further historical research is necessary before any true scientific conclusions can be drawn from the variant paths of non-European development'.[10] Hobsbawm and Anderson would probably agree with Habib's critique of the thesis of Asiatic immutability. This point of view was endorsed also in F. Braudel's polymathic researches into the nature and evolution of capitalism.

There exist much more intricate refutations of the AMP. B. Hindess and P. Q. Hirst analysed it, as they claim, within the conceptual universe of MOP itself. This meant, according to the rules laid down in their scrutiny, that no touchstone other than the definition of mode of production was applicable, not even the evidence of history. They found that the AMP as conventionally defined did not exist because 'the appropriation of surplus labour by the mechanism of the tax/rent cannot define a set of relations of production'. M. Rodinson based his critique on the distinction between MOP and socio-economic formation. The latter is the result of the integration of the economic base – the essential concretion of mode of production in any given social situation – and the socio-political superstructure. The only MOP which in Rodinson's view actually engenders a superstructure proper to itself is the capitalist MOP. All the other MOPs can function with a variety of different superstructures, and that includes so-called feudalism, which Rodinson called an MOP based on serfdom, hence not exclusively defined by its European social structures. Marx's AMP was based on the idea of communal or village property, and Rodinson considered this a universal predicate of any human group at an early stage of technological and social development. Furthermore, the AMP, which, always according to Rodinson, can best be described as 'primitive communal mode of production', is compatible with institutions other than those (Oriental despotism) that Marx conceived in combination with it, so there again AMP lacked precision and specificity. In an exhaustive study of the international ideas and positions of Marx and Engels, M. Molnar found that the AMP is but a preamble to the vast subject matter of pre-capitalist formations, which Marx and Engels did not sufficiently clarify because their acquaintance with them was mainly haphazard. From these inklings to a fully formed theory, Molnar considered that there was 'a large bound', which he certainly would not dare attempt. Molnar's main point, however, was that the Marx/Engels outlook was totally Eurocentric, from which he argued that Marx and Engels considered European world expansion a necessary part of the capitalist 'civilizing' integration of the world.[11]

A haven in the maelstrom of Eurocentrism

If then Marx and Engels themselves, and the Soviets at a time when the Soviet word still carried the greatest authority among Marxists, disallowed the idea of the AMP, which subsequently has been demolished by specialists in different branches of Marxism, what is left, if anything, of the Marxist theory of the long-term historical origins of economic inequality among nations? When inequality is alluded to here, it is the inequality of underdevelopment. The concept of underdevelopment, in the sense of a condition that implies human equality but is refractory to a process of self-sustaining economic development, is of recent origin. It did not exist at all in nineteenth-century Western intellectual history, which oscillated from the prevailing acceptance of extreme Eurocentric racial and cultural prejudices to the particular but implicit Marxist idea that the evolution towards capitalist development was inevitable once the dirty work of the colonialist destruction of traditional social formations had been achieved. The complicated contemporary diagnoses and issues of underdevelopment were unknown to Marx and Engels – perhaps even, in some respect, inconceivable to them – and, in fact, the economic stagnation of Asian societies commanded their interest only sporadically and briefly. They were committed to universal egalitarian ideals and therefore they spontaneously came up against the problem of Indian economic backwardness in comparison with Europe. The common Eurocentric explanation of inequality was a naked affirmation of superiority on all grounds, that is, it amounted to saying that Europeans were superior because they were.

Marx and Engels accepted Europe's material and even intellectual superiority, but this did not square with their evolutive, orthogenic concept of history. In order to explain this paradox, they had recourse to environmental theory in the broad sense that climate conditions and determines social responses, and to the concept of an Asiatic or Oriental despotism superimposed on self-sufficient, unchanging village communities. To this socio-economic formation in the Rodinson sense, Marx and Engels gave the name of AMP, a category which they later, and definitively it would seem, subsumed under the more general heading of communal or ancient mode of production. Subsequently, critics have upheld the latter attitude by denuding the AMP of any singularity or usefulness. In addition to trying to find a rational explanation for inter-cultural economic inequality, Marx and Engels condemned the brutal side of colonialism in no uncertain terms, recognized its violent destructive nature, and encouraged nationalist resistance to it. They could not go any further given the perspectival limitations of their times, from which they could not escape altogether.

It must be admitted that their rejection of the AMP did leave a gap in Marxist socio-historical analysis, but it is a gap that we perceive with the benefit of hindsight. Their concern was not inequality but the process of history as they saw it, into which it is not easy to insert the existence of an underdeveloped Third World. On the other hand, Marx and Engels would probably have been at a loss to explain the appearance and co-existence of social-welfare conditions in one part of the capitalist world with the simultaneous condition of sub-exploitation of the greater portion of that world, a paradox that clashes with the Marxist idea of forward, uniformizing historical movement. Any number of dialectical constructs and inferences could be derived from these two blind spots in Marxism.

One important neo-Marxist alternative, favoured by critics of the AMP, is that capitalist development fed on colonialist and neo-colonialist exploitation and is therefore responsible for today's underdevelopment. But given the unresolved ambiguities of their varying criteria in judging colonialism, Marx and Engels did not propose this theoretical solution and they could hardly have adumbrated the contemporary theory of 'underdeveloping' economic imperialism. Their statements on the relations of the industrialized nations with the rest of the world run the gamut from outright condemnation to unstinted encouragement of colonialism, but the condemnation is usually based on humanitarian or moral grounds and their scattered negative judgements – with which today's dependency theorists tend to make mountainous systems – must be considered against the fact that in Marx's explicitly systematic writings nothing really gainsays the view that capitalism is an agent of universal historical progress whose contradictions eventually lead towards general misery, internal conflict and collapse. On the question of the origins of international economic inequality all that can be said, in sum, is that Marx and Engels covered the territory superficially and in haste, because it was not central to their studies, and that if in the end they did not elaborate a finished theory, they at least proposed the rudiments of a rational explanation of the origins of international economic inequality and this makes them a safe haven in the maelstrom of rampant Eurocentrism.

Soviet debate on the AMP

The relative fragility of AMP theory, which can be traced to the difficulties in articulating it with Marx's fundamental perception of historical movement as expressed by him and as interpreted by Marxist expositors, does not invalidate the fact that Marx did contemplate it and that it had an undeniable if blunt-edged socio-historical foundation in the economic world hegemony of Europe. Therefore, it is not surprising that it retained a certain unpretentious prestige with Marxists even during Engels' lifetime. Plekhanov and Lenin, although they differed on how applicable it was to Tsarist Russia, subscribed to it. It had a period of dormancy in the years before and after the Bolshevik Revolution, but it came back into the mainstream of debate in the USSR after 1925 and at least until Stalin in 1938 definitely came down in favour of a conventionally unilineal schema of historical stages.

The Soviet debate was about Asian societies, China in particular, and their historical evolution, and as such it was not devoid of interest or merits. It can even be said that it established the agenda for all future discussions of the subject. The debate that was rigged against the AMP starting in 1931, touched on such basic points as the Marxist legitimacy of the theory, unilinealism v. multilinealism in history, the defining features of the AMP, its conceptual assimilation or incompatibility with feudalism, and the necessity of reconciling it with Marxist class theory and analysis. As far as it went, it proposed at least four basic features for the AMP: environmental or ecological determinism, bureaucratic despotism, the immutability of the autarkic village system, and economic exaction in the form of tax/rent. The issue of class remained undefined, but on the whole the defenders of AMP theory attributed to despotic bureaucracies the characteristics of a class of exploiters. The concept of AMP was especially controversial on two fronts: ideologically, because of its assumptions about Asian exceptionalism and, politically, because it went against the thesis of the progressive/nationalist front. One of the foremost participants in the debate (who entered into it through his affiliation with the Comintern) was the German Marxist theoretician and historian K. A. Wittfogel. It was Wittfogel who gave the thesis its most elaborate and systematic contours with the publication in 1957 of his work *Oriental Despotism*, unfortunately in the guise of an anti-Bolshevik philippic, for by then his recantation of Stalinism had led him to become a fanatical supporter of McCarthyism in the USA. None the less, Wittfogel did single-handedly make the AMP an important subject of intra-Marxist discussion and his work is probably still the principal contemporary exposition of the thesis.[12]

Marxist theoretical blind alleys

Wittfogel and Oriental despotism

Wittfogel made the theory of the AMP his particular fief in various articles published from 1925 to 1962 and in his thick 1957 tome. The political motivation behind *Oriental Despotism* was his pretension that, first, Marx committed a crime against objectivity by declining to develop the concept of AMP when he realized its affinity to his own political programme, which supposedly prefigured the dictatorship of the proletariat, and, secondly, that Lenin and the Soviet state belittled and suppressed the thesis in the interest of Soviet legitimacy, because it constituted an indictment of Soviet totalitarian practices. In his large work on the AMP, Wittfogel brought together all the evidence he could find in history, anthropology, sociology and politics on the characteristics and the prevalence in all non-Western cultures of the repressive, anti-individualist and non-progressive despotic form of government. In Wittfogel's vast and exhaustive summarization, the reader is laboriously and unflinchingly led on a journey through millennia of history and into the darkest cultural grottoes, producing the deeply engraved representation of a hellish, tentacular, omniscient and omnipotent monster called the autocratic state, more powerful than society itself. The profligate and indiscriminate use of examples propounds the argument that despotism was of one piece from Cuzco to Samarkand, its frontiers beginning where those of Western Europe and its surrogates ended.

This vast and multifarious yet curiously homogenous historico-political panorama had but a single cause: socially necessary, collectively-built and bureaucratically-run hydraulic works requiring the efficient social disciplining of the masses. Wittfogel retained the equivalence between bureaucracy and exploitative class, but this was only a minor feature in what was essentially a monolithic, immutable organization. The roots of his construct were decidedly Marxist, but his obsessive concentration on a single theme, in effect, negated that Marxism was an instrument of integral social analysis, for it made most of its concepts irrelevant to the history of the majority of humanity. Since large-scale hydraulic works are hardly exclusive to Oriental autocracies, Wittfogel claimed that the same sort of works undertaken in Europe did not produce similar social consequences as in Asia, because of the fragmentation of political power achieved under European feudalism.[13]

The waterworks motif in the Oriental despotism schema is indeed the weakest link in Wittfogel's theoretical chain, and it in fact seems less a proof of the necessity and reality of Oriental despotism than a necessary escape hatch in order to avoid the 'special mentality' cul-de-sac. After all, what if not some psychological quirk could explain that tyranny flourishes in some lands and withers in others, if a necessary explanation such as hydraulic works fell by the wayside? The notion of Oriental despotism will always contain a powerful secret inducement to racism, which will certainly prevail if the only defence against it seems embarrassing and unconvincing, as the reliance on hydraulic works often seems in Wittfogel. However, the weakness in the cause/effect linkage that Wittfogel established between hydraulic works and political despotism does not necessarily invalidate the individual elements in his analysis, and in assessing his fully elaborated theory it is possible to approach its two flanks separately.

Despotic states and hydraulic works

Wittfogel's theory can be read as an explanation for non-Western economic backwardness in contrast to Western economic development, especially since it originates in Marx's and Engels' attempt to explain Asiatic economic stagnation, but it would be a distortion to emphasize this aspect of it for it is primarily a political thesis about the origins of despotism, or as Wittfogel himself called it in the subtitle of his major work: 'A comparative study of total power'. Therefore, since politics is its primary concern and since in politics lies the immediate determination of non-Western societies, including their economic organization and performance, we shall start by considering the Wittfogel concept of despotism. The idea fairly bristles with controversy. For one thing, Western history is not without its quota of despots, the word itself going back to the sources of Western civilization in ancient Greece. Wittfogel got around this with what in substance amounts to arguing from anomaly: if despotism flourished in the East and not in Europe, it was because feudalism, which for some reason appeared in the West but did not take root in Asia, laid the basis of Europe's political liberties and relegated despotism to exceptionality.

Japan and the USSR present historical difficulties. If despotic pre-modernization Japan were anything to go by, despotism would be as suffocating and inept at development as Wittfogel claims. Since Japan developed from its own despotic roots with, at most, a moderate degree of external prodding, Wittfogel (and, *obiter dicta*, also P. Anderson and F. Braudel) endowed it with a truly feudal past. There is, however, a certain degree of inconsistency in this argument inasmuch as economic development did not do away with political despotism in Japan, an objection which both Anderson and Braudel anticipated and disarmed by removing the concept of freedom from politics and fusing it entirely with the economic rights of private ownership and of private enterprise, while Wittfogel did not budge from his rigid political stance. How could Japan have developed under despotic political power both before and after industrialization? Wittfogel's attribution of feudal liberties to Japan seems forced and artificial from his premisses and definitions, the result of the *post hoc* necessity to explain its economic development rather than of consistent research criteria. The explanation he gave of Japanese feudalism – that 'Japan's irrigation agriculture was managed by local rather than by regional or national leaders' – would either invalidate the waterworks/despotism formula, or come perilously close to an exceptionalist, quasi-racist stance.

In relation to Soviet economic development, Wittfogel claimed that in 1917 absolutist, pre-Bolshevik Russia, which he compared favourably with the successor Communist regime, was on the verge of democracy after years of rapid economic development, and that what the Bolshevik coup did was to bring back and perfect old despotic habits. The extremely speculative character of this argument – would Russia have industrialized faster under Tsarism, if it had not been overthrown, than it did under the Soviet regime? – is as suspect as his affirmation that despotism is extremely efficient at certain activities, such as tax-collecting and the social control of the population of a country. Unfortunately, history tends to refute even these relatively unassuming propositions. The Ottoman tax-farming system, a prototypically despotic institution, was inefficient and originated in a lack of sufficient centralized political control. And Imperial China, the prototypical example of political despotism, which Wittfogel uses abundantly, is a good example of social cohesion and stability only if we ignore its periodic political disintegrations.[14]

Montesquieu and the mode of propagation of despotism

Wittfogel cannot have been unaware of the many historical inconsistencies involved in the abstract correlation between waterworks and despotism. In order to at least paper some of them over, he recurred to the idea, which can be found originally in Montesquieu, of the artificial (in the sense of not materially explicable or justified) perpetuation of social or political traits. According to this argument despotic habits acquired by a people in one environment could be carried to and imposed in a different environment by a conquering horde. This was particularly the case of Russian despotism, which originated not in the necessity of building hydraulic works but through Tatar imposition. This special line of reasoning was crucial to Wittfogel because it supported his contention that Bolshevism had adopted for its own ends the political system left in place by the Tsarist autocracy, which in turn derived from a dark and remote part of Russia's history.

The affinity with Montesquieu of some of Wittfogel's arguments (including the association of despotism and nomadic peoples) reveals their ultimately eighteenth-century *rationaliste* origin, although no doubt his immediate sources were Marx and Engels, but whereas their speculations on economic inequality were a tentative and relatively flexible adaptation of pre-nineteenth-century concepts in the age of capitalism's European apotheosis, Wittfogel's adoption and elaboration of the sketchy Marx/Engels thesis represented a rigid and unjustifiably generalizing attempt to carry the same ideas over into the twentieth century, in order to do which he had to posit some dubious hypotheses about the mode of propagation of despotism. These hypotheses involved the perdurance and transference of social quirks in a manner suggesting, despite the ultimate appeal to the environmental causation, a special psychological tendency in peoples outside the pale of Western civilization, and this could have been interpreted as a reversion to some of the more suspect nineteenth-century Eurocentric speculations on racism and polygenesis.[15] He was certainly not alone in denouncing Soviet autocracy, but from this to reducing its origins to some pristine Asiatic font and underestimating or neglecting other, perhaps more pertinent and immediate influences and circumstances, there is an inadmissible and vulnerable theoretical impulsiveness, to say the least.

As we shall see, Braudel recurred to despotism as the final explanation for the failure of Oriental civilizations – specifically, Islam, India, and China – to reach the upper levels of capitalist development, but he posited despotism as such and did not attempt any further theoretical elaboration, certainly nothing like Wittfogel's totalizing and subsuming vision of non-European cultures, and although this still leaves a blank area in Braudel's world-historical canvas (Why was despotism so prevalent in the East? Why did it not prosper in Europe?), it is overshadowed by the richness of his total representation, in which those self-same Oriental cultures, which Wittfogel relegated to absolute obscurantism, had the potential for and showed signs of an incipient but eventually unavailing movement towards capitalism. The pretension that Wittfogel's appeal to despotism was at least rationally based on the determinism of the environment, which Braudel's is not, is invalidated by Wittfogel's frequent and arbitrary unmoorings of the concept from its initial and fundamental environmental post, a theoretical looseness in his apparently rigorous correlation which comes out even more palpably in connection with its other flank, the one involving hydraulic works per se.

P. Anderson and the importance of 'superstructures'

In order to validate the assumptions that non-Western cultures and civilizations were despotic and that the political system of despotism was configurated by the social necessity of harnessing collective efforts to the construction and maintenance of agricultural waterworks, it is necessary to determine if all historical despotic systems were indeed based on the environmentally imposed need for hydraulic works. Such, however, is not the case. Pharaonic Egypt did build some major canals – in fact, the extent of irrigation in modern Egypt is almost exactly what it was in ancient times – but its sustenance depended on the natural rise and fall of the Nile and it probably dedicated most of its surplus and its physical energies and technical prowess to the construction of temples and monuments. Central Asia, where, according to both Montesquieu and Wittfogel, despotism was incubated and from where it supposedly spread to the Asian fringes, is notably devoid of waterworks and canals. The early conquering Arabs, purported propagators of Islamic despotism, are reputed to have wrecked, or at least neglected, the irrigation canals that even the barbarians spared in North Africa. In India, which was a centrepiece of the AMP both for Marx and for Wittfogel, 'centralized hydraulic agriculture' was significant neither for the Mauryan and the Vijayanagar empires nor for the later Islamic social formations: the sultanate and the Mughal Empire.

Probably the most telling succinct refutation of Wittfogel, in English at least, was accomplished by a fellow Marxist, P. Anderson, who, like Wittfogel, believes in the historico-political blessings of feudalism. Anderson found no basis in history for the waterworks-cum-despotism correlation. 'Very crudely', he wrote, 'in relation to the historical evidence with which they [Marx and Engels] were originally concerned, those countries which were marked by the absence of private property in land – Turkey, Persia, and India – never possessed any public irrigation works of importance, while that which possessed major irrigation systems – China – was vice versa marked by private property in land.' Anderson perceived the disregard of property rights under Islam as a consequence of its nomadic origins, which also led to the 'economic spoliation of agriculture': the exact opposite of the

European feudal order with its reliance on land both for power and wealth.[16]

Anderson's refutation of Wittfogel was embedded in a theory of Western capitalist development which deserves mentioning for its own merits. In Anderson's view, feudalism as an economic system only begets more feudalism, as in Japan, and forward historical movement necessitates an impact external to the system itself. This impact can only proceed from the political, legal, and ideological superstructures: 'What, then, was the specificity of European history which separated it so deeply from Japanese history, despite the common cycle which otherwise so closely united the two? The answer surely lies in the perdurable inheritance of classical antiquity.' The instrument of this all-transforming influence (in fact, a product of it) was the absolutist centralized state, from which, again, Japan never benefited in the strictly Western sense. 'The haphazard multiplicity of political unity in late medieval Europe', wrote Anderson, 'became in the early modern epoch an organized and interconnected state system. . .The increase in the political sway of the royal state was accompanied, not by a decrease in the economic security of noble landowners, but by a corresponding increase in the general rights of private property.'[17]

Anderson adheres to an intellectual tradition – historicist, *rationaliste* and Marxian – in which Wittfogel also claims a place. When all is said and done, their essential shared position is that inequality is rooted in historical determinisms: it arises as a natural consequence of the economic development of capitalism, but not because of the external economic and political repercussions of Western capitalist expansion. From their outlook, dependency theory, which affirms that the West produced underdevelopment in the rest of the world for its own economic benefit, inverts the order of things, because inequality already existed when Europe took the way of world expansion, and the proof of this lies in the possibility itself of that expansion. Marx and Engels, who, in the final reckoning, never really turned their back on their basic original persuasion that nineteenth-century colonialism was ultimately progressive, would probably have accepted these ideas as fair and accurate enough. They were of a piece with the concept of Asiatic despotism, with which Wittfogel tried to go further than historical evidence allowed, but which Anderson, in applying a corrective to Wittfogel's excess, did not disallow, preferring instead to concentrate, in connection with the general issue of disparities in economic development between East and West, on the beneficent social legacy of feudalism in conjunction with the bracing influence on Europe of its classical past. It can be said, therefore, that whereas Wittfogel, on the prompting of tentative Marxist texts, took a wrong turn into a theoretical blind alley, Anderson wisely cut the AMP down to size, choosing instead the application to the question of inequality of a more flexible Marxist methodology based on the concepts of MOP and social superstructure. His emphasis on a specifically Western line of historical evolution can be considered part of a tendency of thought on intercultural and international inequalities that seeks primarily to explain the comparative reason behind Western economic success while not neglecting the analysis of non-Western values and structures. It manifests an unmistakably but moderate Eurocentric attitude, whose roots go back to pre-nineteenth-century assessments on the political significance of feudalism, such as can be found, according to Anderson himself, in Machiavelli, Bacon and Montesquieu.[18]

The contemporary AMP debate

As of the future controversies that Marx made possible when he invented the formula AMP, it can be said of Wittfogel's Oriental despotism that it set the cat among the Marxist pigeons. Although some researchers tend to play down Wittfogel's importance in the contemporary AMP debate, the fact is that his mammoth work in comparative history preceded most of the mainly intra-Marxist research done on the subject. In the early 1960s the French Communist Party spawned a brood of AMP theorists, who in turn stimulated further discussion in the USSR itself. From this period, too, comes the main body of essays by the Hungarian, F. Tokei, vindicating the necessity of the AMP for a true understanding of history. In 1972, the Italian, U. Melotti, produced a much debated work defending multilinealism and the AMP. There has been a regular output of theoretical works in English since the 1960s, of which we have mentioned concepts and arguments in Hobsbawm, Lichtheim and Anderson, who placed the AMP in a wider context of historical and social issues.

Other theorists have restricted their perspective to the idea of AMP itself and its place in the development of Marx's thinking. The principal points of debate have been whether or not Marx and Engels eventually repudiated their tentative formulation of the theory and whether it expresses a unilineal or multilineal approach to historical and social analysis. Among these writers, the consensus is that there was no repudiation, even when they allow that the theory was principally ancillary to the major concerns of its originators. In 1975, L. Krader made a thorough examination of Marx's sources for the AMP, and concluded on the basis of Marx's ethnological readings and notebooks that he had a more than superficial commitment to it, but that it served principally to clarify his understanding and critique of 'the political economy of capital as a whole'. H. Lubasz ratified this approach when he wrote in 1984 that Marx's observations on India 'are what one might call auxiliary statements whose purpose is to help Marx make a point about the capitalist, not the Asiatic, mode of production'. In 1977, M. Sawer made an appeal for the 'openness of history' from her reading of Marx, which rejected the 'quasi-teleological view. . .that world history consisted in a unitary process of development'. In a doctoral dissertation published in 1989, B. O'Leary expounded a systematic critique of the AMP both from historiographical and from internal Marxist perspectives. He did a thorough job of demolishing Wittfogel's hydraulic hypothesis as it applies to India. However, his contention that neither Marx nor Engels abandoned the AMP was inferential and open to serious questioning.[19]

Imperialism idealized

According to M. Molnar, the AMP with its implication of historical immutability was a useful but not a necessary argument for Marx and Engels in their consistent view of colonialism as a callous but inevitable force for world progress. Pulling out that prop did not provoke the collapse of the other, wider and more important idea. Lenin, who accepted the AMP theory up to a point, was particularly hostile to colonialism, as indeed was a strong current of opinion inside the Second International. In order to justify his position within an orthodox Marxist context, Lenin, always according to Molnar, had to ignore the Marx/Engels texts, and moreover he had to affirm that 'They had not lived long enough to fully observe the imperialist side of world capitalism', a demonstrably exaggerated claim in view of their perfectly explicit perception of the global nature of capitalism. Nevertheless, the Leninist view gained wide acceptance within Marxism, and it is, as we shall see *in extenso*, the cornerstone of dependency theory. Even if we were to consider Molnar's view too extreme in the opposite direction, it would still be necessary to take into account that Marx's and Engels' critique of colonialism was halting and ethical in character, that is, not addressed to its transforming and dynamizing socio-economic impact, and this left open another tantalizing theoretical opening that, as in the case of the AMP and Wittfogel, could lead to another intellectual cul-de-sac. It was into this opening that the British sociologist, B. Warren, entered.[20]

Warren was apparently a fully committed Marxist intellectual, who also managed to defend imperialism and to deny the existence of underdevelopment. In his posthumous and controversial *Imperialism: pioneer of capitalism* (1980), his main contention was that Marx had formulated a coherent theory according to which the inevitable spread of capitalism throughout the world by means of colonialism and of formal and informal imperialism represented a progressive movement and would in the end usher in the stage of worldwide socialist revolution. He based his thesis mainly on Marx's early journalistic statements in *The New York Tribune* on the predatory but modernizing British presence in India. He also cited other pronouncements by Marx along the same lines, but he could not allege an actual body of theory on economic imperialism in Marx's works, and in fact his dogmatic assertions rest on a glaring scantiness of sources, even in a field where each phrase from the master can be stretched to inordinate lengths.

Marx himself did not use the word imperialism, and what later came to be known as the Marxist theory of imperialism was an elaboration by Lenin of J. A. Hobson's idea that the flag follows capital, which flows outwards when it finds obstructions in the way of its gainful or profitable placement at home. Marx did believe, of course, that capital sought outlets when profits fell, but he saw this as a general feature of capitalism and did not relate it specifically to colonialism or expansionism, or at least he did not expressly do so. There is no such a thing as a direct or original Marxist theory of imperialism, but on the other hand, there is a Marxist/Leninist theory of imperialism that practically has acquired the status of doctrine. Warren, who dissented vehemently from Lenin as Wittfogel had from Stalinism, got around this orthodoxy by arguing that Lenin turned his back on the pristine Marxist doctrine for reasons of international political strategy and later asked for and got sanction for his views from the Comintern. What Lenin did that divided him from Marx, according to Warren, was that he chose to posit that international capitalism, rather than progressive or modernizing, was exploitative and retardatory. Lenin did not actually espouse this view to the hilt, but he gave it revolutionary bonafides and respectability. During the 1920s, when communism was being blocked in Europe but gaining adherents in

Asia and Latin America, the Leninist alternative was adopted and 'officialized' for the revolution by Comintern congresses.[21]

An imaginary but useful confrontation

Despite his repetitive invoking of Marx, Warren had handicaps from the start in the defence of his thesis. Marx entertained few if any doubts on the cultural as well as on the material superiority of the West to the other important world cultures. This superiority had been possible because of the ripening of economic trends and forces, and the creation of a capitalist world market by hook or by crook contributed essentially to the righting of a historical imbalance. In that sense, and only in that sense, could Marx conceive of something akin to Warren's imperialism and, moreover, this was mostly implicit in his work. In brief, even if Marx's perception of colonialism had been unalloyed by misgivings and recriminations, which Lenin's of course was, it lacked the compulsive, specific economic motivation with which Lenin endowed late-nineteenth-century colonialism in transfiguring it – and capitalism as a whole in its alleged final phase – into imperialism. Warren seemed to be pushing Marx too hard in the direction of a fully developed theory of imperialism, in doing which he was also stretching too far Marx's supposed complacent attitude towards European colonialist expansionism. If Marx welcomed the capitalist world market, he could also be an implacable critic of colonialism and this always latent antagonism became more pronounced and more manifest with the passing of time and the intensification of colonialist pressures, which both Marx and Engels did live long enough to perceive.

It was once again I. Habib who took on the task of vindicating the anti-colonialist Marx. In the 1983 essay 'Marx's perception of India', he presented a convincing case negating the Warren version but not overly biased towards any specific theory of economic imperialism. Even though there is no question of a deliberate confrontation, Habib and Warren have written as if they were aiming at each other, and their writings on the subject of Marx the imperialist and Marx the anti-colonialist can be usefully paired and contrasted. Warren affirms that Marx posited a progressive imperialism; Habib claims that Marx understood the imperialist nature of capitalism and that he condemned it as brutal, harmful and reactionary. Habib quotes from *Capital* and from *The Poverty of Philosophy*, among other Marxian sources. He also, like Warren, quotes from the articles in *The New York Tribune*, but it is obvious that, on the whole, Habib and Warren were rummaging in different Marxist sacks. In order to reach their conclusions, they had to purposefully reject each other's emphases. Who then is right? Warren bases his thesis on a few direct and unambiguous statements by Marx, but he tends to build too high on that minimal foundation. In order to do so, he posits a once-for-all-times Marx, and then he has to do a lot of extrapolating on the strength of that static, unchanging Marx. Habib admits that there did exist a Eurocentric Marx who felt that colonialism, though brutal, fostered socio-economic change, but he plausibly claims that Marx did not adopt Eurocentrism either as a banner or as a permanent intellectual attitude. With more material than Warren uses, Habib builds an evolving Marx sensitive to the implications and meanings of events and trends. Perhaps he cannot prove that Marx was a theorist of economic imperialism *avant la lettre*, but he makes a good case for the idea that Marx was neither an ally of colonialism nor an unconditional believer in the generative powers of international capitalism. The least we can derive from the Habib/Warren textual confrontation is a healthy scepticism about the existence of a truly Marxist orthodoxy on the subject of economic imperialism.[22]

The statistical denial of underdevelopment

Warren can be found even wider of the mark in the extrapolation of his so-called Marxist theory of imperialism to the period after the Second World War, in specific connection with the Third World. To start with, Warren denied the existence of underdevelopment. He took two lines of approach: (a) the historical argument that colonialism and imperialism improved the overall conditions of existence for humanity the world over; (b) the thesis that international capitalism has stimulated economic development in every society where it has been either adopted or implanted.

To defend these propositions, Warren embarked on a veritable statistical crusade against almost every flank and parapet erected by development studies in the last forty years. This is not necessarily proof that he is wrong – wrongheaded, perhaps, but not necessarily wrong. However, his statistical legerdemain is self-defeating for the simple reason that what he specifically tried to demonstrate – that the non-industrialized nations have been growing since the Second World War at a faster clip than the developed capitalist nations – begs the issue in various ways: in admitting the statistical functionality of the group he pretends to deny; in giving self-serving definitions of growth; and in using special, almost doctored series. In the end the reality is still there, for no amount of special pleading can modify the actual fact of the co-existence of capitalism and extreme underdevelopment. Warren's ultimate absurdity is his statement that the concept of underdevelopment was a product of the pseudo-Marxist theory of economic imperialism, concocted for strictly politico-subversive strategic purposes. In point of fact, the concept of underdevelopment is, if anything, a child of a Western capitalist developmentalist outlook, and its implications are anything but revolutionary, close indeed to Warren's own position: that economic backwardness can be overcome, that it is merely an accidental historical lag, and that it can be made good without deviating from an essentially capitalist model.[23]

The paradigmatic theory on the origins of international economic inequality between the contemporary developed and underdeveloped blocs of nations is the neo-Marxist/Leninist long-view theory of economic imperialism. It holds that underdevelopment is the direct, deliberate and systematic historical result of capitalism operating on a global scale. No other theory besides this one, not even Marxist/Leninist theories before the Second World War, make such a categoric and sweeping statement. Basing his thesis on fragments of Marx's works, Warren made precisely the opposite claim: that the world influence of the more developed Western capitalist countries was not retardatory but stimulative of growth. Except by implication, there is nothing in this pertinent to an explanation of inequality. Because Warren, however, proclaimed his faith in a pristine Marxist doctrine on expanding world-capitalism, it can be inferred that, like the early Marx, he would have been inclined to attribute backwardness to a combination of climate and despotism. At any rate, his dogged efforts to validate one arguable, disputed and limited side of Marx's thought, places his theory, in a general sense, on a very precarious footing, and although, as we shall see, there has occurred, in view of the deficiencies of dependency theory, a contemporary re-evaluation of Marxist MOP and class-struggle ideas that seems to contemplate the possibility of real capitalist development for the Third World, Warren's position is also not welcome within this trend, because of its neglect of internal social processes in underdeveloped countries.

In closing our discussions of Wittfogel and Warren, we cannot refrain from wanting to emphasize how, despite the seeming disparity in their outlooks and approaches, they represent two aspects of the same Marxist construct, and they are, therefore, closer to each other than they are individually to Marx, who proposed that construct with all the doubts and reservations in the world. The conceptual and programmatic complementarity between the

AMP and the transforming effects of Western expansion – like historical forces inevitably bound to confront each other, one timeless and immutable, the other dynamic and iconoclastic – presented two distinct avenues of research for these two authors, although in following them at different times and independently of one another they were never very far apart, and what is really most crucial, the enticing vistas that attracted them were reduced at the end to what we have described as intellectual or ideological blind alleys. Both are zealous (and over-zealous) Marxists, who fished in the same Marxist waters. Both have a driving sense of the virtues of Western ways. Both finally sinned through excess: Wittfogel by making too much of the idea of despotism; Warren by unduly idealizing the process of world capitalist expansion. Would it have made any difference if, rather than Oriental despotism and colonialism/imperialism by themselves, these concepts had been taken up and used as inseparable halves of one integral historic vision? Marx and Engels renounced this scheme. Others have found its individual parts much too rough-cast to be able to assemble them smoothly. It does not do, however, to underrate Wittfogel and Warren excessively. Political despotism has been resurrected in recent research – perhaps in less politically prejudiced research than Wittfogel's – as the only viable explanation of non-Western economic stagnation. And Marxists today are going back to the idea that capitalism, devoid of imperialist intentionality, may indeed be inching towards the full industrialization of backward lands. Therefore, it could be put, as a sort of indulgent envoi to these authors, that they erred not in falsifying but in distorting reality.

The evolution of environmental theory

Toynbee's challenge-and-response version

Well into the nineteenth century, the geographic context of Western speculations on inequality was not, as today, the division of the world into two blocs of nations, one developed, one under-developed, but a small group of different higher cultures with the West on a pedestal among them. The integration of the world by Western capitalist forces did not, of course, effect an instantaneous transformation of the political and cultural diversity of mankind, but it did propagate ideas, values and habits, and it did put in place the means for modernization and its further spread. Some traditional political and economic structures that functioned only in the context of non-Western cultures became obsolete or obsolescent as a result of world integration. Despotism as a quintessentially non-Western political system retreated to the degree that imperialism either imposed its own one-sided rule or was responsible for indirect change in other countries. The adoption of Western practices and values did not mean the sudden suppression of despotic habits, but it modified them and tended to put them into a *sine die* legal limbo. In general, cultural relativism, or the Western acceptance of exotic customs and values as embodying a valid logic of their own, suffered grievous damage at the hands of Western world hegemony during the nineteenth century.

These practical and intellectual trends were inevitably also damaging to the pre-nineteenth-century ideas on which Western thought had built its explanations and rationalizations of cultural differences and inequalities. Some of those concepts, like the ones that went into the Marxist formulation of the AMP, survived into the twentieth century, but mostly as relicts: the dying gasps of exhausted, wheezing analytical apparatuses. Although the direct and unadorned notion of despotic political power has been making a theoretical comeback, its more problematic juxtaposition to hydraulic works has been discredited. The multifarious group of theories on environmental influence that had prevailed since the beginning of Greek classical thought, ceased to matter much during the nineteenth century, at least in their old physiological and cultural versions, as a result of Western intercultural ascendancy and of progress in the biological sciences. Nevertheless, of all the pre-nineteenth-century concepts used in the West in dealing with other cultures, the one idea that has retained a dogged, polymorphous validity is that human behaviour has somehow to do with the place and the climate in which people live.

Closer to contemporary perceptions than the dubious arguments in Montesquieu is the cultural role of the environment in Arnold Toynbee's *A Study of History*. It is defined by the formula challenge-and-response, and although this is not entirely original (for what it does is reiterate the very old notion that cushy environments make for decadence and hardscrabble ones for toughness) in the flexible, probing Toynbeean grip it uncovers a plethora of examples and illustrations. In the end, though, what emerges is not the historical demonstration that environmental theory was lacking, but a reaffirmation, after the long Eurocentric interlude, of cultural relativism, almost though not quite as it was practised by the Encyclopedists, because the planet that Toynbee knew was in general more homogeneous, more integrated than before, closer to the notion of one world, and at the same time, more diverse, its corners and pockets less obscure and remote. Relativism had been a product of ignorance. It was rejected by and large in the West, whose espousal of it was never quite unreserved, as soon as it had demonstrated its own superiority over all other cultures. As Toynbee applied it (and it was a crucial aspect of his historical approach), relativism was post-Eurocentric. It was affirmed in the face of evident economic backwardness and on the basis of hard-to-define, non-material values. For our purposes, however, precisely because of his universal outlook, Toynbee has nothing to say on the origins of international or even intercultural inequality.[24]

The comeback of environmental theory

Challenge-and-response need not be taken only in a context in which civilizations and high cultures form the irreducible units of history. In fact, it seems to be part of the general awareness of theorists on underdevelopment that environmental influences are crucial in their field. The impartial and equable P. Bairoch had to fall back on climate in order to explain the origins of the development gap. Guy de Bosschère partly attributed underdevelopment to 'excessive climates'. The ultimate cause lay in what he called 'the Aryan invasion', which parcelled the globe and the climates among the peoples and determined the eventual separation between the rich and the poor nations. More specifically, though less explicitly, Bosschère was claiming that the white races started making the world their own when they swept into and settled in the European extension of the Asian landmass. He was not alone in claiming that the foundations of inequality were laid long before written history began, in the fate-ridden, unknowable and probably fortuitous process by which the earth was originally shared out, but most speculation on climate has more immediate concerns.

What A. K. Biswas called the 'correlation' between climate and development has been made time and again by development economists. J. K. Galbraith did so in a 1951 article entitled 'Conditions for economic change in underdeveloped countries'. C. P. Kindleberger succinctly expressed it in *Economic Development* (1965). K. F. Boulding wrote in 1970: 'Development, like economics, has been very largely a Temperate Zone product.' P. Streeten and G. Myrdal have both made the connection between climate and economic activity. Streeten in particular presented a book by A. M. Kamarck, which makes explicit some of the crucial specific effects of the tropical climate on economic development: 'Compared to the Temperate Zones, there are certain effects of the Tropical climate that, up to the present, hinder agriculture, handicap mineral exploration, and make the population less vigorous through disease and, possibly, through the direct physiological impact of temperature and humidity.' Kamarck adds significantly: 'The effects of Tropical climate are not absolute obstacles to economic development, but they do make many of the problems of economic development in the Tropics sufficiently different from those in the Temperate Zone countries so that an additional hurdle has to be overcome and, consequently, all other relevant factors being equal, the pace of development in Tropical countries tends to be slower.'[25]

The implications of these ideas are vaguely deterministic. P. A. Baran posited the notion that the environment merely retards development. In Baran, the environment both explained underdevelopment and was a denial of its existence. It was the ultimate explanation of why the West surpassed all other cultures, but since its effects were retardatory and not permanently handicapping, as some environmental theories would have it, development was inevitable everywhere and the persistence of underdevelopment could be explained only as a result of economic imperialism.[26] Climate theory is a vast non-specific awareness and claim. Biswas tried to pinpoint the influence of climate through a development strategy centred on agriculture. Implicit here was a theory of the purest environmental tenor. Its main contentions were that farming is fundamental to development and, obviously enough, decisively influenced by climate. Always as contributing to a development strategy, but giving support to environmental theory as well, Biswas handled figures and arguments showing the adverse influence of tropical climates on soil management, pest control and human labour. He did not specifically trace underdevelopment and inequality to the environment, but the inference is inescapable.

We shall return to climate, because we have only used these references to illustrate briefly the full circle of environmental theory from its robust Greek beginnings through its diverse and honest Western avatars to its racist Eurocentric misuse and finally back to its groping, tentative rebirth as a last-resort explanation of the origins of underdevelopment and international economic inequality. Climate theory began as a human response to foreignness and diversity, and it fulfilled this role diligently up to the eighteenth century. When the perception of differences gave way to the superior/inferior dichotomy, climate was employed to support Western racism and cultural prejudices. Climate theory fell into disrepute among 'Westerners' as it did among radicals and Marxists. Eventually, however, climate resurfaced on the strength of its theoretical legitimacy, but it did so by allowing itself only very cautious generalizations and by eschewing a commitment to specific physiological explanations.

Is climate theory then correct as the final instance on the issue of the origins of international inequality? To come out and say so without having explored other avenues would be overbold and prejudicial, but we can point out that the contemporary writers on underdevelopment who make use of the concept of the environmental influence on economic development do so as an ancillary, almost philosophical complement, and not as an end in itself in their researches, with significant exceptions such as Kamarck, or the economic historian E. L. Jones. Nevertheless, when climate does come up, its implications belie the casual or even subordinate manner in which it tends to be put in context. Climate, in brief, is in some manner related to inequality, but it can be an awkward associate in an era of boundless faith in bounding technology. The environment today from a certain angle seems like a trifling manageable quantity, and yet it is the environment that still scythes through communities and nations with a devastating force that is a reminder of its underlying empire, as when London built a barrier to stem flooding tides from the North Sea only to be hit by an unexpected hurricane from the south four years later. A more telluric perspective would have to admit that man's historical fate has always been bound to the environment, which to a considerable degree still remains attached to him, exerting its forces pitilessly on him.

2 *The anti-imperialist reaction and the Marxist pre-emption of economic-imperialism theory*

Colonialism and social imperialism

The history of nineteenth-century European economic and military expansion and conquest has an *in crescendo* quality that is not easy to reconcile with Little-England and other theories about respites in the advance of colonialism. It is this observable fact that makes Lenin's claim concerning Marx's and Engels' relative ignorance of imperialism seem rather feeble, apart, of course, from the overwhelming textual evidence that, far from not being aware of European expansionism, they used this tendency as a recurrent motif in their writings on politics and on history. It was in fact inescapable even in Marx's cold sober economic analyses, such as those in *Capital*, a work in which colonial issues from the start of colonialism and onwards come up time and again to illustrate technical arguments.

It is, however, true that after 1880 there was an indisputable intensification of colonialism coincident with a growth of nationalist tendencies in the major European powers. Ideologically, it is not easy to find a lack of continuity in the history of European nineteenth-century colonialism. For example, the altruistic 'white man's burden' motif had never been absent from the literature of colonialism. In one way or another, before and after 1880, the violence of colonialist conquest always submitted to the gloss of world unification or of human progress or of some such fragile idealization. However, the scramble for colonies in the late decades of the nineteenth century had produced incidents and confrontations between powers, and this presaged war, which ill fitted anyone's definition of idealism even if it was itself a social Darwinist paradigm. The idea of the inevitability of international rivalry and struggle led to the doctrine that has been dubbed social imperialism, a phrase first used by the Marxist K. Renner in 1919, although it applies to positions and ideas that were very much in vogue in Western Europe from the 1880s onwards. Social imperialism, which did away with the idealistic and humanitarian jargon of colonialism and colonialist imperialism, had as its manifest immediate objective the harnessing of mass support in the advanced capitalist powers to the cause of colonialist expansion and inter-imperialist contentiousness.

The distinction is frequently made between social imperialism in an empire-building power like Germany and in a power such as Great Britain with an already built-up empire: in Germany, social imperialism, relying on social reform, funnelled national energies towards colonial acquisitions; in Britain, it promoted belated social reforms in the metropole and high tariff walls all around the empire to confront the challenges to its existing position. The interwoven strands of social Darwinism and social imperialism can be observed in a writer such as the eugenicist Pearson, for whom international struggle was the *fons et origo* of social reform and of a programme of applied eugenics. For both forms of social imperialism, one of the crucial ideas was that colonies existed for the benefit of the imperialist centre rather than being in some degree the object of metropolitan care and concern. It was also a proclamation to the effect that the world at large (powers such as the USA and Japan excepted) was to be the battleground of the European empires. Given the bluntness of its approach, social imperialism could never become the official state policy of any European power; it was, like eugenics at first, a purely intellectual proposition. It became, however, politically influential, and it is probably no mere coincidence that it was at the height of the social imperialist movement in England that the theory of economic imperialism was launched by the liberal politician and author J. A. Hobson.[27]

J. A. Hobson, the patterns of colonialism and the debate over economic imperialism

The fountainhead of anti-imperialism

Hobson's treatise on imperialism, when all is said and done, was less about international inequalities than about social injustice at home, and perhaps the fact that this was his fundamental concern allowed him to disavow in 1938 an international thesis that had such epochal lasting intellectual consequences.[28] Among other targets, for instance, he gave 'biological imperialism' a prominent place in his polemic. But he muddled things somewhat by accepting the distinction, current in the nineteenth century, between imperialism and colonization: the latter concept applied to such cases as the British colonies of settlement, which were considered legitimate expressions of nationality, whereas imperialism was the conquest of countries that had nothing in common with the imperialist power. Hobson further complicated matters by also accepting the Eurocentric colonialist argument that certain very backward colonies could be legitimately held by their conquerors in a sort of humanitarian trusteeship.

What these unnecessary distinctions and qualifications did was to confuse the general issue of colonialism, its origins, history and motivations, because he did not explore the continuities between the past of European overseas expansion and the imperialist present that he observed, a historical likelihood that he at least contemplated. Even if his perception of the special character of the self-governing white British colonies was justified, he was quite nonchalant and even sloppy in his general approach to the complicated and historically far-reaching issue of colonialism. His critical appraisal of imperialism applied specifically to colonialism of the late-nineteenth-century variety, yet he decried British colonialist policy in India long before the appearance of what he called imperialism, and despite the obvious affinity between these two views, he seems not to have been tempted to exert a synthesizing or organizing intellectual effort on them. Likewise, it never dawned on him that if his critique of the British destruction of handicraft industry in India was valid, there was as well the possibility that analogous acts of cultural and economic depredation could have been committed in the case of Africa. In the end, however, it must be recognized that these were side issues for him and that his main contention was centred foursquare on the way the British capitalist economy functioned.

Hobson made the following fundamental claims. He reasoned that the unequal distribution of national wealth led to oversaving, which in turn resulted in overproduction in as much as workers were not being paid enough wages to permit a levelling out of supply and demand. Oversaving and overproduction together in one country created the necessity for foreign outlets, but since all advanced capitalist powers were in the same economic situation, the pressure of competing for external capital and consumer markets contributed decisively to the development of the political will for the acquisition of colonies that would function as the exclusive economic preserves of each imperialist power. This meant that imperialism was motivated by the capitalist pursuit of economic gain and that capitalism in each advanced nation employed politico-military means to ensure its profits. Behind this reasoning lay the notion – first suggested by Adam Smith and later consecrated as a fundamental idea of political economy by an uninterrupted line of thinkers from Malthus to Marx – that over a period of time the rate of profits tended to decline, though generally not the absolute mass of profit, which thus created a problem of realization or investment. The culmination of the imperialist process was the conquest of overseas territories. Hobson used as historical examples the Boer War and the scramble for Africa, which involved the sharing out of the tropical areas of that continent among the imperialist powers. These included tiny and backward Portugal, and this was a dead giveaway on some of the historical and operational flaws of his thesis: Portugal's claims on empire long anteceded the imperialist grab and could not be easily accounted for in terms of internal capitalist pressures, and even less as a sign of British imperialist benevolence towards an old and weak ally if imperialism was being moved by capitalist cupidity.

In judging Hobson's anti-imperialist stance it must be emphasized that he did not propose a wholesale condemnation of colonialism, although it has to be recognized that he was sensitive and sensible enough to condemn imperialism wherever it did more harm than good, as he saw it. He did not use British India to shore up his main arguments – which in effect put India out of the reach of the early, topical theory of economic imperialism, with important theoretical and ideological implications – but he did blame colonialism for disrupting the potential for development of its traditional economic foundations. He was not concerned with what we know today as underdevelopment, and he attributed the differences in development to the environment without elaborating on this. He certainly did not blame economic backwardness generally on imperialism. But he did a sound solidly British job of debunking the hollow talk about the duties of civilization towards the benighted natives of the colonies.[29]

The two sides of Hobson's thesis

There are at least two basic sides to Hobson's theory: (a) its humanitarian anti-colonialism; (b) the logical, well-articulated connection that Hobson established between economics and imperialism. There was nothing really novel about either position, and Hobson's prestige and influence have probably more than anything else to do with the way he combined them and with the sort of statistical and documentary support he proposed. On the issue of the colonies, there had always been in Great Britain a strong opposition movement with a powerful if not always pervasive moral component. After the 1830s, the Little England liberals, led by Richard Cobden and John Bright, went foursquare against empire as a syphon of labour and capital needed at home. Cobden's main argument was that since empire could not pay for itself, it should be let go rather than be allowed to become an economic burden on the mother country. For this he was taxed with parochialism and meanness by the eulogists of the glories of empire-building. It must be said, however, that there were also humanitarian considerations associated with Cobden's views – notably their affiliation to the anti-slavery movement – so that in spite of the overwhelming jingoist attacks against it, the anti-colonialist critique never really lost the moral high ground and, over the decades, even as colonialist imperialism prospered, anti-colonialism itself gained momentum and became particularly strong towards the end of the century.[30] In addition, Hobson's own critique was prefigured in all its parts by the socialist press of the times.

The other side of his theory, the connection between economics and imperial expansion and conquest, has an even older, in fact an ancient lineage. It had been adumbrated in classical Greece and certainly by the time of the Cromwellian Navigation Act of 1651 colonies were forthrightly envisioned as strictly economic entities at the disposal of the mother country, which was really not much different from Spanish colonialist policy in America despite the often unctuous tone of the Leyes de Indias. In the early nineteenth century the political economist E. G. Wakefield defended the convenience of transferring both money and populations from the home countries to the colonies as reciprocally beneficial. Wakefield belonged to the group of theoreticians who believed that a capitalist economy tended to produce excess capital.

He went them one better in proposing that this excess could more profitably be invested in colonies of settlement, and from this to applying the same criteria to colonies of conquest, the only thing that stood in the way was the quasi-semantical distinction between colonization and colonialism. Wakefield had the support of John Stuart Mill, who in turn sympathized with Malthus's demographic catastrophism and impugned J. B. Say's theory of recurring equilibria in economic life. In Germany, the nationalist neo-mercantilist F. List expressed in 1841 the idea that colonies had a strictly economic function for the growth and greatness of the colonialist power. List also defined colonialism as the export of manufactured goods in exchange for raw materials, which was standard mercantilist doctrine but also is one of the basic definitions in today's dependency theory. In France, Leroy-Beaulieu, taking a cue from the Wakefield school, proposed colonies as logical and natural repositories of metropolitan capitals. His countryman, J. Ferry, conceived of colonies as necessary outlets for metropolitan production.[31] Even though most of these theorists walked a thin line between economic expansionism as reality and as doctrine, between 'what is' and 'what should be', the net impression from them is that we cannot separate colonialism from economic interests and considerations.

Hobson had already worked out the essential line of reasoning for his thesis in a series of articles that were published from 1898 to 1902.[32] By then, however, the basic arguments were well known. In 1890 the Socialist William Morris had correlated 'the appetite of the World-Market' with colonial expansion. B. Porter considers that Morris was in fact reiterating old arguments: 'For years it had been the unblushing assertion of capitalists and traders, accepted and implemented by governments, that the "flag" should be used in the service of commerce. Both had persistently stressed the necessity of finding new markets for British manufactures and new fields for investment.' E. B. Bax wrote in 1899, in the socialist journal *Justice*, that 'the one hope of prolonging the existence of the present capitalist system lies in the opening up of new territories to commercial and industrial enterprise, in other words, in the extension of the world market and the acquirement of fresh sources of cheap labour', and therefore 'it is a thing of vital importance to the early realization of socialism to stem the tide of annexation and colonial expansion without delay'. According to Porter, 'The theory was less sophisticated than the one J. A. Hobson was to develop a little later: it confined its attention to commercial capitalism (not financial), and it was never worked out by Bax in any great detail.' A similar call was emitted by the International Socialist Congress, which met in Paris in 1900. In America, C. A. Conant, among others, invoked in 1898 the surplus capital idea as the source of imperialist expansion. He was quoted by A. Thompson in the Socialist magazine *Clarion*. Porter perceives the influence of Marx on British socialist thinking on imperialism in two concepts: in the overproduction of capital and in capitalism's need to exhaust all possible means of surviving, which clearly pointed to imperialist expansion, although Marx had not made that specific connection.[33]

The patterns of colonialism

Hobson had striven to demonstrate his thesis on the basis of a few examples of imperialist expansion, paramount among which was the manipulative and obviously economically motivated British aggression in South Africa. His original paradigm was the big-power China grab in the wake of the Japanese defeat of China in 1895, which also had self-evident economic causes. On another tack, Hobson correlated statistics on capital outflows from Great Britain with the measurable growth of empire in terms of area and populations. From the series he used, roughly from 1860 to 1890, it has been supposed that he referred to the period embracing what was known as the scramble for Africa.[34] However, his theory eventually has had to withstand the test of the entire history of nineteenth-century colonialism, and in fact it has been made extensive in radical contemporary versions all the way back to the start of European colonialism. This means that in effect there are two theories of economic imperialism: (a) the special or specific theory that Hobson formulated, on which V. I. Lenin directly patterned his; (b) the general theory, which echoes parts of Lenin's distantly, and which went through the Comintern phase before being elaborated in its original and general form by P. A. Baran.

We shall see gradually how Hobson's theory mushroomed to the vast intellectual dimensions it has, including such forms as 'world-system analysis'. But in all fairness, it would seem as if Hobson should not be judged except within the confines of his own historical and geographical claims. On the other hand, since European expansion the world over, starting with the Portuguese exploration of the West African coast and the Spanish discovery of America during the fifteenth century, is all part of the same historical continuity up to the Boer War and beyond, if we think of it at least in terms of intercultural relations and confrontations, it would be helpful, before proceeding to examine the critiques of the specific Hobsonian thesis, to cast a sidelong glance at its possible correlation with the long and complex history of European expansionism.

A summary consideration of European expansionism reveals the emergence of at least four historical patterns of overseas colonialism: (a) the commercial outpost or entrepôt; (b) the Iberian, English and French colonies of conquest and settlement in America; (c) the plantation colonies; (d) the Anglo-Indian colonialist pattern of gradual penetration from a peripheral foothold. Dutch Cape Colony and the British colonies of settlement in the South Seas can be reasonably considered to have been variants on the earlier settlements in America. These patterns demarcate overlapping periods in the history of colonialism up to 1870. The first warehouses or trading posts were founded during the fifteenth century, but they became the prevailing form of European colonialism in Asia until at least the mid-eighteenth century, when Great Britain initiated the consolidation of her Indian possessions and in the process made herself the foremost power in the subcontinent. They were also the basic form of the European presence in Africa.

The second period of colonial history is defined by the establishment of the Iberian and the English settlement colonies in the New World during the sixteenth and seventeenth centuries. The third period started with the Anglo-French rivalry for plantation colonies during the War of the Spanish Succession (1700–13) and culminated with the definite imposition of British ascendancy in India during the Seven Years War. Between 1775 and 1825 there was a wave of decolonization in America. During part of this period, the Napoleonic wars monopolized the attention and the efforts of all the European powers. After 1815, colonialism started anew and carried on to the end of the century, but in two waves: during the first, the less rapid phase, variants on the Anglo-Indian pattern were applied in Africa and Asia, with Britain at the head and France a rather distant second; the second, the rapid phase, was basically the scramble for Africa after 1870, during which a new pattern of colonialism appears.

The question concerning Hobson's theory of economic imperialism really is how extensive it can be made to those historical patterns and stages without falsifying its import. Hobson was very specific in his formulations, and this has been the cause of both their prestige and their vulnerability. It is one thing to try to prove with fresh and relatively reliable figures that the flag travels in the hands of Mammon; it is another to make the same assertion for colonial enterprise since Da Gama landed in Malabar. However, if we interpret Hobson as wanting to say that in a general sense individual and collective economic gain is a more potent motivation than politics or religion, or that it takes precedence over policy and over missionary zeal, then a case can certainly be made for a Hobsonian rendering of colonial history. All you need to do is to command a sufficiently impressive array of facts and they are there for the picking.

The entrepôt and the plantation were both strictly commercial in nature. The Portuguese and Spanish colonies in America were milked for taxes, profits and raw materials. British America rebelled over taxes and commercial impositions it had not sanctioned. British India started as the East India Company, a joint-stock company definitely chartered in 1657, that prospered as long as it could set commercial policy for India. It gave up its rather shadowy control in 1857, but by the end of the century it was being claimed that the Raj – the British Indian administration that had officially taken over from the East India Company – had been draining India of a yearly fortune for services the country hardly needed. In fact, the distinction between one British Indian administration and another was illusory, and the proponents of 'drain theory' were not inclined to accept it: under either regime, they said, Great Britain blocked Indian development, squeezed imports from India – which were 'balanced' through the imposition of a common sterling-based monetary system – extracted revenues, interest and transfer payments, and produced misery and famines. One weak response to these charges was simply to deny them on the surmise that the traditional sector of the Indian economy had benefited from economic growth in its margins. According to I. Habib, this was tantamount to claiming that Indian living conditions under the Raj were not so bad because they had not appreciably deteriorated since Mughal times.[35]

Another questionable distinction whose critique also points to the primacy of the economic motivation behind colonialism is that between the 'old' and the 'new' British colonial empires. It is predicated by K. E. Knorr on the parallel changes from mercantilism to economic liberalism and from political liberalism to strict, even despotic, political control, which became effective after the American War of Independence. However, this distinction can be made to stick only if British India is excised from the historical picture, and this can only be sustained on the fiction of an East India Company operating autonomously, outside British government control or interest. In fact, the only real change from one empire to another was the loss of the Atlantic seaboard colonies of North America, whose bonds with Britain were significantly economic but mainly ethnic and political, and the strongest liens that go from one of those purported empires to the other, best exemplified by the British colonialist connection with India, were economic in nature. The economic bonds held true when the ethnic and political bonds were burst asunder in these historical cases. It would not be amiss to conclude on this issue that the empire held because Britain had the will and the strength to make it hold and that underlying this, regardless of political and policy changes, were strong economic liens and economic interests ultimately emanating from Britain.[36]

The scramble for Africa

But if a bland general reading of Hobson poses few difficulties, such is not the case with the specific theory, which he harnessed to a stern programme of proof and verification, and which therefore cannot be carried without many qualifications beyond the limits he himself put on it. The rapid phase of European colonial expansion during the nineteenth century, to which the thesis specifically applies, started by Hobson's reckoning around 1870. Objectively, at least two political trends were evident: (a) empires expanded dramatically in a short period of time; and (b) imperialist governments seemed to take a more active, more direct role in the process of expansion. Hobson's explanation for this was that capitalist interests, both commercial and manufacturing, wanted imperial outlets and could make governments do their bidding. Populated, semi-populated and even empty territories were reconnoitred and acquired as colonies in lightning marches or campaigns. The military led the way, although they may have come after the trader or the missionary. The colonializers fanned out from enclaves to embrace as much territory as they could before encountering other European occupation or serious resistance of any kind.

The French were very nimble at this sort of thing, even before the start of the rapid phase of colonialism, but they were also often checked. They were checked by the existence of Morocco during the conquest of Algeria in the 1840s and they were contained by the British in their dash to the Sudan in 1898. The Germans occupied Tanganyika in 1885 as far south as British and Portuguese zones of influence or occupation, north to British East Africa, and west to Leopoldine commercial occupation in the Congo. The Italians started from Eritrea and were actually defeated and contained by the Ethiopians in 1896. This pattern of colonialism differs from all the others we have defined. The new, late-nineteenth-century colonies may have started in many cases as entrepôts, but that is the only characteristic they retained from other colonial epochs. They were not settlement colonies and were never meant to be. They were not plantations, although in some cases they later became one-crop economies. The analogy with India only extended really to the entrepôt origins of both, and they differed significantly in the speed and the mechanics of conquest: it took centuries to conquer India; the scramble for Africa was over before 1900. British India grew by fits and starts, depending on international conditions, on British home policies, on political opportunities, on strict commercial considerations, and also on man-on-the-spot initiatives. African empires grew in one fell swoop at one specific lapse of time and mainly either by political decision or with the active consent of policy. How does Hobson's theory stand up to the reality of the scramble for Africa? We shall consider first the alternative political theses and then the cliometric critique of the theory.

The principal common contention of the various political explanations of the scramble for Africa is that, at some specific point during the last quarter of the nineteenth century, the European powers – mainly Great Britain, France and Germany – decided to share out the African continent among themselves. This decision was a natural geopolitical extension of their larger big-power rivalries, which also went beyond Africa to China, Oceania and the Pacific. The scenario of world rivalries, originating in intra-European political issues and confrontations, such as Franco-German enmity and the British interest in the balance of power on the continent of Europe, is presented in these theories as a likelier explanation of late-nineteenth-century European colonialist expansionism than the Hobson economic-imperialism hypothesis. Where they diverge is in singling out the specific event and the circumstances that set off the African grab, or to be even more concrete, on the date when it actually started. More for the sake of illustration than of thoroughness – because, despite their multiplicity, these explanations do not at bottom depart significantly from the pattern sketched here – we shall consider three influential ones: (a) the complex interrelated arguments advanced by the British historians, R. Robinson and J. Gallagher; (b) the wide-scope approach of the American historian of world colonialism, D. K. Fieldhouse, who besides his political theses also built up a minute refutation of the statistical arguments for economic imperialism; (c) the chronological approach of the German specialist in social imperialism, W. Baumgart.

The Gallagher and Robinson thesis

Robinson and Gallagher believe that Britain's colonial policy during most of the nineteenth century was one of moderate expansion preferably through informal imperialism, which refers to all the means of keeping less developed nations docile to free trade and Western financial practices without the need for outright military intervention. For them, as for Fieldhouse, when territorial expansion did occur before the rapid phase of nineteenth-century colonialism, it was usually attributable to 'man-on-the-spot' initiatives, or at least to specific local circumstances rather than to metropolitan policy. All of this changed owing to the Ottoman inability to exercise adequate sovereignty in Egypt and supposedly to safeguard operations in the Suez canal, which after its opening in 1869 was Britain's vital link with the Indian Ocean and the bulk of her empire. As a result, and without the hard-to-get co-operation of France, Whitehall unilaterally decided the occupation of Egypt in 1882 in the hope that it would be lenient, beneficial and short-lived. In the event, one thing led to another and, from Egypt, Britain went into the Sudan and France went into Madagascar as compensation for the Sudan, the division of West Africa entered the rapid phase, and Germany decided it could not be left out of this process of territorial acquisitions, and so on. Hovering behind this scenario is, of course, the economic importance to Britain of her Indian empire, but Gallagher and Robinson, in their effort to explain the scramble for Africa, chose not to dwell on this ultimately crucial influence, preferring instead to search for causes in the documented motivations of British statesmen, which as an intellectual démarche lies at the opposite extreme from Hobson's concentration on statistics rather than subjective considerations. Less than a critique of the economic-imperialism hypothesis, the Robinson/Gallagher approach is a modulation of it, but in carrying through their impressive, deeply delving programme of research these authors tilted the balance decisively away from the fundamental economic character of colonialism and presented a view of imperialism which, in depending excessively on the minutiae of history, distorted the perception of historical continuity in the prevalence of long-term trends and forces. Granted for the sake of argument that the British occupation of Egypt in 1882 did signal the actual historical start of the scramble for Africa, where did that leave the wider world-historical circumstances that made British and European hegemony and expansion possible? What Robinson and Gallagher said finally was that for the period they chose (the 1880s) and with their preordained 'frame of reference for colonial motivations' (the 'official mind' of British statesmen), they saw no other political solution for the African grab but the specific time and the specific motives they chose.[37]

Fieldhouse and Baumgart thought that they had discovered the beginning of the scramble for Africa in events different from, but related to, the sequence posited by Robinson and Gallagher. On the question of dates, Fieldhouse prefers 1884, the year of 'Bismarck's sudden claim for German colonies', in fact when Germany initiated its own occupation of African territories; Baumgart, assuming a synoptic stance on general historical research on the issue, seems to opt for 1879, 'when the rivalry between Britain and France became especially intense in West Africa'. When a specific date is identified for the initiation of a historical process, the implication in the nature of things is that politics, which means deliberation, or at the very least, some form of decision-taking, is the underlying predominant force. But Fieldhouse and Baumgart arrive at their final chronological conclusions from different lines of argumentation. Baumgart discards as unconvincing the economic-imperialism hypothesis and, somewhat like Robinson and Gallagher, he goes for the evidence on political motivations within the European powers, where he sees, perhaps with a marked Bismarckian slant, the decisive weight of the latitudinous reading of social imperialism consisting in the attitude that colonialism existed for the aggrandisement of colonialist powers rather than in the Pecksniffian pretension that it was a humane enterprise of Western civilization. Fieldhouse is not quite as contemptuous of economic motivations, but he tends to ascribe these to peripheral, piecemeal initiatives in the colonies themselves, and for the weightier process of the late-nineteenth-century world colonialist grab he plumped unequivocally for political motivations.[38]

The Fieldhouse critique: focusing on numbers

In arriving at this conclusion – which, as we shall see, is not really as final as it seems – Fieldhouse attempted the statistical or cliometric refutation of the economic-imperialism hypothesis. The premiss for this critique was the Hobsonian claim that colonies were sought as outlets for capital, which in turn carried the implication that once colonies were acquired they necessarily had to become the objects of metropolitan finances, investment and commerce. The defence of this thesis rests on precise statistical facts and series that respond to such questions as: Why did the British empire grow by so many hundreds of thousands of square kilometres from such a year to such a year? Or, what was the flow of capital from Great Britain to the Gold Coast during the last decade of the nineteenth century? Theories of imperialism since the Second World War have in general tended to ignore the distinction between colonialism and imperialism. It cannot be ignored in considering Hobson's original theory, in which, however, it is one of the weaker flanks.

Fieldhouse reduced the central issue of the original restricted version of economic imperialism in this manner: 'The question can therefore be redefined: what economic advantage did Europe extract from her colonies which she could not have gained from other countries, however similar in other ways?' In an exercise which many undertook before and after him, Fieldhouse systematically demonstrated that capitals from the colonialist metropoles did not preferentially flow towards their respective colonies. In a particularly telling argument concerning imperial tariffs, he averred that 'not all imperialists were protectionists whereas all protectionists were imperialists', which seemed to show the political primacy of imperialism and the unworthiness of the Hobson thesis. Yet Fieldhouse's refutation was constructed upon an overall analysis which demonstrated that, on the whole, European overseas colonialism had been extremely profitable from its inception in the fifteenth century, and this meant that, for some reason, Fieldhouse seemed to be applying an arbitrarily different standard to late-nineteenth-century colonialism from the one he applied before that period. If colonies had been traditionally profitable for Europe, which meant that their acquisition had an obvious economic base, why discard the same base for the African grab?

Fieldhouse also seemed to be discarding the notion of potential or expected profits and advantages, which had been operative even as far back as the discovery of Africa and the conquest of America. This perfectly reasonable motivation, which has been called 'the pre-emptive mechanism', was described by M. W. Doyle in these terms: 'The chance that those lands might prove valuable in themselves or to another power outweighed the prospective costs of management, and expansion was pre-emptive.' Lenin deduced from technological progress that colonies did not have to be profitable from the start and that their acquisition had probably more to do with future economic exploitation than with short-term profits. He certainly was not the only one to make that logical inference. In fact, Hobson himself must have seen that the logic of his thesis implies a certain degree of precariousness or of chance. No one ever invests a fortune with the assurance of getting it back in five years, but if you are going to make a profit, there is always a chance your money might go into a dud. This was not where the Hobson thesis went wrong. Where it distorts, and carries with it people such as Fieldhouse and Robinson and Gallagher, is in its restricted definition of economic imperialism.[39]

Historically, colonialist imperialism seems to be one essentially unbroken reality, so that the very difficult intellectual task of reducing it to a short period of Western history during the fag-end of the nineteenth century, which was the task undertaken by Hobson and accepted as such by Lenin, makes its refutation all the easier. It is a matter of the harder you try the easier it is to fall. By an inverted logic, the fallacy of the specific theory of economic imperialism gives way to the myth of the political origins of the African grab. But if Fieldhouse's refutation of Hobson is not a valid refutation of the economic causes of colonialism, what is it then? After 1880 colonialism was notoriously political in character, which does not mean that it was not also interested in profits, but that it was motivated not so much by the defence of profits as by the expectation of future benefits, economic ones not excluded. Whatever or whoever set off the late-nineteenth-century scramble for colonies, were it West Africa, Egypt or Bismarck, the question to ask in relation to economic imperialism in a wide sense should be whether or not the rivalries and the issues involved were devoid of economic significance of any kind. To put it another way: the indiscriminate annexation of territories is not per se a contradiction of the causes implied in economic-imperialism theory. It would be if it were possible to affirm that the acquisition of land obeyed only motives and objectives of a rigorously non-economic character. This was demonstrated neither by Robinson and Gallagher nor by Fieldhouse. What Fieldhouse did prove was that a narrow definition of economic imperialism is practically impossible to defend successfully.

Fieldhouse was not alone in expressing those ideas, nor were Robinson and Gallagher the sole proponents of the idea of the nineteenth-century importance of informal imperialism. The prominence we accord to Robinson and Gallagher is based on the impact of their programme of political review of the economic-imperialism theory, and Fieldhouse, of course, wrote the virtually definitive refutation of its specific economic claims. In 1960, J. S. Galbraith defended the man-on-the-spot explanation of

British colonial expansion. F. Crouzet and H. Neisser both probed different chinks in the armour of Hobson's theory: Crouzet denied that the post-1880 colonial expansion contributed to the prosperity of late-Victorian and Edwardian Britain; Neisser said that, apart from a cushioning effect during periods of depression, there were for Britain no other economic benefits from empire. Yet the ghost of Hobson's economic imperialism seems never to be laid to rest. A recent book by L. E. Davis and R. A. Huttenback tackles all the conceivable issues and implications of the specific theory in pages bristling with statistics, tables and all the paraphernalia of cliometrics.[40] It proves, for instance, that the people at large paid for an empire whose most palpable benefits accrued to the economic upper class. But if this indicates a narrow connection between empire and gain, neither the import of raw materials, nor trade, nor emigration, nor overseas rates of return (colonial ones were no better than those to be had at home) argue for the profitability of empire. Even so, according to P. K. O'Brien, the proof that the empire paid or did not pay is not given one way or the other in this work, mainly because it is not possible to quantify the alternatives of dismantling the empire to compare them with the existing facts and determine conclusively that the empire was demonstrably useless. In other words, the only final proof that imperialism was an unnecessary economic fiasco can only be obtained contrafactually, which means that Messrs Davis and Huttenback and their battery of computers may not have exhausted the subject.

The idea of imbalance

It may be that the only way to encompass imperialism, whether pre- or post-1880, whether political or economic in essence, is to be as unspecific as possible and to work with the broadest possible categories. The notion of imbalance very nearly fits the bill ideally. In a 1965 summing up, Fieldhouse wrote: 'The modern empires, however, were inevitable. At some point between 1700 and the mid-19th century, the balance of power between the Western nations and the rest of the world shifted decisively.' This proposition is reminiscent of D. S. Landes' explanation that imperialism is the result of a secular imbalance of power, which he expressed in an article in 1961: 'It seems to me that one has to look at imperialism as a multifarious response to a common opportunity that consists simply in disparity of power. . .So if one seeks to understand the imperialism of the 19th century, one must take into account not only strong economic motives, among others, but even more those technological changes that increased the disparity of force between Europe and the rest of the world and created the opportunity for and possibility of dominions. . .In this sense, the expansion of the 19th century is only the last phase of a millennial explosion that goes back to the turning point of the Middle Ages when the peoples of Europe, long compressed and pierced by stronger enemies, halted their incursions and beat them back – on the plateau of Castile, on the East Elbian plain, along the shores of the Mediterranean.' Related to Landes' 'imbalance thesis' are what Doyle calls 'systemic views' on imperialism, which he summarizes in this manner: 'Disparities in power provide both opportunities and motives for the establishment of empires.' Doyle traces them originally to a 1947 book on Athenian imperialism by J. de Romilly, and also finds them expressed in M. Kaplan (1957) and K. Waltz (1959). All these ideas have a vague resemblance to Schumpeter's 'objectless disposition on the part of a state to unlimited forcible expansion' to the extent that they all posit a lack of specific motivation.[41]

The contemporary reformulations of economic imperialism incline more towards a general concept of economic causation than towards the balance-sheet approach that characterized the specific theory during its first, essentially Hobsonian phase. The idea of imbalance and the general theory of economic imperialism could easily be reconciled and made complementary. Certainly imbalance and the notion of a development gap are apposite. The general theory of economic imperialism, precisely because of its non-restrictive protean character, leads smoothly into the question of the origins of international economic inequality. This issue was in fact totally irrelevant to the concerns of Hobson or for that matter of Lenin, for they were both immersed in strictly European political squabbles: Hobson in the question of British overseas expansionism; Lenin in Marxist factional struggles. Neo-imperialist theory is associated with the Third World: it emanates from Third World concerns, and it has been elaborated to a significant extent in the Third World or from a Third World perspective. The specific theory cannot escape the taint of intentionality given the nature of its contentions, and this carried over into Stalinism and into contemporary theorization. But aside from this – and, of course, the common ground of economic motivation or causation and the negative results of colonialism – they are two distinct systems of conceptualization with different historical and socio-political sources, different themes and objectives, and different investigative methodologies. Modern dependency theory often protests its relatedness to Lenin's concept of imperialism, but the specific contemporary attempts to revive the latter (notably by H. Magdoff, T. Kemp and A. K. Bagchi) have not been very convincing.

Marxist theories of imperialism

Rosa Luxemburg

In part, Hobson has become identified with the specific theory of economic imperialism because of Lenin's avowed debt to him. Marx himself did not formulate anything that could be described as a theory of economic imperialism, but this does not mean that Marxists did not try to found one on his teachings. One who tried to do so, even though it meant proposing a bruising criticism of Marx's main analysis of capitalism, was the Polish-German Marxist Rosa Luxemburg. She was a fiery, brilliant and unyielding intellectual and politician, who founded, with Karl Liebknecht, the communist Spartakist movement in the aftermath of Germany's defeat in the First World War and who was killed in the insurrection of January 1919 in Berlin by the Freikorps under the social-democratic Weimar Republic.

In 1913 she published *The Accumulation of Capital*, a work in which she tried to come to grips with the question of capitalist economic growth and economic imperialism in terms of complementarity. Given Marx's fundamental definition of capitalism (a term, incidentally, which he never used himself) as a discrete and finite historical MOP, he had to explain three processes in relation to it: (a) how it came about, which he called 'primitive accumulation'; (b) how it reproduced its relations of production, which he called 'simple reproduction'; (c) how it evolved and expanded towards its own dissolution, which he called 'expanded reproduction'.[42] As we shall see, the general theory of economic imperialism, or dependency theory, places the start of capitalism's interference with economico-historical processes in non-European lands virtually during or just after the phase of primitive accumulation in Europe. The ambiguity here on the exact point in Europe's capitalist development at the start of European colonialist expansion is due principally to the lack of chronological and functional precision in Marx's usage of his analytical concepts, which appear in his writings as purely abstract and theoretical, hence with at most imprecise references to concrete historical situations, as when he placed the start of capitalism in the late-Medieval Italian city-states active in international commerce. The most, therefore, that can be inferred from dependency theory is that colonialist expansion could have contributed to the drawn-out process of primitive accumulation in the more advanced European states during the fifteenth and sixteenth centuries and that surely it promoted the ensuing capitalist process of self-replication and growth. In the case of Luxemburg's theory on economic imperialism there is no comparable ambiguity, for she explicitly took up Marx's schema when the requirements of expanded reproduction were leading towards the final integration and transformation of the world from its West European centres of power during the imperialist era.

Very synthetically and schematically, it can be said that Luxemburg starts from Marx's division of simple reproduction into a producers' goods sector (department one) and a consumers' goods sector (department two). The first supplies its own and the other sector's needs; the inverse relation holds true as well. This balance, however, was unrealistic, for it did not reflect the reality of economic expansion, and therefore, it implied and required the schema of expanded reproduction. Always following Marx, Luxemburg claimed that any increment in the process of capitalist reproduction had to come from increased production in department one, which meant that surplus value was deflected from hoarding or consumption into increased capitalization, but this created the problem of the realization of capital in that department two would be interested in supplying the growing needs of department one but did not have the incentive to absorb its increased production. The evident reason for this was that capitalists were in the business of making profits for themselves, not for others, and, *a fortiori*, the capitalist MOP did not operate with the target in view of creating jobs for workers. There was also no question of increasing overall demand by raising wages, as Hobson had advocated, because Marxism was built on a series of fundamental psychological axioms that did not include the pursuit of social welfare or the exercise of altruism. This also disqualified the argument of natural population increases, for there were no special provisions under capitalism for new workers, unless they were taken on by capitalists as a result of profit-making opportunities, in which case they were already part of the working force and could not exert new demand. Population increase among workers had to be supported by the workers with existing wages, and this could not be considered an injection of new consumers into the economy. Another, perhaps more direct, way of describing the same problem was that the avid search for profits, even by the sharpest operators, did not guarantee profits in industrialized capitalist economies subject as they were to business cycles and especially to the problem of the declining rate of profits.[43]

Was Luxemburg being faithful to Marx in this analysis? She accepted Marx's premisses on capitalist reproduction and she remitted them with respect and punctilio. Where she parted company from Marx was on the question of the growth and expansion of capitalism. In Luxemburg's view, Marx's schema of expanded reproduction was not a good enough answer to the question, and even though, as she claims, Marx was aware of the insufficiency in his theory he had not tried hard enough to cover it. On the other hand, it is not amiss to wonder in this case, as in the case of the origins of economic inequalities between the West and other cultures, to what extent that really was an issue for Marx. E. Mandel apparently thinks that it was, and despite his admiration for Luxemburg and his tendency to agree with her reading of Marx, he criticizes her on this issue on two grounds: (a) that she makes too much of Marx's schemas, which were after all designed to illustrate the capitalist MOP and how it went on reproducing itself; (b) that at any rate Marx did not finish *Capital* and that his intention had been to explore the problems of 'many capitals', which somewhat inconsistently does seem to imply that Luxemburg had not over-stressed the point of a lack in Marxist theory.[44]

It could be that Marx, who, after all, had offered sufficient reasons to expect the downfall of capitalism, did not feel the need to explain further the mechanics of a system whose expansion must have seemed to him lopsided in its social effects and transitory in time. In whatever modern sense we employ the word development, whether as economic prosperity or as social welfare conditions or in any combination of these complementary ideas, it was foreign to Marx's concept of capitalism. Capitalism had come about historically and it had created progressive and socially rational economic structures and practices, but it had by no means 'developed' either in the sense of abundance or of social justice. This blind spot in Marx's vision invariably leads his contemporary followers into the 'progress dilemma' whereby they feel obliged to criticize and denounce capitalism while at the same time wishing it on the Third World. Marx had seen in the capitalist system a driving need to increase profits, which went about it self-destructively by concentrating capital and laying off workers every time a strong economic crisis struck at its foundations. Luxemburg interpreted the capitalist drive for profits as the need to incorporate more and more consumers and cheap labour, a possibility that was becoming increasingly more difficult in the industrialized nations. The difference between them lay in that Marx had his sights firmly placed on Europe and more specifically on England, whereas Luxenburg as an intellectual product of the age of imperialism was much more aware than Marx of the spread of capitalism to backward nations. Unlike Lenin, she did not make concessions to nationalism because she believed that all it did was to divide the working class. How did Luxemburg formulate her theory of economic imperialism as she solved the problem of expanded reproduction?

'Simple' and 'expanded' reproduction

Her solution to this problem went back to her criticism of Marx's schema of simple reproduction, which was 'that simple reproduction is a fiction not only for capitalist production but also for the progress of civilization in general'. The key to growth and expansion was expanded reproduction, and this was only possible if there existed a 'third person' to absorb the increase in production as foreseen but not developed by Marx in his schemas. Who or what was the 'third person' that other Marxists had also sought without finding? 'The decisive fact', she wrote, 'is that the surplus value can not be realized by sale either to workers or to capitalists, but only if it is sold to such social organizations or strata whose own MOP is not capitalist.' And the difficulties that Marx had experienced in explaining the realization of surplus stemmed from his premiss that once capitalism prevailed it did so 'universally', when in fact 'real life has never known a self-sufficient capitalist society under the exclusive domination of the capitalist MOP'. Nevertheless, capitalism in England and in Germany and generally in what she called the 'old bourgeois countries', was probably at its peak, and this was where imperialism came in, because there were plenty of non-capitalist societies to bring within the confines of capitalism as purchasers of excess production of capital goods, as providers of raw materials, and as sources of exploitable labour. In the long run and by those and other means, capitalism would transform non-capitalist societies into replicas of itself and the 'young capitalist states' would try to shake off the hold of the older ones, but while that happened capital flowing in to them would get its own back. In the end all would be operating under the same system, heading towards the same apocalypse of greed. Her basic point was that the only venue for surplus capital was imperialism: 'Only the opening of immense non-capitalist lands, through the increase in the number of consumers, has allowed capital to pursue enlarged reproduction.'[45]

Here again, Luxemburg showed herself a firm adherent to and a cautious dissenter from Marx. Her use of Marxist definitions and postulates is deferential, even slavish, but the inclusion of the entire globe as a necessary field for the expansion of capitalism before its collapse was carrying Marxist analysis beyond what Marx, who could probably envisage revolution with more ease than decolonization, had foreseen. In doing this she was facing up to something that also troubled other Marxist theorists, and that was the extraordinary tenacity of capitalism in spite of grinding exploitation, cyclical crises and cut-throat political and economic rivalries. In her view of world capitalism Luxemburg was wrong because of something that her analysis did not reveal to her: she had not the slightest inkling of the notion and the reality of underdevelopment and this for the simple reason that for her, as a good Marxist of another age, exploitation and the conditions of life were the same whether in the imperialist countries or in developing capitalist nations such as Egypt or Turkey. A hungry worker in a young capitalist country had nothing to envy his counterpart in a capital-exporting country. To have believed otherwise would have meant for her, as for any true and loyal Marxist, a terrible misperception, indeed a heresy. Whatever else one might have said of capital, it could not be denied that it was an equalizer of working-class conditions, and, as there was no theoretical objection to the export of misery, Luxemburg logically could not conceive the sort of international economic disparities, involving inequalities in employment ratios and dramatic wage differences, that we have become familiar with in our times. This problem has dogged Marxism all the way to the present and Marxists still have not been able to solve it adequately. As is known, those Marxists who engaged in revisionism by recognizing that capitalism could benefit workers by attenuating exploitation were ostracized and expelled from the fold.

Hilferding and the robber barons

The Austrian Marxist, R. Hilferding, had actually taken an ambiguous step towards the perception of underdevelopment in his book *Finance Capital*, published in 1910.[46] Hobson's 'square one' had been the problem of low wages and oversaving; Luxemburg's was the Marxist schemas of capitalist reproduction. Hilferding posited finance capital as the fundamental manifestation of capitalist concentration and, in effect, of 'organized' capitalism. Bankers were like economic planners who took over industry and streamlined it through initially profitable monopolies and cartels. These achievements, however, could not last without their control of the state, which had to be used to protect profits by means of high tariffs allowing higher prices but at the same time resulting in fewer sales. Whereas in Marx production and profits continued punctuated by crises which led to growing concentration and centralization, in Hilferding the combined forces of capitalism within one nation established policies to prevent the decline of the rate of profits. In view of the counter-productive effects of tariffs, exports had to be promoted and provisions made for the safe export of capital. But these measures collided with similar ones introduced by other capital-exporting nations, thus creating rivalries and tensions. The logical outlets were the undeveloped regions of the world, to ensnare which the state was made actively interventionist, and this led to expansionism and finally to conflict.[47]

For some, Hilferding anticipated in general lines the conditions under which the First World War started. His depiction of bankers, whether considered original to him or, what is more likely, as a rationalization of a widespread popular perception, became influential in the 1920s and 1930s. It corresponded to the image of the pudgy, coat-tailed, high-hatted, hedonistic and unscrupulous financiers represented in the Berlin paintings of G. Grosz and in countless cartoons of the times. His theory on the operations of finance capital was illustrated convincingly and entertainingly in M. Josephson's socio-historical chronicle *The Robber Barons* (1934), in which a group of American financiers came within a whisker of taking over the entire economy of the USA. The coincidence between Josephson and Hilferding was probably unwitting, but in any case both authors demonstrate the powerful hold that bankers had on the imagination and the thought of leftist intellectuals during the early decades of the century. Whatever the cause for this, Hilferding undoubtedly gave finance capital a theoretical status and a notoriety it did not have before – certainly not in Marx, whose villains were the generic class of capitalists, although, perhaps, on a more profound ontological level, what Marx really deplored was greed itself – and this deserved or undeserved reputation became something of a folk-myth during the depression years in America. These are no mean achievements, but history has not been kind to Hilferding's theory and today it is generally agreed that banks do not seem to have the power that Hilferding attributed to them. Whether they once had it and then lost it to state control and regulation or to some economic force stronger than theirs is another question, but then Hilferding would have to be faulted for having had an excessively negative and pessimistic view of the state as a tool of special interests under capitalism. Where he commands respect and attention even today is in his pioneering if far from infallible exploration of the relations between developed and backward countries.

On this question Hilferding commenced with the classic Marxist proposition of the transplantation of capitalism to non-capitalist territories, although he singled out a specific scenario in which industrial and finance capital overthrows traditional social relations and introduces capitalist relations of production and exploitation 'at the level already attained in the most advanced country'. But this did not necessarily create homogeneous conditions all over the world, for there were differences between the capital exporters and the capital importing or debtor countries, as there were international differences based on what Hilferding called the size of the 'economic territory', which essentially referred to the ability of an economy to produce and to absorb capital. One of the results of the free flow of capital was the creation of colonies. Another was the establishment of dependency relations, a case in point being the control by foreign capital of the iron mines in Spain and Sweden. Hilferding's fallibility is manifest in his underestimation of Swedish capitalist resilience, although he was not far from the truth in relation to the economic backwardness of Spain.

Finally, and most significantly, Hilferding described certain traits of capital-importing countries as corresponding not to economies growing to full capitalist status but to economies staying at a level of stunted development. A capital surplus, for instance, usually gave a country advantages over less developed economies: 'The export of capital had now become a means of ensuring that the capital-exporting countries will be the suppliers of industrial goods. The customer has no choice: he becomes a debtor and hence a dependent who must accept the conditions imposed by his creditors.' There was also what he called 'absentee ownership', by which he meant foreign capital and the profits it sucks out of 'small economic territories'. 'Naturally, this accumulation did not have to take place', he wrote, 'in the country where the profit originated; but this capitalist "absentee ownership" slows down enormously the pace of accumulation, and hence the further development of capitalism, in the debtor country.' Hilferding even described a typical phenomenon of today's debtor countries: the flight of capital: 'The smaller the economic territory the less the power it has to sustain the competitive struggle successfully by means of large export subsidies, and the stronger is the urge to export capital in order to share in the economic development and higher profits of other greater powers.'

Of course, Hilferding was often wrong. He considered the lack of free labour in a new country (citing Australia and Canada) as the greatest obstacle to its development, which even on the eve of the First World War must have sounded like rigmarole. He referred to a supposed preference by British capitalists for an imperial tariff, although that was the particular hobby-horse of a school of social imperialist thought and was never approved or applied. All in all, one suspects that Hilferding did not lump all capitalisms in the same category and that he considered that attaining to full capitalist status was important and rewarding per se for a country. Likewise, he thought he perceived that the inability to achieve this was engineered by the more developed capitalist countries, and this was a far cry from the point of view of a dyed-in-the-wool Marxist such as Rosa Luxemburg. Marx had said that capitalism creates like wherever it goes. Luxemburg added that capitalism must create like in order to survive. Hilferding implied that capitalism created caricatures of itself from the more developed to the less developed countries.[48]

The harvest of Leninism

Rosa Luxemburg had no doubts whatever about the inevitability of capitalism on a global scale, but it was not a cheery prospect except in that it would presage doom for the system. Hilferding had an equally apocalyptic vision, but he was more interested in the mechanics and the effects of capital flows, not that he had any doubts about what their final exploitative intents were. In the process, however, he observed shades and variations. The impact of capital was not the same in every country. Often, instead of capitalist development, dependence was the result. Likewise, development could be stunted. Hilferding could have been, like the brilliant descriptive economist that he was, on the spoor of under-development as we know it. Lenin's own outlook was influenced by Hilferding. He wrote his treatise *Imperialism, the Highest Stage of Capitalism* in 1916, in the midst of the First World War, which he was sitting out in Switzerland. But he was far from detached about imperialism and, in fact, if his essay had one unifying purpose it was to give the coup de grâce to K. Kautsky's notion of ultra-imperialism, the hypothetical grand alliance between the imperialist powers in order to divide the world, shattered by the occurrence of the First World War, and to offer his own version of why capitalism always carried in itself the seeds of conflict. He was also trying to square what he knew about capitalism with the theory of economic imperialism. For this theory he consulted, besides Hilferding, the seminal work by Hobson, and he followed both closely. However, he was also attuned to Marx's vision of the evolution of capitalism towards its own downfall.

In this respect, it is necessary to retain two principles from Marx: (1) that under capitalism there is a tendency for machinery to replace workers (what Marxists describe as an increase in the 'organic composition of capital'); (2) that, in consequence of this, although profits for a time might increase in absolute terms, over the long-haul the tendency of the rate of profit, or the proportion of labour power the capitalist retains as surplus relative to total capital, is downwards. If the mechanization of industry is a natural and rational tendency of the forces of production under capitalism, capitalist greed turns it unwittingly against itself when it uses machinery to lay off workers in order to save on expenditure on variable capital. This is carrying the trend towards concentration of the means of production – in Marx's words, 'the facility of appropriating other people's surplus labour in great masses' – to irrational extremes. It also leads to the centralization of capital, a tendency summarized by Marx in the lapidary phrase: 'One capitalist always strikes down many capitalists', which resulted in that a tiny few benefited from a system of economic oppression over the vast working majority of society, 'trained, united and organized by the very mechanism of the capitalist process of production'. Eventually, therefore: 'The monopoly of capital becomes a fetter upon the MOP which has flourished alongside and inside it. The centralization of the means of production and the socialization of labour reach a point at which they become incompatible with their capitalist integument. The integument is burst asunder. The knell of capitalist private property sounds. The expropriators are expropriated.'*

* Owens and Sutcliffe offer the following analytical explanation of the organic composition of capital and the tendency of the rate of profit to fall: 'In Marx's analysis of the capitalist MOP the value of a commodity is composed of: first, the value of the constant capital (c), that is, the machinery and raw materials used up in production; second, variable capital (v), the amount of labour used – measured in terms of the wages paid to keep the workers alive; and third, surplus

Loyal Marxists such as Mandel would claim that the process is not quite as simple or as facilely determinist as this, and that, despite his own words, Marx never meant that it should seem that way. Lenin, however, certainly believed in the ineluctability of those tendencies depicted by Marx. If capitalism had not yet succumbed it was because it compensated for its falling profits at home with its exploitation of non-capitalist or semi-capitalist territories abroad. To reach this conclusion he accepted Hobson's 'flag-follows-capital' model and Hilferding's thesis on the primacy of finance capital under modern capitalism and its control over the state in capitalist society. However, the ultimate, and the last, concretion of Marx's centralization process, and the base upon which imperialism rested, was the reduction of the exploiters not to a few individual capitalists but to a handful of capitalist powers in which there was virtually no separation between capital and state.[49]

Lenin believed that the world was ruled by financial capital, concentrated in the 'four pillars' of the system: Great Britain, the USA, France and Germany. Capital travelled to wherever it could make profits, especially backward countries. He was well within the traditional Marxist norm: 'The export of capital affects and greatly accelerates the development of capitalism in those countries to which it is exported. While, therefore, the export of capital may tend to a certain extent to arrest development in the capital exporting countries, it can only do so by opening and deepening the further development of capitalism throughout the world.' When Lenin speaks of 'development', though, it should be borne in mind that it is not 'development' in the contemporary sense, but in the

---

value (s), the excess of the value of a commodity over its cost of production (c + v). . .Technical progress in Marx's view tended to raise the organic composition of capital (c/v) in production, reducing the amount of labour needed relative to capital. With the class struggle tending to keep the rate of surplus value, or the rate of exploitation (s/v), constant, it follows that there is a tendency for the rate of profit in Marx's sense s/c + v to fall.'

Both technical progress and the class struggle must be understood in terms of the capitalist's drive for greater profit. Using the same simple equation, therefore, it is possible to deduce how the absolute mass of surplus can grow while the rate of profit keeps falling, when both c and v grow but c at a faster rate than v, and, finally, how a constantly falling rate of profit will lead to one of two outcomes: (1) a reduction of s to increase s/c + v, or (2) the situation where the stronger capitalists will gobble up the weaker. In the meantime, since v diminished in relation to the growth of the available labour force (in the reserve army and through natural increase), the capitalist MOP arrives at the stage where the tension between the forces of production and the relations of production is such that the system will collapse or will be overthrown. (R. Owens and B. Sutcliffe, *Studies in the Theory of Imperialism*, London, 1972, pp. 13–14.)

brutal Marxist sense of the destruction of old social relations and of traditional economic institutions. What capitalism put in its place was not exactly welfare and social justice but the worst forms of economic subjection and drudgery.

On the other hand, there was no question for Lenin, as there had not been for Hilferding and for Luxemburg, of some kind of 'structural' impossibility to industrialize. In impeccable Hobsonian fashion, Lenin related the growth of colonialism to the age of financial capital, and he cited the fact that social imperialist thought accompanied and justified colonialism. The conquest of colonies was frequently motivated by the need to control sources of raw materials. Lenin refuted the arguments against imperialism based on the non-profitability of colonies: 'Financial capital is interested not only in the already discovered sources of raw materials but also in the potential sources, because present-day technical development is extremely rapid, and land which is useless today may be made fertile tomorrow if new methods are applied. . .and if large amounts of capital are invested.' Finally, Lenin echoed Hilferding's analysis of dependence: 'Typical of this epoch is not only the two main groups of countries: those owning colonies and colonies, but also the divers forms of dependent countries which, officially, are politically independent, but in fact, are enmeshed in this net of financial and diplomatic dependence.' It is not easy to find consistency in all these points of view unless we keep in mind that, for Lenin, financial capital and capitalism in general were unmitigated disasters not 'out of any particular malice, but because the degree of concentration which had been reached forces them to adopt this method (division of the world) in order to obtain profits'. Up to this point Lenin was well within conventional economic-imperialism analysis, but in what follows he tended to leave the beaten track to pursue certain formulations, some basically of practical politics, which were pregnant with consequences.[50]

The highest and final stage of capitalism

Lenin made clear that he considered imperialism to be consubstantial with capitalism at its highest and final stage. The features of imperialism were: (a) concentration of production and of capital; (b) merging of bank capital with industrial capital in a financial oligarchy; (c) export of capital; (d) international monopolist capitalist combines sharing the world; (e) territorial division of the world. This international situation led to war. Far from lessening 'the unevenness of contradictions inherent in the world economy, as Kautsky says, imperialism tends to increase them'. Lenin cited France's longing for Lorraine and Germany's for Belgium, but this is as far, really, as his explanation of the First World War went in concrete terms. More significantly, within this international framework, Lenin looked at the spread of capitalism, which Cunow defended as 'inevitable and progressive', and he responded with a singeing refusal. Yet Lenin himself had said pages before that the export of capital 'accelerates the development of capitalism', presumably in a historically progressive sense. Now he turns his back on this classic Marxist proposition and, throughout the final pages of his treatise, he pounds time and again the same keys: exploitation in the colonies and dependencies, coercion of workers everywhere, resistance to imperialism, and so forth. The spread of capitalism means above all the outright exploitation of workers in backward and subject countries. No improvement there, but this was to be expected in a Marxist political tract. However, there is also unequal development: imperialism does not develop except in so far as it can exploit and, in order to exploit, it has to accentuate inequalities of all sorts. Therefore, it has to be fought politically by all available means in every terrain.

Lenin's message is simple and direct: fight imperialism now and not when it has finished its work as a catalytic agent of social transformations, because it cannot be trusted to be anything but oppressive and rapacious. The form is obvious and the intention more than evident. There are no possible theoretical contradictions, because Lenin's essay is a political tract with an essentially nationalist message: 'Monopolies, oligarchy, the striving for domination instead of striving for liberty, the exploitation of an increasing number of small or weak nations by a handful of the richest or most powerful nations – all these have given birth to those distinctive characteristics of imperialism which compel us to define it as parasitic or decaying capitalism.'[51]

To complete the picture, Lenin remitted the concept of labour opportunism, which was the 'bribing' with monopoly profits of the upper strata of the proletariat. Hobson had already said that colonialist 'parasitism' permitted the bribing of the 'lower classes into acquiescence'. Lenin plays up the idea and puts it on an equal footing with imperialism on a scale of political priorities, because 'the fight against imperialism is a sham and a humbug unless it is inseparably bound up with the fight against opportunism'. If we collate the different parts of Lenin's essay, we can deduce approximately a cross-bred thesis in which the export of capital develops backward societies to some extent, but having entered the monopolistic imperialist phase capitalism is capable only of exploitation, which it does all over the planet from the few centres where finance capital is concentrated.

By toying with the Marxist notion of the export of capitalist forms but giving precedence to the ideas on economic imperialism in Hobson and Hilferding, Lenin came up with a call on the patriotic and nationalist sentiments of backward nations. It was a political thesis in essence, but in expressing it, not without its large quota of ambiguity (in fact, the richer for this), he foreshadowed the contemporary notion of a sort of long-term imperialism by which capitalism does not stimulate development and instead generates underdevelopment. It was also the thesis that some nationalists in Asia and Latin America were arriving at, and Lenin's message was calculated to coincide with them and to produce political benefits for communism. The important point here for the architecture of our own work is that Lenin had expressed to all intents and purposes something approaching a theory on the origins of inequality among nations. The scope of this theory, however, was too restricted. It concerned itself only with the period of imperialism, which in Lenin's terms of reference had practically begun at the turn of the century.[52]

To arrive at these incipient insights, Lenin had had to solve two doctrinaire problems. One was, as we saw, the equation that capitalism equals progress, which he had finally unambiguously denounced. The other was what to do with the so-called bribing of the working class in the centres of finance capital. After all, Lenin could not abandon the call 'proletarians arise' for 'oppressed nations, fight back'. Regarding the latter problem, he placed the fight against opportunism on the same footing as the struggle against imperialism. This was retreating judiciously from the out-and-out nationalist position he was taking, but it was understandable, and the unspoken message was that somehow the proletarians of the world were one class. Lenin was above all a politician, and this was politics of the highest order.

Concerning the other problem, that is, the transformation of capitalism in its international role, Lenin hit on a brilliant and quite frankly a pregnant idea: he said that capitalism had become imperialism and entered its final phase. Capitalism had not yet exhausted the possibilities of worldwide exploitation. In most colonies all it wanted were raw materials, which hardly represents an advanced form of capitalist exploitation. But it had run its course in the centres of financial capital. In both its centre and in the backward nations all over the world, it was the same imperialism, and therefore the fight, whatever the social conditions, was the same. In one stroke, he eliminated two objections – that it was necessary for advanced capitalism to spread all over the world (which was a refutation of Luxemburg) and that revolution had to begin at the core of capitalism. And this was theory-cum-politics of the most efficacious, almost prophetic kind. It is true that Lenin's essay would probably not have gained the influence that it did if Lenin himself had not triumphed as a politician, but surely it would have stood out in any event as a signal elaboration. Of course, the final phase never actually existed as such, and in that sense he was mistaken.

Lenin, it must be recalled, elaborated his theory of imperialism at a time when, first, the world had virtually been carved up by the main capitalist powers and there were signs and symptoms of restlessness and resistance in the subject lands, and secondly, the capitalist Armageddon that Marx had envisioned seemed to be coming true in the sense that the different 'advanced' and 'monopolized' national economic structures were at each others throats in the First World War. But, in fact, he did not proffer any conclusive evidence that capitalism had actually undergone a qualitative internal change that brought it closer to extinction through the working out of its internal self-destructive logic. He accepted Hobson's arguments and figures, reinforced with others he culled here and there in his own research, and poured the mixture into a Marxist conceptual and analytical framework, and after that he thought he found corroboration for his views in contemporary events. Hobson, however, had not proposed a new foredoomed hypostasis of capitalism, and Lenin's evidence for it was highly selective, netted by political revolutionary prejudices rather than by rigorous inductive methods.

The residual virtues of the specific theory of economic imperialism

Where did Lenin go specifically wrong in his historical analyses? He went wrong in dismissing the resilience of the centres of capitalism. Monopoly was not as widespread as he supposed. Financial capital had not taken over the system and was managing it through some kind of irresponsible and secretive *petit comité*. Raw materials were by no means running out. In other words, at the centre there was scope for growth and reform, and revolution was not imminent or even near because of the state of social conditions. This applied to the industrialized and to rapidly developing nations such as Japan, Canada, Australia and New Zealand. On the other hand, even though capitalism was not doing anything spectacular to improve conditions in the underdeveloped world, these nations were working out their own ways and means to resist political control and economic imposition. By and large their concerns were political and, even though these often overlapped with socialist economic objectives, politics had the upper hand. Despite Lenin's sweeping optimism the toiling colonial masses ignored that they were in the grip of the international capitalist octopus, and their leaders wanted above all freedom to run their own affairs, even if under a mini-capitalist proto-system. Conversely, colonialist powers that had them in their grip were hanging on, but they were slowly becoming aware that they could survive without their colonies.

Lenin was also right. He was right in the fundamental vision that revolution could succeed anywhere, given the global nature of capitalism in its imperialist phase; hence he was on the *qui vive* about his own Russia and he did not have the doubts and scruples of the Mensheviks, which would have been fatal for the future revolution. Once in power, Lenin had in place the theoretical basis for the further spread of communism in any direction. He could in good revolutionary law look to the West for more social upheaval, but he could also, if that failed, cast his glance eastwards and southwards in the name of the struggle against imperialism, which in effect happened. His raw and ambiguous theses were the ideal seed-bed for all sorts of practical and convenient theoretical elaborations.

Hobson built his arguments for economic imperialism on statistics. Marxists used statistics, but their arguments were drawn principally from their own persuasions concerning what they called the capitalist MOP. To criticise their position, in fact, implies a criticism not just of their specific theories on imperialism but of some of the fundamental concepts in Marx and in Marxist literature in general. Virtually the only riposte to Marxist dialectics is another self-contained system of theorization, and that is what J. A. Schumpeter proposed with his own overrated explanation of imperialism, whose vague socio-historical character has had only isolated repercussions. He conceived imperialism as an atavistic tendency to expansion or aggrandizement on the part of the state, more or less pronounced depending on the influence or weight of militarism and other practices associated with absolutist political power. Schumpeter was emphatic about two things: capitalism per se was not imperialistic and the British Empire, despite the seeming contradiction, was not a product of imperialism. Schumpeter was perhaps close to home in so far as Fascist Italy and Nazi Germany, whose use of naked bullying force during the 1930s set the pattern of international power politics, were near-perfect incarnations of his model. But on the whole his overt distinction between capitalism and the state, between the economic order and the seat of political power, is frankly untenable as seen from almost any analytical and socio-historical point of view. Only economic marginalists and other strictly analytical equilibrium theorists could entertain such an extreme separation and that only on the basis of their own economic and political prejudices.[53]

In general, not only Schumpeter's but also most non-economic explanations of imperialism fall short of their objective, and economic imperialism at least has a flexibility and a range of applicability that rigidly political formulations lack. Economic imperialism can have a narrow or a wide meaning. It can be read in the pages of Conrad's *The Heart of Darkness* and it can be seen in the murals of Diego Rivera in Cuernavaca. We shall see shortly how it evolved from the Leninist thesis into the principal, almost spontaneous way by which revolutionaries from the underdeveloped and colonial lands framed or organized their perception of the relations between the rich and the poor countries. Economic imperialism is, in brief, one of the fundamental versions of the way intercultural and international perceptions and relations have evolved in time, on the same level of importance at least as environmental theory and Eurocentrism. By way of contrast, could Robinson and Gallagher have applied their going-to-the-political-sources method to the Spanish conquest of America, where the royal cedulas (grants and instructions) said one thing and the adelantados (agents and representatives) did exactly the opposite? Or could Schumpeter's fancy conceptism allow for the likely inference that the British conquest of India could have been nothing other than a purely capitalist enterprise? Yet these two events were in essence not entirely unlike the scramble for Africa, and for all of them the wide or general theory of economic imperialism could conceivably seem the only possible symposium.

The Comintern phase of Marxist economic-imperialism theory

The dawn of a brave, new world

The theory of economic imperialism gained immeasurably in prestige and eventually in practical and ideological influence as a consequence of an event that occurred in the midst of the First World

War hecatomb. On 7 November 1917 (26 October according to the Julian calendar), the Bolsheviks, inspired by Lenin himself, fresh from writing his thesis on imperialism, and implacably led by the redoubtable Leon Trotsky, staged a coup d'état. Before the year was out, Trotsky, the one-man band of the Revolution, signed an armistice with the Germans, which effectively took Russia out of the war and freed a million Germans to man the trenches on the Western front. The Western allies, in an attempt to get Russia back into the war, landed troops in Archangel, on the White Sea, and gave all the support they could to the insurrections that soon broke out all over the country. Thus began the siege of Soviet Russia. This time Trotsky donned the soldier's cap and from his command post on a train like an armoured fortress travelled from one end of Russia to the other leading operations against various White Russian generals commanding Cossack and other counter-revolutionary contingents.

The Bolsheviks were not the only ones in trouble. In November 1918 Germany in effect asked for terms and German revolutionary agitation became active and menacing. Marxist socialists were prominent in the unrest that led to the abdication of the Kaiser shortly after the cessation of hostilities. The republic that followed was thrown into the lap of the social-democrats, who seemed willing enough to accept responsibility for it and for all that it came to mean for Germans as the heirs to defeat and anarchy. The communists hung back and became a vociferous, semi-violent opposition led by Karl Liebknecht and Rosa Luxemburg. For these two there were no half-tints: it was all-out revolution or nothing. In Hungary the situation was even more critical, because there the communists under Bela Kun had actually taken over the government. Revolution seemed to be spreading in the West after the end of the war, following the example of Soviet Russia, and the Russians were intensely aware of it.

The Bolsheviks were hopeful about the outcome of these events for various reasons. First of all, they themselves were being besieged by reactionary forces and had an understandable urge to hit back at the Western sponsors of these forces. There was not a better way to do it than to carry revolution to the heart of their enemies' societies. Secondly, a Sovietized Germany would be an immeasurably valuable ally in the quest for world revolution. Considering the industrial importance of Germany, her radicalization, Russian leaders fantasized, could very well signify the beginning of the end of capitalism. Finally, there were solid doctrinaire grounds not only for wanting Germany as an ally but also for expecting her to enter into revolution: Germany had the most numerous, the best organized and the most radicalized proletarian movement in the world, she was one of the models of Leninist finance capitalism, and her communization would respond ideally to Marxist principles and expectations. Therefore, even as the Bolsheviks were having to stitch their nation painfully back together, they felt encouraged and even optimistic when they contemplated the events taking place in Germany. None was more hopeful than the brilliant and irrepressible Trotsky.

The process of the Comintern

The Third Communist International, or Comintern, was founded in March 1919, in Moscow. Its purpose was to promote world revolution, but also, as a matter of course, to obtain support for the Soviet revolution. For our ends especially, it embraced a second, intermediate phase in the evolution of economic-imperialism theory. Throughout its life (and it was only shut down definitely in 1943) the ambiguity about its ultimate objectives hovered over all its actions and initiatives, both practical and theoretical, so much so that the history of the Comintern has been classified in terms of the tug on its proceedings of one or another of those two purposes.

Another way of defining the same issue is to enquire into the extent to which the Comintern was from start to finish a mere instrument of Soviet policy. F. Borkenau considers that there was a first phase of Comintern history during which the Soviets did not dominate, when the initiatives were in the hand of German communists, of Kun in Hungary, and of various other local revolutionary movements, and the Comintern was strictly a means for furthering world revolution. Successive defeats to initially promising communist bids for power outside the USSR, led to the devolution of control within the Comintern to the Soviets, who used the organization, in a second and longer phase, as one of the crucial stages in the Stalin-v.-Trotsky factional struggle, and in a final and even longer phase, as a mere appendage of Stalinist policy. This thesis is also held, along general lines, by I. Deutscher. A more prevalent opinion is that the Comintern could not have escaped Soviet control at any time, in view of the organizational structure it gave itself at the founding congress in 1919 and at the two successive ones under the guidance of Lenin, whose avowed intention was doing away with any possibility of 'federalism', the cardinal sin, in his opinion, of the Second International. Under the new form of organization all the essential powers in the Comintern belonged to the executive committee, which sat in Moscow and handled affairs from congress to congress and thus could and did turn itself into 'an anti-democratic, self-elected oligarchy'.[54]

Nevertheless, just as the Comintern could not control world events, not even all the actions of its members parties all over the world, so the Soviets could not control entirely at first the twists and turns in the debates that went on in the congresses. Towards the close, under the Stalinist boot, the Comintern became nothing more than a wax seal for Soviet foreign policy and for Stalinist ideology, but before that it followed an interesting process which lurched on towards the configuration of the contemporary neo-Marxist/Leninist general theory of economic imperialism, though it never actually got there, and when it started Lenin had already done most of the theoretical work. D. Boersner divides the historical process of the Comintern into four phases: (1) from 1919 to 1920, when its attention was centred on the West; (2) from 1920 to 1923, when its attention was divided equally between the West and the East; (3) from 1923 to 1927, when it devoted its greatest attention to the East; (4) after 1927, when it 'entered a phase of ultra-leftism in the Eastern and colonial countries'. [55] This internal process, which trod closely in step with the march of revolutionary events after the First World War, corresponded to an ideological process which had as pivot the question of the world role of capitalism/imperialism in the historical movement towards revolution and, in particular, of its effects on the social and economic evolution of backward and dependent lands.

Despite radical opposition to colonialism, the Second International (1889–1914) still lived by the dictum that 'The colonies, too, must pass through capitalism. One does not pass from savagery to socialism in a single leap.' The colonies, and the rest of the backward countries, were not very important in that period to socialist thinking and strategy. Lenin had a different opinion, in so far as he showed himself primarily and intransigently anti-imperialist. He too felt, however, that revolution would take place first in Europe under the leadership of a proletarian-based communist vanguard. The events in Germany after the war were so potent a sign of hope for the Bolsheviks that, despite the bloody suppression of the brief Spartakist insurrection in January 1919, when the First Comintern Congress met two months later the enthusiasm for revolution was virtually intact. It fed on the thesis of the 'permanent revolution' (the belief in the furtherance of revolutionary activism on a continuous basis and across international frontiers), which had its most formidable and influential advocate in Trotsky, although

Lenin too figured as a cautious adherent. The demise in the same year of the ephemeral Bela Kun regime in Hungary did not dampen hopes either. Trotsky was at the zenith of his military career and of his political power. The Red Army was retaking one by one all the cities and the regions previously forfeited to the counter-revolution. Recognizing the failure of intervention, the British had withdrawn from Murmansk. Understandably enough in view of all these events, the colonies received only a passing mention in the final resolutions of the inaugural Comintern congress. With the recapture of Odessa in 1920, the Russian civil war came to an end and, with the alleviation of the military pressure on the revolution, the issue of the colonies (which became known as the 'Oriental question' because it was in the Islamic East that a potential for revolution seemed to flicker) gained considerably in importance and figured with some prominence in the proceedings of the Second Congress, celebrated the same year. A gathering of Comintern representatives and Persian, Armenian, and Turkish delegates met in Baku after the Congress and proceeded to brand imperialism retrograde. It was also at Baku that John Reed, the American revolutionary journalist, proclaimed the solidarity of Latin America with the peoples of Asia.[56]

In the Third Congress, held in 1921, the enthusiasm for revolution in the East was much subdued, owing to the Soviet need to maintain good relations with Persia and Turkey; instead, Germany was once again the cynosure of the debates despite the recent defeat of a workers' uprising in the Ruhr. The claims of Asia upon the revolution, however, were met at the Congress of the Toilers of the East, which was held in Moscow in 1922. According to Boersner, the idea that 'the national democratic revolution of an underdeveloped country was likely to precede the proletarian transformation of the advanced regions' was first expressed at this meeting.

At the Fourth Congress, also in 1922, the colonial question came back strongly on the agenda. The tack taken tended towards the gradualist strategy of communist alliances with local bourgeoisies against imperialism. One of the most prominent theorists of the Comintern, the Indian M. N. Roy, divided colonial and semi-colonial countries into: (a) the advanced with a class-conscious bourgeoisie; (b) those with feudal predominance; (c) the primitive with feudal patriarchalism. Roy also proposed the idea that capitalism promotes decolonization and industrial development in the colonies in order to create markets for producers' goods from the advanced capitalist countries, but this point of view was overwhelmingly rejected. Boersner summarizes thus the proceedings of the Fourth Congress: 'The general theses on the Eastern question stated that the World War had weakened imperialism and that the growth of nationalist fermentation in the colonies was steady and mighty. In opposition to Roy's theory of decolonization, the theses maintained that European capitalism continued to keep the colonies underdeveloped and non-industrial.'[57]

It could be said that as early as 1922 communism had taken imperialism, despoiled it of all ambiguities, turned it gradually into the principal enemy of progress and change, and to round things out, had 'invented' a national bourgeoisie to stand up against it in alliance with the communists themselves. In this scheme the only thing that was lacking was the dumping of the West as a revolutionary focus, and this was practically inevitable with the failure of the communist insurrection in Hamburg in 1923. Revolution was not likely from that quarter any more. The Soviet Union, on its side, had overcome its political birth pangs and was on its way to national consolidation. Revolutionary ferment was strongest in the non-industrialized world, and it was in this direction that Comintern energies seemed to be converging, just as Soviet energies were committed to socialism in one country.

The 'discovery' of Latin America

The Fifth Congress of the Comintern was held in 1924, and it centred primarily on China, which was in the throes of extreme social unrest with the communists in precarious alliance with the Kuomintang. Behind the debate loomed the struggle for power in the Soviet Union between Trotsky and Stalin. Despite defeat in the West, where he had been the principal instigator of extremism, Trotsky still believed in permanent revolution and wanted his strategy, which implied a rejection of alliances and compromises, carried out by communists in China. Stalin preferred a more prudent, less adventurous approach, which meant preserving the alliance with the Nationalists, and his point of view prevailed. For its pains, it suffered Chiang Kai-shek's bloody 1927 suppression of communists in Shanghai and elsewhere. Even after the failure of this strategy, plus that of another Stalin-sponsored, Comintern-inspired uprising in Canton the same year, Stalin still managed to crush Trotsky utterly. The fifth congress also consecrated the revolutionary importance of backward nations, or as Boersner says, it 'placed the national and colonial question at the very head of its basic rules of action'. Among other things it proposed the following slogan apropos of the British Labour government: 'The liberation of the workers of England depends on the liberation of the colonies.'[58]

The Sixth Congress (1928), in the words of M. Caballero, 'showed, with reference to colonial questions, two main trends. The first was the tendency to reverse the tactics which were dominant in the former congress related to the alliance with the national bourgeoisie. This was a consequence of the attitude of the Kuomintang against the communists. . . The second trend was what has been called the "discovery" of Latin America.' What did this discovery contribute to Comintern debate and revolutionary theory? For one thing, there was the tentative denial of the existence of a national bourgeoisie in Latin America in the sense of a capitalist class in potential or actual opposition to imperialist penetration. There was also the emphatic presentation of the category of 'dependencies' of imperialism as the only adequate one for the Latin American countries. It was put forward at the Congress by the Ecuadorian delegate Ricardo Paredes in these terms: 'Therefore a new category must be accepted. This new group would consist of the "dependencies" which have been penetrated economically by imperialism but which retain a certain political independence either because the economic penetration is not very strong or because they are strong politically.'

In assessing the relative significance of this clarification by a Latin American in a gathering of dedicated Marxist revolutionaries, it must be remembered that Lenin, who set the essential rules by which the Comintern lived, had been wont to distinguish, outside the 'four pillars' of imperialism, only between colonies and semi-colonies. The Paredes intervention implied a hierarchy, which had been present in the Latin American awareness of the political division of the world, involving the following categories: (a) imperialist powers; (b) dependencies, which were sovereign nations with backward economies, hence subject to extreme exogenous influence; (c) semi-colonies, that is, internally autonomous countries (not necessarily backward economically) whose defence and foreign affairs were conducted externally, which included the British self-governing dominions, Egypt, *et al.*; (d) colonies proper and other subject territories. Whether this hierarchy was valid or not, whether, say, Australia was more of a colony than Ecuador or the other way around, is of course a debatable issue, but in a purely formal political sense, it could be validly proposed and to a Latin American it also must have seemed prima facie admissible. This forceful presentation of a widely held Latin American point of view did not prosper, however, and, according to M. Caballero, 'In spite of the relative acceptance of the diversity of state forms of dependence, in spite of the formula of Paredes, after 1928 the Comintern tended to use such formulas as "dependency" less and, in fact, to put the accent on the semi-colonial condition of Latin American countries.'[59]

In summing up the relationship between the Comintern and Latin America, Caballero claims that Comintern influence was mainly in the 'theoretical realm' and consisted in positing questions about Latin American society and the Latin American revolution. He refers particularly to the issue of the specific nature of Latin American dependence as differing from the semi-colonial condition.[60] In this, in a contemporary context, Caballero harks back to the implicit Paredes hierarchy, which likewise underlies the entire edifice of the theory of dependence defined and outlined by F. H. Cardoso and E. Faletto, in particular the distinction between 'dependencies' and 'semi-colonies'. However, if the latter distinction in the 1920s relied on perceivable formal features proper to the final stages of the long epoch of European colonialism, in the decolonized post-war world even though it still might have seemed valid it was less easy to apprehend and define.

The Comintern had one final Congress, in 1935, before its dissolution eight years later. It sanctioned yet another volte face with the approval of the 'popular front line', which defended a strategy of political alliances on the left and was a consequence of successive defeats suffered worldwide by the communist movement. The Nazi-Soviet Pact of 1939 made the direction of the Comintern a delicate, almost impossible affair, and the wartime pact between the USSR and the Anglo-American alliance practically condemned it to inoperativeness, thus putting paid to its useful life.

The general theory of economic imperialism

What did the Comintern contribute to economic-imperialism theory? What was this bridging role between the narrow theory of economic imperialism and dependency theory that we attributed to it before? The contemporary general theory of economic imperialism, that is, dependency theory, exhibits the following characteristics: (a) it considers that capitalism does not just inhibit development but that it is actually and historically 'underdeveloping'; (b) it tends to smear over the distinctions between capitalism, colonialism and imperialism; (c) it puts in doubt the validity and/or utility of the concept of national bourgeoisie; (d) it virtually rejects the Marxist feudalism/capitalism schema of socio-historical evolution. It goes without saying that it acknowledges the Marxist concepts of MOP and class struggle, but it places the greater emphasis on the external aspect of socio-economic processes in underdeveloped countries. Already Lenin had taken a few halting steps in that direction. He practically did an outright reversal on the Marx/Engels conception of the modernizing or progressive final effects of capitalism on backward nations. Furthermore, he probably was not completely convinced of the virtues of bourgeois nationalism, and, in fact, he said that the phase of development that the bourgeoisie stood for in a backward nation could actually be skipped with revolutionary help from the outside. Even granting the significant differences in the worlds known by Marx and by Lenin, Lenin's deviations from strict Marxism would still merit the coinage of the term Leninism.

The Comintern went a few steps closer to our time ideologically without actually overstepping the bounds of Marxism/Leninism. This was due to the presence in its deliberations of representatives from the underdeveloped countries themselves, whose experience of economic backwardness and of foreign penetration was practical and direct. Comintern theses and resolutions, once the mirage of permanent revolution was dissipated, placed more emphasis on the retrograde influence of imperialism than Lenin himself had actually done, while at the same time, with the arrival en masse of Latin American delegates, identifying the significance of relative political independence. Comintern debates played up the notion of national bourgeoisie, but they contained different even opposed criteria, ultimately perhaps distrust having the upper hand.

In balance, the most significant contribution of the Comintern to theory was probably formal in character and consisted in the constant collating of ideas and reality, which over the years and despite the presence of the Bolshevik landlord-cum-censor in the background was inimical to orthodoxy and dogmatism. The Comintern debates did not produce the contemporary general version of the theory of economic imperialism, nor did they put forth any theory at all on the origins of inequality, which after all could not be further from their concerns and preoccupations. They had, however, the right conditions for doing it: the reality of imperialism, a fluid theoretical point of view, and the presence of parties which did not need prodding to blame imperialism for all the evils in the world since the beginning of time. The Comintern, however, lacked agility, it lacked the free-wheeling view that came after the Second World War with the era of decolonization and de-Stalinization, and then perhaps too the Soviet gendarme was not there for nothing. Comintern influence cannot be circumscribed to the narrow Marxist revolutionary circles which were its normal intellectual clients. It can safely be taken to have flowed into a mainstream of theoretical work that carried on into the postwar era in conjunction with the momentous historical processes that got their headstart in that conflict.

The humane face of Eurocentrism and the progress of the West

During the interwar years what had happened to Eurocentrism, which we last saw on its social-imperialist high horse? Marxist theory and anti-imperialism hardly affected the pride of Eurocentrism, but the First World War did, and so did the Bolshevik Revolution and the threat of revolutionary unrest in the West. Furthermore, the 'inferior races' in the colonies and in semi-colonies such as Egypt and Persia were getting edgy. Violence is a dangerous leveller, and the First World War left the scent of violence in the air. Racism had not disappeared but it was no longer aired so openly. After the trenches and the slaughter and the indecisiveness of war, social Darwinism would have one last insane fling in Fascist Italy and especially in Nazi Germany. It was like a deadly caricature of militant Eurocentrism: Italians bombing Ethiopian hamlets from the air and Nazis carrying out the logic of race supremacy in the extermination camps.

However, Eurocentrism had more humane and rational aspects. One that touches indirectly on the question of the origins of international economic inequality was the theoretical work on the subject of the development of the West. Marx's oeuvre, which spans the period when industrialism entered a mature pan-Western phase, was significantly, perhaps crucially, responsible for making capitalism aware of itself, but awareness is not necessarily admiration and capitalism was admirable in many ways, at least on its own ground. Just how admirable was the task that a group of theorists straddling the twentieth century set themselves. These theorists were, principally, Max Weber, W. Sombart and, well past the start of the century, J. A. Schumpeter. All of them believed that capitalism was rational; the first two also believed that it had ethico-religious foundations. All three thinkers can be placed in the category of enlightened Eurocentrism through their tacit but unequivocal negation of racism and social Darwinism. Their myopia, if we can call it that, consisted in the restriction of their lines of sight, in being perhaps culturally star-struck by the West to the exclusion from their vision of the rest of the world (except in a relatively marginal way in the case of Weber). Our interest in mentioning them in passing lies in that their intellectual progeny are the works of those who in our days have carried on with the exploration, from different angles and with varying degrees of historical range, of the process and the evolution of Western capitalism, and this, as we shall see in Chapter 5, offers in the last analysis possibly the most reliable approach to the study of the origins of international economic inequality.

3 *Policies and politics in the struggle for the Third World*

Economic development and world history

There is a three-stage sequence of ways in which the world can be roughly divided historically from the perspective of Western economic development into large conceptually manageable categories: 1 Before the nineteenth century, mainly into different comparable high cultures and civilizations. 2 During the nineteenth century and up to the Second World War, into the advanced capitalist nations (which might or might not include Argentina and Uruguay depending on the measurements applied) and the politically and culturally backward rest of the world, which was made up mostly of colonies, a handful of semi-independent states in Africa and Asia, and the remaining Latin American republics (and in a category of its own, the rapidly industrializing USSR). 3 After the Second World War into the economically developed and the underdeveloped blocs (the communist bloc excepted).

These classifications are essentially 'Western' as opposed to Marxist or 'Third World' perceptions of history and of economic development. They betoken wide cultural, economic and political perceptions. They are also the sources of theories and explanations. In the case of the pre-nineteenth-century dominant Western perception of cultures, the theories referred to the differences between Western culture and the other world cultures. The relativistic perception of cultural differences engendered principally theories on the environmental causation of social and behavioural traits, although of course ethnocentric claims of Western superiority were never absent from pre-nineteenth-century inter-cultural contacts. Even though environmental or climatic theory ideally suited a world of cultural relativism, it survived in the Eurocentric climate of the nineteenth century as an explanation of Western superiority, and it was still going strong in modified, more enlightened versions after the Second

World War. During the nineteenth century, Western progress and expansion made relativism unsustainable and Eurocentrism became the expression of the West's certainty of its cultural superiority over what were uniformly described as 'backward nations' and 'inferior races'.

Eurocentrism, in the rather prejudicial guises it tended to assume, came under fire from the theory of economic imperialism. It did not fare well during the two world wars, but it too survived in a humanitarian, toned-down version, as we shall strive to show in this chapter, which revolves crucially around explicit post-1945 theories on the origins of international economic inequality, as distinct from the explanations implicit in Eurocentrism and in the specific, short-term theory of economic imperialism. In other words, it is here that we enter, properly speaking, into our principal area of research, which however cannot be fully understood if it were not made part of long-term intellectual continuities, just as today's world division between rich and poor countries cannot be fully understood without the Industrial Revolution, nor can the latter be sequestered from its Western cultural cradle.

Before ceding its place to a less invidious 'economic' perception of the world, the rigid Eurocentric outlook had come under pressure and critical scrutiny from different quarters. The First World War, which left Western civilization exhausted and disillusioned about itself, effectively claimed social Darwinism as one of its casualties. By the time that another world conflagration became imminent, the superior/inferior dichotomy was wearing thin. It was about then that a new conceptual classification that obviated the increasingly untenable contrast between civilized and inferior peoples was being elaborated: it divided the capitalist world into the same two blocs as before, but these were now economic blocs, not overtly based on race or cultural disparities, but on the distinction between the economically advanced and the economically backward countries. The West still viewed the rest of the world with dim sceptical eyes, but this scepticism was more plausible than extreme Eurocentric prejudices, and it was conceivable that it could be substituted by some sort of rational, progressive and 'hopeful' conceptualization. The compass to the new intellectual terrain was the idea of 'underdevelopment'. It elbowed aside the old jades of 'inferior races' and 'backwardness' and it also lent itself ideally to tracing sensible, bridgeable frontiers in a world of economic inequalities, even if in the end they followed in the main the old dividing lines.

The 'birth' of underdevelopment

Of neologisms and socio-historical clues

'Underdevelopment' and 'underdeveloped' more than mere postwar neologisms are socio-historical clues. Whoever actually put the word 'underdevelopment' together was probably slaving away before the Second World War in some university cubicle, and writing in English.[61] However, the invention of the word is not as significant as its general acceptance and wide diffusion during the years immediately after the war. This happened either because the term designated some meaningful reality, or because it gave a special sense to an old intellectual perception. Does underdevelopment have a basis in reality wider or different in any way than that which underpins the notion of economic backwardness? In point of fact, yes: underdevelopment refers to a measurable, numerically comparative backwardness. It is perhaps the same phenomenon as backwardness but seen through a fine wire-grid.

'Underdevelopment' has come to grief in recent times. The oft-heard assertion that 'underdevelopment' is a mere euphemism is only partially correct. At the time when the word first became current there was little concern in the West for the opinions of the politicians or the public in backward lands. 'Underdevelopment' takes on the appearance of an euphemism mostly in the critical review of postwar developmental dogmas and by comparison with older designations. But, in fact, it is not as a euphemism that it has fallen into ill repute but because of its patronizing overtones. This engendered, through the repeated exercise of what G. Myrdal calls 'diplomacy by terminology', a variety of new phrases: 'developing countries', 'less developed countries', and so on, which have entered the vocabulary of international agencies, politicians and pressmen. Among the reasons for its downfall are some that have to do with the corrosive effects of time and failure. In its origins, however, 'underdevelopment' was not condescending, as it later came to seem, and it was not associated with stagnation and defeat. It implied the capacity to grow and catch up, a state of potentiality which could by rational means be taken to a higher level of economic organization.

Areas of research

But if underdevelopment conjures up such a diversity of attitudes, it is probably because its principal historical raison d'être was to offer a 'mediation' for a global change that occurred in the material and conceptual relations between the West and the backward lands and which had the Second World War as a fulcrum. The change itself admits of different interpretations. For one thing, it substituted the traditional vision of socio-economic backwardness for a more hopeful if more abstract condition. But principally 'underdevelopment' firmly established the economic implications in the Western awareness of the relations between the advanced and the backward countries in the capitalist world. The pre-1939 diversity in political perceptions played down the weight of economic issues, so that even imperialism theory, with its firm grounding in economic analysis, functioned as an instrument of political action in so far as its underlying critique was contingent upon political domination. Instead of the old Western conceptual ordering, which had been gradually coming round to the primacy of economic differentiations but still hung on to political categories and definitions, the postwar capitalist world rapidly came to see itself as exclusively divided by economic inequalities. By the same token, under the general intellectual guidance provided by the idea of underdevelopment, the previous conceptual separation of the backward lands into colonies and politically and economically backward independent nations tended to coalesce, in rhythm with the process of decolonization, into not precisely a bloc-concept but an awareness of common basic economic interests.

In sum, the old Western racial and cultural prejudices had self-destructed even before they were seen to be inadequate in a world where colonialism was bowing out and Eurocentrism no longer had the field to itself. A new wave of theorization on the relations between the strong and the weak, the rich and the poor countries was on its way. This can be divided into two general currents: (1) development economics and the sociology of development; (2) the long-view or general theory of economic imperialism, otherwise known as dependency theory. A third field of study touches on a whole range of issues on the origins of underdevelopment, but it is not primarily concerned with them. It is what we have called here 'the development of the West', and it was begotten in the work of the pioneering authors whom we mentioned collectively before as presenting the humane face of Eurocentrism because of their deliberate disengagement from racism and social Darwinism.

Chapters 3–5 of this book are organized around these three areas of study. We shall start with the creation of development economics and its growing importance and influence after the Second World War. After following the evolution of development studies to the late 1960s, we shall trace the parallel if tardier process of dependency theory to its recent culmination in the work of I. Wallerstein. We shall then take up again the thread of development studies and close the two intellectual processes with the 'dependency debate' and a general critique of dependency theory. To round things out on the Marxist side, we shall consider what can best be described as MOP and class-struggle Marxism, which is the latest approach of this ideology to the issues of underdevelopment. And we shall close with an attempt to elicit from the study of the development of the West, principally but not exclusively in the work of F. Braudel, pertinent observations on the origins of underdevelopment and economic inequality.

Pre-1945 theoretical work on economic development

C. Clark and the per capita measurement of poverty

If the concept of underdevelopment was a crucial instrument for the West in re-focusing its relations with the non-industrial remainder of the capitalist world, development economics was its necessary disciplinary framework. In time, development economics would become a part, the main part, in the general field of development studies, but during the war, when it effectively started, it was strictly on its own. There is a special place in the canon of the literature on economic development for the category of pre-1945 works on underdevelopment and development policy, even though the word 'underdevelopment' was barely in use then and the concept was still unfolding its diverse connotations.[62]

One of the outstanding names in that early phase is that of the British economist Colin Clark, author of the *The Conditions of Economic Progress* (1940), a book that was being quoted on the statistical definition of underdevelopment long after the end of the war. G. M. Meier and D. Seers, in *Pioneers in Development* (1984), include Clark in a gallery of the then-surviving founders of the discipline. What Clark did in his studies was to work out a means for determining the per capita real income of workers all over the world. From these it emerged that the seven countries with the highest standards of living were the USA, Canada, Australia, New Zealand, Argentina, Great Britain and Switzerland (in that order), comprising 10 per cent of the world's population, followed by 'the principal industrial countries of Europe', comprising 9 per cent of the population, and finally by the low-income countries, accounting for the remaining 81 per cent.

To measure income, Clark used what he called an 'international unit' (I.U.), which was defined 'as the amount of goods and services which could be purchased for $1 in the USA over the average of the decade 1925–34, or an amount interchangeable with them'. Clark further clarified: 'For international comparisons of real income, the incomes are reduced to a 48-hour week basis by a simple proportion between the current prevailing working hours and 48 hours.' The average wage for poor countries was below 500 I.U. a year, and for the top seven, above 1,000 I.U. 'Summarising these figures', Clark said, 'the world is found to be a wretchedly poor place.' Despite the rueful tone, however, the figures themselves were less discouraging than reality itself would probably have warranted in his time or, at least, so they seem in retrospect from a world in which poverty seems manageable only by establishing distinctions between the poor and the extremely poor. But Clark did go to the heart of the matter when he lamented that 'very little attention has been devoted to ascertaining the causes of the tremendous differences in real income which prevail between different parts of the world'. Looking back in 1984, Clark considered that the two most important merits of his book were to have emphasised the significance of tertiary sector growth as an indication of development and to have pointed out that capital alone does not produce growth. Significantly, Clark's acknowledgements include S. Kuznets, G. Myrdal, and V. K. R. V. Rao, all of whom would later become influential names in development studies.[63]

J. H. Boeke and the foundations of 'economic dualism'

In moving from C. Clark to the Dutch economist J. H. Boeke we undergo a radical change in perspective. Boeke's *The Structure of the Netherlands Indian Economy* was published in 1942 by the Institute of Pacific Relations in New York. It was part of the concern in both America and Britain with the postwar order and in particular with the less developed, larger part of the planet. If C. Clark's study was statistical and global, Boeke's was regional and descriptive: it was what you would get or expect to get by applying a magnifying glass to one of Clark's statistical items.

Boeke's work, based on various decades of colonial experience, is significant in two respects at least: in the thorough descriptive exposition of a 'dual economy' and in the presentation of the effects of culture on economic activity. 'In dualistic countries', Boeke wrote, 'we find pre-capitalism embodied in the indigenous social system even at the present date. . . But here – in the Netherlands Indies for instance – it is brought into direct contact with capitalism in its full bloom, and this it is that gives it the double character which is indicated by the term dualism. We are here dealing with a clash between two social periods – a clash the economic aspect of which we shall discuss and analyse in the present paper under the name of 'economic dualism', although it finds expression in other departments of life besides the economic – in legislation, in government, in the administration and formulation of justice, in social organization – as well as in men's conception of what they need, in their evaluation of things, in work and recreation, in religion and morals.' Boeke's observations derived from his study of the economy and social structure of villages, which he claimed were as alien to the modern urban milieu as different planets could be to each other.

Boeke was not, of course, the first to notice this. The British had observed Indian villages closely from the eighteenth century at least, especially when it came to the question of how best to exact tribute or taxes from them. The concept of dual economy was described vaguely by Marx. It was clearly recognized by Marxist theorists of imperialism such as Hilferding and Lenin, but it was never developed by any of these authors, who indeed would have found it untenable beyond a certain stage: in Marx's system different modes of production were mutually exclusive, the more progressive one inexorably displacing its predecessor. However, the possibility of overlap or simultaneity could not be entirely ruled out, and in Latin America, for example, the Peruvian social critic J. C. Mariategui in 1928 explored further the feudalism/capitalism form of Marxist dualism. But Boeke's was undoubtedly the 'classic' non-Marxist expression of dualism. The dual economy idea became the theoretical framework for the different growth models and strategies that were predicated on the existence of excess population in the countryside.

Since rural–urban migration became one of the key concepts in development economics, Boeke was actually poking at its roots in his research, although the notion that a labour surplus existed in backward countries owing to the inefficiency of their agriculture was fairly conventional and apparently solidly established, and what Boeke contributed was a social model that included different, even antagonistic operative modes, such as that the profit-incentive did not function in the villages in the same way as in the cities. In this respect, that is, in the weight which he attributed to culture, he was a forerunner of what became known as the modernization school of American sociology, which was the principal alternative to development economics as a source of Western strategies for progress in the underdeveloped world.[64]

P. N. Rosenstein-Rodan and the concept of the 'big push'

For some, P. N. Rosenstein-Rodan laid the foundations of development economics in his 1943 essay 'Problems of industrialization of Eastern and South-Eastern Europe'.[65] He was born in Poland in 1902, emigrated to Britain before the war, and eventually settled in America as an elder statesman in the discipline. In London during the war he proposed the study of the problems of underdevelopment at the Royal Institute of International Affairs, and in the USA in the late 1950s he was among the more influential defenders of American economic aid to Latin America.

What Rosenstein-Rodan did in his famous war essay was to establish upon what then seemed like unassailable foundations the hypothesis that industrialization is the best and most efficient road to economic development. He gave a variety of reasons for this. One was that it would absorb the rural slack. This was a theme that tied in with the dual-economy motif in a rather general way. It was later taken up in a more precise manner by W. A. Lewis and other economists. The general proposition that derived from it was that in exchange for taking a back seat to industrialization the agricultural sector would eventually reap the benefits of accelerated economic growth. Another basic argument for industrialization was the so-called externalities. This was a marginalist concept according to which the growth of a branch of industry will of itself lower costs for individual firms within the industry. Rosenstein-Rodan applied it to entire national economies in the sense of external savings which were made possible by industrialization and which were in turn absolutely indispensable for the continuation of the industrial process. Externalities were to be augmented by 'indivisibilities' and economies of scale. This meant that the demand generated by one factory required the construction of another, and this one in turn of two more, and so forth. The foreseeable increase in demand required that these plants be of an 'optimum' size in order to maximize the externalities. The 'market mechanism' was not a reliable guide to these projects – for who would build a plant twice or more as large as a market required on account of future demand? – so planning of the 'indicative' sort was required.

In retrospect, Rosenstein-Rodan would defend his ideas on industrialization in these simple terms: 'Industrialization has to be promoted not because of terms of trade, but because external economies are greater in industry than in agriculture alone', but the fact remains that the implications of his early model were of daunting social complexity. D. Avramovic believes that the example of Soviet planning must have had some influence on it. Rosenstein-Rodan himself mentioned Keynes and Harrod/Domar among the 'predecessors of the theory of development' – although his own work was contemporaneous with post-Keynesian analytical research – and this reinforces the idea that he was more inclined to stimulation than to coercion, and makes almost unavoidable the critique that the means he had in mind were disproportionately small compared with the goals he proposed for poor nations.

A third argument for industrialization was that it led to the investment of what Rosenstein-Rodan called 'social overhead capital' in the creation of infrastructure, which made modern transportation and trade possible and industry viable. It had also other obvious social advantages, from the employment it gave during its construction to the permanent services it rendered to the communities within its reach. The fourth argument, and one to which Rosenstein-Rodan was especially partial, was the impulse that it gave to education and to learning skills, which he called 'technological external economies'. In the Meier and Seers book he reiterated that the 'process of industrialization of underdeveloped countries was and is largely based on the advantages of training, learning on the job, and the formation of human capital'. In retrospect, these ideas seem like truisms, but in their time they were part of a successful new system of conceptualization. The trouble was that these ideas also were simplifications that in practice have proved ineffective or misleading. Whether the 'excess agrarian population' existed or not, the situation in most Latin American metropolitan areas after many decades of siphoning off rural 'excess' is not one of rural–urban harmonization or even of social integration in the cities, but of 'excess' unemployed or under-employed urban masses, in other words, that the 'excess' was if anything merely transferred from one part of society to another. The 'external economies' have transpired in some cases but the co-called 'indivisibilities' are probably as vaporous today as they were vague on paper when Rosenstein-Rodan defined them. The 'technological external economies' sounded and still sound as inevitable as breathing, but the truth is that lack of technology is probably today, almost half a century after Rosenstein-Rodan wrote, the one principal obstacle for the majority of the industrial projects in the LDCs.

The crowning all-embracing idea in Rosenstein-Rodan's model of development was the 'big push', for it brought together all the previous targets and it summarized what the model was all about: a sufficiently large bloc of investment from different sources applied in such a vast scale over such a compressed time-lapse as to overcome not only the drag of private marginal net product, which was determined by ordinary market mechanisms, but also any shortcoming or lag that might arise from any of the sectors or areas participating in the process of development: agriculture, infrastructure, finance, industry, training, and so on. For Eastern and South Eastern Europe he proposed an 'Eastern European Industrial Trust' and he estimated an investment of 6,000 million pounds, nearly half of which would have to come from outside. The concept of a 'big push' was jargonized in the postwar literature of development economics as a 'critical minimum effort', although this could not dissimulate the fact that from its theoretical launching by Rosenstein-Rodan it partook of the nature of a pipedream as far as foreign assistance went and sounded quite incongruous juxtaposed to the unanimously perceived insufficiencies of domestic savings in underdeveloped countries.

In following the intellectual trajectory of Rosenstein-Rodan one cannot help thinking that he became an expert on Latin American development by default. In 1943 his sights were firmly placed on the underdeveloped countries of Europe. By 1944, he was taking in other areas: the Far East (which in truth he had mentioned in his 1943 essay), the colonial empires, the Caribbean area, and the Middle East, besides Europe. By the 1950s he was mainly interested in Latin America – understandably enough in view of the communization of the Balkans, Eastern Europe and China – but his recipe for development had not deviated in any significant way from his original model, and, in 1957, in an article that was part of a collective work published by the Massachusetts Institute of Technology (MIT), he went back to the 'big push' concept, with a touch of Rostovian imagery, and defined it thus: 'There is a minimum level of resources that must be devoted to. . .a development program if it is to have any chance of success. Launching a country into self-sustained growth is a little like getting an airplane off the ground.' Significantly, 'take-off' and 'big push' are analogues of the idea of 'primitive accumulation' (in the sense of a decisive amassing of disposable capital), which dependency theorists borrowed from Marx for their own ends and in their own interpretation during the following decade. More to the point at hand, what we have in this essay are various useful indications. It revealed: (1) that Rosenstein-Rodan had remained consistent over the years in his criteria about development and that it was in America and during the early 1960s that his ideas were coming into their own; (2) that there existed an intellectual mainstream in development economics, which was flowing then between MIT and the State Department, and on which Rosenstein-Rodan and Rostow effortlessly sailed; and (3) that this was probably a heyday and a culmination in development economics because the policies involved, which were being preached and occasionally applied all over Latin America, would not have results commensurate with the optimism that engendered them, and would never again get such an opportunity to prove themselves as the one they had during those years. But the most significant indication is that what Rosenstein-Rodan wrote in 1943, two decades later would still seem valid, if not indisputably as truth at least as a mover of wills.

Some may consider Rosenstein-Rodan a precursor rather than a begetter, and perhaps not even a precursor but an influential systematizer, the right sort of advocate in just the right spot for policies that many considered inevitable. The individual ideas that he espoused and wove together had been expressed before and they were developed with greater rigour and precision after him, but there is no denying the coherence and the force of his reasoning, its greater efficacy in contrast to what before had been mostly pious exhortations, so that finally, as often happens, the statement of the obvious was the beginning of the new.[66] The obvious was that monetary and technological 'externalities', infrastructure, and 'excess agrarian population' had all been at one time or another among the priorities of independent underdeveloped countries before the Second World War. The new consisted in bringing all these ideas together as a recipe for accelerated development, and in doing so from a vantage which permitted bridging between areas as disparate as Eastern Europe and Latin America.

The 'four truths' of pre-1945 studies in economic development

What made the Rosenstein-Rodan project problematic was the disparity between goals and means. The tentative solution was planning, but in Rosenstein-Rodan planning was cautious bordering on coy, and it was not even called planning but 'programming'. It was indicative and supplementary, neither socialist nor propitiatory to free-market extremists.[67] K. Mandelbaum, like Rosenstein-Rodan also working in England during the war, constructed a 'hypothetical model of an industrialisation process in South East Europe', which of course never left the pages of the book, but which was a paradigm of what development economics would consider to be its task in the postwar world. It defined targets, quantified resources and their allocation, estimated outputs, and set the whole thing in motion with a snap of the fingers. The fact that it referred in a general way to South Eastern Europe did not detract from its relevance to the preliminary foundation-building of development economics.[68] The theoretical work accomplished at that point was undeniably thorough and solid, not so much in the sense of completeness, although the work done during the war was admittedly comprehensive, as in the sense of a relatively finished set of hypotheses none the less susceptible to further research and elaboration.

It could be seeing too much into the short period covered, but the temptation is irresistible to depict an expanding progression from C. Clark, who did the quantitative definition of underdevelopment (on the basis of per capita statistics, which is the way we still mainly define it), to J. H. Boeke, who dealt with the problem of an available under-used work force, to Rosenstein-Rodan, who proposed a strategy to absorb it, and finally, to Mandelbaum, who described the means to make that strategy workable. It sounds too pat because, for one thing, these authors were not discovering anything that was not known before them and, for another, they (with the possible exceptions of Rosenstein-Rodan and Mandelbaum) were not working in one venue towards one specific objective, but were moving in different directions in different places. Nevertheless, a pattern of sorts can be read in the facts described and, anyhow, the important thing is that we can recognize in them an abstract meaningful intellectual structure despite the diversity of the contributions to it.

The historical context for the growth of development studies

The Second World War placed the United States not just at the head of the West, but also in such a commanding position in the world at large as to seem to ensure the prevalence of capitalism everywhere outside the USSR and its area of influence. However, it did not make the world any easier to deal with than it was before. In relation to the economically backward, non-communist lands, there were two trends that were complicating the future for the

US and Western powers in general: one was the start of decolonization and the other was the strengthening of the communist world movement. Together they posed political uncertainties and policy quandaries. Decolonization came about when the European colonialist powers attempted without success to start as if from scratch in their former Asian possessions. As it spread gradually to all corners of the world over three decades after the war, it was usually associated with aspirations to rapid economic progress and social reforms, and that is where communism came in as a threat to Western influence or control.

The USSR had been taken to the brink by the Nazis. The thoroughness of Germany's defeat afterwards enhanced the prestige of the Soviet victory, in particular in the eyes of the leaders of newly independent countries, who thought they saw in the Soviet command economy an example worth studying and even applying. The self-evident risk existed that the imitation of communism could lead to political and economic alienation from the West, which was something that native communists in the underdeveloped countries, with or without external support, were trying to impose. The West, therefore, was being confronted after the war by the crumbling of the prewar colonialist order and by the rise of the world communist challenge. One of its responses to those challenges was to give full sanction to the economic and developmentalist Western optic that had been focusing on the world since before the war and which had acquired a definitive urgency and relevance as a consequence of the international processes that the war set in motion. To give substance to this attitude there already existed the wartime work on economic development, and in addition, new theories and new arguments were being elaborated after the war, which ratified and strengthened the essence of what had been said before.

The United Nations Organization was created in 1945 as the successor to the League of Nations, but with a different outlook on the relations between larger nations, the Western powers in particular, and the colonies and the so-called semi-colonial countries. Even in its infancy, when it was power politics that mostly mattered, it was significantly attentive to the political concerns of its weaker members, owing mainly to the convergence of America's desire to assume an anti-colonialist stance and the USSR's outspoken support of anti-colonialism, all of which resulted in the approval of general principles of international political equity. Some of the principles sanctioned the idea of national freedom and self-determination. Others had to do with the desideratum of economic development for all nations. They were a reflection of the relatively fluid postwar international situation, especially as it affected the old colonial empires. In the area of economic development, the UNO was stimulating the formulation of the economic doctrines that had to go with it, and by 1949 it had created different organisms devoted to the issues of underdevelopment, including the Economic Commission for Latin America (ECLA; CEPAL in Spanish), and it counted on the services of R. Prebisch, H. Singer, and V. K. R. V. Rao, among others.[69] Two memorable concepts emerged from the work on underdevelopment sponsored by the UNO. One concerned a purported secular trend of international commodity prices to decline in comparison with the prices of manufactured goods to the benefit of the industrialized nations and to the detriment of the less economically developed ones. This was mainly Singer's doing. The other was the stroke-of-genius presentation that Prebisch did of developed and underdeveloped capitalist countries as 'core' and 'periphery'.

The genesis of 'core-periphery'

In the brief but brilliant and far-sighted *The Economic Development of Latin America and its Principal Problems*, published in 1950 by ECLA, Prebisch, who had been influential in shaping economic policy in a rigidly 'neo-classical' direction in his native Argentine before the war, described not only the process leading up to his advocacy of industrialization, but also the possible consequences, good and bad, of an all-out industrializing policy. The core/periphery motif was employed throughout his analysis, although not with the ideological connotation that it would acquire in the hands of dependency theorists, but as a conventional designation for a geographical arrangement underpinned by historico-economic circumstances that had evolved in the 'natural' course of events. It definitely did not constitute an argument for the sort of deliberate long-term world process of underdevelopment of the Third World that economic-imperialism theory later contemplated, which was latent in Marxist texts and debates and which Prebisch could have drawn on. What he said, signalling a radical change from his previous thinking, was that primary production for international commerce had very nearly reached the end of its possibilities for internal growth because of various factors: due to higher productivity and the advantages of technical progress in the core (explicitly, in this case, the USA), the prices of primary export commodities were deteriorating in relation to those of manufactured goods, and even though recourse could be had to inflation for capital accumulation, sooner or later the disparity in the terms of exchange would catch up with marginal gains and would tend to produce stagnation in underdeveloped economies. The cycles in the periphery had to be countered either with foreign savings or with savings from the production of substitute industrial goods inside Latin America. This was, of course, a denial of the international specialization or division of labour principle dating back to Adam Smith, and it was not really the first (F. List had done the same thing at the high tide of classical political economy), but it was the first one based on economic analysis rather than on nationalism or neo-mercantilism.

In justifying this position Prebisch admitted its 'unorthodoxy' but countered that, since the core/periphery order of things went against a Pareto equilibrium in the international factors market (which was one of the inescapable implications of the 'invisible hand' philosophy), it was permissible to strike down also the absoluteness of the principle of the free international circulation of goods. Prebisch was not assuming this stance out of purely nationalist feelings (or at least he disclaimed that he did, employing a sober 'scientific' tone of presentation). For him, industrialization was only justified if it served to procure more goods than were being obtained through the export of primary production. In this, and perhaps not unbeknown to each other, Prebisch coincided entirely with Rosenstein-Rodan. The suspicions that cling to the reasonings of both authors is that they answer the same enquiry affirmatively without the benefit of supporting historical, statistical, or other evidence. Prebisch was probably more aware than Rosenstein-Rodan of the formidable problems involved in an all-out industrial development policy. For instance, he affirmed categorically that 'The centre must not lower its import coefficient', which, with his experience in government, cannot have seemed a pre-ordained assumption, and he ruled out the creation, at the start of the process, of a capital goods industry, there being 'still ample room for current consumption'. In the end, and really at the base of his presentation, he chose import substitution industrialization (ISI) crucially because 'we are of the opinion that industrial development will bring out the consequences of the cycle more clearly by accentuating fluctuations in urban employment'.

This particular theme would become a cornerstone of theories based on the dual-economy model, particularly, though hardly exclusively, in W. A. Lewis, who by then had been doing substantial work in industrial development problems in some of the British colonies in the Caribbean. In the context of Prebisch's concerns, it basically meant that he was probably thinking in terms of the ultimate application of Keynesian economics to the economies of Latin America, and specifically to that of the Argentine, and this was a far cry from anything even remotely resembling the dependency model that Marxists later adopted.[70]

Even if there is room for debating whether or not some Latin American economies jumped the gun in the matter of heavy industries, it is a reasonable assertion that the general Latin American process of development adhered quite closely to the Prebisch formula. Even more to the point, though, to what extent was this an original programme or a reflection of policies already operating in Latin America? The ambiguity of development economics, whether it is original research or a synthesis of previous experience, whether it is a 'science' in its own right or merely an accumulation of sanctions and eloquent exhortations, has never perhaps been better illustrated than in the early work of Prebisch, which is itself one of the essential pillars of the discipline. Ironically, or perhaps inevitably, it was from within ECLA itself, by then operating out of Santiago de Chile, that Prebisch's theses came under siege in the late 1960s, with pleas and arguments for more national economic autonomy through more state action and more heavy industries, as on behalf of more free trade it would be attacked in the 1970s by the critics of the idea of general, all-fronts industrialization. In later years, Prebisch would blame the flaws in the system on 'the serious socioeconomic bias of the mechanism for income distribution and capital accumulation in favour of the high social strata'. He would also insist on his criticism of the American 'hegemony' in international trade, and doff his hat to those of his colleagues in ECLA who 'have dealt much better than I with the political and strategic significance of this hegemony'.[71]

H. W. Singer and the exports of underdeveloped countries

The essential premiss in Prebisch's system was the idea of the imbalance in the terms of trade sustained in the also UNO-sponsored work *Relative Prices of Exports and Imports of Underdeveloped Countries* (1949). Its author was H. W. Singer, and although neither he nor Prebisch remember having known at the time about each other's work, their shared interest in the subject is frequently referred to as the Prebisch/Singer thesis or effect. It was faulted by P. Bairoch on two counts: lack of originality and lack of accuracy. Bairoch traced the Singer essay to the League of Nations study *Industrialization and Foreign Trade* (1945), which states, in Bairoch's words, that 'between the last quarter of the nineteenth century and the eve of World War Two, or more precisely between 1876–1880 and 1936–38, there had been a 43 per cent reduction in the price of primary products compared with the prices of manufactured products'. Against this accusation, Singer in 1984 made a very good case in three directions. In one he attributed his interest in what he called 'the problem of distribution of gain from trade and investment' to deeper sources than mere statistical analysis. Keynes, whom he acknowledged as a basic influence on his thought, had in 1938 'advocated buffer stocks for primary commodities'. He had 'come back to the idea when he started thinking in 1941 about post-war reconstruction', and, at Bretton Woods in 1947, in anticipation of a 'long-run downwards trend' in primary commodity prices, 'had considered the creation of (an) organization to increase and stabilize' them as 'the third pillar, in addition to the World Bank and the International Monetary Fund, of the international system he envisaged'.[72]

This concern geared smoothly for Singer with the idea of 'structural backwash effects' from industrial economies 'on the trade of the primary exporting countries, with prices and terms of trade acting as a mechanism of transmission', which he credited to the Swede G. Myrdal. In his turn, Myrdal had been influenced by his compatriot, F. Hilgerdt, 'who had already shaped the League of Nations publications on the Networks of World Trade' (surely the origin of the work cited by Bairoch), but from whose attribution of the 'backwash effect' to cycles in the industrial countries Singer shied back, preferring Myrdal's 'structural' hypothesis. These ideas closely resemble the Prebisch centre/periphery construct, and they are undoubtedly the basis of the Prebisch/Singer *ex post facto* pairing. In the other two rebuttals of the Bairoch critique, Singer in effect implied that his study was more thorough than the League of Nations one and that it made accurate projections up to 1973. But especially he claimed for it the condition of a 'policy guide', advocating for underdeveloped countries, if needs be, 'temporary delinking. . .until a better basis for trade with more evenly distributed gains could be developed' and an 'engine for growth' could be constructed on 'a shift from primary products to manufactured goods and the development of a system of international aid', a clear foreshadowing of the New International Economic Order (NIEO), to whose support Singer later became deeply committed.[73]

Before considering the accusation of lack of accuracy, which others besides Bairoch have advanced, we would like to emphasize at least one aspect of Singer's basic stances, in 1949 as now, and that is his insistence on the 'structural' nature of the unequal trade relations between the rich and the poor countries. It is not in his view just a cyclical or conjunctural phenomenon, but the result of something inherently tenacious in the way it functions or malfunctions, not unlike the depiction of the deliberately exploitative international processes in economic-imperialism theory, although Singer does not incline in that direction and he is dismissive of the 'phraseology' of the 'dependency school'.

If Singer has sought support for his ideas, it has been among fellow development economists. In particular, he recognized in 1984 that he had extended the reach of his original thesis, from being about the relative deterioration of the prices of export primary commodities, to encompassing the terms of trade in general of developing countries. This was on the basis of investigations by C. P. Kindleberger in the early 1950s, showing that the value of primary products tends to deteriorate more when these are exported by developing countries than by developed countries, and that manufactured exports of developing countries tend to be worth less per unit than those from developed economies. 'Thus,' Singer wrote, 'the deterioration of the terms of trade of developing countries can be attributed to the combined effects of three factors: the relative deterioration of unit values for primary commodities exported by developing countries in relation to primary export unit values of developed countries; the relative deterioration of manufactured export unit values of developing countries relative to manufactures exported by developed countries; and the lower proportion of manufactures in total exports of LDCs (for which unit values have increased less).'[74]

Whatever Singer's reservations on dependency, the fact remains that the terms-of-trade hypothesis has gained more and stronger pledges from the Marxist side, where it is probably an article of faith, than from the Western developmentalist side of the divide between approaches and attitudes to Third World problems. Bairoch denied the original unequal terms-of-trade hypothesis outright, although he at first ignored Singer and restricted his criticism to the League of Nations study that was the basis of the latter's work: 'The chief bias in the League of Nations world trade price indices is that they use British prices only, and that some three-quarters of the prices used in the British indices are import prices. So, in fact, what is measured is notably the price of the products but also, and mainly, the transport costs that fell very considerably during this period. Since those import prices are more numerous for primary products, and since for those products transport costs are of particular significance, this involves a major distortion of the prevailing trend.' From his own studies Bairoch 'deduced that between the 1870s and the 1926–9 period, the terms of trade for primary products relative to manufactured goods improved by some 20–25 per cent, instead of worsening by about 20 per cent as had been calculated by the League of Nations'. Bairoch admitted that 'from the early 50s and until 1961–2, there was a real deterioration in the terms of trade of primary products, and even more so of those primary products exported by less developed countries', but added that there was a stabilization afterwards, although the 'negative evolution' was still there. He explained the 1950s downturn as being the combined result of sluggish demand, the competition of synthetics, policy restrictions, and 'last but not least, the Singer/Prebisch effect'.[75]

The 'unequal exchange' controversy

The list of critics of the Singer/Prebisch thesis is quite long – and does not necessarily exclude Marxists, such being the case of G. Kay – but the really all-stops-out statistical assault on it was co-ordinated by B. Balassa, who asserted in 1984 that not only have the terms of trade not been unfavourable to LDCs, but that in fact there was 'a decline of 10 per cent in the terms of trade of the developed countries in their exchange of manufactured goods for primary products other than fuel with the developing countries during the 1953–1977 period'. Furthermore, there was 'no change in the terms of trade of industrial Europe relative to the developing countries between 1872 and 1953', as per research and adjustments on UN figures done by I. B. Kravis and R. E. Lipsey in 1981, reinforced by M. Michaely for the first period in question. Whoever is right on this strictly quantitative issue (and the entire Third World with its programme for a NIEO vociferously supports the Singer/Kindelberger theses – not to mention the support of its generally enthusiastic Marxist partisans), the controversy, like all those involving the origins and the perpetuation of underdevelopment, has passed from the realm of the technical to the domain of the ideological and the political.

This would seem not to be so from the reams of material devoted to the technical side of the debate, yet let us consider how it stood up to the early 1980s. J. Spraos accepted with many reservations and qualifications the validity of the adverse trend in the prices of primary products – 'a deteriorating trend is detectable in the data for the period 1870–1938. . .but it is questionable when the period is extended to include the post World War Two decades' – and he presented long-term series from which it would seem that, indeed, there was no noticeable long-term trend in what Spraos calls national barter terms of trade. However, the series for the postwar period, which coincided along general lines with statistics in Singer, did seem to show a certain downward trend. In both the long-term and the short-term series, however, and in two authors who would appear inclined to agree rather than to disagree, there is really no basis on which to sustain a secular downwards trend, although it would seem from these exercises as if, on the whole, exports from the Third World do tend to be valued less than those from the developed world in international exchanges. To any impartial observer this would appear to confirm B. Balassa's position that there is no adverse trend in the merchandising of the products of developing countries, yet not content with this, Balassa insists that technical adjustments (very technical, in fact, such as that 'changes in unit values do not appropriately represent changes in prices') demonstrate that, if there is a trend, it is against the exports of manufactured goods from the developed countries. This has the appearance of a counter-thesis at the other extreme of the Prebisch/Singer effect, a further positioning very likely influenced by Balassa's championing of the strategy of growth-through-trade against growth-through-ISI. It seems inevitable to conclude that 'ideologies' can hardly be discounted even in the higher and more abstract reaches of the debate. At any rate, on the question of Third World economic backwardness it is probably true, as H. J. Bruton wrote back in 1955, that the Prebisch/Singer thesis 'has surely been asked to support a heavier argument than it can bear'.[76]

While the UN-based economists were preparing a forceful theoretical case in defence of the industrial development of the underdeveloped economies, the wolf-stalking-sheep situation that the postwar aggressiveness of communism in a world of mounting decolonization appeared to create for the West, was making an even more urgent point of its own. In the absence of direct intervention where and when danger loomed, the Western powers had to rely on local ruling classes, and, to consolidate friendly political power, they were banking on material progress and improved standards of living, to all of which development economics held the soi-disant key. There was, therefore, a convergence between theoretical work such as that of Prebisch and Singer and Western political concerns, and it was from this circumstance tht development economics got its head in the 1950s. In lieu of something akin to the Marshall Plan, the economically backward countries were offered technical advice, often becoming hosts to development economists from America and from Europe.

In one way or another, whether in the groves of Academe or in ministries of the Third World, whether turning foreign aspirants into fully-formed boffins or actually advising on policies and plans, development economists and development economics were recruited in the West's campaign to improve the world's living conditions and to keep communism at bay. The political context of development economics need not be considered the only guide to its evolution, especially as it has its own inherent logic and its proper field of study, but that context should never be underestimated or neglected. Development economics and development studies in general should not, therefore, be interpreted as ever straying very far from Western political orthodoxies, even if they often proposed a much-tampered with model of capitalism. In our exploration of the history of development studies, we shall try to determine how far they went in disassociating themselves from Eurocentrism, and if in doing so, they also posited an explanation of their own for the origins of economic inequality between nations.

The history of development studies

Two analytical approaches

In order to explore these themes, the voluminous productions of development economics have to be put into some sort of manageable order. The two methods most frequently recurred to are: (a) by conceptual emphases and tendencies; (b) by chronological sequences or stages. The former approach can be found in, among others, H. B. Chenery and P. W. Preston.

Chenery is the originator of the useful concept of 'structuralism. 'The structuralist approach', he explained, 'attempts to identify specific rigidities, lags and other characteristics of the structure of developing economies that affect economic adjustments and the choice of development policy.' He identified the following as structuralists: Rosenstein-Rodan,Nurkse, Lewis, Prebisch,

Singer and Myrdal. Besides the structuralists, Chenery also recognized two other tendencies: the neo-classical and the neo-Marxist. However, these two groups represent a virtual denial of development economics itself, the neo-classical by reducing it to orthodox mainstream economics, and the neo-Marxist through its refutation by dependency theory, so that what Chenery really proposed was a classification of 'approaches to the analysis of developing economies'.

Preston suggested two different but related classifications of development studies and theories, one according to definitions of progress, the other according to an ideological classification of the theorists themselves. In the first classification, progress can be defined in three ways: as 'growth', and this definition corresponds to the 'positivists' of the second classification (Lewis, Rostow, the sociology of development and modernization theory); as 'ordered social reform', corresponding to the 'radicals' (A. G. Frank, C. Furtado, G. Myrdal); and as 'disengagement from world capitalism and the pursuit of planned socialism', corresponding to the Marxists (P. A. Baran, G. Palma, Frank again). Without entering into the validity of the conceptual sequence involved here, the groupings of theorists by this system are outlandish and incomprehensible. What can Frank, who figures in two different, almost antipodal categories, be doing in the same group with Myrdal? And why should Myrdal, to start with, be considered a 'radical' (which he certainly was not) and not a 'positivist' (which he more likely was, as per Preston's references)? There is a closetful of bones to pick with Preston, and we think the problem is his refusal to admit the fundamental opposition, even incompatibility, between Western developmentalism and Marxist dependency theory. There is a huge difference in outlook between these two groups of theories, which extends to almost all aspects of Third World reality and which in our opinion can most eloquently be brought out through the consideration of the problem of the origins of international economic inequality.[77]

P. Streeten and K. Basu are in general agreement on how to organize chronologically the contents of development economics. Streeten said: 'The history of development economics can be regarded as a progress from large generalizations and high abstractions to greater specificity and concreteness.' He attributed this change to 'two discoveries – that many problems of the countries of the South are shared by the North, and that few problems are common to all countries of the South'. Basu was more specific on the same transformation, which he perceived as gravitating from the study of the process of development to that of 'the problems and structure of underdevelopment', involving 'an increasing use of rigorous analysis and concepts and results from economic theory'. Both authors seem to discover in development economics a pattern in which something resembling order emerges out of nebulousness.[78]

As the only full-scale monograph on the subject of the history of development economics, H. W. Arndt published in 1987 the work titled *Economic Development: The History of an Idea*, which is a chronological depiction of the basic doctrines on the economic development of the Third World. Arndt divides the concept of development into two branches: growth and social objectives. Under growth, he places capital accumulation, the development of human capital, and trade as the engine of growth. He recognizes a variety of strategies that he categorizes under the general heading of social objectives, among them the creation of employment as the first priority and 'basic needs'. Arndt describes capital accumulation as 'the orthodoxy of the first phase of postwar thinking about economic development'. He considers that all the significant departures from the orthodoxy occurred during the 1960s, although he does not make a completely convincing case for some of the tendencies of thought that he identifies. Finally, and rather late in his exposition – because of the light it throws on the theoretical origins of the research on economic development – Arndt included a section on 'structuralism', a concept that he defined with a formula from I. M. D. Little: 'In economic terms, the supply of most things is inelastic.'

Basically what structuralism involved was a critique of price mechanisms as a means to correct balance of payment crises and other distortions, all of which had to be approached from government planning and controls. Associated with this general outlook, dating from before the Second World War, were M. Kalecki, T. Balogh, E. F. Schumacher, D. Seers, H. D. Henderson, N. Kaldor, Rosenstein-Rodan and apparently Arndt himself. The idea all these economists shared was that the price mechanism works 'even less well in underdeveloped than in developed countries and that classical economic theory was therefore largely inapplicable to LDCs'. Since this general version of structuralism was undoubtedly also held by many other economists, what we think that Arndt was indicating with his choice of names was the 'structuralist' origins in mainstream economics in England of development economics, although the placing of this important chapter in his scheme is undoubtedly eccentric as it comes after he has covered the full range of what he and others call the orthodoxy of development economics.[79]

From mainstream to disillusion

By way of introduction to our interpretation of the history of development economics and, at the same time, of our criticism of the Arndt version, we agree that there is an orthodoxy of development economics or economic development (either way is equally valid for us), but unlike Arndt we think that the orthodoxy was not successfully challenged in the West from within or from without until the 1970s, and that in the Third World even now it still largely expresses the dominant outlook on development, although two provisos must be made: first, that there are important exceptions to its prevalence, and, secondly, that the orthodoxy of development economics in the Third World was often encumbered by principles and practices that were not originally contemplated in it, so that it has often also been transformed out of all recognition, closer at times to the model of a command economy with capitalist traits than to a free economy with indicative planning as was originally envisaged by that orthodoxy.

In the West, and sometimes in the Third World or from a Third World vantage, the orthodoxy was challenged during the 1960s in different ways. There was the permanent challenge flung by P. T. Bauer during its inception, consisting in a rejection of 'statism' and planning, and consequently of the notion of induced industrialization and all the political paraphernalia of development economics. This challenge was reinforced at different times, as by the Haberler Report (1957) and the UN-sponsored Little/Scitovsky/Scott Report (1970), but it became increasingly strong in the 1970s in view of two circumstances: the awareness of inadequacy and failure that gripped development economics, manifesting itself in the social orientation of development studies, which dates tentatively but not significantly from the late 1960s; and the rise of the 'gang of four' (Hong Kong, Singapore, South Korea and Taiwan), and with them the notion that a totally free-market economy was behind their success. We also reject Arndt's tripartite division of the concept of growth and his reduction of it to an obsession with capital accumulation: the 'revision' that he calls 'investment in human capital' can be found almost anywhere in the early literature of development economics and the 'revision' proposing trade as the engine of growth was part of the critique formulated by J. Viner and others in the 1950s, and not an issue that came up originally in the UNO or in research done in the 1960s.

Without renouncing Arndt's exposition entirely, in doing the history of development economics we shall follow a chronological multi-phase scheme, and within each phase, we shall rely on the emphases or tendencies approach used by Chenery and Preston. The first phase of our own scheme has already been discussed. It can be described as the initial gestation phase extending from the war years to 1950, during which the basic ideas, methods and attitudes of development economics were elaborated.

After this phase, we enter what we shall call here the mainstream phase of development economics, which is an extended unfolding of the implications of the development process. As Streeten and Basu have said, the mainstream phase, which covers mainly the 1950s decade, was indeed concerned with generalizations. It also was oriented towards definitions and basic principles. It came up with the idea itself of development studies as a wider research endeavour than what was being contemplated within the strictly economic field. The means for that conceptual expansion was principally the launching in the USA of modernization theory under the umbrella of the co-called sociology of development. The 1960s decade contains, in our opinion, another phase in the evolution of development studies, for it was a time of external influences on the discipline, of experimentation, and of second-thoughts. Towards the end, the doubts and the shuffling and the daring cross-breeding of ideas (not always felicitous) were gaining the upper hand. After 1970 and up to the present, development studies became almost obsessively concerned with immediate, starkly down-to-earth research and policies, as reflected in such issues as 'basic needs' and the 'informal sector'. We think this phase can be accurately described as the 'onset of disillusion'. It was also the time that brought back into force the old 'rightist' denial of the development-economics project. This last phase can be seen as a kind of negative, near-despairing gloss on all that had come before. The 'great white hope' of the 'right wing' in development studies was the 'gang of four', but the economic performance of these fringe Asian countries could be interpreted in different ways and by no means exclusively as the Golden Apples of the free-enterprise, free-trade, export-substituting Hesperides.

The 'mainstream' phase

Of 'vicious circles' and 'poverty traps'

The mainstream phase had a central preoccupation and a fundamental outlook. The preoccupation was to build on what had been achieved during the gestation phase about the reality and the meaning of underdevelopment. The act of building – in the various senses of further explorations of the reality of underdevelopment, of the elaboration of specific policies and mechanisms, and of the erection of syntheses and conning towers for theoretical overviews – was undertaken with an optimistic, rationalist and voluntarist outlook. On the question of the definition of underdevelopment, the quantitative approach pioneered by Clark was reaffirmed and refined. There had been from the beginning the temptation to think of development in terms of major industrial projects, including the manufacture of weapons and munitions. For the developing countries that could afford it, it was a matter of national pride in the 1950s to construct a steel mill regardless of profitability or of domestic absorptive capacity. Volta Redonda, in Brazil, was the premier example that others in Latin America strove to imitate. J. Viner's famous 1950 stricture on the per capita distribution of the national product as the meaning of development made so much sense that it is hard to believe that economic development could have ever been understood as anything other than expanding social welfare.[80]

The trouble with underdevelopment was that it did not seem to allow for economic growth of the spectacular sort that European countries had known after the start of the Industrial Revolution and which alone could permit the acquisition of social welfare. Admittedly, many underdeveloped countries were too backward even after the war to really be able to utilize the technologies of a modern Western economy for their own benefit, but what of the countries that were not so backward and that could have theoretically followed in the footsteps of the more advanced nations? The temptation was there to put the blame on external influences, but for development economics the problem was not one of external impediments because it was not engaged in a historical search for origins and because it simply could not believe in possibilities it did not contemplate seriously. Its basic approach was to describe, in the field if possible, why underdeveloped economies did not produce a socially acceptable degree of economic growth, and the explanation to hand was structuralism.

Structuralism is one of those Protean archetypal concepts that mean different things in different contexts. We have seen in Arndt that in prewar economics it meant the critique of the price mechanism as the instrument to correct economic distortions. It was probably from this perspective that it spread to development economics. However, it became better known in the 1960s in connection with a theory on inflation in Latin America that differed from the traditional monetary explanation.[81] In 1975 Chenery brought back the use of structuralism in its original prewar meaning to describe a specific approach to Third World realities. These realities were of general acceptance in development economics since its early years; in fact, it could be said that 'rigidities and lags', plus bottlenecks, disparities and disequilibria in general, were the daily bread on which the discipline was fed and raised from birth. But even with this description in view, it is possible to have two readings of structural underdevelopment. The more extreme version means that underdevelopment is such a hopeless historical malformation that only a social upheaval can cure it. This is the view of economic backwardness that Lenin came close to stating, the one that Comintern proceedings either suggested or tacitly ratified time and again. It disqualifies the ability of capitalism to develop any economy outside of where it is already entrenched on a foundation combining social bribes and complicities. The other less extreme version of structural underdevelopment does not go to that length, but it does say that the internal malfunction in underdeveloped economies is of such magnitude as to necessitate considerable reconstruction, and, furthermore, than the untreated or unfiltered norms and conventions of orthodox economics do not apply to it. It is essentially this version that quickly became standard developmentalist doctrine and went untouched down to the mid-1970s, when the doubting hit home.

One of the basic early motifs of the structural vision of underdevelopment (the less extreme, which we shall be using in this part of our analysis) was the 'vicious circle', later translated into technical terms as a 'low-level equilibrium trap'. It derived from the awareness even during the optimistic gestation phase of development economics that Rosenstein-Rodan's model might have been somewhat too sanguine. In 1949 Singer wrote an article – incongruously or ironically titled 'Economic progress in underdeveloped countries' – which enumerated a long list of vicious circles present in backward economies. These were beset by health problems, but medical improvements increased population, which made the economic situation more difficult, which over the long haul made the solution of endemic health problems more complicated. Social legislation to mitigate the scourge of poverty diverted resources needed for economic development. Low production hindered the possibility of acquiring capital equipment that could have served to increase production. Singer synthesized the discouraging nature of underdevelopment in these simple terms: 'An underdeveloped country is poor because it has no industry; and an underdeveloped country has no industry because it is poor.'

The solution to these problems was no less subject to the vicious-circle logic than were the problems themselves. The solution for underdevelopment required a 'big initial effort', yet underdevelopment by definition only allowed small-scale measures. The highly unequal distribution of income resulted in savings being wasted in luxury imports or in the export of capital, but redistributive policies tended to diminish savings capacity. Finally, development could not take place without political stability, which required unpopular policies, which resulted in social discontent and political instability. One vicious circle did not exclude another, and they could be made complementary or concentric.

In his highly influential lectures, *Some Aspects of Accumulation in Underdeveloped Countries* (1952), R. Nurkse reiterated or elaborated on some of the previous examples of the vicious circle. Lack of capital and low productivity made for low real income and low saving, which resulted in lack of capital. Alternatively: low income led to low savings and lack of capital, which made for low productivity and low income. Nurkse too envisaged the obstacles in the way of solutions, in particular those stemming from the operation of the 'demonstration effect', which was the jargon equivalent of 'keeping up with the Joneses' and explained why, in the USA, the growth of income did not generate a correspondingly higher savings-to-income ratio (known as the Dusenberg effect). In the case of the underdeveloped countries, Nurkse reasoned, foreign investment could paradoxically diminish the relative level of real income and increase the distance between the rich and the poor economies through diminished savings in the poor economies resulting from the spending of income gains according to patterns of consumption imported from the developed countries.[82]

The 'low-level equilibrium' trap

Like structuralism, the vicious circle was less a theory than an idea, and perhaps even less than an idea, an image eloquently in the service of an important cause. At a pinch, it could pass muster as a technical definition of underdevelopment. This was, in effect, what some theorists attempted to do during the mainstream phase of development economics. R. R. Nelson's mathematical model of 'the low-level equilibrium trap in underdeveloped economies' emphasized the relations between the production function and population growth. 'At an equilibrium level of per capita income', he wrote, 'both capital and population are constant, or are changing at an equal rate so that their ratio is constant.' If the ratio of population increase to capital accumulation at equilibrium was less than one, 'then equilibrium is unstable and there is no trap'. Otherwise, the economy would show no growth and it would remain trapped at a constant ratio of income to population. The model was somewhat more complex in that it also took into account the availability of arable land and the relative efficiency of production, but on the whole it basically described the fairly obvious principle that development required investment, food production and technological progress. Another model in general use was called the 'two-gap approach' because it correlated the savings/investment function in an underdeveloped economy (which usually did not suffice for development targets) with the flow of foreign resources, which showed in national accounts as an excess of imports over exports.

The implication in these models was that underdevelopment manifested a condition that backward countries tried to escape but kept falling back into owing to the pull of its accumulated deficiencies. A frequent underlying assumption for these pessimistic projections was that, whereas in a developed economy the attainment of full employment with high productivity required viable adjustments in certain quantifiable magnitudes, in an underdeveloped economy each new investment was afflicted with disproportionality, owing to the much narrower production and income bases. In characterizing economic backwardness as a whole, H. Leibenstein, relying on the concept of the vicious circle, contrasted its condition of quasi-stable equilibrium with the state of disequilibrium in advanced economies.[83] There was, however, something nugatory, and perhaps inaccurate, about these exercises. They were aggregative and descriptive, hence they analysed neither in depth nor in detail, and it could be argued that the real concrete problems of underdevelopment eluded them. The notion itself that underdevelopment was a state or quasi-state of equilibrium was useful perhaps in constructing a mathematical model, but on balance it seems profoundly unsatisfactory as a representation of reality or as an approach to the problems of economic backwardness.

Despite these technical models, underdevelopment was in various ways closer to a state of disequilibrium than to a condition of stability. There was, to start with, the essential imbalance between development and underdevelopment, which in the normal course of events made for instability on a global scale. Within underdevelopment, there was the permanent imbalance between the reality of low-level economic performance and potential development, and this condition implicated a whole series of specific disequilibria and disproportionalities: between means and ends, between the urban and the rural sectors, between the income/saving ratio and a desired input/output relation, and so on. If one compared these disequilibria with the articulations in a developed economy, the only way to perceive underdevelopment as a state of equilibrium would have had to be through the prism of history in the sense that economic backwardness represented the permanence in time of very old traditional ways, but this was perceivable from the vantage of industrialization and economic progress in general, which in itself made the indefinite survival of those ways either problematical or unlikely. Development economics existed precisely to come up with solutions for these problems, and that is perhaps what explains the greater influence in its proceedings during its mainstream phase of formulators of policy such as Rosenstein-Rodan, Prebisch, Singer, Nurkse and Lewis compared with those engaged in general descriptive analysis.

Working in the field of foreign commerce, G. Myrdal used in 1957 the 'vicious circle' metaphor but gave it a further twist with the 'principle of circular and cumulative causation'. What he meant was that without corrective measures the working of the market made for growing inequality, and this was particularly relevant in international trade. Myrdal was partial then to regulations and arrangements that biased conditions in favour of underdeveloped countries. With most other development economists, Myrdal believed that without help from the developed world underdevelopment could not be overcome. This did not involve dolloped programmes of foreign aid, but a truly massive effort that would affect the industrialized nations' overall rate of growth. This outlook, which had been foreseen by Rosenstein-Rodan in 1943, presupposed that you could not have real significant growth at the same time on both sides of the divide. Myrdal was always a prolific researcher and writer and he later modified this approach by conferring a crucial importance on the question of modernization and of social reform in underdeveloped countries. His initial impact on development studies, however, was much greater than his later somewhat acerbic opinions on the Third World. There is one constant throughout his work and that is a sense of moral outrage at misery and suffering, and this gave strength in his early work to the idea that economic aid was an ethical obligation. This concept had its sharpest expression in a vision of poverty and backwardness continuing or getting worse over the years. This was the essence itself of the vicious circle. Although firmly inclined towards free trade, Myrdal could not bring himself to accept the advisability of free trade as the sole motor of growth for underdeveloped economies.[84]

Of rural–urban flows and industrialization

Industrialization was defended in many ways during the mainstream phase, even though it was already a foregone conclusion before the basic texts from this period were written. In fact, even for Rosenstein-Rodan and Prebisch it probably had been an inevitable if problematic choice in view of the Western penchant for equating collective wealth and manufacturing, which concretely goes as far back at least as the age of mercantilism and has its most resounding historical validation in the Industrial Revolution.

The doctrine of industrialization did not necessarily include a denial of the advantages of international commerce as an instrument of development – certainly not in Prebisch, whose rallying cry for underdeveloped countries had to do with the imbalances rather than the 'backwash effects' of trade – but it did involve a strategic choice between three alternatives: (1) the export of primary products through the old international division of labour system; (2) manufacturing for exports; and (3) emphasis on the development of the domestic market on both the supply and the demand side. The third possibility could be said to be at the heart of the idea of economic development itself, although, as we shall see, it did not enjoy universal acceptance even during the mainstream period of development economics. Nurkse explicitly defended it because he identified primary exports with the vicious circle, and he did not believe that underdeveloped countries were in a position to compete in the international market with manufactured goods. Since underdeveloped countries, unlike the historical cases of Great Britain and the other early industrializing nations, did not generate enough surplus for their own endogenous industrialization, foreign capital resources in the form of foreign investment and capital goods were added as 'indivisibilities' in the development process. This had been known since early in the game, but during the mainstream phase of development economics it became an indissoluble part of the dogma of industrialization.[85] More complex elaborations of the industrialization model required the notions of social overhead and economies of scale, all of which came straight from Rosenstein-Rodan and the gestation phase of developmental thinking. On the whole, these ideas were incompatible with a system strictly activated by profit/loss calculations and had to be part of a planned development programme.

Capital, whether for industry or for infrastructure, was not, however, the only precondition for industrialization. Even though in the early literature of development economics it often seems as though industrialization were an end in itself, it was in fact always a response to the excessive importance of the primary sector in weight of numbers and of production ratios in underdeveloped economies. Underdevelopment could have been defined during the mainstream phase as the prevalence in a national system of the low-productivity rural economy over the high-productivity urban economy, and development consisted in the orderly transfer of under-utilized factors from the country to the cities. We shall see later that one of the basic changes in development economics, leading to disillusionment and to the search for concrete issues and solutions, came about when it was seen that the rural–urban process did not result in harmonious development but in the transfer of rural unemployment and poverty to the cities. However, at this stage, the rural surplus population was seen as the fundamental problem to be tackled.

Rosenstein-Rodan and Nurkse tailored their ideas on industrialization to the existence of rural unemployment, but it was W. A. Lewis who presented the situation of the rural sector in an underdeveloped economy in such a way that it became part of fundamental doctrine. For this he translated the awareness of rural excess population into two technical formulas: 'unlimited supply of labour' and 'zero marginal productivity'. The first permitted a set of subsidiary inferences, such as that wages in the rural economy had to be 'institutionally' determined rather than market determined in order to guarantee a constant flow of labour power towards urban industries. This required that the supply of labour in the rural sector should be of a certain magnitude, at least during the early phase of industrialization, in order to prevent a fall in agricultural production and at the same time a rise in rural wages to the levels prevalent in the urban sector. The operative principle behind this balancing act was the second factor, 'zero marginal productivity': this meant that agrarian productivity in an underdeveloped economy was so low that workers could be subtracted from the agricultural labour force, up to a certain point, without affecting overall production, although this did not mean that, at any given time, a unit of labour could not be more productively employed.

Lewis's oft-repeated concern was productivity – in the sense that more production per capita redounded in a more equitable share of goods and income – because he believed that in the long run it was trade that would allow for steady growth through export competitiveness. The overloaded rural sector did not allow much room for improvement as it was, but there were trade benefits to be had from an expanded industrial sector. The countryside could contribute cheap agricultural produce to sustain the rural–urban migration. In the end it would benefit from a lessened human burden on its resources and from higher per capita output. Nurkse was in substantial agreement with the idea that agriculture should keep its prices down. Following these recommendations Latin American economists would argue that 'food prices are irrelevant to the long-run development process since both producer and consumers are insensitive to changes in prices', a fallacy that would cost developing countries dearly in future.

J. C. H. Fei and G. Ranis became identified during the 1960s with 'labour-surplus economy' theory, which they derived from Lewis's unlimited supply of labour ideas and summarized in this manner: 'In a word, the vital real resources function of the agricultural sector in the dualistic economy is performed when the released agricultural worker fed by the agricultural surplus is enabled to create new output in the industrial sector.' Without surrendering the premiss of the low-productivity rural sector, they tended to emphasize the overall necessity of balanced growth between agriculture and industry, and in 1969, in view of the frequent misapplication in underdeveloped countries of the orthodox norms of development economics, they wrote: 'While the modernization impulse may well have to come from outside agriculture, without the mobilization of that sector and its full interaction with the rest of the economy in an ever broadening net of human and market participation, development is difficult to sustain.'[86]

Development economics did not deal with a 'natural' or spontaneous process of industrialization or with the reasons why this process had not occurred. Its main concern was development through induced industrialization. From the study of its fundamental texts, we have tried to extract certain basic doctrines by singling out and interrelating the ideas which best exemplify the process of induced growth and which by all logic are the least ascribable to a real historical process of industrialization, such as the British eighteenth- and nineteenth-century paradigm, since those ideas by definition had to do with historical lags and were meant to provide correctives for them.

The concept of structural underdevelopment characterized by vicious circles and poverty traps is foreign, not to say antipodal, to the process of material growth in the industrialized countries. It is true that capitalism was afflicted by relatively short-term economic cycles, which reached a depressive paroxysm in the 1930s, but these periodic downturns were also by definition surmountable, and this seemed not to be the case with the sort of continuous low-intensity rhythm of activity that defined underdevelopment. Likewise, induced industrialization is not consonant either with the historical norm. Foreign investments were required to industrialize and this again did not reflect an invariant historical pattern. Neither economies of scale nor social overhead (except in terms of profits, as for the latter, in British toll roads and canals) were operative historical functions. We have refrained from indicating other developmentalist concepts, such as infant-industry protection or policies for monetary stimulation, because they are either self-evident or they were part of historical experience. Finally, we have seen development economics attempting to model short-run replications of the complex and historically long-term process of Western urbanization that came perilously close to being distortional in the light of historical experience. Yet these daring prescriptions were still not enough by the canons of development economics to ensure industrialization. At least two more coordinative principles were necessary: one practical, the other a guiding theoretical light.

Planning and balanced growth

Early development economics was as committed to planning as it was to any other of its basic principles. However, Rosenstein-Rodan always seemed diffident about the subject, despite the fact that his views on induced industrialization seemed to clamour for strong economic *dirigisme*. Nurkse like him sounded coy and uncommitted on the subject, although the policies he advocated also required not just planning but planning that was both precise and far-reaching. Lewis probably expressed the general attitude of his peers when in 1949 he wrote for the Fabian Society a book on planning in which he practically defined it as 'targeting' and as having to do with 'the means which the government uses to try to enforce upon private enterprise the targets which have been previously determined'. Lewis was only marginally pro-planning and inclined strongly in favour of 'mobility of resources'.

Here again we see that development economics required of its practitioners an ethical commitment that went beyond the mere exercise of a profession or the use of scientific instruments. Despite their very real and very profound misgivings, Rosenstein-Rodan, Nurkse and Lewis had to admit that planning was a necessity in order to combat poverty, and planning duly entered development economics on an equal footing with induced industrialization and rural–urban population flows. Theorists like the Indian P. Mahalanobis and the Dutchman J. Tinbergen did their best to make it practical and acceptable. Mahalanobis in particular became influential through his crucial involvement in the choice in post-independence India of a policy of all-out heavy industrialization, that is, in favour of the construction of the steel mills and the engineering and tool plant that Third World countries were yearning to possess. Ironically, early gung-ho industrializers took for granted in their planning models one of the tools that has proved least amenable to the control of underdeveloped nations: a practical, self-multiplying fund of modern industrial technology. Conventional wisdom had it that education would provide the resources needed in that area, but few economists apparently suspected how complex technology would become, or to what extent the centres of gravity of technological research under capitalism would shift over the years from the universities to the laboratories of multinational corporations. This exclusion from the sources of vital knowledge for survival in the international market place would become in due time the crowning aggravation in the career of failures and frustrations that economic development has turned out to be for most of the countries in the Third World.[87]

If planning was supposed to offer the superior means to stimulate and control the process of industrialization, 'balanced growth' was the open sesame with which development economists hoped to crack open the gates of progress. It had been spelt out first by Rosenstein-Rodan in his 1943 essay, where it was proposed as an all-purpose guide for those involved in the process of economic planning, and it was of a piece with the idea of the big push. After the war, when economists started to perceive the quagmire on which Rosenstein-Rodan's grandiose edifice of industrialization had to be built, balanced growth and the big push were invoked as the two sledge-hammers with which to break the vicious circle and the poverty trap. Nurkse had few illusions about the big push, but he was the foremost advocate of balanced growth. In his view it was the necessary approach to attack the fundamental dilemma that any input into an underdeveloped economy, whether of capital, labour or foreign currency, was never sufficient for self-sustained growth because it generated additional needs and requirements as, for example, when investment A generated a demand that could only be satisfied domestically by investment B, except that by the time that B was in place the output of A could not supply the aggregate demand of A + B. In primary-products exporting economies, balanced growth was the ideal strategic alternative for stagnating exports by means of diversified and mutually complementary industrial investments.

There was an even more basic application of the same principle, which incidentally showed that Nurkse was not unaware that agriculture could not be entirely neglected in the process of development: 'The relation between agriculture and manufacturing industry offers the clearest and simplest case of balance needed for economic growth.' But Nurkse also drew from the notion of balanced growth an additional justification for the principle requiring that cheap food should keep flowing to the cities at all costs in order to support industrialization. The reasoning behind this was apparently that increasing demand would stimulate productivity in the agricultural sector and bring it in line with industry. In practice, however, the policy of supporting urban industrialization was interpreted as either underpaying producers or subsidizing them where fiscal resources permitted it, and resulted in agriculture becoming the poor handmaiden of industry and eventually in parasitic, ramshackle and volatile urban economies, which came to seem like the millstone around the neck of development theory. Whatever the distortions that were later introduced, Nurkse rested his case in this fashion: 'The case for balanced growth is concerned with establishing a pattern of mutually supporting investments over a range of industries wide enough to overcome the frustration of isolated advances in order precisely to create a formal momentum of growth.'

Balanced growth, then, was a sort of compendium of all the norms and dicta of development economics. It was specifically contrasted to international specialization by Nurkse, which was about as complete a statement as could be found of the internal-market orientation, as opposed to trade-oriented strategies, of development economics. The idea was fertile in possibilities and influences. No other policy made planning so absolutely indispensable, and not just of the indicative sort that Lewis seemed to favour. H. B.

Chenery understood that it had to be the moving force behind industrialization or development programmes. In line with his heavy-equilibrium view of underdevelopment and despite evidence on the limitations of foreign aid and investments, H. Leibenstein in 1957 still insisted that in order to break the vicious circle of poverty it would have to be attacked through a critical minimum effort oriented by the guiding idea of balanced growth.[88]

Modernization theory, or a controversial expansion of development studies

G. Myrdal's change of heart

In 1972 G. Myrdal wrote of his disenchantment about the increasing socio-economic inequalities within Third World countries themselves. His moral fervour on market inequalities and international injustices had been buffeted by events and grievously offended by the social reality in some underdeveloped societies. He had in effect come down from the Elysium of figures and intentions to the mire of corruption and bureaucracy. In his own words: 'After the war and the avalanche of decolonization, the ideals of modernization were adopted almost everywhere as a sort of state religion. A prominent role among these ideas was played by the egalitarian doctrine. There is a strong flavour of the Enlightenment philosophy colouring most public pronouncements in these countries concerning the goals for planned development.' Reality, however, was a painful let-down. 'In sharp contrast to these declarations for greater equality', he went on, 'stands the fact that almost everywhere in the non-communist underdeveloped countries actual development has moved towards increasing inequality. Even when egalitarian reforms have been legislated for in some of these countries, they have not been carried out, or they have been permitted to work in the interest of the not-so-poor.' The basis of these observations was an in-depth study of social habits and institutions in some South Asian states, which he undertook when his wife Alva was named Sweden's ambassador to India in 1957. From this immersion in the day-to-day reality of developing societies, Myrdal concluded 'that social and economic institutions and attitudes should be changed in order to: increase labour efficiency and diligence, effective competition, mobility, and enterprise; permit greater equality of opportunities; make possible higher productivity and well-being; and generally promote development'.

The new emphases in his approach to the problem of underdevelopment were decidedly grimmer than they had ever been, even granting that he was never really a Pollyanna on the possibilities of development, and they led him to a terrible dilemma: 'Observing the broad correlation between degree of inequality and poverty in South Asia, it is legitimate to ask whether or not poverty breeds inequality.' He surfaced with three concepts, which explained for him in part the causes of the observed deterioration: environmental influence, cultural determinism, and the 'soft state'. The last two put him smack into the middle of an important Western intellectual stream. Cultural determinism was exemplified by religion, which, on the popular level, was 'a ritualized and stratified complex of highly emotional beliefs and valuations that regularly give the sanction of sacredness, taboo, and immutability to inherited institutional arrangements, modes of living and attitudes. . . [and] acts as a tremendous force for social inertia.' The 'soft state' was a crucial derivation from this psycho-cultural complex. Within it there was neither solidarity nor social discipline. Western juridical principles and practices were foreign or incompatible with it. But above all it was arbitrary and corrupt. And Myrdal mentioned the irony of Third World corruption, which made the profit motive operative in the public sector while tending to stifle it in private business. Myrdal cited the case of Indonesia, where corruption was reputedly absent during Dutch colonial rule but had picked up dramatically after independence. By some recondite means, climate was the ultimate cause of social and economic backwardness, but the immediate determinant influences were 'reformable' social practices. The offshoot seemed to be that more could be done about underdevelopment from within than by changing the structures of international commerce.[89] We shall refer later on to the implications of Myrdal's change of heart about underdeveloped countries, but let us explore now the intellectual frame of reference in which it came about. What had happened between his plaintive pleas on international inequities and his later schoolmarmish attitude towards non-Western developing societies?

The concept of 'pattern variables'

There is a line of reasoning going back at least to Max Weber, which explains development as the result of certain collective mental attitudes and the resulting social habits. The essential idea of the psychological origins of progress reappears in J. A. Schumpeter's thesis on the importance of the entrepreneur for the optimal working of a capitalist model. American sociology had been examining these ideas since the 1930s without extending its conclusions beyond what could be described as the field of its immediate social implications, but during the 1950s it had begun to enlarge its vision to take in the problems of underdevelopment.

The starting point for this analysis was T. Parsons' concept of 'pattern variables', which clustered related traits into divergent groups of varying social efficacy. D. Lehman considers that modernization theory, which, in this context, is a conventional name for the Western sociological concern with underdevelopment, is 'Talcott Parsons' reading expounded in his *Structure of Social Action* of Weber and Durkheim'. D. McLelland (1961) drew from this research the idea that 'community development' was a function of an individual desire to do well, which he called 'n-achievement'. Social progress depended for each group on the number of 'n-achievers' that it produced. E. Hagen (1962) saw the possibility of applying these concepts to the condition of economic underdevelopment and he proceeded to do so in connection with 'peasant societies'. As B. Higgins (1959) put it: 'In contrast to the technologically advanced society with its high n-achievement, high autonomy (need to be independent of others) and high need dominance (need to be a leader), the peasant society is characterized by a high need-affiliation (need to please friends and to have their affection, to co-operate with them) and high need-dependency (need to feel inferior to someone; to have ideas and attitudes approved by persons regarded as superior).' Furthermore, said Higgins: 'The lack of Schumpeterian entrepreneurship in a peasant society is a direct reflection of the value system in such a society.' Hagen cited as high-achievers the lower-order of Samurais in Japan and the antioqueños of Colombia.

Other pattern-variables were proposed, always according to a scheme contrasting progress to stagnation. B. F. Hoselitz (1960) attributed to the 'first world' a pattern of behaviour defined by universalism, achievement-orientation and functional specificity, and to the Third World the opposite traits: particularism, the inability to generalize or discover productive analogies; adscription, the acceptance of one's station in life; and functional diffusion, the lack of concentration and method. It was believed by the theorist of this tendency that if the n-achievement mystique could be instilled in a general and systematic way into a society it could help it escape underdevelopment. The programme for doing this was known as the 'sociology of development', and the designation 'modernization theory' probably derives from looser, non-technical analyses of developing societies, such as those by D. Lerner (1958). In essence, this method sought to substitute traditional habits and values, which were seen as retarding, with new, progressive, essentially Western ones. Myrdal has admitted that the work he undertook in Asia was specifically oriented towards modernization, that is to say, towards the study of 'attitudes and institutions' which he 'found to be largely responsible for those countries' underdevelopment and would have to be changed in order to speed up development'.[90]

Modernization theory did not have the acceptance in economic circles, or the success in general, its authors and defenders envisioned. Myrdal's *Asian Drama* (1968) was probably both its hightide and its swan song. The diffusion of the sociology of development during the 1960s permitted the creation of the wider category of development studies, but the sociological approach to underdevelopment has not prospered either academically or in the area of policy. Its influence on development economics has been minimal, although not entirely null. There are elements of sociology in the re-orientation of economic development studies in the 1970s towards social objectives, but on the whole development economists, while accepting the existence of non-economic factors in underdevelopment, have tended to put them on a 'lower order of variables', or to use them only as discrete or ancillary aspects of the entire picture. Even though they agree that underdevelopment has endogenous causes, development economists, habituated to interpreting behaviour in terms of rational self-interest, do not as a rule see it as psychological in origin.

As was to be expected, the greatest opposition to modernization came from those who believed that underdevelopment was not primarily a self-generated phenomenon, but a product of international inequalities and forces. This takes us a step closer to the contemporary theory of economic imperialism, and it is apposite in this respect to mention the A. G. Frank critique of the sociology of development because of its precise targeting and because, despite Frank's radicalism, it probably reflects the widest possible spectrum of Third World opinion on the subject. Frank, of course, denies the assumptions about the origins of underdevelopment in modernization theory, but he goes further and impugns the theory itself in that it posits a 'psychological dualism', which goes against the fundamental idea of the unity of humanity. His criticism consists in attributing to modernization theory an implicit racist discriminatory content, which he then proceeds to demolish with a mixture of sarcasm and common sense. Was his victim really racist though? One supposes it was not by intention, but, like the IQ test, it laid the burden of the proof of its egalitarianism on the shoulders of the people it deprecated. Even if its influence had gone further than it actually did, the sociology of development would always have been a difficult doctrine to preach in the context of economic theory and policy.[91]

The W. W. Rostow synthesis and its critics

The figure who brings together all the main strands of development studies is also the most controversial because of his theoretical contentions and because of his political clout. With the publication and wide dissemination – to no small degree due to the quasi-official backing of the US government – of his book *The Stages of Economic Growth* (1960), W. W. Rostow came to seem like the incarnation of the quintessential development economist, but before that he had been associated with the theory of modernization through his participation in the CIA-funded, MIT-based Centre for International Studies (CENIS). CENIS was a policy-research institution pursuing that objective with one foot in economics and the other in sociology. It also exemplified the tight bonding in the USA during the 1950s between government and academe on Third World development issues. This is Rostow's own description of its operations: 'CENIS's work on development began formally in 1952 and included intensive studies in India, Indonesia and Italy. Aside from [M.] Millikan and me, the members of the senior staff engaged in economic development problems were Everett Hagen, Benjamin Higgins, Wilfred Malenbaum and P. N. Rosenstein-Rodan. Rodan had, of course, been at work in development problems longer than any of us – since his research on Eastern Europe in London during the Second World War. We were also closely in touch with our colleague Charles Kindleberger, whose wide portfolio of interests included the field of economic growth in both a historical and a contemporary context.' However, even before his attachment to modernization as a strategy for development, Rostow had been interested in the 'application of economic theory to economic history', in particular in connection with economic growth.

By fishing in three different ponds – the history of economic development, development economics and the sociology of modernization – he came up with his special theory of stages in economic development. Rostow's contribution in this area consisted in defining and describing five stages through which economic modernization supposedly went. Starting from traditional society, itself classified as the initial stage, these were: the transitional stage, the take-off stage, maturity, and high mass consumption. From the angle of underdevelopment, the take-off stage was the principal concern and target of policy. Thirlwall summarized it in these terms: 'Since the pre-conditions of take-off have been met in the transitional stage, the take-off stage is a short stage of development during which growth becomes self-sustaining. Investment must rise to a level in excess of 10 per cent of national income in order for per capita income to rise sufficiently to guarantee adequate future levels of saving and investment.' Conventionally, Rostow accepted that resources had to be transferred from the rural to the urban economy. Less conventionally, he was not in favour of balanced growth. In development, he found, certain key industries led the way, generating forward, backward and lateral linkages. This meant, therefore, unbalanced growth in its most elementary sense.

In his study of stages of growth, first adumbrated in an article in 1956, Rostow wove together strands from different, even opposed tendencies within development economics, an approach which gives more substance to the notion that his work was a conscious attempt at a summation of all the basic themes and areas of development studies. The sociological aspects of a strategy of development, which could be defined as the political, social and institutional frameworks for industrialization, had to do with change and stimulation of traditional societies or of large traditional residues within changing societies. Ultimately, for Rostow as for the other intellectual pillars of development economics, change and progress were dependent on the assimilation of technology, which was the process itself of learning, and economic growth was not an end in itself but a symptom, 'one manifestation of a society's total performance', as he stated in *The Process of Economic Growth*, published in 1952.[92]

There was a blandness about all this that belied but could not do away with the fact that it was near-official American foreign policy doctrine for Latin America and the rest of the Third World during the late 1950s and early 1960s, and Rostow himself made no bones in 1984 about his clear perception of the stakes in East–West power politics: 'It was vice president Nixon's difficulties in Lima and Caracas in May 1958. . .that shifted the balance of power within the Eisenhower administration towards support for the Inter-American Bank and other positive responses to Latin America's development needs, long urged upon it. Castro's emergency in 1959 as a working ally of Moscow was not irrelevant to easy congressional acceptance of the Alliance for Progress.'

Rostow was, of course, completely identified with this ill-starred programme for aid and counselling in Latin America. His ideological position has provoked more attacks and denunciations than the actual contents of his academic work, but his published work has not had easy sailing either. In putting aside (or down) Rostow's claims to having given due recognition to non-economic factors in development, A. Fishlow inveighed against Rostow's reliance on quantitative measurements to define economic stages and, in particular, the so-called take-off stage, which is the crucial step in the development ladder, and he cited nations such as Mexico and Argentina that have entered the transition phase to take-off and relapsed or stagnated without apparent cause. Fishlow explained: 'The national capital input ratio lacks behavioural content. Its constancy subsumes complementary changes in other inputs, such as labour or entrepreneurial skills, not to mention technological progress. It excludes the important category of human capital.' Furthermore, Fishlow argued that Rostow's quantitative measuring rods were useless to stabilize his stages because the historical evidence for them was at best patchy and at worst contradictory. S. Kuznets, whom Rostow recognized as an influential teacher, nevertheless castigated Rostow's historical data as well as some of the conclusions that he derived from the historical process of industrialization. Kuznets disputed Rostow's estimates on the savings ratio (marginal propensity to save) characteristic of the take-off stage, but worse, he compared unfavourably today's data from the LDCs and the estimates for the pre-industrial phase of the industrialized nations, and he concluded that Rostow's optimistic sequence of stages was probably unrealistic. In short, what Kuznets was saying was simply that history does not repeat itself. But he also faulted Rostow for applying to economic history the Procrustean bed of development economics, as, for instance, with his (Kuznets') claim that industry and agriculture during the pre-industrial and the industrial phases in Europe presented a reciprocal growth pattern, rather than agriculture being skimmed for industry's benefit, as development economics seemed sometimes to suggest. We shall see more of Kuznet's pessimism, but his final answer to Rostow on underdeveloped countries was that they could be in 'a sequence of long-term growth separate and distinct from that of the Western European cradle of the modern economic epoch'.[93]

An interesting analytical adjunct to Rostow's historical approach to economic development was a Ranis and Fei article in 1961, in which they attempted 'to make a contribution towards the theory of growth by rigorously analysing the transition process through which an underdeveloped economy hopes to move from a condition of stagnation to one of self-sustaining growth'. The authors stated that they took as their basic reference 'an economy's first departure from quasi-stagnation or the initiation of the so-called take-off process. Rostow defines this as a period of two or three decades during which the economy transforms itself in such a way that economic growth becomes, subsequently, more or less automatic; its characteristics are a reduction of the rural proportion of the population, a doubling of savings rates and the first marked and continuous flowing of industry stimulated by the availability of surplus labour.' Considering that the authors made liberal use in their analysis of the ideas of balanced growth and of the critical minimum effort, it can be considered as an attempt at an analytical synthesis of the principal doctrines of development economics. Their elaborate mathematical framework yielded, as most models of that sort did, fairly self-evident, even simplistic results. In concluding, they said that 'the take-off can only occur if $i > r$; if $i = r$ or $i < r$, no matter how large a t is permitted, take-off becomes impossible', where i was the rate of growth of the industrial labour force, r was population growth, and t a conventionally assumed time-period. For the rest they underlined the necessity of increased investment in agriculture as development materialized and the application to industrialization of the 'critical minimum effort' thesis, although what this really meant was 'that, for every value of t, a certain investment activity must be carried on in both the industrial and the agricultural sectors during every year of the take-off process, from year 0 to year 5'.[94]

The balance to 1960

The pride of the here-and-now

What was the intellectual balance of development economics to around 1960? It had been built on a series of co-ordinated assumptions that amounted to one large theoretical construct, which is frequently and on the whole accurately described as the orthodoxy of development economics. In future it would subject itself to a mordant critique of those assumptions, even to raising the question of its own legitimacy, for what if not the assumptions in question was development economics? Few on the outside (or even inside it) accorded it the title of science, or even of academic discipline, separate, that is, from the wider science of economics. But it was not downgradeable to a mere chapter or section on the concept of growth, as Meier, Baldwin and Kindleberger had implicitly suggested.[95] It was therefore a theory. Its first assumption was that all men could and should be capable of the same productivity, and were consequently entitled to a commensurate standard of living. It assumed that underdevelopment, which was measured in per capita terms, could only be understood and described through the concept of a social duality: on one side, a modern urban society with the basic economic traits of more advanced Western societies, but with a much lower register of activity; on the other, a traditional rural society with a high degree of hidden or overt unemployment, and therefore a very low level of productivity.

The values of the rural society were antithetic to those of the city, and of the West, a contrast on which modernization theory and the sociology of development were built in the 1950s and 1960s. It was assumed that it was necessary to promote industrialization in order to modernize all of society, which in essence meant integrating the two badly articulated sectors on which underdevelopment thrived. This was a very convenient assumption, because it supposed that the human-input needs of industry could be supplied by the rural masses, and that therefore one and the other ideally complemented each other. The capital needed for industry would come from domestic savings and from foreign investment. The guiding principle in this process was dubbed balanced growth and the instrument chosen for its application had to be economic planning, but of the targeting persuasive kind.

Why didn't development economics choose development through export specialization or growth-through-trade? Because most of its leading lights had actually accepted the thesis that developing countries were being deprived or swindled out of the profits in their commerce with the industrialized nations and would not be able to raise sufficient surplus in that way to escape the vicious circle of poverty, whereas through the principle of balanced growth they expected that the internal consumer market could grow in tandem with an increasing supply of goods. It was expected that development would become self-sustaining, which on the assumptions about the terms of trade, it simply could not be. Was development economics biased against agriculture? Defenders of its mainsream phase, such as D. Lehman, claim that it favoured industrialization but did not neglect agriculture. However, the facts speak quite clearly: while development economics had all sorts of prescriptions on the technology of planned or stimulated industrialization, it had nothing but contempt for agricultural commodities or it went out of its way in nurturing the expectation that the urban economy would of itself in the end stimulate agricultural productivity.[96]

Having said all this, we must go one step further. Development economics had one fundamental outlook and assumed one significant philosophical stance in such a way that it informed all its undertakings and all its objectives from the very start, and was in fact consubstantial with its very existence, and that is what we shall call the phenomenological attitude towards reality. Development economics above all strove for and stood by the claim of having achieved objectivity. It prided itself on its impartiality and purported lack of biases. And yet we have seen that the orthodoxy of development economics consisted of mostly a priori choices and manifested biases in matters of policy and method.

In what then did the phenomenological attitude consist? It consisted in the pride of the here-and-now. Development economics virtually rejected history as a dimension in its research. It accepted the past hesitantly or in rigid cliometric dimensions, but mainly it saw time in terms of the abstract future involved in policy and planning. However, even if it did not openly state or acknowledge it, development economics was an attempt at replicating the European Industrial Revolution in the Third World. It harboured a model for replication obtained by superimposing the historical experiences of the principal national industrialization cycles in Western Europe. The model could be a bad copy, or what is more likely, it could be that it was the wrong model to throw at the Third World, but the historical involvement of development economics in this sense cannot be ignored.

To what then does the here-and-now attitude specifically apply? In which respect is it valid, if at all? Development economics had its biases and it did not entirely ignore history, despite the apparently abstract, intemporal character of its injunctions, but it did tend to avoid as if from principle the issue of the origins of underdevelopment. We shall see that this is not entirely true either, that some development economists did write on that subject, categorically if briefly; but taking all in all, the attitude of the literature itself in its mainstream phase could be synthesized in this manner: we have a problem that needs solving; we have identified the problem; we know how the problem can be solved, because it has been solved in the past; but frankly it is none of our concern how the problem came about. This spurious 'ahistoricity' goes to the root of the fundamental differences in approach between development economics and the contemporary theories of economic imperialism.

Does development economics contain an original theory of growth?

Did the gestation phase of development economics actually produce an original theory of economic growth? Setting aside the vexed issue of what exactly is a theory of economic growth, it is possible, we think, to identify different aspects of the subject: the why and the how of growth. The tradition of political economy since the physiocrats dealt with the why of growth. For example, W. A. Lewis wrote in 1955 that 'the last great book' to deal with economic growth was John Stuart Mill's *Principles of Political Economy* (1848), and it is true that Mill did make a clear distinction between growth and the distribution of wealth: growth was possible in backward countries; allocation was the proper study in developed economies. Economic marginalism and equilibrium theory deal with the how of growth. Besides its concern with equilibrium levels of employment and income, Keynesianism has been passionately dedicated to applying correctives to economic dysfunctions. In this sense, there does not exist a unique theory of growth, but different categories of valid theories on growth to the extent that they address themselves not exclusively but predominantly to one of the different aspects of economic growth.

Development economics in its mainstream phase did have underlying ideas on the how of growth, but they were taken by its practitioners from what they perceived as the process of modern European development. In order to describe underdevelopment, development economists borrowed the Keynesian idea of equilibrium with unemployment and transformed it into the unstable or low-level equilibrium trap. As to the why of growth, they harked back to the classical industry-oriented models of Ricardo and Mill, and they (including now the sociologists) also reflected the more modern preoccupation with the utility of technologies and the importance of the entrepreneurial function. There was also a tendency to identify economic development with the Harrod/Domar formulation on growth, but although the shared emphasis on savings and investment did seem to indicate some kind of concordance, it was easily seen that the social circumstances of underdevelopment did not warrant an unrestricted scope of applicability.

Where development economists did seem to break new ground was in the obvious area of correctives and stimuli, because here they had no classical or Keynesian precedents to go by, yet even in this they borrowed old infant-industry and other neo-mercantilist precepts. In the mainstream of the orthodoxy of development economics were the orderly transfer of labour from the countryside to the cities, the indispensability of foreign aid and investments, and the co-ordination of growth through planning. These 'recipes', except to some degree the one referring to foreign investment, were not part of 'standard' Western growth models. Some precedents were to be found in the Soviet Union, but it would be unfair and inaccurate to say that development economics advocated Soviet policies, or that it 'lifted' its doctrines in one piece from a communist model. Development economics was fully and unambiguously committed to capitalism and private initiative. The development assistance it advocated was Western capitalist assistance. The planning it contemplated was an indicative *pis aller*, not the coercive totalitarian type. The trouble with its programme was that precisely because of its ultimate libertarian, easy-going character, it could not cope with the sweeping historical movements it foresaw, like the shifting of population masses or the conversion of sleepy old Andean towns into whirring industrial dynamos. Nevertheless, with all its shortcomings there did exist a 'corrective' development-economics theory of growth, with what seemed like a rightful place in the firmament of academic disciplines. Would it hold up against the hammering of reality?

The critics of the orthodoxy of development economics

Even before time had its say, the orthodoxy of development economics had come under fire from all directions, even from those who could be considered to be intrinsically involved in its affairs. S. Kuznets had been researching into the statistics of growth since before the Second World War. In fact, C. Clark mentions him as a source of advice for his pioneering book on world statistics. During the mainstream period of development economics, Kuznets took to it like a duck to water, and thus he can be credited with having been an early starter both in cliometrics and in development economics. His original field had included the late-nineteenth century and onwards, but he also went backwards much beyond this point. What Kuznets found in his long trek was that there did not appear to be as was usually believed a noticeable or dramatic change in net capital formation in the period prior to the clear emergence of the Industrial Revolution in the eighteenth century. However, there had been a considerable increment in gross capital formation, which meant that much of the investment leading to industrialization had gone into the yearly renovation of the existing stock of capital and into social overhead. When Kuznets in 1953 came to face with the assumptions of development economics, he pointed out that 'Output per capita is much lower in the underdeveloped countries today than it was in the presently developed countries at the date of entry – a period rather than a point in time – into modern economic growth'. But even more significantly he concluded that the major obstacle in the 'rapid spread of the industrial system' was that it required a 'marked break in established patterns of social and economic life', and he was not optimistic about the possibility of such dramatic changes in societies attached to traditional values. In his opinion, the comforting developmentalist assumption that industrialization was like 'a slowly moving glacier whose course cannot be stopped' was a historical delusion. Finally, he himself had no illusions about discovering a formula for development, 'some invariant pattern of economic growth of nations' that would permit 'distinguishing between the necessary and accidental conditions of the effective adoption of the industrial system'.[97] What Kuznets was telling his peers then was that European development had been a process of '*longue durée*', in Braudel's phrase, not the result of a sudden spurt in growth, and therefore, it was highly unlikely that there would be a replication of it in the compressed time-scale of development economists. This was a much-needed cautionary note that few heeded and in the event was to prove premonitory. It also meant that Kuznets was a defender of the notion that the Third World could not be considered a homogeneous lump to be kneaded and shaped in any way development economists wanted.

If Kuznets assailed the heedless optimism of development economics, A. O. Hirschman's equally basic criticism was directed at the crucial principle of balanced growth. Hirschman was a 'front-line' or in situ development economist, in the sense that a decisive part of his formation took place while acting in his professional capacity as economic adviser in Colombia from 1952 to 1956. He had, of course, his career prejudices, but he took the trouble to observe how Colombians themselves were managing their economic affairs in their own '*al revés*' fashion (the other way around), in which he discovered merits that went against the grain of standard development doctrine. For one thing, whatever development economists propounded about the simultaneous advance of different branches of industry in an underdeveloped economy in order to achieve all-round complementarities and provide maximum employment, the existence of high-technology, high-efficiency enterprises seemed to be defensible through unquantifiable advantages. Hirschman called them 'pressure mechanisms' and 'pacing devices', because they set standards of productivity and were means for passing on efficiency to other sectors. He used the example of airlines (Colombia's at the time was considered one of the most advanced in Latin America), and he generally included as illustration of his idea industries with a high capital-to-labour ratio, precisely those that orthodox development economics considered unadvisable for high-unemployment developing economies. Another Hirschman proposition was the 'investment sequence', based on an advanced industrial activity which complements itself by creating backward and forward linkages, again in rank disregard of the co-ordinated frontal advance envisioned in balanced growth.

Hirschman applied the principle of imbalance to other areas, such as inflation and balance of payments, always trying to see the more salutary and exploitable side of real events rather than trying to squeeze reality into a preconceived mould. What Hirschman's approach amounted to was in effect a rationale of what Latin American countries were laboriously striving to implement by themselves, that is, to foment industrialization by all available means and to simultaneously control inflation and produce enough trade surplus to fuel growth. The concept of import-substitution industrialization, which Hirschman considered a fundamental if flawed development strategy, was compared by him to the Hansel and Gretel situation in which the 'fatter' the imports of a specific sort a country had, the likelier it was that they would be swallowed up in its industrializing efforts.

Hirschman carried his diagnosis of the reality of development in Latin America to the decision-making process in government in his book *Journey towards Progress* (1963). Here he proclaimed himself an enthusiastic subscriber to modernization theory, specifically to its Schumpeterian emphasis on the entrepreneur as the initiator of progress, the entrepreneur, however, as decision-maker in the public as well as in the private sector. Above all, he was arguing for improvisatory development from within as against development by formula, or as he put it: 'I am trying to show how a society can begin to move forward as it is, in spite of what it is.'[98] Hirschman's work was undoubtedly a denial of the orthodoxy of development economics. What he claimed was that the developing countries were doing things their own way, regardless of balanced growth and the rest of the development-economics shibboleths, because they really had no other choice. In spite of the constraints, however, they were not doing so badly, in Latin America at least, and the task of developmental research was to observe and to cull the good from the useless. Hirschman was an acute and persuasive expositor, and his approach, its refusal of preconceived models and well-intentioned but unpractical abstractions, would be influential when the time came for development economics to take a starker look at itself.

How Marxism and developmentalism fell together

It is possible to exaggerate Hirschman's alienation from orthodox development economics, because both had things in common, like the convenience of discreet government planning and prodding or the necessity for foreign investments. It is nearly impossible to do so in regard to the critics that development economics had on the right. These were out-and-out partisans of *laissez faire* and its corollary of growth through the comparative advantages of foreign trade specialization. Their icons were Adam Smith and *Homo economicus*. They did not believe in economic planning or in strict modernization theory, but in the profit motive, in free enterprise, and in the free movement of factors. The leading light of this group was and has remained to this day P. T. Bauer, a hard-to-beat record in the history of the trends in development studies. Bauer believes in the retardating influence of the state. To the argument that the state merely supplies the lack of the entrepreneurial function in an economy, he replies that bureaucrats can hardly do as a substitute. He blames the West for the politicization and the social distortions in the Third World. His ideas on underdevelopment sound sometimes like a mini-theory on despotism, comparable in some respects to Wittfogel's except that Bauer puts the blame not on 'hydraulics' but on development economics and on 'the establishments in most Third World countries'. J. Viner and H. Myint were both defenders of the market and the doctrine of growth through trade. Viner was also very keen on the defence of agriculture in the midst of the development-economics high tide. He saw actual social and economic harm occurring as a result of government-induced misallocation of resources between agriculture and manufactures, which consisted in the 'diversion of agrarian-produced resources to the support of parasitic cities'. Myint employed the formula 'balanced growth', mainly in the sense of equal weight in development policies for agriculture and manufactures. He did not believe that the international trade in primary products had exhausted its potential for contributing to Third World development and he denied that the transfer of rural masses to the cities was devoid of social costs.[99]

How influential were these critics? Bauer was active in Washington in the 1960s, in general pushing for aid programmes in Latin America that favoured free enterprise regardless of the politics of the recipient countries, and his insistence certainly did not go unheeded. The well-intentioned, relatively innovating policies of the Kennedy administration in the early 1960s, associated with Rostow and the mainstream of development economics, were scrapped or modified by Lyndon Johnson, but this was probably just a question of going back to traditional American policies oriented towards maintaining the status quo in Latin America, although the Kennedy programme, it must be said, was not fundamentally different in that respect. Within development studies the preachings of the pro-trade, pro-agriculture lobby became influential as the optimism of the mainstream phase waned in the 1960s. But this influence really came into its own in the late 1970s and the 1980s with the electoral deluges that brought Margaret Thatcher and Ronald Reagan to power in the United Kingdom and the USA respectively, with their monetarist and supply-side policies. The sanction all this gave to radical anti-state, pro-market administrative philosophies was also a tacit recognition for the same approach to development problems and in Western relations with the LDCs. These political changes in two of the most important capitalist countries coincided with the strengthening of conservative academic trends and with the rise of a phalanx of economists and specialists on LDCs, some new, some converted, who denounced development economics as a bankrupt statist ideology. Their influence today probably means that development economics as a theory of growth will probably stay dormant for a long time to come, unless some dramatic political changes bring it to the fore again.

But the decisive factor in the decline of the orthodoxy of development economics as the nearly 'official' Western approach to the problems of the Third World was probably the failure of the revolutionary Marxist alternative to capitalist development. We saw that the expansion of development economics was chiefly a response to decolonization and to the rise of communist world influence after the Second World War. However, the communist record in the Third World has been lamentable. After three decades of Marxism,

Cuba remains as underdeveloped as when Batista and the Mafia left. Vietnam's heroic freedom struggle produced national integration but also extreme poverty, and the country probably deserves the dubious accolade of being the most militarily powerful among the poorest nations of the world. Angola and Mozambique have not advanced much since independence in 1975, though admittedly they had to cope with the siege from racist South Africa and from their own armed dissidents. The Soviets compounded their own serious problems and the problems of communism in the Third World with their December 1979 invasion of Afghanistan. The communist spectre no longer seems to be haunting the world. The LDCs apparently can take care of themselves if not actually develop. They have their own powerful interests, as they in fact always have had, in not becoming communist. The West's economic help is not needed urgently. It has been severely chastised as useless or actually counter-productive by the critics of development economics, and the underdeveloped countries themselves have often hindered and sabotaged its operation. Neither are Western specialists and their advice and their policies required and welcomed as they were in the past, partly of course because LDCs have had time to prepare their own people. Politics is now, as it was after the war, what is determining the rise and fall, the influence and the eclipse, of development economics. Are its critics on the right correct, therefore, in calling it an ideology? Perhaps, but if so they themselves must admit that they share in essence the same capitalist ideology and that their polemics are about means rather than about objectives. Let us see, to close the mainstream phase, what the practical balance-sheet of development economics was.

The practical balance sheet

The parallels between the strategies put forward by development economics and the policies and social tendencies within developing countries after the war concern such crucial areas that it is tempting to infer a vital, even a causal connection. Throughout the world there was a significant rural–urban movement in underdeveloped countries. Cities grew much faster there than in the industrialized nations. For the LDCs, urbanization became both a goal and a badge of progress. It was possible to argue that it should be stimulated even if the cities did not have the immediate resources to integrate the rural emigrants, because at least these would be settling where makeshift work could be had and where eventually social and economic reforms would be easier to implement.

Industrialization, likewise, was an objective pursued in almost every independent underdeveloped country. From this time came the images of thousands of Indian peasants carrying wicker baskets weighed down with earth and rocks for the construction of a steel mill in Bihar. The same pride in and devotion to vast industrial projects was shown in all the other LDCs that could allocate funds to them, or could attract or borrow the necessary capital. Those nations that could not afford a steel mill actively pursued or stimulated less ambitious enterprises as long as they were in manufacturing. To promote them, all sorts of financial institutions were created and to protect them tariffs were raised and restrictions on free-flow were devised. Although, grounded on rational arguments, industrialization shone in their eyes with the fervour of religious dogma.

One thing that was absent from all this, no matter how hard the LDCs and their experts and foreign advisers tried, was the achievement of the cherished principle of balanced growth. Inequalities, disparities and distortions kept tugging and squeezing things out of shape, like the work of a maladroit taxidermist. For a seemingly endless time – in fact, it still is the case of most developing countries – they could not escape the single export pattern, but investment in agriculture was not keeping up either with manufactures or with the demand for foodstuffs in the cities. In the industrial sector, the rolling mills and the sheet metal plants were producing uncompetitive goods for domestic consumers that had not come on stream. Industrialization was a kind of slapped-up monstrosity with some very powerful looking limbs but with others that were either shrunken or made of rotten wood. Planning was going on all the time, but it was not achieving much except an endless flow of inaccurate statistics. It quite seemed as if Hirschman had been absolutely right: underdevelopment had to be taken on its own terms, not forced into moulds, and development had to be nurtured and raised like a fragile plant.

Indeed, the only development economist who appeared to have got the right measure of underdevelopment in his works was Hirschman, to the extent that he perceived that the real striving for development was not imported into but generated within underdevelopment itself. At the time he wrote his classic work on unbalanced growth, fresh from his Colombian stint, it was obvious to him also that the more appropriate development tactics being applied to Third World countries had not been invented outside, but had been elaborated there from experience and from needs.

However, even his own ideas on 'pacing devices' and 'pressure points' and on productive, spontaneously arising linkages were actual observed events he hoped would happen again, and even today the sad fact is that there have been as many or more cases of linkages either not taking place or doing so incompletely as of fully realized chains of linkages in any individual underdeveloped country.

Hirschman himself said that ISI was the cant-phrase development economists gave to a process that had been going on in Colombia before he got there. It is very likely, therefore, that what development economics did in Latin America and elsewhere was to give sanction to, and perhaps to modulate somewhat, certain fundamental policies that had already been chosen and were already being applied as practical measures. It would be very hard to claim that development economics influenced or determined any sort of fundamental choices in the Third World. It might have channelled some of those choices, like tendering proposals on how to stimulate an orderly rural–urban flow, but it could be argued as well that postwar circumstances were probably favourable to spontaneous worldwide urbanization. Latin American governments in general believed in it. Newly independent states agreed with it because it made ruling easier. The West in general did not want the sort of communist-sponsored rural agitation that had incubated in Malaya, Indochina and Indonesia. Even the communists still believed that revolution was more likely in the cities than in the country. Urbanization, like industrialization, was a global aspiration: for modernity, for prestige, for development. Jawaharlal Nehru in India, to put it succinctly, wanted industrialization, and industrialization of sorts would have come with or without Mahalanobis. These trends were as important and as irresistible as nationalism. It is not very likely that development economics had anything crucial to do with them, or the way they were working themselves out all over the underdeveloped world. *Mutatis mutandi*, it would be like placing the historical responsibility for the Industrial Revolution on David Hume or on Adam Smith, or like explaining Western economic history in the decades before the First World War through the medium of equilibrium analysis. Of course, if development economics did not significantly affect the postwar evolution of underdeveloped economies, it was not the Dr Frankenstein that created the monster of Third World industrialization.

It could be argued that developing countries did not apply correctly the principles of development economics, but this would be complicating the issue with a series of useless contrafactual possibilities. And in the end the fact will remain that development economics, despite its claims to originality, was merely following historical trends which it did not undertake to criticize unambiguously and, on the contrary, did the utmost to abet and encourage, as when, as often happened, Third World countries intent on applying statist strategies called upon Western development economists to give their blessing to policies that had already been selected and were practically in motion. Finally, it is also very likely that the highfaluting idealized conditions that development economics envisaged, such as balanced growth, were self-defeating in that they were used by its critics to highlight the disparities between targets and real achievements, and this was, when all is said and done, the ultimate explanation of its downfall.

Development economics and the origins of international economic inequality

Does development economics include or imply a theory on the origins of economic inequality among nations? As we saw, a common nineteenth-century Western European way of thinking about the relations between cultures and nations was founded on the notion of inequality, or, as we have called it, the superiority/inferiority matrix. Inequality was seen as the product of a struggle for survival in which the decisive advantage was race. This was fundamental to Eurocentrism. The break with this extremely prejudicial outlook came with the politico-economistic world perspective, succintly expressed in the concept of underdevelopment, that had been gaining ground in the West prior to the start of the Second World War. The war itself contributed to strengthening this attitude, and after the war, development economics made it explicit, and in doing so assumed part of the burden of defining the terms of the relationship between the West and the rest of the non-communist world. Just as it had been biology and race that gave form to imperialist doctrine in Victorian Britain and during the Second Empire and the Third Republic in France, so gradually before and much faster after the Second World War it was economics that shaped the ideas influencing a wide gamut of relations between the industrialized and the underdeveloped capitalist nations. This may be because, of all the social sciences, economics is the only one that is fundamentally committed to a rock-bottom definition of human nature, and can thus deal with diversity and with all the grades in the scale of social progress with the utmost steadfastness and self-assurance. Development economics was, in sum, the best instrument the West had to hand for managing intellectually an explosive piebald world. In this respect, it would be idle to explore the ideological propensities of individual development economists one by one. Development economics, of which it can accurately be said that it represents more than the sum of its individual thinking parts, had its own overarching political engagements, to which its practitioners as a rule subscribed. The latter sometimes came close to but never edged into socialism. Shared cultural attitudes are another matter. On the whole, development economics was resolutely Eurocentric, but not so much in the old way that we have so often seen in this book as in presenting the West as a socio-economic paradigm.

Take the case of Myrdal. He had two attitudes towards the Third World: in the first he blamed underdevelopment, in part at least, on 'cumulative causation' and he called earnestly for redress; in the second he blamed the 'soft state' and vented his moral indignation on corruption, which he seemed to attribute to the brain-withering power of the tropic sun. What was the difference between the first and the second Myrdal? A stay in the Third World perhaps? At any rate, the cultural prejudices of the second Myrdal were always implicit in the first Myrdal, so it is probably true that there wasn't that much difference. Yet a caveat is in order. Myrdal was neither racist nor a social Darwinist. His moral feelings were sincere. He was what in America is called a 'bleeding-heart liberal', that is, someone who will sympathize with the poor but never sanction rebellion. He had, in Marxist parlance, a 'petit bourgeois' mentality. And in this he was very much like his unimpeachably third-worldist Latin American colleague Prebisch, who towards the end of his life was still decrying poverty and injustice but having to accept the system because, although unfair, it was somehow compatible with freedom. Both, the Argentine and the Swede, the theorists of 'core/periphery' and of 'cumulative causation', in the final reckoning turned for the causes of underdevelopment towards the inside of underdeveloped societies. They were in fact upholding Western developmental paradigms and, in particular, they were being loyal to the principles of their academic discipline. The case of both these passionate developmentalists serves to illustrate convincingly the limits of speculation on the origins of international economic inequality within development economics and development studies in general.

On a deeper level – and here too Myrdal, though not Prebisch, concurred – Western developmentalism had, as we have seen, the nagging awareness that tropical climes were related if not causally at least consistently to economic retardation, and many development economists during the mainstream phase and afterwards (Streeten perhaps foremost among them) kept making asides in the course of their researches to bow respectfully in the direction of environmental theory. In the end this did not produce more than *obiter dicta* amounting to an endorsement of the truism that (since Montesquieu) had ascribed indolence and backwardness, partially at least, to the effects of adverse environmental circumstances. Development economics and development studies as a whole were not interested in origins but in the here-and-now, in analysis and in policy, and this undoubtedly prevented them from an engagement with further, deeper research in that area. Even the work of A. M. Kamarck, which we described in Chapter 1 as relating minutely the adverse effects of climate on economic performance, was strictly analytical and contemporary, totally lacking in historical and cultural dimensions. Development economics limited its say on origins to positing endogenous causes, at times, as in Myrdal, through concrete social analysis and criticism, but mostly by default, through not saying anything on the subject and letting the eloquence of its socio-economic paradigm speak for itself.

If a verdict were required from development economists on the relations between the West and the rest of the world and their economic consequences, it probably would be the express exoneration of all Western responsibility for Third World backwardness. The sociology of development was much more declarative in this respect, which in itself had the merit of forthrightness, but it overstepped the bounds of reasonable cultural and social differentiation in that its premisses closely bordered on a kind of psychological superiority in the West, and although the distinction between psychological and cultural or social attitudes is often hair-thin (how separable, from an economic point of view such as Kuznets', are social and psychological habits and attitudes from their cultural matrixes?), it is valid enough to have kept economics and the sociology of development clearly apart on the issue of the causes of underdevelopment. Though garbed in modern sociological jargon, modernization theory was of the purest Eurocentric stock, and could have been related historically to the more obscurantist nineteenth-century pronouncements on Asian despotism and on non-Western cultural backwardness in general. As such it made an easy target for anti-capitalist polemicists and more generally it bared itself to a complete, clean-conscience repudiation by anyone connected to or affiliated in any way with the Third World.

Development economics in the 1960s

Despite the carping, development economics went almost intact through the 1960s, which was probably the time of its greatest political clout. There were, however, significant stirrings of dissatisfaction with previous doctrine, some even perceivable in the original upholders of that doctrine. Arndt underscores the significance of T. W. Schultz's orientation towards the formation of human capital instead of the accumulation of physical capital. But you could not honestly fault development economics for not being aware of the benefits of education, and besides, with this theme Schultz was more interested in economic growth in the USA than in the underdeveloped countries. However, he aimed much closer at development economics in his no-holds-barred repudiation of the idea of the zero marginal productivity of labour in the rural areas of backward countries. In this he was adding to the growing bulk of the literature that was picking holes in, or simply putting down, the established priorities for development economists between the rural and the urban sectors in developing nations. D. W. Jorgenson at the start of the decade and on the heels of Lewis and others, stated flatly, but with the benefit of a mathematical model for dual economies, that 'there is no "minimum critical effort" of investment in dual economies in which substitution between capital and labour in manufacturing is possible', a statement that apparently seemed to undercut the advantages of the touted rural–urban flow. In 1967 H. M. Southworth and B. F. Johnston wrote what seemed like a self-evident truth, but which development economics in the 1950s, with all its ingenious inventions and complicated models, apparently did not grasp: 'Most of the underdeveloped areas are predominantly agricultural. It is now recognised that increasing the productivity of their agriculture is essential to their economic development.'

This was but one blow away from bashing the other icon of the rural-excess school, and this one M. Lipton dealt in a 1968 collective work on the crisis of Indian planning, where he spoke of urban bias and the useless diversion of manpower to the cities. This general volte-face in development studies was even evident in the noticeable shift of emphases that we observed in Fei and Ranis, who were the principal exegetes of the Lewis canon. They were not the only ones re-assessing the orthodoxy from within, or at least some of its emphases, as could have been observed when Prebisch in 1964 took a mincing sidestep away from all-out ISI towards manufacturing for exports. Finally, in this short list of uncollected arrears, G. M. Meier put his finger on another trend when he went for international trade as the engine of growth from a Rostovian angle and in step with other favourable international reports on this subject.[100]

If it is accepted that development economics is a legitimate discipline of study and research, less than a science but more than an ideology, which exhibits sufficient identificatory traits in the past and still has a claim to recognition, whether because of its field or its methods or for whatever other valid reasons, then more pertinent to its evolution during the 1960s than the critiques and reassessments were certain burgeoning trends within the mainstream of the discipline itself. Since, however, the orthodoxy carried on virtually undisturbed from its mainstream phase until the advent of disillusion in the 1970s, we shall refer here summarily to three significant trends that arose in the previous decade.

The Brazilian economist C. Furtado, who held reasonably conventional views on development, introduced a historical perspective, something which was usually lacking in the discipline, by purposefully seeking the origins of Latin American backwardness. He proposed that underdevelopment resulted from a 'hybridization' between capitalism and earlier and more primitive economic structures, an idea which could be related to the dual-economy model but which also anticipated some Marxist theories based on the application of the concept of MOP to underdeveloped economies, although Furtado's position was fundamentally anti-Marxist. His historical outlook from a developmentalist position brought developmentalism to proximity with dependency theses and also presaged the dependency debate.

Another development theorist who found a rapport with the endlessly fertile dual-economy concept, was the Frenchman J. Freyssinet, in whose 1966 work, *Le concept de sous-développement*, economic backwardness is presented as the 'non-convergence' or 'non-articulation' of economic spaces within an underdeveloped general context. This conceptual approach, favoured by French students of development, which can probably be traced to the so-called spatial economics going back to the early nineteenth-century work of the German economist J. H. von Thunen, cannot however conceal its limited practicality in the elaboration of concrete policy alternatives and indicated (as well as the abstract almost philosophical enquiry contained in Freyssinet's treatise) a tendency to either evasion or ossification.[101]

One way out of the dilemma between the exigencies of the real world of underdevelopment and the tendency to build theories upon it, was offered by the coincident views between the British development economists D. Seers and P. Streeten. Streeten took a significant siding away from the developmentalist mainline when he negated the 'advantages of being a latecomer', which was about the only thing that underdevelopment had going for it in the tacit view of many development economists. Seers, for his part, had theorized about the 'special' nature of development problems, although, as Streeten puts it, by the 1970s he tended to acknowledge the 'universal' nature of the issues concerning poor countries. Be that as it may, the combination of Seers' view on the singularity of underdevelopment with Streeten's pessimism constituted one of the theoretical mainstays for the formulation of the 'basic needs' approach, which became influential during the 1970s and beyond as an alternative to the old orthodoxy of developmentalism. The 1960s then held *in ovo* the tendencies that were to characterize the onset of disillusion during the next decade, when developmentalism, even as it went on theorizing about underdevelopment, had to turn and face the attacks of dependency theory and in desperation at its own shortcomings virtually gave up on massive industrialization to champion instead the alleviation of extreme destitution in the Third World.[102]

4 *The Marxist response to Western developmentalism*

Introduction

The world as seen by New Times

Before the 1960s, Marxist or Marxist-derived theories on imperialism, though they could contain an underlying concept of underdevelopment, were usually designed as instruments of politics and not as purely academic representations of reality. If we substitute 'policy' for 'politics', it would be possible to discover a certain similarity between that and the concerns of development economics during its mainstream phase, but of course in a totally different direction: the theory of economic imperialism had always pursued radical social change, and development economics was created to stabilize the status through change within the status.

We have so far covered two phases of economic-imperialism theory: the phase from Hobson to Lenin, and the Comintern phase. Neither of these phases was influential on the dominant Western conceptualization of the relations between the advanced capitalist nations and the rest of the world. The Marxist conception of the backward countries was, of course, vastly different from the old Eurocentric clichés, but in the West in the decades before the Second World War, there were few influential Marxist thinkers, their influence was marginal, and often they managed to reconcile their Marxism with undisguised though moderate Eurocentrism.

In explaining the relative intellectual isolation in the West of Marxist thinking on colonialism and on international economic inequality, it must be recognized that the greatest individual influence on the theory of economic imperialism came from Stalin himself, hardly an impartial, objective theoretician. Even at the height of Marxist proselytizing among intellectuals during the 1930s, the 'scientific' authority of this theory did not extend beyond the leftist press. It had a much greater latitude in literature, but what obtained here were images and representations rather than new ideas. Stalin had been Lenin's spokesman in 1917 on the question of national self-determination. From this vantage he deduced the revolutionary significance of colonies and 'semi-colonies' in so far as they rebelled against imperialism and wasted some of its strength. He remained faithful to this doctrine and even tended over the years to emphasize its importance, affirming that the fate of capitalism depended on its hold on the colonies and backward lands. By 'hold', of course, he meant actual physical domination. Postwar events would force the Soviets to backtrack discreetly while trying to preserve Stalin's 'infallibility'.

For a short while after the war the Soviets adopted a conciliatory tone towards their erstwhile Western allies, and this was reflected in their attitude towards the colonial empires and the other underdeveloped lands within the Western orbit, which they habitually described as 'dependencies'. In general, 'dependency' rather than 'imperialism' was the term used to denote in the magazine *New Times* (the English language version of *Trud*) the relationship between the principal Western powers, mainly the USA and the UK, and their client states. There was thus created a grey area in which dependency and colonialism seemed to merge and blend. As the Cold War froze over, however, the tone changed and the Soviet condemnation of the West in all its guises and in all its policies henceforth became unsparing, unremitting and unrestricted. It was particularly noticeable in the Soviet doctrine of economic imperialism, which became set in a cluster of principles and attitudes of universal and inflexible application to the underdeveloped world. One of the constant motifs of Soviet analysis was the supposed Anglo-American imperialist 'act', in which Britain sometimes co-operated as junior partner and sometimes tried to be the rival and got its knuckles bashed. According to *New Times*, Latin America was the area where after the war imperialism (as opposed to outright colonialism) had achieved its fullest bloom. In the view of *New Times*, which not only reflected official Stalinist doctrine but occasionally even printed Stalin's own statements, all of Latin America by 1951 was 'under Washington's control' and 'American imperialism has deprived the Latin American people not only of their economic, but also their political independence as well'. As to decolonization, at first Stalinist analysis did not accept that it was taking place, but finally it went from its initial pertinacious scepticism to graduated denials of the reality of independence: outright in the case of Indonesia, partial for Burma, and qualified for India as independence with economic subjection. In all cases, however, imperialism retained ultimate control.[103]

Western Marxists/Leninists had been toeing the Soviet Stalinist line since before the Second World War. They seemed willing to go on doing so, and showed no signs of introducing innovations after the war. The villains in the Marxist economic-imperialism scenario did not vary, whether they were seen from Moscow or from Paris. Communist ideology managed to leap effortlessly across the Iron Curtain in a way that capitalism could not do, owing to the totalitarian nature of the Soviet regime. The Latin American version of Stalinism had had a go at achieving a kind of regional identity, but it was not really extremely original at it. The ideas involved had been there since the 1920s in the work of J. C. Mariategui and in the tenuous influence of the Comintern; in fact, what the postwar Latin American communists did was to make them more rigid and more dogmatic. Their standard view of underdevelopment was based on the infliction on powerless nations of a dual mode-of-production structure, in which feudalism was strong enough to dominate an incipient often venal bourgeoisie through an alliance with imperialism. As in a musical score for organ, you could play with the buttons and the keys and come up with variations – like making the bourgeoisie stronger and more promising as an agent for progressive economic forces, or, as was more frequently the case, assuming that imperialism was the ultimate king-maker and arbiter. The basic concepts and the principal enemies of progress were always the same: feudalism, capitalism, imperialism, etc. This model was extremely ideological and mechanistic. It defined terms like feudalism loosely or not at all. And above all, it was incurious about basic causation and, in general, contemptuous of serious historical research. In other words, it was propaganda with a smattering of Marxist jargon.

Stalinism out of its depth

But even as Stalinism kept its hold on the minds and wills of its adherents, it was losing touch with reality fast. There was the unresolved issue of decolonization. Even if it was claimed, as *New Times* was wont to do, that newly independent nations were not as sovereign as they should have been, to deny decolonization entirely was plain obstinacy. There was also distortion. The Stalinist portrayal of Latin America was sweeping and strident, so close in places to absolute falsehood that it was probably not possible to separate lies from near-truths in it.

One thing that was definitely distasteful to communist dogma was the theory and the practice of developmentalism and, in particular, the idea of foreign aid. The Marshall Plan rankled the Soviet Union both as the showcase of American aid and because it was a reminder of the frustrated Soviet project for a manipulable European order. In Latin America nothing even remotely comparable had been initiated, but *New Times* let loose a barrage of invective at the slightest hint or mention of foreign aid. It was argued untiringly and without proof that American aid was the cutting edge of economic imperialism and that it was specifically intended to open the way for resource exploitation by the 'big monopolies'. This argument left standing as many questions as the answers it pretended to provide on the issue of Latin American economic backwardness. It was indeed the absolute poverty of Stalinism on the issues of underdevelopment in general that indicated its inadequacy as theory for the Third World. Stalinism simply stuck to Leninist and Comintern theses that denied capitalism any stimulative power in backward countries and that did not accord bourgeois nationalism much recognition without the support of local communists in each country. *New Times* expressed this line in a direct and unsophisticated manner: 'In bygone times, when the fight was against feudalism, capitalist initiative helped to develop the economic resources of society; capitalism was then a step forward compared with medieval economic forms. But today capitalism is incapable of being a constructive force.'[104]

This explanation was profoundly unsatisfactory, even taking into account the context and the intention behind it, which was primarily propaganda. Supposing that this 'fight against feudalism' had taken place in Europe, why had it ceased operating in the rest of the world? Why did capitalism achieve so much in some countries and so little in others? Was capitalism then promoting feudalism in Latin America and elsewhere instead of displacing it? The underdeveloped world simply seemed to have been left out of Marxist analysis in a cloud of anti-imperialist gas, and the Latin American version of the Stalinist imperialist model, in particular, with its persistent invocation of the fight against feudalism within national frontiers, contained a *contradictio in adjecto* in so far as it also insisted that the only visible enemy of contemporary social change was imperialism itself. Even granting the elementary nature of Stalinist ideological formulations, one could have expected some minimal degree of theoretical consistency.

The theoretical shortcomings of the Marxist view of the Third World

P. A. Baran and the critical analysis of underdevelopment

The problem was even more complicated than it seemed because the communist attitudes towards underdevelopment never faced the issue squarely. They blamed capitalism or imperialism in a ritualistic way for perpetuating economic backwardness, and they made no attempt to discover the origins of economic inequality, for which development studies had a least some half-baked explanations. The Marxist historical perspective was either diffuse, impossible to circumscribe in accordance with a precisely oriented theoretical model, or else it had a clear if unconvincing point of view with a myopic visual reach.

Lenin's imperialism was a specific historical manifestation of capitalism, in which capital had become nationalistic and managed to combine a two-tier system of labour exploitation with the wholesale exploitation of entire national entities. Would knowing how capitalism had got there have made any difference? Did the study of the origins of economic inequality have any theoretical importance for Lenin? Apparently it did not and there was a hitch to all this. As we saw, development economics arrived at a theory of sorts by default or by inference: the West was definitely not to blame for underdevelopment; therefore, underdevelopment had secular endogenous causes in the underdeveloped countries themselves. This simple formalistic approach left much to be desired, and the least that was to be expected was that Marxists should respond with a deeper historical explanation of underdevelopment rather than with the tired political slogans on the immediate oppressive consequences of economic imperialism. Something more rounded, more meaningful and more far-reaching was needed.

The person who limned an answer was the Russian–American Marxist economist, Paul A. Baran. The importance of Baran has been bruited by those who worked with him, such as H. Magdoff and P. Sweezy. Magdoff considered Baran to be a significant innovator within Marxist thought because of his criticism of 'relayed stereotypes'. At the zenith of his polemical career, A. G. Frank admitted Baran's decisive influence on him, which was no mean compliment. R. B. Sutcliffe credited Baran with being the first warrior against the myths and mirages of development economics. G. Palma considers him the 'father' of dependency theory. A. M. Hoogvelt explains: 'From about the late 1950s theories of imperialism began to address popularly the effects of imperialism on the overseas territories in an attempt to explain the roots of backwardness. The dependency theory that emerged from this exercise thus became a counterpart to Marxist theories of imperialism.' Hoogvelt's reference to 'overseas territories' is at first confusing because of the implication that he might have meant colonies alone. The use of 'counterpart' is also imprecise, as it suggests a strong differentiation, but further on he makes his case explicit: 'The original version of "dependency and underdevelopment" theory, as outlined by first Paul Baran, and next more popularly and grandly by André Gunder Frank, concentrated on locating the cause of backwardness of Third World countries, more especially of Latin America, within the dynamic growth of the world capitalist system.' There is an unjustified chronological compression in attributing dependency directly and originally to Baran, but Hoogvelt is nearly right in saying that the 'genesis of dependency thinking and its continuing qualifying essence was its criticism of bourgeois modernization theory', although again it would be more accurate to speak of a criticism of Western development studies in its two branches of economy and sociology. The point well taken is that Baran led the way in the formulation of contemporary dependency theory. From Wallerstein's optic he 'introduced "the long view" into the core/periphery conception', which was a bit like recognizing Baran too as Wallerstein's intellectual progenitor.[105]

Baran's early explorations of the persistence of underdevelopment are contained in two essays, one on economic causes (1951) and the other on social analysis (1952). The first of the essays did not once mention economic imperialism. It aimed to prove that economic development was impossible in a capitalist underdeveloped country, contrary to the donnés and expectations of development economics, solely from the inhibiting mechanisms of capitalism itself. This was nothing less than *lèse majesté* to Stalinist imperialism theories, but the Soviet credibility gap in the West was then so large, even among Marxists, as to make the offence less heinous than it would have seemed in other circumstances. Baran's claim was that in any 'profit-determined economy' there exists a large divergence between what Arndt calls 'the social and private marginal product', or, less technically, between social ends and private motives, and this difference was 'particularly striking in underdeveloped countries'. Development policies had to fail because they would have to curtail upper-income corruption, including the prevention of foreign currency flight, and this was something that the system in place would not tolerate.[106] This does not sound very original on the surface, but in fact it was something that neither development economists nor Stalinists were emphasizing: Stalinists because what they wanted to prove were the evils of 'Yankee' imperialism, not those of local bourgeoisies; and development economists because they did not go about antagonizing their patrons in the Third World, no matter how strongly they may have felt *in pectore* about social injustice. Western developmentalists in the best of cases usually preached to people whom they probably knew would either bungle or sabotage any stringent programme for economic growth, and in fact some of them were merely proposing timid policy measures with the understanding that radical programmes of social reform were unnecessary. As a result, you seldom got to hear or to see in print simple, almost self-evident statements such as Baran's, which almost no one wanted to hear anyway.

The second of Baran's two essays did approximately the same thing as the first, but by concentrating on the collective behaviour of the upper classes in a social situation somewhere between feudalism and capitalism. Baran gave no names, used no dates and cited no figures. The thesis was the same as before: that under capitalism underdevelopment could not be overcome, and, as before, the culprit was capitalism and not some maleficent, all-mighty imperialist juggernaut.

According to the Baran outline, capitalism 'reoriented the partly or wholly self-sufficient economies of agricultural countries towards the production of marketable commodities', but it did not wipe out feudalism, leaving instead mostly dual-economy situations: 'an economic and political amalgam combining the worst features' of feudalism and capitalism. And who introduced capitalism into the social equation? The imperialist genie, at this point in Baran's thinking, was discreet but he was out of the bottle anyway. The 'ruling coalition of owning classes' could not increase output by employing the manpower in the countryside or by transferring it to industrial jobs in the city for various reasons: potential investors either feared the risk or they lacked the necessary technology for industry; wealth was squandered in conspicuous consumption; measures to stimulate development were nearly inconceivable. 'The mere listing of the steps that would have to be undertaken in order to assure an expansion of output and income in an underdeveloped country', wrote Baran, 'reveals the utter implausibility of the view that they could be carried out by the governments existing in most underdeveloped countries.' Large landowners were the only potential investors in industry, but even if they were willing to invest, the problem of infrastructure was beyond them both in principle and as a possibility. Government planning and investment, on the other hand, would only breed corruption and inefficiency under capitalism. And Baran underlined: 'The crucial fact rending the realization of a development programme illusory is the political and social structure of the governments in power.'

This was turning all the fundamental precepts and principles of development economics upside down. Baran's underdeveloped country was a pure model, a distillation of all the negative traits in a backward society, but it was also a never-never land, and therefore this second article was perhaps less good than the first one, in which the arguments rested on economic logic, that is, the logic of either individual or collective self-interest. But it was also effective in that it based its arguments on solid social grounds and in that it skirted the imperialist controversy and went to the root of the question, which was underdevelopment itself, and faced off development economics on its own terms. Aid, Baran said, whether policy advice or external monetary aid, was no substitute for endogenous growth.[107] Why there had been no endogenous growth in the Third World in the first place would be his next endeavour in this field. Something momentous happened before that, however.

The 'atomization' of Marxist dogma and the rise of the Third World

Joseph Stalin died on 5 March 1953. The process of the 'atomization' of Marxism had started before then, but his death gave it further licence and momentum. Atomization presented two aspects: actual international political decentralization and its correlative ideological fragmentation. From its birth the USSR had every right to consider itself the Vatican of Marxist communism and no one dared to dispute this for a long time. There was some disappointment and some grumbling in the West when Stalin signed a non-aggression pact with Nazi Germany in 1939, but Nazi barbarism soon cleared away the fog and the ambiguities, for most Marxists at any rate. The crimes of Stalin were not as well known and documented during the war as they later became.

After the war, the USSR had as much world prestige as it had ever had in its short history, but Stalin had not changed his stripes and he was bound to slip. Yugoslavia was the one and only slippery slope in his lifetime: Tito bucked the Stalinist yoke in 1949 and the USSR reacted with all the fury of a thwarted super-power, but the situation between East and West was still fluid and Belgrade offered the capitalist powers the olive branch of a neutralist foreign policy. Thus was born Titoism. It was premonitory of future events in the communist political world, where the Yugoslav initiative was followed by failed insurrections in East Germany (1953) and Hungary (1956), by the defections from the Soviet orbit of China in 1960 (if she had ever been actually within it) and of Albania (1961), by the Prague 1968 Spring, and by the civil war in Afghanistan (1979).

Ideologically, Titoism became influential through the decisive participation of its founder in the deliberations that launched the non-aligned movement. This movement is very significant. The Afro-Asian nations had met in Bandung in 1955 and had approved the basic general principles of non-alignment. In 1956, Tito was host to Nasser and Nehru for the preparations of the first non-aligned summit meeting, which was held in Belgrade in 1961. Marxist Yugoslavia thus contributed meaningfully to the formation of an international doctrine, proclaiming that nations not only could but in fact should steer a course between the extremes of American capitalism and Soviet communism. This, of course, did not go unobserved by Marxist theoreticians in the West. The influence of this approach to international issues was further enhanced by the revelations about the crimes of Stalin made by Nikita Krushchev during the 20th Congress of the Communist Party of the USSR in February 1956. At about that time, the USSR also adopted the principle of peaceful coexistence with capitalism, which put the Leninist/Trotskyist doctrine of uneven development and permanent revolution into *sine die* abeyance. But perhaps the greatest impact on Marxist theorization about underdevelopment was the rise of the Third World.

Opinions on the Third World run the gamut from forthright scepticism and denial to sympathetic understanding and 'official' self-affirmation. Marxist radicals have been wont in the past to describe third-worldism as, in J. Sebreli's phrase, a 'bourgeois myth', or in R. Debray's own dressing-down, 'as a statistical gap'. Western scepticism is on the whole less ideological, more attuned to the *realpolitik* insufficiencies of the Third World. The anthropologist and sociologist P. Worsley illustrates an evolving perception of the Third World, which went from hopeful acceptance – in his 1963 book *The Third World* – to frank disillusionment ten years later. In this personal intellectual process, the Third

World passed from being a historical awareness of itself allied to a will for change into the bottom-line belief in 'the economic strategy of a mixed economy'. An extremely critical view of third-worldism, manifesting a curious convergence between the right and a relatively consistent interpretation of Marx, holds that it was begotten after the war through Stalinist influence and support and depicts it as a simplistic, maladroit proto-version of dependency theory in its reiterative, emotion-laden blaming of underdevelopment on the capitalist West.[108]

As against these critiques, there exists what might be called the 'official' literature of the Third World movement, which principally encompasses the voluminous proclamations, statements of principle and 'action' programmes emanating from Third World conferences, conclaves and more or less permanent international organisms such as the United Nations Commission on Trade and Development (UNCTAD) or the also UN-sponsored economic commissions for Latin America, for Africa and for the Pacific. The contents of this literature can actually be boiled down to what came to be known in the 1970s as the New International Economic Order (NIEO).

The political scientist K. Nweihed has prepared an instructive outline of the evolution of Third World solidarity, starting with the Bandung Conference and branching out into a political and an economic cycle (see Table 4.1). On the political side he places the non-aligned movement from Belgrade to the 1973 Algiers conference. The economic cycle covers mainly the actions and proceedings of the Organization of Petroleum Exporting Countries (OPEC), created in 1960, and of UNCTAD, founded in 1964. In this outline, the two cycles, which were evidently not unaware of each other, moved fully into phase with the approval by the General Assembly of the UNO in 1974 of the NIEO. Nweihed considers that the essence of third-worldism consists in the principles of non-alignment and of international economic justice. What the latter means had already been stated by Prebisch and Singer in the gestation phase of development economics – better prices for Third World raw produce, and non-reciprocal concessions on trade from the industrialized nations – and it was also a theme that came up in all the reunions of the non-aligned and of UNCTAD.

However, beyond these general principles, there was also an ideological undercurrent that received full expression at the sixth non-aligned conference, which met in Havana in September 1979. Its concluding declaration was not subscribed to by the entire Third World – many governments were present only as observers

Table 4.1 Third World solidarity table to 1974 (simplified version).

Bandung (1955)	
POLITICS	ECONOMICS
	1960: OPEC (Baghdad)
1961: Non-aligned movement (Belgrade)	
1964: Non-aligned conference 2	1964: UNCTAD 1 (Geneva)
1966: Tricontinental conference (Havana)	
	1967: UNCTAD 2 (New Delhi)
1970: Non-aligned conference 3 (Lusaka)	
	1972: UNCTAD 3 (Santiago) 1972: OPEC Teheran meeting on oil crisis
1973: Non-aligned conference 4 (Algiers)	
Declaration of the 'New International Economic Order' at the sixth Special Session of the General Assembly of the UNO on development and primary products (1974)	

Source: Courtesy of Dr K. G. Nweihed.

and others expressed reservations about its contents – but it was fairly representative of widespread Third World opinions whether official or not. Its tenor, despite the facade of impartiality, was definitely anti-Western and anti-capitalist. It defined non-alignment as 'the fight against imperialism, colonialism, neo-colonialism, apartheid, Zionism', and so forth, and it harped on this theme time and again in virtually unvarying language. It devoted a substantial part of its considerable extent to a review of the struggles for liberation. It proposed a 'new international informative order' based on national (as opposed to international) news media and sources. It pointed to the 'widening breach' between the developed and the underdeveloped countries. It sanctioned, as a matter of course, the NIEO, and then it practically turned this into an indictment of 'imperialism, colonialism, neo-colonialism', etc., of MNCs, and of capitalism in general, in other words, it was what might be called an exercise in applied dependency theory. Was this, however, a true expression of basic Third World positions?[109]

Unanswered questions and a doctoral dissertation

There is a valid connection between third-worldism and dependency, but we believe that it is not to be found in the fellow-travelling pieties of the Havana Declaration but in the nature of the questions that the Third World started asking on the origins of international economic inequality from the moment it became conscious of itself. It may even be that these questions themselves are the only reliable definition of third-worldism. Since doubt and query are often the liminary stances to the emergence of valid correlatives of reality, they may not have been a flimsy basis on which to construct, and whatever some views on the Third World may have claimed, the Stalinist theory of imperialism was not giving sufficiently good answers to those questions. It simply did not go deep or far enough. There was, of course, a general Third World consensus that colonialism blocked development, besides being racist and unjust, but it was also admitted that economic retardation was there before colonialism had the run of the planet in the late nineteenth century.

Colonialism was capitalism in action, but it was not the only form of capitalist expansionism. There was, among other means, informal imperialism. This concept had wide acceptance on the left and was employed by K. Nkrumah, H. Magdoff and even the magazine *New Times*. The theories that began to appear in the late 1950s, and which expanded and crossbred and clashed in the 1960s and 1970s, were meant to be, to a considerable extent, answers to Third World queries. That is also why, for the first time, many of the theorists who were involved in their elaboration came from the Third World, the vast area on which the speculations this work deals with have mostly centred, but engaged in at a distance, in the context of strictly Western preoccupations. The death of Stalin and the loosening of the previously adamantine ideological bonding of Marxists (what we have called the atomization of Marxism), in conjunction with Third World political and intellectual dissatisfaction and unrest, were the mainspring of this theoretical dispersion and search; in fact, these circumstances were primarily crucial in starting the process of revision of the theory of economic imperialism in the West.

Before the publication of Baran's cornerstone long-view of dependency and underdevelopment, the French-speaking Egyptian theoretician S. Amin, in an unpublished but influential dissertation written in 1955, which presaged the accession of Third World thinkers to the front rank in economic-imperialism studies and research, analysed the circumstances that prevented economic development in the Third World, although he did not use this expression, as he did not use the term imperialism either, and dependence only in an elementary, non-ideological sense. Subsequently, Amin would become much more of an intellectual radical, but in this scholarly work – which still contains the seeds of some valid theses, such as the analysis of colonial and post-colonial monetary systems and his study of the economic cycle in underdevelopment economies – he hewed meticulously to achieve an academic, non-political method and approach.

Even though his starting point was a distinction between 'economic structures' that was analogous to Marxist MOP analysis, he did not stake any claims on systematic Marxism or Leninism. The difference between development and underdevelopment (the latter being given the global definition of 'poverty') was the operation in the former of 'creative savings': under 'autocentric' capitalism, savings were put to use in production and in demand-generating circulation. Because of their backward economic structures (based on land-rent, on subsistence agriculture and on artisanal industry, and involving in addition a different 'psychological structure') underdeveloped countries did not use savings to improve or expand production, although Amin did admit that the potential was there. But the crux of Amin's argument really was that once advanced capitalism integrated these economies into the world market their ability to develop, precarious at the best of times, simply evaporated. Initially they were utilized merely as outlets for industrial production to mitigate cyclical imbalances between production and demand in the developed countries, but even the external flow of capital, which came on the heels of manufactured imports, although it did have some 'multiplier' effects, went into the exporting sector and flowed right out as profits that easily compensated for the initial outlays.

Amin accepted the monopoly theory of capitalism – which he derived unquestioningly from Lenin, as he accepted the idea of the decisive outward expansion of capitalism in the late nineteenth century – and he ruled out any possibility of competition, either between exporters of goods and exporters of capital (who were the same in his view), or between foreign articles and local manufactures, which could not prosper because of inherent disadvantages in the latter. The few gains that went into underdeveloped economies either entered the tertiary sector, which was interpreted by Amin as a sign of backwardness, or into what he called 'thesaurisation' that is, accumulation for consumption by land-owners.[110]

There was a significant ambiguity in that Amin, despite his radicalism, in the end consented to the development-economics model in nearly all its parts. He accepted the dual-economy theory, in fact he made it the basis of his entire analysis, and not an alternative Marxist formulation of it based on the MOP concept. He came out in favour of delinking in terms comparable to those used by Singer. Although he attacked the Nurksean idea of the vicious circle and the concomitant notion that external capital and aid could foment development, he agreed with the principles of balanced growth and of planning, perhaps in a more committed and enthusiastic way, but in essence such as development economists were proposing at the time. With reservations, he gave sanction to Prebisch's ideas on the growing imbalance of trade between centre and periphery, and on the potentially reproductive results of internal inflation. His insistence on the absolute necessity of transforming precapitalist social structures coincided with Kuznet's emphasis on the same point, and could even be read as an anticipation of modernization theory. And, finally, he even ratified the assumption in development economics that underdevelopment was not originally produced through the action of external forces but was begotten endogenously.

It could be said of Amin, in effect, that he, more even than development economists, took their hypothesis and assumptions to their ultimate intellectual consequences, and in doing so demonstrated how close they could be to radical anti-capitalist ideas on development. But whereas development economists, as we saw, never even contemplated shaking off their bottom-line adherence to capitalism, Amin did not labour under that inhibition and he did not rule out that the Soviet model could in the end be the one valid instrument for the development of the Third World.[111] In this remarkable coincidence of criteria, more than in any other instance that we shall study, it is possible to appreciate how the differences between developmentalism and Marxism in their final definitions and approaches to underdevelopment were more a matter of ideological choice than of purely academic preoccupations. When we meet Amin again, it will be as a contributor to the foundations of dependency theory. As in most aspects of it, however, it was Baran who pointed the way for his successors.

Baran's long-view of underdevelopment

'Transpositional' Marxism

Baran had a talent for utilizing the technique of conceptual transposition. A case in point was the idea of 'uneven development', which in the Lenin canon refers principally to the disparities in economic and military strengths between advanced capitalist powers, but which Baran, and many others after him, used to refer to the economic gap between developed and underdeveloped nations. Another concept was 'primitive accumulation': in Marx it was the process whereby producers were divested of their means of production at the onset of the capitalist mode of production, but Baran used it to refer in a crucial way to colonial booty. The transposition of Marxist concepts became in due time a regular practice of dependency theorists, who would turn almost all the basic ones into equivalences in relation to underdevelopment. It could be argued that these were simply latitudinous readings of Marx and Lenin, but if you combine all the transpositions you do not get the same results as you do with the same concepts in their pristine ordering. 'Uneven development' gave rise to the inevitability of war under capitalism. Khrushchev banished the latter with the formula of 'peaceful coexistence'. Shortly afterwards, Baran used 'uneven development' again, but out of its original context and subject to any arbitrary interpretation. It could refer indistinctly to war or to exploitation or to both at the same time. The 'reserve army of the proletariat', another Marxist concept transposed in the Baran manner, referred to the growing legions of unemployed as a consequence of the increase in the organic composition of capital and of successive capitalist business crises. It was supposedly the mechanism whereby capitalism kept wages low and ensured its profits beyond the point of exhaustion of its real productive potential. In the transposed version (which had been adumbrated in Luxemburg's analysis of enlarged reproduction), it was loosely used to refer to the unemployed in the underdeveloped countries, who had no actual role to play in the mechanics of developed capitalism, or, alternatively, it designated the underdeveloped economies themselves, presumably capitalists and all.[112]

The work that contains the fundamentals of Baran's thinking on underdevelopment, *The Political Economy of Growth* (1957), was principally another attempt to explain how it was that capitalist relations of production hampered growth yet still managed to subsist. In this sense, it was conceived in the spirit of Hilferding and Luxemburg. Baran's explanation was founded on the concept of surplus, which is related to but not quite the same as Marx's surplus value. In his shorthand definition, surplus was the difference between production and consumption, and it raised once again the classic Marxist problem of realization.

The trouble originated in that the monopolistic and oligopolistic structure of the capitalist system did not allow for the rational and socially beneficial investment of surplus (such as, Baran believed, would obtain under socialism and planning, though not necessarily Stalinist-type socialism) and encouraged instead wasteful spending on publicity, which acted as a substitute for competition; on trashy and unnecessary output; and most significantly, on armies and weaponry. The last item was crucial in two respects: it demonstrated how government functioned under capitalism as the crucial prop of the system and it pointed towards the 'international relations' of advanced capitalist countries, which were likewise an indispensable area for the irrational disposal of surplus. Given the inability of the system to utilize surplus rationally in its own maximization for the benefit of society, it streamed out to underdeveloped lands, where it could exploit at will and obtain exceptionally high rates of return. Capitalist surplus was, then, but a fragment of its potential size, and at the same time, it operated as the safety net that kept the system, like a fat ageing acrobat, from landing on its face. Through its employment for military purposes and in its outlay in foreign economic relations, which were complementary functions, it constituted 'the central core of government intervention on behalf of "full employment"'. But this of course was nothing but a 'glittering façade of economic prosperity and social and political cohesion'. At the time this was written, Marxists believed that, after Korea and on the doorstep of Vietnam, capitalism was living on time borrowed from militarism. Baran sounded as Marxist as one would expect, yet the quotes from Marx were either so general and abstract, or so specific and technical, that they could not be easily grasped or refuted. The old Marxism was dead, you seemed to feel, but here was a new version of the old dogma, a non-Stalinist, libertarian, ultra-modern Marxism.[113]

Capitalism, or the root of all evils

When Baran came to consider the problem of underdevelopment in Marxist terms, he did not have to do much fiddling with Marx, as he had had to do in dealing with the surplus, because there was not much there to tamper with. In fact, what he had to do was to answer questions that the theory of imperialism, which had not been Marx's doing, fudged or simply did not consider. Baran knew what underdevelopment meant as a new conceptual mediation in the relations between the industrialized and the poor countries in the capitalist world. He knew that development economics had espoused aggressively in the name of capitalism the idea that economic development was possible, and he had tried to refute the essential suppositions behind that project. The West had substituted 'underdeveloped' for 'backward'. It was making a strong bid for support in the less developed countries, while Stalinists were still talking about colonies and 'semi-colonies'. On the other hand, colonialism per se could not explain the full meaning of the social condition of underdevelopment. Baran wanted to prove that underdevelopment, the very concept practically patented by development economics, was consubstantial with capitalism, that development and underdevelopment were the two faces of the capitalist Janus, and that underdevelopment was as eradicable under capitalism as marrow was from bone. That a relation of dependence existed few would have denied, and Baran's intention was to make it as explicit and tight as possible.

Baran subscribed to Marx's principle that the countries of the first rank of history have shown the way that the others were to take: 'The country that is more developed industrially only shows to the less developed the image of its own future.' But this was not the way history had taken. There were disparities to start with: 'Differences not only in the natural pre-requisites of economic development, in geographic location and climate, but also in political, cultural and religious background, were bound to create divergences in levels of rates of increase and of productivity.' Western Europe had gone ahead of the rest of the world because its geographical location stimulated overseas mercantile enterprise and, strangely enough, because of its lack of resources. However, its 'large leap forward need not necessarily have prevented economic growth in other countries'. What happened was that once capitalism started operating all over the world, which had happened long before the Industrial Revolution and the advent of the classic Marxist model of a capitalist economy, the laws of exploitation and accumulation inherent in the system put a stop to economic development in all the less advanced countries. This in turn served to consolidate the West's progress and led to the economic breakthrough of industrialism, which in effect meant the permanent subordination and backwardness of today's underdeveloped economies. Baran was not too precise about the exact magnitude of the world's tribute to the development of the West, but he had no doubt about its importance: 'The intensity of the boost to Western Europe's development resulting from the "exogenous" contribution to its capital accumulation can hardly be exaggerated.'[114] It was like saying: 'we know it is true but we cannot prove it.' This sort of tactic would come up time and again in dependency arguments against historical capitalism.

The plundering of India was of special concern to Baran. With Hobson, he believed that colonialism, a quintessentially structured form of capitalist international exploitation, had disrupted the cohesion of its pre-capitalist society for the sole purpose of extracting profit. India was, of course, less advanced than Great Britain when its conquest started and so less capable of utilizing its own economic resources, but even so 'there can be no doubt that had the amount of economic surplus that Britain has torn from India been invested in India, India's economic development to date would have borne little similarity to the actual sombre record'. Furthermore, 'it should not be overlooked that India, if left to herself, might have found in the course of time a shorter and surely less tortuous road toward a better and richer society. That in that road she would have had to pass through the purgatory of a bourgeois revolution, that a long phase of capitalist development would have been the inevitable price that she would have had to pay for progress, can hardly be doubted.'[115]

In reading Baran's text the question persists: but why Britain and not India? Surely being an island and lacking resources was not enough. Throughout dependency literature, these residual interrogations will always seem like the final metaphysical Achilles heel of dependency explanations of underdevelopment. What must be emphasized about Baran's speculations on Indian underdevelopment is that they at least try to give it a historical rationale rather than to use it solely as an unconditional condemnation of colonialism or of Anglo-American imperialism. In the balance, Baran's was the first attempt at a systematic if summary theory on the origins of the contemporary inequality between the advanced capitalist nations and the rest of the non-communist world, on the assumption of the relative comparability between East and West before the advent of colonialism. And the fact that it was simplistic and schematic does not detract from its originality.

Finally, there was the question (which in retrospect seems premature when applied to the newly independent ex-colonies) of the persistence of underdevelopment in a world in which colonialism was becoming a thing of the past or for that matter in nations with a long history of independent life, like those of Latin America. Why did sovereign nations avid for economic development fail to increase their productivity and improve their standard of living? Baran on this issue tried to light the candle at both ends. On one hand, he argued that 'colonial and dependent countries today have no such sources of primary accumulation of capital as were available to the now advanced capitalist countries'. This proposition he balanced with the claim that potential economic surplus in underdeveloped lands was large enough for a very high rate of growth. Apart from the scepticism about national elites expressed in his articles in 1951 and 1952, there was also the problem that sovereignty in the Third World was often an illusion and, as R. B. Sutcliffe explained in a lengthy exposition on Baran's ideas, that when a nation sought to oppose foreign economic domination 'all leverages of diplomatic intrigue, economic pressure, and political subversion are set into motion to overthrow the recalcitrant national government and to replace it with politicians who are willing to serve the interests of the capitalist countries'. These interests were that economic frontiers should remain open to foreign investment for the extraction of raw materials, for the unrestricted marketing of manufactured goods, and for the acquisition of profitable assets either for direct surplus-extraction or for the crushing of competition. The only form of capitalism allowed by foreign capital were minor merchandising and other trivial services. 'The principal impact of foreign enterprise in the development of the underdeveloped countries', Baran insisted, 'lies in hardening and strengthening the sway of merchant capitalism, in slowing down and indeed preventing its transformation into industrial capitalism.' And as to Third World reformist planks, such as the thesis of the unequal terms of trade, Baran belittled the tapage around them with the argument that they had no bearing on development for what counted was who benefited from trade in the Third World and not what the benefits were. Even if the terms of trade could be evened up or made favourable to the underdeveloped countries, as long as the benefits from trade belonged to a privileged class of accomplices in the capitalist system of trade relations, development would remain an ignis fatuus.[116]

A time of political radicalism

The historical circumstances in which Baran divulged his ideas on underdevelopment were crucial to the influence that they achieved as well as in connection with the basic targets that they aimed at. Of these targets, one was technically within the purview of Marxism, and the other could fairly be described as one of the main intellectual adversaries of violent change in the Third World. Baran gave, if not proof, at least colourable arguments against the notion that capitalist development in the Third World was possible, or as G. Lichtheim had put it, that there was nothing in the laws of the system to prevent it. B. Warren later would say that capitalist development in the underdeveloped countries was inevitable, that it was, in fact, happening. Even later, N. Harris would adduce that he had proof of it.

But from Lenin's day the bulk of Marxist opinion had been that capitalism not only did not develop but also prevented development by any other means and even tended to immiserate. However, until Baran this was dogma and propaganda. It was founded on images and feelings and not primarily on reason. Baran gave reasons. Latin Americans were torn between hatred of Yankee imperialism and the Marxist logic that feudalism engenders capitalism. Baran explained that feudalism was not the primary cause of the condition of underdevelopment, because endogenous capitalist development could evolve from it, as it had in the advanced Western nations, and that it was capitalism imposed from the outside as a system of exploitation and of lopsided trade relations that had been producing backwardness and poverty over the centuries from the start of European expansion. In proposing these explanations, Baran fused Marx's sometime-negative view of colonialism with a vast historical expansion of Lenin's theory on the reactionary nature of imperialism.

The other target singled out by Baran was development economics: the whole wide myth that all that Latin America needed was social reform, some state intervention and plenty of investment in order to develop without tampering with private property or with the incentives to private enterprise. It was against this more than anything else that Baran flung his missiles, because here was an enemy that had to be destroyed, and that was the idea of potential progress at the heart of the concept of underdevelopment. Before Baran, the left had been content to castigate the colonialist and semi-colonialist Western domination of the world, and it had done nothing significant to counter the specific threat in the idea of a potentiality for development in the Third World that only had to be stimulated. This was an ideological and policy approach that bid fair to move and, in fact, was moving the relations between the industrialized and the non-industrialized nations from the old

Eurocentric and colonialist patterns on to a new basis of possible dialogue and collaboration, certainly of strong intellectual and political complicities. This was not a promise of instant change, and thirty years ago it was not even much of a possibility, but underdevelopment nevertheless needed to be defined by Marxists differently from the way Western developmentalism had defined it when it created the idea during and after the Second World War. Baran understood how important it was to scotch any notion that being underdeveloped meant that development was possible, which was the philosophy behind an anti-Marxist, anti-socialist programme like the Alliance for Progress, and that is what, in Marxist terms, he tried to accomplish in his book and in some three basic articles he wrote on the subject.

Fidel Castro came to power in 1959, less than two years after the publication of Baran's book. The Cuban revolution became radicalized in less than a year. By 1961 it was trying to export subversion all over Latin America. The ideological prestige of Stalinism, which, in spite of Cold War vociferation, was basically conservative in that it placed Soviet interests above all else and in that it at times contemplated progressive inter-class nationalist alliances in backward countries, had died with the Soviet despot, and the Soviet Marxist ideological centre was not holding. All over the Third World there was a tendency to try out new ideological formulas, usually with radical often irresponsible or adventurist practical implications. *New Times* did not have the same readership and influence as before. In Latin America in particular the New York-based relatively unorthodox *Monthly Review* had a reach and commanded a respect out of all proportion to its scant circulation (probably around 10,000 copies per issue). Some of the forces for renovation in Latin American Marxist thinking irradiated from its pages, in which L. Huberman, S. Nearing, P. M. Sweezy, H. Magdoff and others regularly expressed their views. It was used by Baran as a vehicle for his ideas, and it was the firing range in which A. G. Frank later tested his most explosive arguments. The shock of the Cuban revolution on Latin American politics and society after 1960 had something to do with the spread of the ideas that *Monthly Review* had been expounding during the previous years. In particular, there was a special complementarity between theories that postulated a complete rejection of capitalism and a political strategy that spurned all alliances and compromises in favour of revolutionary radicalism and even violence. The theoretical rationale to armed insurrection might have been the strategic ideas of R. Debray, but Baran (or something akin to his work) was the necessary ideological linchpin on which everything hung.

In the wider Third World, Baran's ideas (or again, an orientation similar to them) were likewise at work, though in a more subtle fashion. The non-aligned movement manifested a decidedly anti-Western bias on both political and economic issues. In conjunction with the call for the end of colonialism, it proposed that the world capitalist economic order be restructured. The communist world emerged unscathed. The USSR was now much involved in the Afro-Asian countries: it had mended relations with India, it was building Egypt's Aswan dam, it was in general in the midst of its Krushchevian Third World offensive, and it was brandishing its space triumphs and its revolutionary self-confidence. The Third World felt assisted in its inchoate intuition that it was not to blame historically for its underdevelopment, that it was the victim of Western cupidity, and that the West had a responsibility for which it had to make amends, and part at least of this was what Baran had been claiming since at least 1957.

A dispassionate assessment of Baran

What can be said of Baran's work from a less passionate vantage than the political confrontations of his time? In general his approach to history was abstract, diffuse and subsuming. Less than a fully worked-out interpretation of 'historical underdevelopment', what he proposed was a gigantic and unspecific programme of research. Frank attempted this for Latin America and Wallerstein for the entire world, with the results that we shall see. W. Rodney followed through on Baran's idea of frustrated nationhood in the countries colonialized by the Europeans. Baran merely threw out what amounted to hints and clues, and his texts, like Amin's dissertation, are shot through with ambiguities. In general they have not produced consistently quality fruits. The idea that capitalist primitive accumulation took place at the expense of the colonial world is pure impressionism of the sort 'it would seem as if' or 'it evidently had to be'. He did not have an iota of proof, and the idea itself lacks even clear definition. His speculations on the contemporary relationship between the developed capitalist countries and the Third World, what he specifically called 'dependency', have failed, as we shall see, both the proof of investigation and of subsequent historical events. His insistence on the notion that the prosperity of the West depends on the exploitation and the misery of the Third World seems with hindsight nothing short of pious and arbitrary, that is, with no other basis than the intense desire that it be true. When all is said and done, for all his superficial unconventionality as a Marxist thinker, Baran was essentially a prejudiced pro-communist Marxist observer. What is his standing as such?

Baran did make what seem like two significant contributions to Marxist/Leninist thought. He cut through the contemporary tangle concerning the theory on the meshing of disparate MOPs in underdeveloped countries. This scheme, especially recurred to in Latin America, permitted a series of inferences on possible political alliances between Marxists and the property-owning or the rising middle classes or different combinations of these classes. The explanation was that imperialism somehow had a special affinity with 'feudalism', which in turn was the enemy of industrialization. There were special definitions of what in Latin America constituted feudalism, but they were mostly too vague or too abstract and certainly had nothing whatever to do with the Marxist feudal MOP, although, ironically enough, they were elaborated by Latin American Marxist intellectuals in an effort to mould their thinking to Marxist and post-Marxist theory. Baran, who had himself also initiated his study of underdevelopment with a rather bloodless feudal-seeming social model, had come around to seeing the essential vacuity of the concept of feudalism outside of its Marxist Eurocentric context. He therefore cast it aside and pointed out that external capitalism took on as ally any class that had an interest in the capitalist system of exploitation. To emphasize 'feudalism' was anachronistic and inaccurate, and, worse still, it was unnecessary because feudalism, capitalism, imperialism and other related concepts were equivalent in so far as the creation of underdevelopment was concerned.

Baran's other contribution related to Lenin's idea of labour opportunism, which implied some degree of nation-to-nation exploitation. Imperialism exploited workers in the colonies and in the 'semi-colonies'. The benefits were hoarded by the ruling classes in the 'four pillars' of imperialism, but some wage benefits trickled down to the workers there through the agency of opportunist labour bosses. This had made Lenin livid. Baran was somewhat more resigned to the fact that some of the spoils of imperialism were part of a working man's pay cheque in the USA. He did not like it, but the alternative for him was the Soviet myth of the starving masses under capitalism, and Baran knew the lie behind this. What he did was to make an analysis of the way nation-to-nation exploitation worked, and this made the Lenin intuition explicit. Imperialism exploited entire countries to the extent that even its ruling classes, which were the collaborators of imperialism, received only the crumbs. These profits were added to surplus in the developed world and made possible a superfluous production, principally in war industries, which created jobs and the illusion of prosperity. The idea was that for its own preservation capitalism could not afford not to share out with its wage-earners part of its ill-gotten gains.

Baran refrained from calling his historical system 'imperialism'. The Marxist tradition was to stick to Lenin's terms, according to which 'imperialism' had started around the beginning of the century. Lenin had relied for general purposes on the term 'dependency', which, as we saw, was used during the nineteenth century to designate colonialized territories in contrast to colonies of settlement. Despite the definition of 'dependency' by the Ecuadorian Paredes in the Comintern as referring to a country that is not a colony and in which imperialist penetration had not managed to subvert national sovereignty entirely – which responded to a peculiarly Latin American view of hierarchical international categories – the term still retained the connotation of subjection or absence of effective sovereignty, and Baran opted for it to indicate the historical impact of Western capitalism on the world at large. The Leninist touchstone for imperialism was that capitalism in its final stage had to look for areas to exploit beyond its own backyard. But, for Baran, capitalism had always gone overseas to seek out profits necessary to its own advancement. The Industrial Revolution would not have taken place as it did without the exploitation of India and other colonies. (This left unanswered questions on why Spain had not kept in economic step with the rest of Western Europe, but that was an issue that came under the province of more precise historical research, such as Wallerstein initiated with his world-system analysis.) It is logical, therefore, to conclude that when Baran explored the distant origins of underdevelopment and related them to capitalism, he was formulating the long-view, long-term version of economic imperialism that is known as dependency theory.

The historical context of radicalism

The left takes the offensive during the 1960s

The Western counterpart to the spread of Marxist and generally anti-Western radicalism in Latin America and the wider Third

World during the 1960s was a strategy combining softness and hardness. On the soft side there was decolonization. Algeria acceded to independence after many years of struggle. More peacefully, so did most of Africa and all of Asia, as well as Guyana and the former British West Indies. It was also the time of the widest and most intense application in the Third World of the Western strategy of aid-and-advice. The Alliance for Progress reached its apogee during the first half of the decade, and, on the whole, the US government tried to stimulate private investments all over the underdeveloped world while inter-governmental assistance banks evaluated projects and lent funds. On the other hand, the hard side of all this, Washington armed and financed in 1961 a failed invasion of Cuba, which was the culmination of countless raids and attacks on Cuban territory, and in 1963 the US Marines actually invaded and occupied the Dominican Republic to thwart a perceived leftist take-over threat in that country. The former Belgian Congo at one time during the 1960s was in the grip of European mercenary brigades, later displaced by a peace-keeping contingent of the UNO. France currently sent its paratroops into its unstable former colonies in Africa. Massively supported by US military aid, Israel in 1967 occupied the West Bank, Gaza, Sinai and the Golan Heights. If anything, what all this showed were the limitations of the Western developmentalist approach to its relations with the Third World, and the left was not slow to notice.

Leftist intellectuals tried to counter the capitalist West in at least three ways: by revamping or updating the theory of economic imperialism as Baran had done, with the denunciation of 'neo-colonialism', and through the stimulation of Third World anti-Western attitudes. The French ideologue P. Jalée wrote in 1965 that colonialist military and political dependence had been replaced by extreme economic dependence, which was but a reincarnation of the old 'colonial pact'. One of the founding fathers of the Afro-Asian non-aligned movement, Kwame Nkrumah, the first head of state of Ghana, (which became independent in 1957) was arguably the principal intellectual supporter of the idea of neo-colonialism, which he defined thus: 'The essence of neo-colonialism is that the state which is subject to it is, in theory, independent and has all the outward trappings of international sovereignty. In reality its economic system and thus its political policy is directed from outside.'[117] Sovereignty, independence, even decolonization were at most dubious concepts. Ex-colonies had to be kept under observation to see whether they could slough off the condition of dependence. H. Magdoff summed up the ultimate intent of neo-colonialism: 'Imperialism without colonies'.

One of the ways to combat dependence was to stimulate Third World solidarity, which was based for most underdeveloped countries on a common colonial past and on current capitalist/imperialist penetration. In order to achieve this, as Baran had shrewdly perceived, developmentalism had to be discredited. Jalée cited the French Marxist economist C. Bettelheim as having 'unmasked the concept of underdevelopment' by denouncing its implication that underdeveloped countries were catching up with the advanced capitalist economies. This was a direct onslaught against development economics. The countries of the Third World, Jalée affirmed, unlike the industrialized nations, did not possess and did not exploit their own resources. By way of contrast, according to Bettelheim, today's industrialized nations had never been economically dependent. Jalée supported Bettelheim's suggestion that the Third World was integrated not by 'underdeveloped' countries but by 'exploited, dominated, and economically deformed countries'. E. Ruiz Garcia, following P. Moussa, suggested that they should be termed 'proletarian nations'. For Ruiz Garcia, a radical Spanish demographer with a wide-ranging and sympathetic interest in the Third World, Third World unity reposed on the awareness of colonial outrages, with special emphasis on racism, whose wounds decolonization had not permanently healed. The French historian G. de Bossechère, who was not a partisan of dependency or economic imperialism theory, also emphasized the poisoned legacy of colonialism and the painful after-effects it had during and after decolonization. In so far as his writings, like those of Ruiz Garcia, who was much nearer to Marxism/Leninism, consistently pursued a structural conception of Third World, they, and those of many other sympathetic intellectuals, contributed subsidiarily to the propagation of the theoretical model of dependence between the developed and the underdeveloped nations posited in dependency theory.[118] The concept of Third World in the 1960s was not exclusively Marxist revolutionary property, but the moral indignation against the West and the enthusiastic cheering that it evoked from different quarters usually served to feed the mill grinding out radical leftist theses.

Perhaps the most important of those theses concerned neo-imperialism, whose basic assumption was that Lenin's doctrine was still valid and needed only the 'retouchings' that the times called for, mainly having to do with decolonization and the capitalist global developmental strategy. Baran and P. M. Sweezy published in 1966 an essay in which they substituted MNCs for the Hilferding/Lenin concept of finance capital. In 1967 Sweezy again forayed into the area of neo-imperialism to describe how international capitalism assigned underdeveloped countries the work of raw material production, and even then sought to control those resources through the investments of giant corporations. T. Kemp also believed that MNCs had taken over the running of imperialism. His thesis was addressed specifically to the epoch of decolonization in the sense that the new imperialism was relaying the colonialist states in turning newly independent countries into economic neo-colonies.

H. Magdoff devoted most of his research, published in the late 1960s, to the nitty-gritty of imperialist control and exploitation. The strictly theoretical side of his work was standard neo-imperialist fare. According to W. J. Mommsen, Magdoff saw imperialism as following upon colonialism, which had 'served only to adapt the social and economic institutions of the dependent countries to metropolitan needs'. Magdoff explored the different liens fastening underdeveloped countries to imperialism. US banks went international due to 'a relative shrinkage of business opportunities in the domestic front and attractive opportunities overseas'. This was a conventional contemporary reiteration of the thesis on the tendency of rates of profit to decline. In the Third World these institutions used subsidiary corporations to acquire controlling interests in native enterprises. Likewise, US firms dealing in raw materials operated in those countries to secure a strategic share of world production. As a consequence, raw materials were produced, priced and exported there on decisions made by MNCs.

American foreign aid also functioned as an instrument of imperialist control. The objectives of the US aid programme in the Third World were twofold: (a) 'to keep the outer rim of the imperialist network as dependencies of the system'; (b) 'to stimulate the growth of capitalist forces – economic and political – within these countries'. The deficit in the US balance of payments put these considerations out of focus, but Magdoff explained it away by adding to foreign investments military spending abroad, especially in Vietnam, and the cost of military assistance and economic aid, all of which were indispensable for the maintenance of the international capitalist system. His arguments were all backed by abundant statistics, the overall trend of which was to prove the growing share of US participation in foreign placements and in world trade, especially with underdeveloped countries.[119]

Revolutionary radicalism and other not-so-radical political trends in Latin America

In the context of Marxist thinking on economic retardation, the special features of Latin America merit mentioning. With nearly a century and a half of independent political life, these republics could not in good faith blame colonialism for their underdevelopment, and in fact when traditional or academic Latin American historians turned their eyes in search of causes of economic retardation they tended to blame endogenous traits and processes. The combination of economic-imperialism theory and class analysis that the Comintern applied to colonies and other backward nations had been relatively influential in Latin America. Mariategui's pioneering socio-analytical approach to the problems of latifundia and of the Indian population in Peru was undoubtedly a creative and stimulating use of Marxist methodology. However, in the 1930s, and especially in the years immediately after the Second World War, Latin American Marxists, completely and willingly under the thumb of Stalinism, went over to an extreme form of anti-imperialism that ruled out any possibility of objective social analysis. Reality could not be entirely obviated, and there arose an early form of Latin America dependency theory – well exemplified by a group of Venezuelan writers active in the early 1960s – resulting from a cross between anti-imperialist clichés and the unavoidable awareness that Latin American republics had independent histories of their own. Social analysis, however, remained stuck in the over-use of the concept of feudalism imbedded in Latin American Marxist thought, and often accepted by non-Marxists such as Furtado and the Mexican writer C. Fuentes. In general, Latin American theorization on international economic inequalities stemmed from the 'chemistry' within this melange of views on external dependence and on internal social structures, in which the former category in its radical anti-imperialist form was the dominant element.[120]

Political events in the 1960s were impelling Latin American Marxist intellectuals in opposite directions: one towards extreme subversive positions, fostered by the Cuban revolution and out-and-out anti-imperialism, and the other towards a more moderate approach to social and political issues. Even though Castroite subversion was being checked by the mid-1960s, the literature of insurrection tended to proliferate, influenced significantly by the ideas of F. Fanon on the revolutionary potential of urban slum-dwellers and those of Debray on the strategy of *foquismo*, that is, the notion that guerrilla bands could act as leavening in the mass of discontented peasantry.[121] But on the whole the cause of revolution seemed to be losing momentum: the USSR had suffered an important setback in the missile crisis of 1963 and not long afterwards L. Brezhnev inaugurated a discreet policy of Soviet retrenchment in the Third World. The USA under the administration of L. B. Johnson cut back on the Alliance for Progress and shifted to a policy of indiscriminate recognition and support of repressive military regimes.[122] These trends further goaded Marxist subversive radicalism – which resurfaced bloodily and futilely during the 1970s in the Argentine and Uruguay – but they also paved the way for a dependency theory that represented in various ways a break with the traditional nostrums of anti-imperialism. There were good reasons for this, too, grounded in the evolving reality of Latin America.

There were symptoms suggesting that the image of economic imperialism as an unfettered and unstoppable kingmaker all over Latin America was losing its power. The Peruvian military had taken over in their country in 1965, with the excuse of covert oil-company machinations, and they had decreed a programme of defiant nationalism and radical socio-economic reforms, which at the time was compared to Nasser's Arab revolution and was widely studied in Latin America as an alternative political and developmental model. Despite heavy pressure from Washington, Mexico never broke with the Cuban revolutionary regime even at the height of its promotion of guerilla activities. Allende's election itself was decided in the Chilean congress against heavy conservative and American opposition in 1970. In addition, clear indications existed that capitalism had not entirely exhausted its industrializing and developing potential in spite of the combined refutation of Soviet propaganda, of dependency arguments such as those used by Venezuelan Marxists, of the neo-imperialism thesis defended by *Monthly Review* theorists, and of the long-view anti-capitalist perspective expounded by P. Baran. If anything, some radical Latin American Marxists in the early 1970s were in secret sympathy with the idea that history and class struggle had to run their course and the bourgeoisie had to achieve its historical tasks before revolution could come about. Even though it has been said repeatedly that dependency got its winding up from the prevalence in CEPAL circles of the Prebisch core-periphery paradigm, it is more likely than not that *cepalistas* in the late 1960s were concentrating more on the development side of their economic studies and policy researches than on imperialism theory, and the former in the final analysis were not incompatible with modified versions of national capitalist structures. This seemed particularly true of Brazil, where economic development in spite of glaring social lacunae seemed to be taking on a new lease of life under the auspices of 'technocratic' military authoritarianism.

A controversial revision of dependency ideas

What F.H. Cardoso and E. Faletto saw that others did not want to see

The concept of dependency has had different avatars within the pages of this work. We saw it used by Lenin as an all-purpose designation for the relations in the capitalist world between the centres of imperialist power and the rest of the world. In the Comintern it was proposed as a half-way condition between complete colonial status and economic and political independence. Baran employed it to describe a world-historical condition created by the expansion of capitalism from the start of colonialism in the sixteenth century. Finally, some Marxists defined dependency basically in terms of all-embracing, all-powerful economic imperialism. According to some observers, the definitive Latin American version of dependency was formulated by F. H. Cardoso and E. Faletto in their famous and controversial work *Dependency and Development in Latin America*. This work was written between 1965 and 1967 in Santiago de Chile, when its authors were working at the Latin American Institute for Economic and Social Planning, an offshoot of ECLA. The book was apparently first published in Mexico in 1969 and reprinted there in 1971. It was not published in English until 1979, on the basis of the 1971 edition but in an 'expanded and amended version', which included a lengthy and almost defensive but illuminating 'Preface to the English Edition'. This edition retained the original 'Conclusions' plus an added, minutely explanatory 'Post-Scriptum', and we shall use it as the mainstay of our analysis.

P. J. O'Brien affirms that 'the original formulation of dependency in Latin America began within ECLA in the mid 1960s' and that the Cardoso/Faletto 'text is classic in the sense that it was the first clear, comprehensive, ambitious and rigorous attempt both to formulate the concept and to analyse a variety of dependency situations in Latin America'. C. Abel and C. Lewis praise Cardoso and Faletto for 'the breadth of their canvass and in the sustained exhilaration of their presentation'. On the other hand, neither G. Palma nor R. Thorp seem to attach more than a moderate significance to the Cardoso/Faletto contribution to social analysis in Latin America, giving pride of place instead, in the context of dependency, to A. G. Frank and, Palma especially, to T. dos Santos.[123] In our opinion, Frank and dos Santos to not meaningfully depart from the radical long-term economic imperialism ideology, whereas Cardoso and Faletto at least made a stab, a very restrained and not finally a very successful one, at reinterpreting Latin American history, both from the socio-political and from the international point of view, under a more modulated, less intransigent 'dependency' illumination.

In a brief somewhat pedantic critique of Cardoso and Faletto, the American professor R. A. Packenham made three points concerning their ideological position. He said: (a) that Cardoso and Faletto were hard-line defenders of the neo-Marxist economic-imperialism line; (b) that their work was probably influenced by A. G. Frank's theses on Latin America, or that at any rate their theories were nearly indistinguishable; and (c) that in the English language 1979 edition of *Dependency and Development in Latin America* they went out of their way to emphasize the 'autonomist' aspect of their position, after they had seen how economic and political events were going in Latin America, presumably also to ingratiate themselves with an American audience. Cardoso and Faletto have disclaimed any influence from Frank on purely chronological grounds and others have endorsed their allegation.[124] Their position, they affirm, was defined and expressed before Frank's main works. The important distinction to be made on this discrepancy is that whereas Cardoso and Faletto were trying to insert Marxist analysis into a Latin American socio-historical tradition, Frank was doing his utmost to pour Latin American history into a mould that combined the long-view general theory of economic imperialism derived from Baran and the neo-imperialist analyses of the *Monthly Review* theorists, among whom he could rightly count himself. Having said this, however, it does not do to start by stressing too strongly an aspect of the Cardoso/Faletto analysis with which they themselves sometimes seem to feel uncomfortable.

Of what exactly does their malaise consist? To start with, they define their work as belonging to a 'radically critical Latin American heritage'. They even go as far as to give blanket 'at least' approval to the Latin American guerilla movements, and they conclude that their main concern 'is how to construct paths towards socialism', which in Latin American ideological parlance is little different from communism. However, they did admit, as Abel and Lewis put it, 'that socialism was not on the immediate agenda'. All of this probably means that Cardoso and Faletto took note, as few of their fellow Marxist intellectuals had, that contemporary events did not warrant a revolutionary optimism, or even a die-hard ultraist 'you-just-wait-and-see' attitude, which was quite common among radicals either putting down or taking up arms in the late 1960s.

The other set of facts Cardoso and Faletto worked with, elicited from social and economic processes in Latin America, concerned the nature and the potentialities of capitalist industrialization. They shared the developmentalist outlook on this point and they participated critically to some extent in ECLA's dogged search for developmental formulas and strategies, which were inevitably affiliated to the assumptions and the programmes of development economics in its mainstream phase. They went about expressing this in words that committed without putting them too far out on a limb that other Marxists could easily saw behind them. They made tentative, ambiguous statements such as that 'when foreign capitals start to promote development in dependent economies some deepening of internal markets occurs and some forms of income redistribution benefit upper levels of middle sectors', benefits which they 'might expand to include. . .alienated parts of working classes'. In brief, 'a real process of dependent development does exist in some Latin American countries', a form of discriminatory lopsided development, which none the less empowered them to criticize 'those who expect permanent stagnation in underdeveloped countries because of a constant decline in the rate of profits or the "narrowness of internal markets", which supposedly function as an impassable obstacle to capitalist advancement'.

This form of development, even though it was characterized by the influence of MNCs, did not conform to the 'belief that the internal or national socio-political situation is mechanically conditioned by external dominance'. On the contrary, peripheral industrialization, they argued, reduces 'typically colonial exploitation' and incorporates into the modern economy all the 'social groups tied to modern capitalist production', from entrepreneurs down to wage-earners. This was then a picture of convergence and conciliation of internal and external interests rather than one of dominance and submission, and one that 'makes possible political analysis'. The evident awareness of the Latin American historical juncture in Cardoso and Faletto was expressed in a judgment which seemed to exclude the violent radicalism of the previous years: 'There are structural possibilities for various types of social and political movements.' When they spoke of 'historically viable goals', they were in effect saying, like Marie-Antoinette: 'Give them cakes instead of bread.'[125]

The 'metaphysical principle' of imperialism

Despite the implied reformism and the sketchy politics of participation, which in themselves were not unknown among certain Latin American communist movements and tendencies, Cardoso and Faletto were not throwing out all the traditional Marxist imperialist motifs. If anything, they reaffirmed some of the more persistent ones in their own conception of what they were attempting to express. Dependency was still dependency, even in its extreme anti-imperialist meaning. Their definition of it is eloquent enough: 'From the economic point of view a system is dependent when the accumulation and expansion of capital cannot find its essential dynamic component inside the system.' This meant that capitalist development had very limited possibilities. It was impeded by the stumbling block of the capital goods sector in countries like Brazil and Mexico. It did not lessen the underlying irreconcilabilities of the class struggle, and it did not even act in a significantly long-haul redistributive manner. It had nothing in common with the 'theoretical schemes concerning the formation of capitalist society in present-day developed countries'.[126]

So in what way did Cardoso and Faletto distance themselves from the Baran-style or the more current extremist Latin American Marxist definitions of dependency? To answer this it will be necessary to bring into sharper focus the way in which the various versions of the Marxist theory of economic imperialism conceived the relations between the centre and the periphery, to use the handy and ultimately accurate Prebisch duality. For this, in turn, we have to insist on the distinction between the narrower Leninist thesis and the general long-view theory of economic imperialism outlined by Baran in the form of an explanation of the origins of international economic inequality.

In simple terms, the Leninist thesis propounded an overwhelming, almost sudden turning of advanced capitalism towards backward countries, with the intention of preventing the decline of profits through the exploitation of labour in the extraction of raw materials and other primary products. This tendency resulted from either the 'laws' or the inherent mechanisms of the system, driven at all costs towards the realization of surplus value in whatever terrain was accessible to it. It was not something that had been initially decided in boardrooms or other decision centres of social and political power and control, but once the process got in motion it was difficult to escape the impression derived from the *loci classici* that it was being planned and conducted deliberately and infallibly towards its specific, perfectly defined targets.

The effects of imperialism fell on already backward nations, but they further resulted in that no development or, at most, only rigorously controlled, inconsequential forms of development would occur. For imperialism there were no frontiers and no sovereignties. It dealt mostly in colonies, and, in those territories that hung on to the external trappings of nationhood, it brought down and put up puppet governments at will. Bourgeoisies, if they existed, had no backbone and no economic roots. There were class conflicts, of course, but they were rudimentary and unclear; it was imperialism itself that ultimately decided who had the upper hand. According to Marxist/Leninist ideology, there was usually an alliance between imperialism and something extrapolated from European history called feudalism. Only communist political action could change this scheme. The only difference between this ideology and its Stalinist variant, was the vociferous and simplistic extreme to which the latter carried it, and also perhaps the absolute reliance that Stalinist postwar political strategy placed on anti-imperialism everywhere, which had been muted in the case of Western Europe during the anti-fascist period before the war.

The long-term general theory was more vague about how the process got started, because it traced its origins back to the initial post-medieval expansion of 'merchant capitalism', or as some put it, when capitalism took the first steps towards becoming a world system. Here, things were much more impersonal. Laws and forces and all sorts of influences external to the system were taken into account, but the *primum mobile* of expansion was still and principally the part of surplus accruing to profits. Given the diffuse and erratic nature of the process, due to technical, financial and resource limitations, it was more difficult to speak of intentionality or deliberateness, but again results bespoke causal uniformity and this was exactly as if history took place according to a carefully drawn blueprint. And in the case of the forces involved in the general theory, which have been identified as 'world market', 'world-system', or simply 'capitalism' according to who does the expounding, there was no room for the uncertainties that Lenin allowed through Marxist revolutionary political tactics: capitalism, in whatever form, prevented or scotched any potentiality for economic progress or change. Despite its vagueness about the origins of capitalism, the general theory was even more fatalistic than the narrower original version: nations were pawns and hostages, social classes and politics outside the imperialist centres did not count in the balance of history. Here were the origins of international economic inequality. Only revolutionary social change could achieve economic progress and independence.

The two theories, rightly considered by many as basically Eurocentric, arrived at the same revolutionary conclusions, and this was one of the rubs, because the revolution in Latin America was stalled or seriously stalling. And there were other even more grievous problems. There was no consistent historical evidence to the effect that imperialism had been manipulating the politics and the economic policies of Latin American nations against their will from the start of independence. Even the evidence on the direct imperialist exploitation of those countries, as defined in Lenin or Baran, who were totally agreed on this point, was not (*pace* E. Galeano and the other muckrakers of Latin American history) conclusive for the nineteenth century and much less so for the twentieth. There was, however, plenty of evidence on political instability and local complicity in foreign capitalist penetration, although the latter did not conform to one universal pattern. In addition, if the Marxist alternative of classist political analysis and tactics were based on the premiss of imperialist domination, it was virtually emptied of efficacy. In the course of the 1960s, then, radical Latin American theories of economic imperialism were urgently in need of revitalization, and that is what Cardoso and Faletto tried to do in the interest of a broader Marxist analysis of realistic socialist politics.

The 'now' dependency and the Latin American historiographical tradition

The historical scope of their book is restricted. It delves superficially into colonial history and in general it downplays the 'external connection' in Latin American nineteenth-century history in favour of internal political events and processes. The authors' fundamental source for these processes was T. Halperin Donghi, a Marxist in the MOP class-struggle tradition. Instead of the all-or-nothing schematic approach of economic-imperialism doctrine, Cardoso and Faletto preferred to categorize what they called 'basic situations of dependency', of which they described two: the 'enclave economies' and 'economies controlled by local bourgeoisies'. In the former, capital 'originates in the exterior'; in the latter, 'capital accumulation is. . .internal'. For the twentieth century they created an additional modality, which they called 'contemporary dependent industralizing economies controlled by multinational corporations', in which a substantial part of 'industrial production is sold in the internal market', their distinguishing feature regarding enclave economies. Local control of capital ensured a greater degree of development, but significantly the other modalities did not indicate total imperialist domination.

'We conceive the relationship between external and internal forces', they wrote, 'as forming a complex whole whose structural links are not based on mere external forms of exploitation and coercion, but are rooted in coincidences of interests between local dominant classes and international ones, and, on the other side, are challenged by local dominated groups and classes.' Or more explicitly: 'What we affirm simply means that the system of domination reappears in "internal" forces, through the social practices of local groups and classes which try to enforce foreign interests, not precisely because they were foreign, but because they may coincide with values and interests that these groups pretend as their own.' This was, in effect, a laboured recognition of the fact that Latin American societies, whatever their terrible inequities, had lives of their own, even the power of decision-making with regard to their own evolution. Political action within underdevelopment was not entirely subservient to imperialist intervention or even to covert string-pulling. Therefore, leftist political practice had to proceed on the basis of this supposition if it was to have some efficacy. Dependency was still very much in operation, but it had to be fought at the grass-roots political level so to speak, rather than with the tiresome reiteration of the slogans on external domination. In particular, dependence had to be considered in the manner in which it affected the social structure in each dependent country. Class struggle was paramount, but it did not respond to special 'laws' pertaining only to dependency situations. It could only be understood and interpreted within the framework of a 'general economic theory of capitalism'.

What, in the final analysis, Cardoso and Faletto were trying to destroy was the image that we described before, of imperialism as the supreme arbiter in the destinies of all underdeveloped countries. 'Conceived in this manner', they said, 'imperialism turns into an active and metaphysical principle which traces out the pattern of history on the sensitive but passive skins of dependent countries. Forms of local societies, reactions against imperialism, the political dynamic of local societies, and attempts at alternatives are not taken into consideration. This type of analysis, although it uses Marxist vocabulary, is methodologically symmetrical to interpretations based on the "logic of industrialization", or on the "stages of modernization", or even on the phases of "political development", which foresee change as a result of mechanical factors.' The key words, we think, are 'change' and 'metaphysical': the latter because it embodies the refutation of the old inadequate representations in economic-imperialism theory, and the former because, although like Baran's *The Political Economy of Growth* this is a programme for research and inquiry rather than a finished, perfected construct, it is also above all a strategy for political change. In fact, behind all Marxist-affiliated theories on international economic inequalities there is a project of radical social transformation, and therein lies the reason why in our times, with respect to the Third World, no rational reconciliation or coexistence is possible between the theories that posit endogenous causes and those that stress, however modulated, the external connection. They are all basically incompatible political choices.[127]

Dependency and Development in Latin America is a work riddled with equivocations and yawning gaps. Political independence led to the 'consolidation of external linkages', yet these were no obstacles to a considerable degree of autonomous development in some countries. Capitalist development was definitely possible, but it was dependent development. This echoed the dilemma that Marx willed on his twentieth-century followers of trying to reconcile the denunciation of capitalism *in toto* while seeking for underdeveloped countries the blessings of developed capitalism. You could not denounce interminably the developed core of capitalism for 'causing' underdevelopment without at some point coming to terms with what it was that development really meant. It if meant 'capitalist development' or some aspects of it, then why denounce capitalism globally? Apparently it worked in some countries and in others it did not. If it was 'socialist development', then two problems came up: one, the core could not really be in a developed state despite appearances, and, two, given the balance of political forces, it was practically a will-o'-the-wisp for the Third World, or at least, in the case of Cardoso and Faletto, for the Latin American part of it.

The simple solution for these contradictions was that for Marx 'capitalist development' per se was an alien concept. For him, there was a historical process determined by political and economic forces within successive MOPs towards some sort of ill-defined workers' millennium. There was no development in capitalism outside that process. As it turned out, capitalism did develop. It did not culminate in a final showdown between antagonistic social classes. It somehow engendered social welfare, and it wore down social asperities and antagonisms sufficiently to obtain a consensus approval for its continued operation.

Of course, long-view Marxists believe that the historical process is still going on and that everything will eventually turn out the way Marx expected it would. This point of view is fraught with complexities and risky analytical profundities about the contemporary world. Standard Soviet Marxism peddled the 'starving masses' theme, which it pretended to apply equally to the core and the periphery of the capitalist universe, with the only perceivable difference being that capitalists in the core were richer and more rapacious than those in the periphery. Baran tried to make this seem plausible with his own definition of surplus, which implied a precarious equilibrium in the core sustained by militarism and conspicuous consumption. Cardoso and Faletto probably believed they had the answer in 'dependent capitalism', which is integral to the one and only capitalism, yet in some way a lesser variety of it. They invoked 'socialism', but the term was not elaborated or explained. Perhaps they meant Cuba in the first version of their book, but later on they were hedging their bets, as Packenham correctly pointed out. The advent of socialism implied previous class struggle but they did hardly more than mention it repeatedly. In this sense, their analysis was not unlike E. Laclau's 1985 Gramscian essay 'The hegemonic form of the political' as it droned on interminably about 'hegemony' and new forms of 'socialist strategy', which could be, indeterminably, peaceful or violent, without once saying what it meant, unless it was the incorporation of 'marginados', gays and feminists into the political arena.[128]

In part what they were saying about Latin America was something that non-Marxist Latin American historians and social analysts had known for a long time, which was that the history of the region could be interpreted in the light of endogenous political events and social movements in the widest possible sense, to the exclusion of any form of economic determinism including that put forward by the theory of economic imperialism.[129] Despite its shortcomings and its shilly-shallying between a radical dependency outlook and political reformism, the Cardoso/Faletto interpretation became highly influential, particularly outside Latin America, through its diffusion by sympathetic commentators. However, it fell far short of being an adequate understanding of Latin American underdevelopment, even on the mundane problems raised by developmental strategies such as ISI, of which a more telling and eloquent critique can be found in O. Sunkel.[130]

The persistence of radical theory

Even as Cardoso and Faletto were exerting themselves to extricate dependency theory from the clutches of its own contradictions and distortions, other Latin American theorists were doing their utmost to prevent it from straying from its rigid adherence to the dogmas of economic imperialism. The Brazilian T. dos Santos, whose major contribution dates from 1969, is credited by Palma with initiating 'an interesting attempt to break with the concept of a mechanical determination of internal by external structures which dominated the traditional analysis of the left in Latin America, and which particularly characterized Frank's work', but in the same breath Palma admits that Santos' analysis 're-establishes, little by little, the priority of external over internal structures', and dos Santos himself, in his 'Introduction' to a 1974 rehashing of his previous work, recognized that he and Frank were in the 'same camp' and shared the same interest in finding 'a theoretical alternative destined to serve as basis for the revolutionary transformation of Latin America'. The origin of their 'marginal' divergences was the priority which dos Santos gave to the exploration of the 'process of social transformation' under the external weight of dependence. Also from 1969, R. Mauro Marini's *Underdevelopment and Revolution*, which, in line with ultra-leftist dependency was oriented towards revolutionary struggle more than towards any serious academic pursuit, was chiefly significant because it gave theoretical formulation to the concepts of 'subimperialism' and 'superexploitation of labour', both used extensively by Frank. Apparently Marini began developing his 'subimperialism' thesis in an article in *Monthly Review* in 1965, in which he argued that the military take-over in Brazil the previous year was leading to the 'imperialist integration' of that country and the USA. However, the most strenuous efforts within this ideological tendency were undoubtedly those of Frank himself.[131]

A. G. Frank

The primacy of political action

One approaches A. G. Frank with some trepidation. He is a formidable polemicist. He is a man with a conscience. He himself admits his 'middle-class North American' background and his conventional even reactionary roots in development studies (one of his teachers in Chicago was Milton Friedman). He credits his contact with the reality of underdevelopment in Latin America with his political and intellectual radicalization. We shall try to be as accurate as possible in describing his positions and in remitting here his basic arguments, although this is a fearsome task given the capaciousness of his intellectual embrace, the volubility of his utterances and the trenchancy of his mind. Before starting, it is convenient to make some commentaries on his oeuvre, based on his usually preliminary claims on the time sequence and on the circumstances of his numerous works and theses. We shall propose a threefold division for the almost uninterrupted flow of his productions, which is not at odds with anything we have heard or read.

In the first group in our classification, we include Frank's early works specifically on Latin America, including his 'apprenticeship' in *Monthly Review*, comprising: *Capitalism and Underdevelopment in Latin America. Historical studies of Chile and Brazil*, published in 1967 but written in 1963–65; the brief 'The sociology of underdevelopment and the underdevelopment of sociology', part of a larger work on the Latin American revolution published in 1969; and the also brief *Lumpenbourgeoisie, Lumpendevelopment*, published in 1972. The trouble with this category is that, as Frank explains, while he was in Chile and presumably immersed in the Latin American *problématique*, he initiated his attempts to carry his researches on to a world stage from which eventually resulted works that go significantly beyond his initial historical and conceptual perspectives, although this did not detach him from his Latin American preoccupations and he published *Mexican Agriculture, 1521–1630* in 1979.

Be that as it may, and as this lingering interest in Latin America can be described as a quite common case of dialectical overlap indicating mere changes of emphases, the second group takes in a trio of works that have as fulcrum *Dependent Accumulation and Underdevelopment*, written in two laps in 1969–70 and 1972–73, and published in 1978: *Towards a Theory of Capitalist Underdevelopment*, a derivation from the previous work in the first lap, published in 1975; and *World Accumulation, 1492–1789*, also derived from the first work but from the second lap, also published in 1978.

The third general category of Frank's works are those which, following upon the fundamental labours and cornerstones of previous years, have undertaken the analysis of contemporary interrelated world events and processes. The most significant of these works are *Crisis in the World Economy* (1980), *Crisis in the Third World* (1981), and a collection of essays on a variety of themes chronicling the ebb-and-flow of his politico-intellectual fortunes, entitled *Critique and Anti-critique: essays on dependence and reformism* (1984). To be quite thorough we should also mention a long list of 'discussion papers' which Frank published while at the University of East Anglia, but these are, in the main, chapters taken from the works in the third group.

From the start, Frank was clear on two points concerning Latin America: his own revolutionary ardour, which was partially a contagion from the Cuban revolution, and his conviction that capitalism underdevelops, expressed in the opening salvo of his work on Brazil and Chile: 'I believe, with Paul Baran, that it is capitalism, both world and national, which produced underdevelopment in the past and which still generates underdevelopment in the present.' From this it followed, as day does night, that he would also do his best to stimulate and defend revolutionary change, and that the best way to do it intellectually would be to refute the concept of feudalism as applied to Latin American history. Baran had toyed with a 'feudalist' model to explain underdevelopment, but he had discarded it for the wider notion of world capitalism. Aside from that, he never actually took a strong stand on the issue of feudalism. Frank would. Halperin-Donghi surely exaggerates when he attributes to Frank 'a violent rejection of all Latin American intellectual and ideological tradition'. Frank's iconoclasm and rebelliousness were perfectly in line with a tradition of Latin American 'nay-saying' going back even to such pre-independence figures as Manco Capac, A. Nariño, M. Gual, J. M. España, J. M. Morelos, M. Hidalgo, and many others, who manifested a sometimes rootless lashing out at the system and at its established conventions.

Halperin-Donghi is perhaps closer to the truth when he suggests that Frank represents the perfect ideological pendant to Debray's musings, later recanted, on the correct strategy for the revolutionary conquest of power in Latin America. Frank's fulminations, which probably began with his onslaught in *Monthly Review* in

1963 on one more of countless repetitive appeals by Latin American intellectuals to the explanatory value of the idea of feudalism, despaired of any fruitful political action other than the decisive triumph of the 'massess'. They were emitted at a time when, as Cardoso and Faletto perceived, such a possibility had been proving futile, as it would go on doing during the following decade. In 1984, Frank would admit that his essays from 1968 to 1973 were done 'in an attempt to defend a hopefully still revolutionary position against reformism and the necessarily reactionary and successful reaction it generates'.

It is important to keep all this in mind, because the ideological debate in Latin America during the late 1960s and early 1970s was as much about political action as it was about the reality of Latin American history and society. Here again it is inaccurate to displace Frank from his well-earned Latin American patch, and his further Marxian admission 'that the point in interpreting the world is to change it' harks back to Mariategui's defiant statement that all his essays, regardless of the subject, were political.[132] How did Frank's war on the socio-historical category of feudalism, which after all was a long-standing Latin American Marxist near-dogma, contribute to his vision of a revolutionary strategy?

Given its briefness, Baran's critical presentation of world-historical capitalism was necessarily sketchy. It did not go into details on how capitalism actually underdeveloped. Marxists in Latin America had usually accepted the idea that capitalist relations of production were a historical step forward. What they defined as 'feudalism' – a mixed-bag concept fusing colonial institutions such as *mita* and *encomienda* with the useless dilapidation of surplus – was considered to be retardatory especially in alliance with imperialism. Therefore, the bourgeoisie and the urban middle classes were sometimes seen as objectively progressive and potentially revolutionary in the long run. Frank took it upon himself to demonstrate what he saw as the essential kernel of truth in Baran's position. To do this he had to ablate from Latin American Marxism any residual illusion it still had about capitalism, and this necessitated making deductions and extrapolations from the 'wider Marxist canon' and applying them to Latin American history. (This was, incidentally, his only real departure from what Halperin-Donghi calls the 'Latin American intellectual and ideological tradition'.)

Latin American history, in Frank's view, was subject to the forging of two sets of chains of domination and exploitation: the first of these chains was the colonial satellization of nascent countries such as Brazil and Chile by the fully operative forces of international 'merchant capitalism', starting in the sixteenth century. But this subjection was economically meaningless without what he called 'domestic polarization', in which the second set of chains were clapped on the 'internal colonies' of the subsidiary centres of metropolitan political and economic control.

The over-arching structure led to different 'concrete' situations. In Chile it produced latifundia in the interior and some rudimentary manufacturing activity with owner/worker relations in the towns. In Brazil, with its potential for a European-style internal economic evolution in the eighteenth century, it established underdeveloping industrial monopolies and it placed the colonial economy on the frail foundations of sugar production in the North-East and gold-mining in the central interior. With the coming of independence, Chile's efforts to develop were undermined by free trade and the externally imposed reliance on the export of nitrates and minerals. This was a replication or a carry-over of the colonial metropolis/satellite relationship. In Brazil, coffee was the instrument of further international satellization, and industry instead of being socially integrating became the catalyst of sharper internal polarizations, to which foreign capital contributed decisively. Imperialist retrenchment provoked by the Great Depression of the 1930s resulted in what Frank labelled 'active involution', which finally dissolved in the intensification of foreign capitalist penetration and control.[133]

These processes were given the catchy overall designation of 'the development of underdevelopment'. They were the specific playing out of the scenario that Baran outlined, in which underdevelopment was the other side of the European-minted coin of development. The die of economic progress had been cast with the two sides: on one side, it showed that once capitalism got going it could only beget underdevelopment outside its metropolitan centres; on the other side, it showed that the development of capitalism could only continue on the sweaty backs of the inhabitants of underdeveloped lands. In Baran's murky vision the personae of history were like spectres entering and exiting national stages, especially so in the countries of the Third World. That is why his ultimate explanation of the origins of the inter-cultural development gap was vaguely 'environmental', vaguely 'culturalist'. Frank's fulfilment of his 'programme' in so far as it referred not to underdevelopment in general but to the underdevelopment of Chile and Brazil (applicable by analogy and research to all Latin America) had to be more specific than that. Frank also had to contend with the seemingly superficial but really crucial objection that in his 'satellization' outline, the Chilean/Brazilian pattern, had not obtained everywhere.

'From the Netherlands down to the Indian village'

Frank did not agree with the Cardoso/Faletto distinction between 'enclaves' and less manipulable national economic structures. For him, Argentina was not developed – point blank. Brazil, despite its social complexities and its gigantic geographic mass, was simply a satellite. The Brazilian upper classes were wasteful and sluggish coffee-vendors; the Chileans, incompetent brokers of solidified dung. In his view, Brazil had had various opportunities to develop: during the late-nineteenth-century coffee boom, during the world depression in the 1930s, and during the Second World War. In all cases, after an initially promising beginning, external capitalist forces had intervened to strangle industrialization and to reinforce Brazil's status as an economic satellite, and the internal forces and tendencies that could have propitiated growth were either too weak or too compromised to do anything about it. This etched deeper the Baran image of the spectrality of the political and economic actors in underdeveloped countries, but Frank accompanied it with a model including the following hypotheses: (1) that economic satellization limited the possibility of economic development; (2) that the link of dependence between metropoles and satellites was weakest, and less obstructive to development, in times of world economic crisis, but also that it could not be cut entirely and in due course full dependence would be reimposed; (3) that the degree of underdevelopment was directly proportional to the closeness of a region's ties to the metropolis in the past.[134] These propositions were mostly proffered without historical substantiations. The concepts involved were imprecise or undefined. But what was really most damaging was that there were sufficient historical examples to disprove the gist of what they were claiming, that is, that the functioning of the world capitalist system – whatever exactly that was, for Frank had not actually taken the trouble to circumscribe it with precision – made economic development impossible or useless and that politics that were not revolutionary and violent were impotent or useless.

Frank could get away with ladling out these ideological lumps because Latin American Marxists were willing to accept them in the lingering radical climate of the late 1960s and they flocked to his field kitchen in droves. But he could not escape the dilemma of the developing to metropolitan status of a nation that, like the United States, had the same satellite roots as its southern neighbours. Here was the real historical and ideological crux and here too one of his basic ideas on the 'development of underdevelopment'; he referred to it in the opening chapter of *Lumpenbourgeoisie, Lumpendevelopment*, in the third chapter of *World Accumulation and Underdevelopment*, and in the 'Preface' to *World Accumulation, 1492–1789*. He discovered two possible solutions: one was 'Weberian', intimating differences between the colonizers themselves, which he haughtily dismissed; the other one was 'suggested by Smith and Marx', and it applied particularly to Mexico and Peru. In these countries, the Spanish discovery of 'gold and silver and a pre-existing socially organized and technologically knowledgeable work-force whose exploitation through less-than-subsistence wages. . .permitting the expansion of commerce and the accumulation of capital in the European metropoles, required a certain mode of production and diverse institutional forms in the colonies in changing historical circumstances'.

Why didn't the English colonies follow the 'Spanish example'? In his first treatment of the issue, Frank averred that English colonists had not found those 'factors' in their own territories, but on further examination he discovered that the absence of those 'productive and exchange relations' in New England, which was due to the 'benign neglect' of the metropole, had permitted its development in combination with 'its particular "semi-peripheral" intermediate (as per Wallerstein) or "proto-subimperialist" insertion and participation in the process of world accumulation, associated with its particular role in the triangular trade, which permitted an important merchant capital accumulation and its subsequent investment in industrialization in the New England and Middle Atlantic colonies'.

Frank did not explain exactly why such a powerful metropole as Great Britain had allowed this to happen: why it had allowed the North American republic to prosper, and why it had preferred to underdevelop the less productive Latin American republics. So he went back again to the Latin American colonial situation and asked why its creators had implanted 'single-crop export economies activated by low-salaried labour establishing thus a mode of production and a colonial relation of interchange, not unlike the Mexican and Peruvian, that generated the development of underdevelopment in Brazil, the Caribbean and the South but not the North of the US? Because these regions offered the potential for this sort of exploitation of labour and capital accumulation although only with an initial outlay of capital and the importation of manpower that could not be justified and would not have been without the resulting benefits and the necessary degree and kind of exploitation.' His theory, therefore, combined the natural and social determination of externally imposed underdeveloping 'modes of production', which apparently carried in them the seeds of irresistible historical perpetuation through changing historico-political situations and circumstances. It seemed to apply squarely to Latin America, but only by negative inference to the USA, which had developed mainly in the absence of the unfortunate circumstances that had determined Iberian colonialism. Political independence in Latin America did not change the basic underlying economic structure, and the continuation of the external linkages had only served to reinforce it. Whatever changes occurred in the 'superstructure' had little effect on the 'base' and on the nature of the imperialist connection, and none on the foredoomed nature of Latin American underdevelopment.[135] Even if we obviate the rather imprecise utilization of the concept of MOP, all of this still left standing the quintessential Marxist category of Latin American feudalism.

Every time that Frank employed the phrase 'mode of production' in the Latin American colonial context, the temptation was there to read 'feudalism' into it, at least from an 'orthodox' Marxist point of view. In opposing this, Frank raised the primary set of chains that fettered Latin America. Disregarding the vexed issue of what exactly is capitalism and when it came into being (which Baran had also done), he claimed that it was 'capitalism' that had discovered and colonized America. It was also capitalism, therefore, that had created the plantations and the mining centres everywhere, and it was capitalism in two incontestable ways: in the sense that the surplus from exploitation accrued to the home of capitalism in Europe, and in the sense that in whatever form it took, whether through wages or through enforced labour or even through slavery, exploitation was ultimately the handiwork of capitalism. After Frank, it became a commonplace in Latin American revolutionary tracts to illustrate the structure of capitalist/imperialist world domination by invoking the calloused hands of the lowliest peasant picking the lowliest cotton-bud or coffee berry in the remotest corner of the remotest plantation in the globe, or as Bagchi ironically put it: the 'Netherlands down to the Indian village' view. Frank was slightly less hyperbolic: 'Even the indigenous people of Latin America, whose supposed non-market subsistence economy is so often said to isolate them from national life, find themselves fully integrated into the same capitalist international imperialism.'

What Frank was in effect proclaiming through his ostensibly academic research programme was that capitalist exploitation, having already reached out to all accessible mankind in all possible and conceivable ways of life and work, had gone the limits of its possibilities and was ripe for overthrowal. If the lowliest peasant was already 'fully integrated' into the 'system' and as fully subjected to exploitation as the most over-zealous Detroit card-puncher, what strength could the whole evil global machine have left in its nuts and bolts? There was really nothing remaining but to liberate them. Lenin had implied approximately the same thing, but Frank had the advantage in that his call to revolution came after fifty years during which capitalism had had more time to tighten the noose around its own neck. In all this there was even the glorious underlying historical absurdity that since, as Frank claimed, capitalism was behind the whole Spanish enterprise in America, then it could be inferred that revolution had been advisable and theoretically possible in the sixteenth and in any of the subsequent centuries. But Frank was not really interested in these ideological minutiae. His exertions were 'specifically directed at important problems of political analysis and policy'. His criticism was peppered with phrases like 'scientifically unacceptable', 'politically disastrous', and 'real national liberation movements'. His real target was not so much 'feudalism', the communists' own bugbear, as the 'national bourgeoisie', which in his view was the political lotus-flower that was paralysing the will of the revolution.

The conundrum of the bourgeoisie

What was this 'bourgeoisie' that so exercised Marxists on so many different fronts? For Marx, the bourgeoisie operated behind the scenes of power in each European country. He never explained whether the bourgeoisie was one or many, whether the bourgeoisie of all advanced capitalist countries would eventually merge or fight it out behind their respective frontiers, whether, in brief, it put profits or politics above all else. In the event, he tended not to distinguish between them, and for that he had been accused of neglecting the question of nationalism.[136] Bourgeoisies were self-generated through burgeoning capitalist forces and the concept of 'local bourgeoisie', in the twentieth-century sense of 'lesser' or 'artificially created', would probably have been problematic for him.

For Lenin, the concept presented fewer difficulties, because he was convinced that capitalism in its imperialist stage had reached its historical pinnacle and that, whether bourgeoisies existed or not in the colonies and 'semi-colonies', the centres of capitalism could mostly do with them as they wanted. They were ideologically irrelevant but not strategically so, since they could act as a bulwark against imperialism with the right sort of communist stimulation and support. Consequently, the Comintern and afterwards Stalin, who were both to a significant extent Lenin's creatures, acted in accordance and sometimes played up and sometimes played down the importance of 'local bourgeoisies', which were like a flowering of mushrooms around a rotted tree trunk. By contrast, local communists on their own, though they were often obliged to accept Moscow's changes of moods, normally inclined to view 'local bourgeoisies' with some respect (some of the exceptions, as in China in the 1920s and in El Salvador in the 1930s, paid bitterly in blood and suffering), and this was especially so in Latin America after the Second World War. The fear of the bourgeoisie abated somewhat with the victory of Castro in Cuba (there was also then in circulation the Maoist dictum about 'paper tigers'), but 'true' Marxists, those who had read the master or knew their history, were never truly convinced that you could just snap your fingers at the bourgeoisie. Besides, Latin Americans were used to hating 'Yankee imperialism' and even Latin American Marxists never felt comfortable when it was suggested that their principal enemy could be at home sleeping beside them.

For a long time Moscow had obliged by blaming everything on the USA not coincidentally at the height of the Cold War. During the 1960s, however, the insurrectionary strategy that the left flirted with and frequently adopted, *ipso facto* brought it into conflict with the bourgeoisie, and this had to be justified and understood if extremist momentum was not to be dissipated. Not all were interested in this. Cardoso and Faletto were not. But Frank's theories were expressly designed to that end. To start with they did not give up 'Yankee imperialism'. On the contrary: they offered a streamlined if history-laden version of world capitalism. Capitalism was at the base of underdevelopment and it still was the principal brake on economic progress. Only socialism could save Latin America, and Frank denied that socialism had to wait for the bourgeoisie to finish its work as the historical agent of economic progress. Capitalism had already done its best and worst, and the bourgeoisie's task was ended: 'If the structure and development of the world capitalist system have long since incorporated and underdeveloped even the furthest outpost of "traditional" society and no longer leave any room for classical national and modern state capitalist development independent of imperialism, then the contemporary structure of capitalism also does not provide for the autonomous development of a national bourgeoisie independent enough to lead (or often to take part in) a real national liberation movement or progressive enough to destroy the capitalist structure of underdevelopment at home. If there is to be a "bourgeois" democratic revolution and the elimination of capitalist underdevelopment, then it can no longer be the bourgeoisie in any of its guises which is capable of making this revolution. The historical mission and role of the bourgeoisie in Latin America – which was to accompany and to promote the underdevelopment of its society and of itself – is finished.'[137] This was a 'logical' if far-fetched deduction from the idea that capitalist exploitation had reached the farthest recesses of the territories under its domination and was extracting as much surplus from its masses as could be expected, and the 'logical' ideological riposte to this situation was to pair total exploitation with the total superfluity of the bourgeoisie, thus closing the cycle of history and the revolution.

But was it true that peasants all over Latin America had reached on average the peak of advancement that they could aspire to, which in Frank's scheme was no advancement at all but eternal miserable servitude? And had capitalism truly exhausted all possibilities of further development? Had the bourgeoisie in Latin America run out of ideas and of capital and of all other resources for industrialization and economic development? And even if all these questions were to be answered in the affirmative, did this necessarily mean that revolution was around the corner and 'that the role of promoting historical progress has now fallen to the masses of the people alone' and that to play along with the bourgeoisie (the alternative inevitably having to be armed struggle) was 'treacherous or treachery'? Needless to say, these statements put Frank's writings into the correct context, which was academic and investigative only in form.

The problems of world accumulation

Frank's Latin American period ended with the overthrow of Allende, but by then he had already shifted his attention towards the mightier problems of historical capitalist accumulation and the origins of world underdevelopment. What motivated this shift? Frank wrote in the 'Preface' to *Capitalism and Underdevelopment in Latin America* of the 'need in the underdeveloped and socialist countries for the development of a theory and analysis adequate to encompass the structure and the development of the capitalist system on an integrated world scale and to explain its contradictory development which generates at once economic development and underdevelopment in international, national, local and sectorial levels'. Whether this implies or not a burning concern with accumulation per se, the facts as he described them are that he felt at the time that placing Latin America (and specifically Chile and Brazil) in a historical context that explained underdevelopment, left virtually untouched the complementary question of how the underdevelopment of Latin America and of the rest of the Third World, on the one hand, was made possible in its origins by world capitalist accumulation, and how in turn the process of underdevelopment became forcibly integrated as a necessary component in the ongoing historical process of world capitalist accumulation. In other words, he had not made clear enough that development and underdevelopment are parts of the same process. This lack was also pointed out to him in 1969 by S. Amin – at the time busily writing his own *Accumulation on a World Scale* – with his criticism that in Frank's approach to accumulation he was 'failing to differentiate and analyse the main stages of capitalist development adequately'. From this self-critical awareness emerged the two 1978 books that we have mentioned as being part of the second phase in Frank's intellectual evolution: *Dependent Accumulation and Underdevelopment* and *World Accumulation, 1492–1789.*

In the first, Frank explained that he was working towards 'the integration of dependence and underdevelopment within the world process of accumulation', which he divided into three stages or periods: mercantilist (1500–1770), industrial capitalist (1770–1870) and imperialist (1870–1930). The specific object he had in mind was 'to proceed historically from one stage of world capitalist development to another and through the analysis of the relationship between production and exchange relations. . .to examine on the one hand the differential contribution of each of the major world regions to the world process of capital accumulation during each of its major stages of development, and on the other hand to analyse the underdeveloping consequences of this participation in world accumulation for each of the major regions of the now underdeveloped "third world"'. This work included three theoretical essays, each one juxtaposed and corresponding to one of the three periods mentioned, on what Frank considered to be the essential issues raised by world accumulation in those periods. They were titled respectively: 'On the roots of development and under-development in the New World: Smith and Marx v. the

Weberians'; 'That the extent of the internal market is limited by the international division of labour and the relations of production'; and 'Multilateral merchandise, trade imbalances and uneven economic development'.

The other work, *World Accumulation, 1492–1789*, was a more profound historical exploration of the first period delimited in the other book. It was part of an exhaustive project that would have explored the process of capitalist accumulation to our days, but it was cut short by the events of 1973 in Chile. It can be considered definitive, at least for the period concerned, in a way that *Dependent Accumulation and Underdevelopment* is not because of the relative brevity of its historical studies. However unfinished Frank may have considered his speculations from the perspective of his original intentions, it can hardly be denied that both works contain a thorough examination of the issues that were foremost in his mind. To understand them fully, it is necessary to do a bit of backtracking.[138]

The process of 'primitive accumulation'

Given that Marx defined capitalism as a discrete historical mode of production, that is, one among various analogous historical formations, he had to explain, and indeed partially explained, three things: (1) primitive accumulation, or how the capitalist mode of production came to be; (2) simple reproduction, or how it replicated itself in time; and (3) expanded accumulation, and reproduction, or how it tended to evolve historically. For her theory on imperialism, Rosa Luxemburg started with the second of these concepts and with the idea that in any stable Marxist reproduction model there always arose an excess of surplus value that predicated the existence of non-capitalist formations. Baran suggested that primitive accumulation already implied or involved a form of capitalist exploitative expansion from Europe to the rest of the world. In a murky and unspecified way capitalist accumulation in general, which might or might not have been the same as reproduction, perpetuated colonial, semi-colonial and neo-colonial exploitation. Marx had defined primitive accumulation as the process whereby producers were alienated from their means of production, and even though he hinted that colonialism contributed to reproduction (or accumulation in the vague Baran sense) – allusions which Frank collected throughout the text of *World Accumulation, 1492–1789* – nothing in his work warrants modifying his essential definitions of primitive accumulation and of reproduction, which means that he saw the process of the birth and replication of capitalism as essentially self-sustaining and West European, and it also means that Baran's latitudinarian view of these concepts was transpositional and theoretically unfounded, even if there might have been hermeneutic precedents for his usages.[139]

These conceptual manipulations entered in a not-too-rigorous manner, as did other transpositions of Marxian ideas, into the motley realm of dependency ideology, where all that was required of ideas was that they should serve to prove, and reprove, the polymorphous 'reality' of economic imperialism. It is likely that S. Amin – on the direct or indirect prompting of Baran, for Amin was indisputably in the large group of theorists affiliated to *Monthly Review* – was the first to work systematically with these conceptual transpositions, as we shall see further on, but it is also true that Frank's entry into the field of accumulation theory was spontaneous and perfectly consistent with his dependency concerns. It could even be argued that, in order to defend and sustain all of his work on Latin American underdevelopment, it was absolutely necessary that he explain how it was that he saw underdevelopment generally as indispensable to the functioning of the world capitalist economy from its start, and even perhaps to the origins of capitalism itself. Accumulation for him, therefore, was not a superfluous area of study but an intrinsic part of his ideological system, and it was inescapable, to boot, in order to bring some coherence and logic into his reiterated if always inferential affirmation that capitalism was fully operational in the European conquest and colonization of America.

The one thing that Frank can never be faulted on is not stating problems explicitly or not making direct precise questions, and this was a practice he applied in *World Accumulation*, the work which, more than the others of the same phase, grapples directly and *in extenso* with these issues. This is not to say that his answers were equally precise. To start with, he managed in his 'Conclusions' to evade the problem of the origins of capitalism, and he did it without giving in to his critics or giving up on his pretensions of fidelity to Marx. In order to do this he visited the usual places where Marx himself wiggled and fudged with nebulous references to medieval Italian city-states or to the creation of a world market in the sixteenth century. But he could not really cope with the conundrum of how to square his vision of capitalist colonial plunder with the process of primitive accumulation, which Marx saw occurring principally or even solely in Europe, so he took a saving way out, declaring that 'The extent of the single, worldwide process of capital accumulation and of the capitalist system it has formed over several centuries remains an important open question', or that 'The question of when and how original precapitalist, primitive accumulation of capital became [the starting point of] the capitalist process of capital accumulation remains substantially open'. Frank's deliberate equivocations disengaged accumulation per se from the convolutions of primitive accumulation, in fact he fused accumulation and reproduction, and this freed him to cut a wide swath in skirmishes in which he could put all his polemical skills into action.

There were two doubtful questions to be disposed of here. One had to do with Frank's insistence on the essential or ultimately capitalist nature of exploitation through non-capitalist economic formations, which to any Marxist ear would have sounded heretical or even nonsensical. The other was the emphasis he placed, in situations of underdevelopment, on the decisive influence of external forces, which again some Marxists found one-sided and exaggerated. On the first point he had various arguments to hand, some of which plunged the depths of Marxian sophistry. For instance, he argued that, depending on how it was defined, 'precapitalist' could signify 'non-capitalist' or 'part capitalist', 'but in either event, non-capitalist need not be pre-capitalist, since it can also be simultaneous with capitalist accumulation or even post-capitalist', with which he apparently was adducing both evidence from historical facts and deduction from abstract logic. (If precapitalist equals non-capitalist and part capitalist, then non-capitalist did not rule out capitalist.)

To make the argument stick Frank distinguished between 'primary accumulation', to which non-capitalist production could contribute, and 'precapitalist primitive accumulation and production', by which he retained the original Marxist concept without diminishing the importance of non-capitalist colonial booty to general capitalist accumulation. 'Such primary accumulation, based in part on production through non-capitalist relations of production', he concluded, 'has been a frequent, if not constant, companion of the capitalist process of capital accumulation even in its developed stage of the dominance of wage labour and later of relative surplus value.' What was more, even in our times non-capitalist relations of production were important for the capitalist process of accumulation (reproduction in Marx's schema) through: '(1) the sustenance and, in time of need, provision of a potential reserve army of labour and pool of labour power; (2) the contribution to the sustenance and the reproduction of wage labour power for which capital pays a less-than-subsistence wage that is too low for the wage labourer's sustenance and reproduction (as in "non-capitalist village production" in underdeveloped countries); and (3) the use of non-capitalist "socialist" relations of production to produce value that enters into the world capitalist process of capital accumulation'.

This last point had to do with the question of the extent to which the communist world participated in or contributed to the capitalist world market, which had already been raised by Amin when Frank adverted to it and was to be taken into account also by Wallerstein. The finished statement on the whole issue was summarized in this matter: 'In so far as relations of production – in relation to exchange and realization – are the significant criterion, it is the transformation of the relations of production, circulation, and realization through their incorporation into the process of capital accumulation that is, in principle, the relevant criterion of the existence of capitalism.' But, in the end, Frank went back to the beginning of the discussion when he reaffirmed his position, stated in *Capitalism and Underdevelopment in Latin America*, that, whatever the formal manifestations, the exploitation of peasants and slaves was ultimately capitalist because it 'contributed to the primitive and then the industrial accumulation of capital concentrated in particular parts of the system and times of the process'.[140]

The other large question Frank felt compelled to consider – the one 'posed by those who argue that relations of production are "internal" and therefore determinant' – he translated into the relative opposition between production and circulation, that is, whether internal relations of production or external relations of exchange were determinant in the development of underdevelopment (although the specific reference to the latter phenomenon was only implicit in the text). His answer was that, since both modalities were part of 'a single mechanism of accumulation and the development of a single world capitalist system', the question was 'irrelevant', but that the thesis of the predominance of internal relations was 'questionable'. In fact, though, what he did was to beg the question by assuming that internal relations of production were subservient to the general process of capitalist accumulation, which in his unshakeable view was crucially dependent on imperialist exploitation. Rather than to point out the inconsistencies and the tortured logic, we feel it is more instructive to indicate that what Frank achieved was to incorporate the history or more accurately the 'prehistory' of the Third World into Marx's sequential scheme of primitive accumulation and reproduction and to make it a necessary if subordinate part in the historical process of capitalism since its inception.

This was somewhat analogous to what R. Luxemburg had done, except for two points, one of which made Frank's construct problematical: Luxemburg attributed the same necessity for non-capitalist socio-economic formations to the expanded reproduction of capital, but she expressly limited it to the period of full development of capitalism during the nineteenth century, whereas Frank took it back to the start of colonialism; and while Luxemburg foresaw that the equilibrium that the non-capitalist areas permitted capitalism to maintain (in the sense of absorbing excess surplus) would eventually be broken – when these areas in turn became capitalist, thus raising once again the problem of surplus – Frank's system did not have an escape valve, because, since under capitalism underdevelopment was fixed for eternity, capitalism could carry on indefinitely by squeezing the Third World with varying strength according to the needs of the capitalist centre, and the only conceivable way out was the only one not forthcoming, despite Frank's intense gropings: the revolutionary political action of the masses. It could be said that the circumstance that made all the difference between Luxemburg and Frank was that in the years intervening between them the USSR had come into existence, and with this a most authoritative precendent for the possibility of accelerating the world revolutionary process.

Finally, in connection with these ideas, another flaw in Frank's scheme was that it established, with regard to the hypothesis of the interaction between the developed centre and the underdeveloped periphery, that the centre loosened its hold on the periphery in times of recession or warfare, precisely when it would have been logical to expect the tightening of economic bondage. Without regard for consistency, Frank would espouse precisely the opposite point of view in his *Crisis* books.

The 'crisis' of capitalism

If Frank had two unassailable attitudes towards Latin American reality, he had one single conviction concerning world capitalism in the late 1970s, and that was that capitalism was exhausted and on the brink of a historical collapse. This reflected traditional Marxist millenialism, which was something that could be read into Marx himself and which motivated much of the writing on turn-of-the-century imperialism, including Lenin's, and Trotsky's ideas on permanent revolution. Millenialism was at a peak in Latin

America after Castro, and Frank carried with him, if not his Latin American revolutionary illusions, his Marxist hopefulness about the final scuttling of capitalism when he climbed the heady heights of the world-system. His two *Crisis* books are founded on this persuasion.

Crisis in the World Economy is devoted on the whole to trends and policies in the capitalist core, although it touches on their consequences for the Third World; but it is *Crisis in the Third World*, a companion volume to the first, that centres on the main themes of our research, and it is the one that we shall briefly consider. The principal idea there, and one which in one way or another pervaded every Marxist work on the theory of economic imperialism since its inception, but which Frank apparently did not share at first, was that when international capitalism enters a 'crisis of accumulation' it intensifies its exploitation of the labouring masses in the less developed parts of the world. According to Frank, the world crisis he had in mind had started in 1967, it had become acute in the early 1970s, and it had been given a sort of *coup de grâce* with the oil crises of 1973–74 and of the late 1970s. If this meant austerity and unemployment in the first world, it provoked the implantation of 'new' forms of domination and exploitation in the Third World, which became a necessary prop for the survival of world capitalism. This was made possible by the further thwarting of development. Mexico, owing to its nearness to the raw power of the USA, had always been a storehouse of raw materials and of agricultural produce. Argentina missed the historical boat because it had preferred exports to high tariffs, which its powerless labour movement could not impose and which, by way of contrast, had been possible in Australia. Brazil had left Argentina far behind in industrialization, but it had failed to expand the internal market despite more than two decades of classic capitalist development policies.

One significant effect of world capitalism had been the distorting influence of 'agribusiness' in the Third World, which steered underdeveloped economies away from self-sufficiency and towards the export of cash-crops. To keep the system in working order, capitalism had fostered the formation of regional 'subimperialist' powers such as Brazil, Israel and Iran. Political interest stimulated development from the outside in the Asian 'gang of four'. These peripheral manifestations of economic vitality were analogous in reverse to the way in which historically the core of capitalism had shifted from Northern Italy in the High Middle Ages through Spain and Portugal in the fifteenth and sixteenth centuries to Northern

Europe in the seventeenth and eighteenth centuries, resulting in the 'semi-peripheralization' of the previous core regions. The modern 'semi-peripheries' were a working backwards of the process, as it were, but with no real development content. In the periphery itself, the greater the exploitation the greater the need for internal political repression and, to that end, peripheral states were activist and strong, although always willing to defer to the pressures of the multinationals.[141]

History and contemporary reality were at odds with these interpretations. There was no proof that capitalism was hanging on by the skin of the Third World's teeth. The 'crisis' that Frank diagnosed was a cycle trough, and if profits and rates of return were down they subsequently bounded back to the heights of the late 1980s. The problem of development in the Third World does not seem to be so much one of external 'super-exploitation' as of a lack of efficient utilization of both natural and human resources, and at any rate, as J. Robinson, G. Kay and others have pointed out, developed capitalism is more interested in its own markets than in those of the Third World.[142] Capitalist ups-and-downs in the core occur without significant long-term effects in one way or another on the permanently depressed conditions in the Third World, whose industrial 'mini-booms' often happen either against cycle trends in the centre (as during the depression in the 1930s whose peripheral effects Frank on the whole analysed correctly), or as a result of anomalous market conditions (as in OPEC countries during the late 1970s). If Frank's new-fangled theories on a core 'dependent' on the exploitation of the Third World to overcome its crises were true, the logical expected result, from his belief in the importance of external determination, should have been the thorough development of underdeveloped economies, or else their importance to the capitalist centre was being inflated.

The idea of 'peripheralization', which Frank borrowed from Wallerstein and which is a logical ideological correlative of 'sub-imperialism', does not stand up to historical scrutiny. The process of historical peripheralization of parts of Europe did by no stretch of the imagination deter the more significant and forward process of long-term overall European economic development, and the analogous inverse process of 'sub-imperialization' can hardly be read as a global accentuation of underdevelopment, even taking it on its own dubious terms. 'Subimperialism' has had a short and lamentable existence. The attribution of the 'subimperialist' condition to Mexico did not prevent the Sandinista victory in Nicaragua. Brazil's supposedly privileged position in the capitalist checkerboard did not preclude it from becoming the Third World's number-one debtor, experiencing periodic bankruptcy crises. Israel's existence is arguably the most destabilizing influence in the Middle East. And Iran's unforeseeable Islamic revolution put an inglorious finale to its regional hegemonic role.

In reference to the 'four Asian dragons', there can be no question that the seed of 'doomed' Hong Kong's development was nurtured internally, and that in the cases of the other members of the group external economic support would have gone to waste without the policy choices that those countries made. No labour movement in history has ever been the motive force behind protectionism, and Australia in particular did not develop behind a specially formidable tariff wall. It is true that the technological 'stinginess' of multinational corporations (MNCs) contribute significantly to Third World industrial stagnation, but it cannot be said that it is its principal cause. Third World political repression is a fact of life that cannot be correlated with periods of capitalist 'super-exploitation', and the notion that Third World governments habitually defer meekly to the interests of MNCs can be disproved with many examples, among which those of India and the Andean Pact, with their 'cordilleran' barriers to foreign capital, have front-rank value.

In fine, if A. G. Frank's intellectual evolution can legitimately be read as an attempt to interpret and apply P. Baran's outline on the origins of international economic inequality, it can only be described as very nearly a dismal failure, and was probably a throw-back, unwitting if you will, to some of the cruder levels of postwar Stalinist anti-imperialist argumentation. This interpretation gains considerable force from the fact that for Frank, at all stages in his intellectual evolution, the so-called socialist world and in particular the USSR have always seemed to represent a valid political and economic alternative model to capitalism, both in its advanced centres and in the Third World, an attitude, perhaps derived from his years in Latin America – where indigenous Marxists have usually had no qualms about condoning Soviet totalitarianism – which is not shared by fellow intellectuals such as Amin and Wallerstein, who incline towards an idealized but hazy notion of world socialism.[143]

The definition of dependency

In our analysis of Cardoso/Faletto and of Frank we have encountered two related but significantly divergent intellectual outlooks claiming the mantle of dependency theory. Before proceeding on our survey of neo-Marxist thought on underdevelopment, it would therefore be advisable to formulate a more precise definition of the concept and the theoretical contents of dependency. During the nineteenth century, the condition of dependency referred to colonies of conquest, at least in British usage. To Lenin it referred indistinctly to colonies and so-called semi-colonies, including the Latin American republics, a usage that continued through Comintern congresses and on to Stalinist dogma and propaganda. Baran, who respected the Marxist/Leninist historically restricted definition of imperialism, recurred to the idea of dependency for his long-view interpretation of the historical effects of capitalism on non-Western nations. This in effect raised dependency to the category of a theory.

In the early 1960s, some Latin American Marxist intellectuals were using the concept of dependency to designate the relations between American imperialism and the backward Latin American economies, which amounted to the application of Marxist socio-economic analysis and Marxist/Leninist imperialism theory to the independent history of Latin America. Somewhat loose, even fanciful, definitions of feudalism were an integral part of the model, which, however, mainly postulated the direct domination of Latin America by capitalist, principally Yankee, imperialism. Subsequently, Cardoso and Faletto took the idea of dependency and used it in a theory that attenuated the external imperialist connection and upgraded internal social processes and mechanisms in Latin America. Underdevelopment was still a function of dependency, but the possibility of capitalist development, albeit beset by distortions and social inequities, was not discarded. Finally, at this point in this work, Frank appropriated the dependency designation for a theory that, following Baran, traced the origins of underdevelopment to the early expansion of capitalism and posited that, under international capitalist relations, development was out of the question for the Third World. Frank accepted the idea of imperialist domination, but he rejected outright previous neo-Marxist Latin American social and historical analysis based on the operation of so-called feudal relations of production.

What in this pot-pourri 'legitimately' represents dependency theory? A definition encompassing all the above criteria could be that dependency is a national condition of economic alienation engineered through diverse means by international capitalism either producing or perpetuating underdevelopment, or at the very least, making development, even capitalist development, an uphill barely

Table 4.2 The evolution of dependency.

THE CONCEPT OF DEPENDENCY	
19th century	Dependency = colonies of conquest; two outlooks on colonialism/imperialism: positive (colonialist theorists) and negative (Hobson and the Socialist Press)
Lenin to Stalin (inc. Comintern)	Territories subjected to imperialist control and exploitation either as colonies or as semi-colonies (dependencies)
Latin American version (Paredes)	Sovereign countries subject to imperialist penetration

DEPENDENCY THEORY

THEORIES	Time and space references	Effects of dependency	Historical agents	Politics of dependency
Baran (1959)	World; from start of capitalist expansion in the 15th century	Permanent under-development	Capitalism	Revolutionary social change
LA theory (early 1960s)	Latin America: 19th and 20th centuries	Economic and political subjection to 'Yankee' imperialism	'Yankee' imperialism	Revolutionary social change
Cardoso/ Faletto (1960)	Latin America: 19th and 20th centuries	Internal socio-economic distortions but development possible	Capitalism	Political reform
Frank (1967–1979)	World; from start of capitalist expansion in 15th century	Permanent under-development	Capitalist forces and processes	Revolutionary social change
Wallerstein (1971–1989)	World; from start of capitalist world-system in 16th century	Peripheralization	Capitalist forces and processes	Vague thrust towards world socialism

possible struggle. If we denude dependency of its nineteenth-century and its Marxist/Leninist colonialist and imperialist overtones, then one crucial observation springs to mind, which is that economic development of the most sophisticated kind is possible even under conditions of extreme dependence, as in the case of Canada and, less markedly, of Brazil. However, in dealing with dependency theory we cannot simply go by semantical criteria, that is, we cannot escape its ideological context and, therefore, we are inevitably drawn back to the fact that dependency is a traditional Marxist designation for all backward countries, a condition barely less derogatory than that of colony. In other words, regardless of the abstract connotations of dependency, which would make the term applicable to nations across the development/underdevelopment divide, dependency theory must apply to underdeveloped lands. The examples of Canada and Brazil cannot serve to determine which analytical outlook rightly embodies dependency theory. It is from within the dependency camp as a whole that some guidance must be found.

Within dependency two basic versions can be discerned: (1) the extreme version with these features: external economic determination of internal socio-economic processes; political independence nearly meaningless; usually in our times, one general form of dependence contingent upon one basic international imperialism (rather than the 'four pillars' Leninist concept implying diverse rival imperialisms); inequality imposed; in sum, no development possible under capitalism; (2) the moderate version in which: the local ruling classes were and are as exploitative and as dominant as is economic imperialism in the other version; political independence creating social and political complications and ambiguities, not excluding class antagonisms and internal political manoeuvring; different types of dependency; in sum, inequality built into a system of interacting national and international forces that allow some margin for capitalist economic development (see Table 4.2). The first version is global in scope and historically dilated; the second is founded on the relatively limited model ideally but not necessarily exemplified solely by some Latin American countries and their histories. If we assume the validity of the moderate version, then dependency tolerates a wide choice of ideological stances, which brings it into close proximity to 'third-worldism' and could even be its most apposite expression. There are various obstacles to this assumption.

Some alleged 'dependentistas' (in particular, at this point in our analysis, those in dependency's radical Latin American wing) share on all points the fundamental criteria in the extreme version, albeit in a Latin American context, and they are reluctant to make a distinction between dependency and long-view economic imperialism. This has led some committed writers such as P. J. O'Brien and A. G. Frank (and some detached critics like C. Abel and C. Lewis) to insist on 'dependency' as a kind of Latin American school of thought on historical and contemporary capitalist imperialism or international capitalism, which for the committed are virtually indistinguishable tags. This classification had gained considerable acceptance. It is, however, subject to some important strictures. If dependency is fundamentally a theory on capitalist underdevelopment, then its specifically Latin American affiliation or origin is not really crucial to its meaning or its import, unless in addition it were postulated that Latin American underdevelopment constitutes a special category of its own, and this is not something that any of the previous writers would probably dare affirm; and even if they did, we would have to go back to the fact that dependency theorists themselves, even moderates like Cardoso and Faletto, do not claim any special traits for Latin American underdevelopment.

Finally, and probably conclusively, the adoption of the dependency category as synonymous with economic imperialism in all its historical and contemporary forms, far beyond Latin America's geographic and ideological bounds, means that, quite apart from the term's rigorously Marxist/Leninist lineage, it refers to a world-historical condition and it expresses a global analytical approach to underdevelopment, its origins and its history. What this connotes is that the specifically Latin American elaboration of dependency offered by Cardoso, Faletto, Sunkel and others, is perhaps not universally valid but applicable in different specific socio-historical circumstances, observed mostly in Latin America, but not necessarily definable exclusively by the condition of underdevelopment, or, at any rate, that it is simply less universally applicable than the second version of dependency. In other words, the only restrictive categorization of dependency is the one to which the concept and the general theory least applies, and it could justifiably lead, from a Marxist perspective, to an intellectual impasse.

Of the analytical trends we posited initially, the Baran/Frank view and the Latin American radicals all seem to have a more valid claim on the idea of dependency than the moderate Latin American version. This seems even likelier from the leftist affiliation of Cardoso and Faletto, which has made their ideas especially vulnerable to Marxist economic-imperialism criticism, and from G. Palma's painstaking but probably unavailing efforts, which we shall consider later on, to rescue the dependency designation from its simplistic over-use by revolutionary radicals. In the final analysis, dependency was and remains a radical anti-capitalist concept in its rightful context of neo-Marxist thinking on international relations, and the attempts to moderate its implications have not really been widely or consistently followed. The concept carries a momentum of its own, which usually ends up putting it in the same category as the general long-term view of economic imperialism.

Third World contributions to economic-imperialism theory

The 'periphery' cracks open an ideological 'core'

The perceptions and theories that both interpreted and affected the relations between, first, the West and the rest of the world's cultures and, afterwards, the relations between the advanced and the backward countries were, as we have seen, unmistakably Eurocentric in nature. This applies to pre-nineteenth-century perceptions of cultural differences, to the overarching concept of Eurocentrism, and to the early topical theory of economic imperialism. The cultures and nations that orbited around the West and around the developed core of the capitalist world willingly often meekly adopted Eurocentric attitudes and ideas. This usually involved a process of internalization of Eurocentric attitudes, which in the case of Latin American intellectuals was nearly spontaneous after a centuries-long connection with Spain and the rest of Western Europe and resulted sometimes in aberrations such as intra-cultural racism, and in the case of even those colonies with their own strong cultural identity, like India, led to the adoption of Western attitudes conducive to modernization, as in the early nineteenth-century Bengali educational movement founded by R. R. M. Roy or in the critical viewpoint of a historian such as Sir J. Sankar.[144]

The Latin American historical process can be described as a perfectly natural if lagging effort to follow in the West's footsteps, although we should not exaggerate this point, as the histories of Argentina and Uruguay are proof that at times it was possible to keep almost in step. The global diffusion of Marxism after its co-option of the theory of economic imperialism and especially after the triumph of Bolshevism in Russia, resulted in the assimilation by intellectuals in the less developed nations of yet new, basically Western ideas, which they adopted to their own ends and needs. Here again we should not, in the case of Latin

America, make too sharp a separation from the West, for after all late-nineteenth century socialism in Argentina was begotten by European immigration, was fostered by that country's considerable economic progress, was in line with the mainstream doctrines of the Second International, and even in a thinker like the Marxist J. B. Justo actively defended the flow of foreign capital for economic development.

In general, however, the coming of Soviet communism fostered the acceptance of new instruments of analysis for the interpretation of social reality in the backward lands. In the larger European Asian colonies Marxism prospered through an alliance with home-bred nationalism. In the pen of a Latin American intellectual such as Mariategui it became a creative tool, but, as in the case of the symbiosis communism/nationalism, Mariategui arguably did not innovate and his importance lies in his extraordinary ability to give patterned shape to a reality that others had been either ignoring or seeing in bulk, as when, for instance, the misery of the Peruvian Indians and peasants was seen to be either of their own making or an offensive manifestation of callous social injustice. All in all, the West taught other cultures and nations how to see and how to discern, and these peoples did it well but did not do it originally. There were few, if any, contributions from the periphery to the core.

This starts to change after the Second World War. The West itself changes. Through the pressures of decolonization and the strong global appeal of communism, apart of course from its own internal spontaneous reassessment of its world role, it steps down from its subjective Eurocentric eminence and transforms the old category of culturally backward into the new enlightened one of economically underdeveloped with a new academic discipline to go with it. But whereas previously the West monopolized the art of teaching and the contents of the textbooks, the periphery now begins to make valid contributions; it does not just assimilate. And this happens progressively in connection even with old Eurocentric concepts. Development economics, which could conceivably be interpreted as manifesting a cleaned-up, 'decontroversialized' version of Eurocentrism, was in truth a joint intellectual venture between the developed West and some of the more advanced countries in the developing world. Latin America had in practice 'pre-tested' all its developmental postulates and, in the figure of R. Prebisch, had given them authoritative sanction as well as the benefit of its experience. India too had experienced some degree of ISI and had its own brood of development economists and ideas. If ISI was a set of trial-and-error policies imposed on Latin America by the force of world events (two world wars and one depression), which was later elevated by development economics to the rank of doctrine, heavy industrialization, that is, the 'logical' move after ISI, was given its justification by Mahalanobis on the basis of 'externalities' plus the example of Soviet economic planning. In Western academic circles, economists of colonial extraction were actively contributing to development studies, as was the case of the Nobel-laureate West Caribbean-born Sir W. A. Lewis, one of the recognised pioneers of development economics, and of the more economically orthodox Burmese economist H. Myint.

The entrance of the Third World into the intellectual inner sanctum of Marxism was mostly barred when development economics was in its prime, in part at least because, from being a sophisticated Western ideology, it had been transformed into a Stalinist dogmatic fief where deviation or innovation was literally a crime. Outside the USSR, there was a great deal of Marxist theorization and debate that was pertinent in one way or another to the Third World, but only in a distinctly Eurocentric, indirect fashion: it contained 'implicit' applications, it 'suggested' or 'insinuated' approaches and angles of vision, the more apposite proposing an 'unorthodox' and 'formalistic' version of Marxism, which was ideally expressed in the Marxist conceptual transpositions in Baran, Frank and others. However, even the influential Baran model of underdeveloping world capitalism was ensconced amid his speculations on the structure and the mechanics of advanced capitalism and his criticism of Soviet practices.

The Third World finally managed to enter the field of Marxist theory through two crevices: the rise of third-worldism itself, in the flesh in Bandung and Belgrade, in theory in the works of such representative spokesmen as Nehru and Nkrumah, whose ideological 'amorphousness' propitiated a rapprochement with Marxism; and the gradual and not always complete emergence of Latin American radical thinking from its Stalinist fealty.[145] The breakthrough en masse came in the late 1960s and, from then on, Third World Marxism has flourished unabated even if, as we shall see, some of the more relevant Marxist work on underdevelopment is still being done, inevitably perhaps, in academic institutions in the capitalist centre. The point is that a core, as has happened before in history, was cracked open and a tendency of thought was widened or modified. Global economic integration, the 'one world' that both imperialism and anti-imperialism envisioned from different optics during the nineteenth century, finally corroded the ligaments of ideological 'monopolies' and 'cartels'.

The reasons for the passionate almost violent assumption by the Third World of Marxist ideology and Marxist instrumentalities are easy to identify: its own material and intellectual progress, even under colonialism, had prepared it for theorizing about itself with a certain margin of freedom from strictly Western moulds; historical Western models about the Third World, such as economic imperialism, had been as much or more about the West than about the Third World and were in need of renovation; and the spread of political independence and the development of political forces in the Third World had made ready the terrain for the transplantation and the flourishing of ideologies. These reasons were as valid for developmentalism as for Marxist theory. In the case of Latin America, that singular heteroclite world, the question should perhaps be why it had not pursued with more vigour its own individuation, or why it had taken it so long to come to its own summations – why, for instance, it had not seen fit, in inventing developmentalism *avant la lettre* to package it for the world at large. Perhaps again it was the pride and the leaden hand of internalized Eurocentrism.

When all is taken into account, these theories grew rank in the Third World not so much because they concerned the Third World, which they in fact most directly did, but because whether on the right or on the left they were basically political and, since the world had evolved into two battling ideological camps, there were interests and tendencies in the Third World ready to adopt them and work on them and with them enthusiastically. It remains to be seen how far Third World theorization really strayed from its Western models and the other ideological constraints from which it was trying to escape.

S. Amin's ambiguous elaboration of dependency ideas

Even as we take leave of Latin America, it will only seem like a fictive parting because by the start of the 1970s world Marxist theorization (again leaving the USSR on one side) was virtually if far from homogenously interlinked through a thick bundle of conceptual capillaries. There is perhaps no better illustration of the inter-connectedness of Marxist currents than the ideological and analytical links between Frank, S. Amin, and the Tunisian economist A. Emmanuel (the last two writing in French), through the mediation of a broad idea of dependency and a shared foundation of Marxist/Leninist convictions. Frank's shift from emphasizing dependency to concentrating on world accumulation, which signified transcending Latin America in order to gauge the advantages that the centres of capitalism derived from dependent economies – theoretically a reorientation of research within the same system – was logical and necessary. Even though Amin's studies of capitalist accumulation anteceded Frank's and were published fully eight years before these, they seem on the whole less crucial as a continuation of the analyses in his 1955 doctoral dissertation. Amin can be considered a pioneer in the Third World invasion of Western ideological fiefdoms, but his further contributions, despite their volume and the acclaim from various Marxist quarters (including Mandel and Frank but not noticeably Wallerstein), were something of an anti-climax. They are contained in two works, both published in English by Monthly Review Press in 1973: *Accumulation on a World Scale* (originally in French, 1970) and *Unequal Development* (also in French, 1973).

In his dissertation, Amin had explained how capitalism during the nineteenth and twentieth centuries prevented the development of societies with 'non-capitalist structures'. Apart from referring to the social, economic and psychological features of such societies, he did not explain how the original differences in development came about, and he did not in any way connect the birth and evolution of Western capitalism with the economic retardation of the rest of the world. In the first of his two subsequent works, there was little change from this fundamental historical perception, but he did shed the notion of 'psychological structure' (which, in fairness, he had not unduly emphasized in his dissertation) and he incorporated some new ideas into his intellectual baggage. There were also some changes of emphasis and of priorities. Although previously he had not perceived development economics per se – perhaps because the policies it envisioned coincided with his own, and he repudiated the essential possibilist persuasions of developmentalism – he now recognized it and consigned it to a sub-heading of 'marginalism', which was in line with his new radicalism. This consisted, among other things, in the importance he attributed to the transfer of surplus from the periphery to the centre of the capitalist system, and in his adoption of the formula of the development of underdevelopment. But these accretions did not mean exactly the same thing as in Frank, although they were part of a similar (but, in Amin, less boisterous) ideological and political rhetoric. The transfer of surplus was indeed related to accumulation in the centre, and it was intrinsic to the mechanics of the world capitalist system, but it did not have the cruciality and indispensability with which it had been endowed by Frank. And the development of underdevelopment referred to a process that had started during the Industrial Revolution, but did not go back earlier than the nineteenth century. It was more accurately the obstruction of development or, as he himself wrote, the 'blocking of transition' from 'pre-capitalist formations' (the phrase he now used in lieu of 'non-capitalist structures' or of mode of production) to 'autocentric' development.

On the specific issues of accumulation – on which Frank had at least clear definitional perspectives – Amin introduced some rather dubiously Marxist explanations. He identified 'accumulation' with 'expanded reproduction', but he described the exploitation of underdeveloped countries through surplus transfer as 'primitive accumulation' in the sense of emanating from pre-capitalist formations, and this had the effect of demoting the importance of the periphery to the dynamics of the centre. (Frank also used this connotation, undoubtedly in Amin's wake, but he did not give it more than secondary value.) Even though Amin acknowledged that capitalism in our days introduced high-technology industrialization into the exporting sectors of underdeveloped economies with a view to lowering its labour costs, he put the brunt of surplus transfer on unequal exchange, but he discarded the Prebisch thesis, which he had used in the dissertation, in favour of Emmanuel's less empirical, Marxist and class-oriented analysis. He elaborated further the sketchy outline he had suggested in his early thesis on the evolution of capitalism, from a robust competitive youthful phase in which the export of goods to the periphery was the norm, to the monopolistic phase in which the export of capital to stave off the tendency of the rate of profit to fall took a place of equal importance next to unequal trade in goods.

Finally, in considering the 'forces that adjust the periphery to the needs of accumulation in the centre', Amin delved deeper into the question of capitalist economic cycles, or the 'conjuncture', in his own terminology, and how they affected the Third World. Once again he arrived at a conclusion that was at the furthest possible remove from Frank's original hypotheses: that it was not the depression but the prosperity phase that permitted 'secondary growth' in underdeveloped economies, although in general he adhered to his fundamental and very likely thesis that, since underdevelopment was not 'dynamic', the cycle curve in the periphery was more attenuated than in the centre.[146]

Amin had still not explained how it was that the West had forged ahead of the other cultures of the world – a problem to which Baran and Frank had responded by stipulating that spontaneous development had been stifled by world-historical capitalism – so in *Unequal Development* he devised a quaint theory that described non-Western cultures as 'tribute-paying formations' characterized by a concordance or compatibility between non-despotic social organizations and productive forces. In Europe, on the contrary, feudalism, despite or because of its violent history, had not achieved such harmony and thus had let loose economic forces leading to capitalism.

In this work, Amin managed the astounding feat of sounding more radical than ever yet at the same time making the economic contribution of the periphery to the centre qualitatively marginal. He reaffirmed the 'autocentric' development of the West, which contradicted the long-view dependency outlook (although he did retain the term dependence to describe the postwar relations between centre and periphery) and, more important, he virtually denied that the periphery was indispensable or vital to capitalism in its evolution from competition to monopoly to its present 'technological' phase. For example, he said of the monopoly phase of capitalism: 'This model reflects the essence of the system. It leaves out of account external relations, which means not that the development of capitalism takes place in a self-contained national framework but that the essential relations of the system can be grasped without taking account of these relations. Moreover, the external relations of advanced regions, taken as a whole, with the periphery of the world system are quantitatively marginal in comparison with the flows that take place within the centre; besides, . . . these relations are a matter of primitive accumulation and not of expanded reproduction.' What was more, monopoly capitalism could actually mitigate 'conjunctural fluctuations' and could produce 'a stable state of quasi-full employment', and the role of underdeveloped countries in the scheme, in the case of the cycle, was to facilitate 'the moment of recovery by providing additional outlets for the exports of the developed countries'.

Amin still clung to the idea that the periphery had been used historically by the capitalist centre for the absorption of surplus in its competitive phase and to prevent the fall of the rate of profit in its monopoly phase, yet if capitalism was 'autocentric' and if it guaranteed full employment through monopolistic 'planning' to which the periphery was unessential, how and why did imperialism arise? The astounding answer he gave, on the authority of Lenin, was: 'The essential reason for the extension of world trade thus lies in the inherent tendency of capitalism to expand markets, and does not arise from any need for absorption of surplus, either in the period of competition or in that of the monopolies.' In other words, it appeared because Lenin said that it was natural for capitalism to create imperialism.

The final image that we derive from a study of Amin's theories is that of a system in which the periphery is of marginal importance to the centre but the centre is handicapping for the periphery, and although Amin does not sufficiently explain why the centre's influence can be so negative and so overwhelming, he comes up with a class-struggle paradigm in which the bourgeoisie at the centre is exploiting the proletariat all over the world and the only valid theory is one of national liberation, with a programme of economic development based on delinking from the world market, balanced growth, and planning. Ironically, therefore, his view of the operation of the world capitalist system, in the light of his attribution of a marginal role to the periphery, is unmistakably tainted with the marginalism he so profoundly despises. Unfortunately, too, Amin's generalizations about Third World societies – which are crucial at every step in his analysis, and which were encapsulated in a 1979 essay by J. Gurley enumerating the main traits as (1) agrarian capitalism, (2) merchant bourgeoisie, (3) large bureaucracies, and (4) incomplete proletarianization – were only marginally viable, and probably as distorting as Frank's Latin American point of view, which Amin had earlier criticized along with the dependency outlook he later himself adopted in form if not in substance.[147]

Is Amin, when all is said and done, a dependency author? Or should he be put in a special category with Frank and Wallerstein as P. J. O'Brien suggests? He himself would probably not turn down the dependency appellation, and he undoubtedly deserved it, because, although one basic side of the dependency equation (the cruciality of the peripheral contribution to the development of capitalism in the centre) is downgraded in his work, what remains (the obstruction of development in the Third World and the radical political stance) sufficiently justified his immersion in the broad meanderings of the dependency flow.

A. Emmanuel and the ideological inevitability of unequal exchange

If Amin used a medium-range 'telescope' on accumulation, A. Emmanuel employed a high-resolution 'microscope' under which he put the microbic slide of unequal exchange. Amin had relied on the Prebisch/Singer thesis in his doctoral dissertation. He had accorded it a recognition tinged with reluctance because of its developmentalist affiliation and because of its merely empirical, as opposed to ideological, foundation. Emmanuel compensated for these shortcomings by transforming the Prebisch/Singer hypothesis into a Marxist theory on international surplus transfer and on the effects of this transfer on the classical or orthodox Marxist definition of the class struggle. He did not entirely forsake the empirical basis of the developmentalist thesis, but he took it as given and irrefutable (which was certainly not the case) and he made empirical debate irrelevant, at least in the Marxist camp. In other words, he was not interested, as Singer was, in proving statistically that prices of primary products tended to decline while those of manufactured goods tended to increase – and he snubbed the Prebisch/Singer effect by putting it literally 'on the fringe' of his own central position – but in creating a tool of analysis with which the Third World could argue conclusively and *sub specie aeternitatis*, so to speak, that unequal exchange between rich and poor countries was inevitable, pre-ordained by the manner in which these separate entities functioned and established their trade relations, more or less analogously to the relations between capitalists and workers.

In order to do this, Emmanuel needed two hypotheses: (1) free movement of capitals, and (2) responsiveness of wages to productivity in the developed countries and their unresponsiveness in the Third World ('fixed wages' hypothesis), or as he put it: 'Instead of equal wages and unequal rates of profit, I adopted the assumption of unequal wages and of profits subject to standardization and tending to equalization.' Why the first hypothesis? Because Emmanuel needed to prove that what were being exchanged in the international marketplace were equal values, and for this it was necessary to show that the organic composition of capital in the Third World (mechanization, automation, call it what you will) was on a par with that of industrialized countries at least. Besides it allowed him to put down the Prebisch thesis as dependent on 'income elasticity of demand and non-uniformity of technical progress', which were unreliable contingencies from the point of view of Marxist analysis based on the 'value of labour power'.

Having done this, the burden of Emmanuel's demonstration fell on the second assumption (fixed wages). This had to do with the better bargaining position of workers in developed economies and, in effect, it meant that these workers were profiting from the labour of their proletarian brothers in the Third World. As there cannot exist an absolutist Marxist doctrine that does not evoke another absolutist Marxist doctrine, C. Bettelheim took up arms for the former (and, incidentally, for the intelligence of exploiters) and wrote in rebuttal: 'The capitalists, who cannot be accused of not knowing how to do their sums, are not deceived: they know that, generally speaking, it is more profitable to exploit the proletarians of the industrialized countries than their brothers in the poor countries.' It was not made clear by Bettlelheim, who subscribed to a straightforward view of imperialism, why, if the rate of exploitation in industrialized economies was higher than in underdeveloped ones, capitalism did not industrialize the Third World and thus try to maximize its extraction of surplus, but such logical considerations would no doubt have been out of place in what amounted to a very specialized debate circling about a core of self-contradictory Marxist semantics.[148]

W. Rodney and the throttling of African nationhood

If the affiliation of Amin and Emmanuel to dependency theory can be considered marginal, with W. Rodney we go back to the mainstream of dependency and the roots of economic inequality. Rodney was a historian's historian. From all evidence he was a generous self-sacrificing man, a Guyanese black writer who spent much of his short life teaching in Dar-es-Salaam, in a corner of the African continent that he loved passionately, and who was killed at 38 years of age in his own country by minions of a pseudo-revolutionary regime that he opposed. He left a sadly brief but admirable oeuvre, including the posthumous *A History of the Guyanese Working People, 1881–1905* (1982), an international paradigm for works in that genre, faultless in research, equanimity and style. He also tried to prove in *How Europe Underdeveloped Africa* (1972) one of the fundamental corollaries of the long-view economic imperialism hypothesis: that the economically backward cultures and peoples of the world could have evolved to modern nationhood by their own means without the crippling trauma of colonialism. Rodney did not, despite the title of his book, principally claim that they would all have industrialized in strict accordance with Western patterns or acquired the dimensions of European economies, although he did not rule this out either, but only that European colonialism scotched their chances for an independent political evolution. To do this, he had to demonstrate two things: that the potential for evolving was there, specifically in Africa, and how it was that Europeans went about extirpating it.

Concerning the pre-colonial ages of African history, Rodney made the following assertion: 'The assumption that will underlie this study is that most African societies before 1500 were in a transitional stage between the practice of agriculture (plus fishing and herding) in family communities and the practice of the same activities within states and societies comparable to feudalism.' To prove this, he described the historical features of African societies from the 'coming of iron, the rise of cereal-growing and the making of pottery' in the first centuries of our era to the production of crafted leather by the Hausa and the Mandinga, of Guinea cotton, of Katangan and Zambian copper, of Sierra Leone iron, and of many other manufacturers, and from *ab origine* communalism to social stratification and the birth of kingdoms and royal lineages, best represented perhaps by the Tigrean and Amharic ruling class in the Ethiopian Empire, but also present elsewhere in Africa in the empires of Ghana and of Mali, the states of Bunyoro-Kitara in the interlacustrine zone, the culture of Zimbabwe, and other formations, not to mention Moslem Egypt and the Maghreb.

Europe's mastery of navigation and its relative economic and political advance on Africa made this self-sufficient and gold-poor continent a part of the incipient world system during the sixteenth century by incorporating it into a classic triangular trade pattern, involving the purchase of cotton goods in India to be exchanged for African slaves, who were then used in the mines of Spanish America to produce silver to finance the cycle all over again. Here Rodney adopts the summarist rhetoric of anti-imperialism to affirm that 'Europe allocated to Africa the role of supplier of human captives to be used as slaves in various parts of the world'. However, he was obviously not unaware that Africans themselves were the actual purveyors of slaves to European traffickers, and he countered by citing instances in which African states either preferred 'normal' commercial relations with Europe, as in Kongo at the beginning of the sixteenth century, or were forced into slave trafficking, as in Dahomey in the 1720s. Slaves, he claimed, were often taken by warlike expanding societies, who would use them as an internal labour force and eventually integrate them into themselves. These societies entered into the slave-trading circuit under the external pressures of the growing and hungry world capitalist system. The profits from the slave trade fuelled the growth of ports such as Bristol, Liverpool, Nantes, Bordeaux and Seville, which later emerged as manufacturing centres significantly influential at the advent of the Industrial Revolution.

Another claim that Rodney made was that racism was in a critical sense a 'superstructural' product of the capitalist mode of production's absorption of Africa through the slave trade. But he was much too sensible to put it all down to Marxist jargon: 'The simple fact is that no people can enslave another for centuries without coming out with a notion of superiority and when the colour and other physical traits of those peoples were quite different it was inevitable that the prejudices should take a racist form.'[149]

Despite the impact of capitalism and the degradation caused by the slave trade, Africa's internal evolution did not come to a stop when relations with the West started. Rodney's programme is above all a relentless refutation of the old Hegelian thesis that non-Western cultures have no history. He wrote: 'The regions of Yorubaland, Dahomey, the inter-lacustrine kingdoms and Zululand. . .are examples of leading forces in the political development which was taking place in Africa right up to the eve of colonialism.' But the undeniable trend of inter-cultural relations showed that the 'slight difference (in development) when the Portuguese sailed to West Africa in 1444 was a huge gap by the time that European robber statesmen sat down in Berlin 440 years later to decide who should steal which parts of Africa. It was that gap which provided both the necessity and the opportunity for Europe to move into the imperialist epoch, and to colonise and further underdevelop Africa.' In doing this Rodney threw Marxism/Leninism to the winds and espoused a thesis not unlike the Landes theory on historical imbalances, which may seem odd in such a punctilious Marxist as he was, unless one understands that above all his interpretation of African history is both African and commonsensical, and this is, we think, what gives it a special place in the ideological congress of dependency and economic imperialism. The discordant note throughout his book is that he keeps falling back on such 'reifications' as 'capitalism assigned' or 'imperialism decided', which brings to mind the Cardoso/Faletto description of external forces and constraints as a 'metaphysical' relation, although it could be argued that in the case of Africa the margin for external decision-making was much greater than in the case of Latin America, and in that sense at least some of Rodney's metaphors are not entirely inaccurate.

For the imperialist phase of African history, Rodney elaborated a ledger with an entry for 'Africa's contribution to the capitalist development of Europe' and another for 'Colonialism as a system of underdeveloping Africa'. The first entry is a 'standard' catalogue, in the Galeano/Jalée/Nkrumah sense, of economic penetration, expropriation and exploitation of African economies by Western capitalism under the aegis of colonial rule. It proves, if proof were needed, that colonialism was profitable in many more ways than macro-statistics about investment and trade can show, because the fact of the matter was (and Dr Rodney made it perfectly clear) that colonialism was not just a matter of having and administering colonies but a two-way system with consequences for the colonialized (mostly bad) and for the metropoles in themselves and as present in Africa (mostly 'good'), and Rodney made no bones about the fact that, yes, definitely, European workers and European middle-classes benefited, and benefited royally as groups, wittingly or unwittingly, from the sweat and the suffering of the African people.

The second entry pretends that, on top of economic exploitation, which was at the base of everything else, colonialism did almost nothing to attend to Africa's socio-economic and educational needs, and that it did nothing constructive towards the creation of independent states but, on the contrary, drew arbitrary boundaries, divided to rule within them, and exacerbated the ethnic rivalries that would have been subsumed under an internal process of autogenetic integration, the same rivalries that are now used as examples of Africa's lingering backwardness. 'So long as there is political power', Rodney cried, 'so long as a people can be mobilized to use weapons, and so long as a society has the opportunity to define its own ideology, culture, etc., then the people of that society have some control over their own destinies, in spite of constraints such as those imposed as the African continent slipped into orbit as a satellite of capitalist Europe.'[150] Rodney's catalogue of grievances is a *summa contra gentiles* that far transcends the works of Fanon, Cabral and Memmi, to whom he of course gave all due credit, as he also did to European Africanists such as B. Davidson, H. Labourit, and B. M. Fagan. Rodney's overview loads the dice, for after all it was a loving work of redress, and much of his reasoning is contrafactual, but the case he made deserves more recognition than a mere benefit of the doubt.

A. K. Bagchi and the denial of 'periphery' from a dependency perspective

One theorist who belonged broadly in the Marxist economic-imperialism tradition, but who, unlike Amin, roundly rejected the dependency tag, was the Bengali A. K. Bagchi. No Indian could ever think of his country, despite its long colonial experience, as a puppet or a sham. India is too big, too varied and too complex for that. Bagchi, however, is too shrewd, like his Moslem compatriot I. Habib, to believe that on its own India would have grown to rival Great Britain. 'For understanding the development of Third World countries', he wrote in *The Political Economy of Underdevelopment* (1982) – a title which seems to echo Baran's main work on capitalism – 'the delineation of non-capitalist modes of production and social formations is essential. For, at the time European merchant adventurers "discovered" the Third World countries, the latter generally had not became capitalist and were not on the path of transition to capitalism.' Even if they had been, however, once capitalism had come into contact with 'lagging societies', these would no longer have been able to follow their own autonomous paths because relations were created that favoured 'mercantile capitalism', promoted international exploitation, and begat 'modes of extraction' of surplus from peasants and artisans that survived beyond the maturity of industrial capitalism in the West: 'Even when native capitalists succeeded Europeans in Third World countries, many of these methods of extraction of surplus from peasantry and semi-free labour were kept alive, at the same time as capacity was being built up in modern mechanised industries. Thus there is no neat succession of stages of mercantile and industrial capitalism in Third World countries.'

In the colonies these imbalances and distortions were part of imposed methods of external oppression, and in countries like those of Latin America, they were the outcome of enforced free trade policies. In both groups, 'much of the investible surplus was transferred overseas, so there was a shortage of funds available to entrepreneurs who might venture into the field of manufacturing catering to the home market'. Bagchi subscribes fully to the thesis of the deindustrialization of the Third World, in the sense both of the destruction of handicrafts and of the prevention of industrialization through, among other means, the creation of railway-and-port enclaves, which propitiated onerous competition from external capitalism. Industrial capitalism 'is not a system that can be simply diffused through countries like, say, literacy', and capitalism in general is 'a deeply unequal system of domination of one class by another, of one nation by the ruling class of another'.

Historical underdevelopment is the result of the unfair advantage that capitalism, which emerged decisively in Europe from the entrails of feudalism, took of less advanced cultures and economic formations and of some of the implants that it carried to foreign soils. Once the system was in place, the Industrial Revolution and the blockage of development beyond its strictly Western confines, through continued exploitation and the perpetuation of non-capitalist modes of production, were its logical complementary offshoots. So far, this sounds like the usual dependency fare with an admixture of MOP theory, but the give-away to Bagchi's difference is the significant fact that he never once uses the bipolarity core/periphery in his analysis. He skirts this possibility in his summary presentation of the failure of ISI in Latin America, but even here he insists on relying on the more comprehensive notion of capitalist forces at work both nationally and internationally.[151]

Bagchi's text continually does a tight-rope act between the pull of economic imperialism and the tug of internal social contradictions. It finally lands squarely in the national arena of competing forces for and against development when he shifts his attention to rural and urban class analysis, and it is here that one realises that, when the colonial night eventually receded, what was left operating was not so much neo-colonialism or neo-Marxist/Leninist imperialism as a reality corresponding to pure undiluted social Marxism and its up-datings on class analysis by Lenin and by Mao Tse-tung. 'At the top of the capitalist pyramid in trade, industry and finance is native big bourgeoisie', Bagchi said, but without putting all his eggs in one basket, because 'in many fields foreign capital still rules the roost.' The experience of India, where effective economic decolonization started during the inter-war years, as shown by native efforts at ISI as a result of Britain's declining economic strength, seemed to underlie this perception.

Bagchi did not at any time abandon the idea of economic imperialism (an expression he himself never uses, for he is a tried-and-true neo-Leninist), but the unmistakable change of emphasis is there none the less: local bourgeoisies fight to drive out foreign capital, even to monopolize production; transnationals encroach and manoeuvre but they do not succeed automatically as they do in most dependency texts. Bagchi admitted readily that, after independence, India effectively if incompetently in a succession of five-year plans took over the running of its economy, not, to be sure, for the benefit of its people but of the capitalist system, for, as in Pakistan, Mahbub ul Haq told President Ayub Khan, planning is not for reducing inequality but for maximizing the surplus and the rate of growth.

For Bagchi, capitalist development, even with the iron fist of the state behind it, is a vain hope, since even in its realization it can only mean more inequality and more injustice. In the Third

World, as anywhere under capitalism, what counts is how society is structured and how social struggles eventually decide the route that economic development will take. For him the development dilemma of most Marxist dependency authors does not exist. A. K. Bagchi, from a 'periphery' that is a virtual denial of the idea of periphery, proclaims that the world process of capitalism is a constant reproduction of itself until it becomes in effect one system with artificial frontiers. The entire underdeveloped capitalist world today is moving, though not smoothly to be sure, towards the pristine Marxist model after having purged itself, as India did, of the relatively short-lived colonialist interlude.[152]

Western syntheses on economic-imperialism theories

One of the West's main contributions in the field of economic-imperialism studies during the late 1970s and early 1980s lay in summarizing, interrelating and criticizing what had been achieved until then in the realm of theory. G. Kitching (1982) and P. W. Preston (1982) attempted from different perspectives to find common grounds for discussing the relative positions of developmentalism and Marxism on Third World structures and processes. Preston opted for a hotch-potch 'theories of development' approach, yielding some rather contestable Procrustean classifications. Kitching contributed to the 'dependency debate' by positing links between development theory and dependency, but he is principally interesting for the curious if uncertain light he threw on a rapprochement between Russian populism (Narodnism), economic development and dependency. The common denominator here seemed to be the Russians' dread of losing their national soul through cultural dependence and the modern Latin American *dependentistas'* quasi-mystic abhorrence of economic dependence. Russian populists were driven to oppose industrialization, preferring instead 'a society and economy in which small-scale agricultural producers (peasants) and non-agricultural producers (artisans) remain in a large majority'. The neo-populist Chayanov had some influence in Soviet Russia, thanks to Bukharin's eminent standing in the 1920s, but Stalin put paid to all agrarian pipedreams through forced collectivization. Kitching perceived in our times sparks of populism in Latin America and in Nyerere's Ujamaa, a kind of Tanzanian rural 'extended family' socialism, but especially in the 'small is beautiful' philosophy of E. F. Schumacher and M. Lipton. That Latin Americans would make light of all this was understandable to Kitching for, whereas Russian populists in their time had something to fall back on within their own culture, Latin Americans had nothing to look for outside industrialization.[153]

More ambitious attempts to categorize the teeming branches of economic imperialism theory were embarked upon by R. Owen and B. Sutcliffe in tandem editorship (1972), by M. B. Brown (1974), and by A. Brewer (1980). Owen and Sutcliffe put together a wide-net anthology of analyses, to which T. Kemp (himself author of the 1967 neo-Leninist book *Theories of Imperialism*), M. B. Brown, H.-U. Wehler (the recognized expert on German social imperialism), R. Robinson, H. Magdoff, P. Patnaik, A. S. Kanya-Foster, T. Hodgkin, R. W. Johnson, J. Stengers and D. C. M. Platt contributed in a not unfair balancing act, and they appended an exhaustive (for the period) commentated bibliography on theories of imperialism divided into these categories: Marxist (in turn subdivided into three time sequences: up to 1914, 1914–1945, after 1945), non-Marxist economic theories, and non-Marxist political theories. Pertinent to our own survey, the only *dependentista* they mentioned in the bibliography was R. M. Marini.

M. B. Brown started his deep commitment in the field with a work published in 1962, in which he defended a historical continuity between the British Empire and the Commonwealth of Nations as an informal structure conducive to international equality within the wider context of the world capitalist system, but by 1974 his interest had centred on Third World policy statements and on an analytical non-Marxist approach to the concept of imperialism, which he used in the wide sense which we attribute to long-view economic imperialism or dependency: 'The concept has thus been associated with an unequal economic relationship between states, not simply the inequality between large and small, rich and poor trading partners, but the inequality of political and economic dependence of the latter upon the former.' Brown's system of categories relied on three heterogenous paradigms: Marxism, Schumpeterean liberalism, and what he described as neo-mercantilist Keynesianism, which roughly corresponded, the first two to 'disharmonic' and 'harmonic' perceptions of capitalist development, and the third to an eclecticism rejecting 'both the inevitable conflicts of the Marxists' capitalism and the harmony of the unregulated classical liberal capitalism'.[154]

From a highly critical stance, Brewer also did a creditable review of economic-imperialism theory, based on the original Marxist concepts that had served as the scaffolding of all later constructs: capitalist MOP, primitive accumulation, world market and anti-colonialism. But Brewer knew that Marx had not formulated *strictu sensu* a theory of economic imperialism of his own (such as the Marxist-derived theories of Luxemburg, Hilferding, Bukharin and Lenin, all of which Brewer analysed), and he made clear the transpositional use that Baran and Frank made of the idea of 'primitive accumulation'. It could be valid, he said, but it is not in Marx. Brewer made a pellucid, no-nonsense division in Marxism: 'Marxist theories of the development of capitalism on a world scale tend to fall into two groups. There are those that concentrate on the progressive role of capitalism in developing the forces of production, and conversely those that present capitalism as a system of exploitation of one area by another, so that development in a few places is at the expense of the "development of underdevelopment" in most of the world.' The former view was that held by 'classical Marxists', 'from Marx himself to Lenin and his contemporaries'; the latter was the Frank/Wallerstein 'response to the failure of capitalist development in many parts of the world'.

In proposing this stark distinction, Brewer underscored the 'progress dilemma' which besets much Marxist thinking on issues of economic backwardness. What was 'progress' for Marx? Certainly not the 'progress' of development studies, so that when Marxists denounce capitalism for denying the Third World its right to 'economic progress' they are in a sense admitting what Marx himself would not have stomached in his time: that capitalism could actually create welfare and promote social justice. Lenin went even further in his rejection because he was not even among those who considered capitalism 'progressive', 'progress' and 'progressive' being of course different ideas since the latter term could signify, as it did in Marx, a step forward or the promotion of a step forward though not necessarily a satisfactory step in itself.[155]

'Orthodox' or, in Brewer's terms, 'classical' Marxists today sidestep this conundrum by arguing that capitalist development was inherent in the dialectics of class struggle and of socio-economic change, to which international capitalism would contribute in one way or another, but that the change did not portend a basic improvement in social conditions or in the intensity of economic exploitation. This argument, however, did not obviate the fact that contemporary capitalism cannot be compared to the monstrous system that Marx had taken apart and denounced. These Marxists were banking on the very long-run exacerbation of the worldwide incompatibility between capitalist relations and capitalist forces of productions, but in the meantime they could not deny that capitalism was not exhausted, even as it tolerated the subsistence of underdevelopment, and thus they had to swallow in their MOP and class-struggle potpourri traces and even floating chunks of dependency diatribe. The interplay of these dilemmas was of the essence in the dependency debate that, during the 1970s, was going on exclusively in the Marxist camp, but before we get there we have to round out our consideration of dependency theory with perhaps its most finished manifestation in the work of I. Wallerstein, and we have to expound the contents of what, in our opinion, is the main if tardier event in the dependency debate: the confrontation between dependency and developmentalism.

I. Wallerstein's dependency summation

Braudel and Wallerstein

On entering the numerous productions of I. Wallerstein, two clarifications on sources and reciprocal influences are in order: in connection with A. G. Frank (and through him with dependency) and in connection with F. Braudel. Why Frank and dependency, which seem quite the opposite of Wallerstein's patient piece-by-piece 'deconstruction' of the economic and political historical cycles of Western Europe? Wallerstein included Frank in the bibliography of his fundamental work, *The Modern World-System* (1974), and he seems to share with him the idea that, despite marginal differences in the way relations of production were organized in the different parts of the world that came under European hegemony or control after 1450, the general picture was that of a fully functional capitalist world-economy. They also coincide, therefore, and with some precedence on Frank's side, on the use of the core/periphery archetype. However, for Latin America, Wallerstein relied on Furtado and other Latin American writers more often than he did on Frank and, of course, core-periphery derives not from Frank, but from Prebisch. Perhaps the focal point of convergence between Wallerstein and Frank lies in the strict equivalence between the verbs 'underdevelop' (which is Frank's neologism) and 'peripheralize' (which is Wallerstein's), but in all justice it would be difficult to claim that Frank influenced Wallerstein significantly.

This is not so in the case of Wallerstein and Braudel, for here we actually have substantial intellectual reciprocity and meaningful formal concordances. Of the two, Wallerstein is justifiably the more appreciative of the other. Apart from using him as a basic source in his historical and economic analyses, Wallerstein freely admits that it was Braudel who set him on the spoor of the idea of 'world-system' by impressing on him the fundamental lesson that the unit of research into economic history must be the 'world economy' and not its individual parts, a lesson which, however, he seems to have boiled down to a synthesis that is profoundly un-Braudelian. As if to leave no doubts about his debt to Braudel, Wallerstein dedicated the second volume of *The Modern World System* (1980) to Braudel, and he named after him a centre for economic and historical studies that he heads in the State University of New York at Binghamton. On the other side of the debit ledger, Braudel no less generously recognized Wallerstein's influence on various definitely major issues. It is these which we should like to explore in some detail.[156]

There is, first of all, the question of Anglo-French nomenclatural equivalences of, on one side, 'world empire' and '*empire-monde*', and on the other, '*économie-monde*', 'world economy', and 'world-system'. To these last Braudel adds, significantly at the start of a discussion of all these categories, the notion of '*économie mo diale*', which he defines with a quote from Simonde de Sismondi, a Swiss political economist who died in 1842: 'Humanity or all that portion of humanity that trades together and today constitutes in a way a single market.' Was this Braudel's subtle dismissal of Wallerstein's 'world-system'? Was he implying that Wallerstein was flogging a dead horse?

There are between them only minor potential disagreements on the definition of 'world empire' and '*empire-monde*'. They are different names for the old 'oriental despotisms' – the Persian, the Mughal, the Chinese, *et al.* – whose definition was that they stuck their political tentacles on all their cities and provinces, sucked surplus unto themselves, and stifled private economic initiative and development. Neither Braudel nor Wallerstein have any doubts that therein lies one of the long-term roots of economic inequality between the West and the other major civilizations of the world. Braudel on this point appears to quibble with Wallerstein on whether pre-eighteenth-century Russia was, as the latter pretends, an 'external area', that is, a 'world empire' that was later forcibly integrated into the 'world economy' from outside, or as Braudel would have it, a 'world economy' in itself that gradually merged of its own into capitalism. This quibble, however, is turned by Braudel into a major discrepancy. For his own concept of *économie-monde*, which he describes as a 'juxtaposition of interlinked zones', he accepts the Wallerstein schema involving a 'narrow center', 'relatively secondary regions', and large external areas. Now, since Wallerstein actually posits four areas – core, periphery, semi-periphery, and the external area – it follows from the above that Braudel does not accept either one or the other of the last two categories. Thus, since the penultimate is the least essential of the four (the 'external area' is necessary for the existence of a precise periphery, or else everything outside the core would be either a general undifferentiated periphery or an external area), then he must be excluding the idea of semi-periphery, which nevertheless plays a highly significant role in the Wallerstein system in two ways: historically, in the building up of the core by positing the existence of what he calls a 'conveyor belt of surplus', and for contemporary political analysis, in providing a functional justification of the idea of 'subimperialist' states, sort of outposts of the core serving to consolidate regional capitalist domination. In a sense, of all the Wallerstein world-system categories, the most germane to the system, the one that exhibits the greatest degree of 'structurality' and purpose (and, in any case, the only one exclusive to his system) is that of semi-periphery, and therefore Braudel's rejection is no mean move. But the differences go much deeper.[157]

Braudel firmly reproaches Wallerstein for the rigidity and the shortsightedness of his system: 'for not having observed through the bars of his grid other than economic realities'; and, even more important, for not having for his world-system 'a temporal unit of reference'. The latter is a strange reproach for a historian to address to another historian, when both tacitly deal in 'temporal references', and what we think that Braudel meant was that Wallerstein's historical world-system, which does not take enough account of politics and other social forces, also came into the world fully formed, with all the formal attributes of reason and will, but incorporeal and without a process of gestation, as if instead of armour-clad Athena, Zeus' brain had produced another brain. Braudel makes light of Wallerstein's rigid typologies. In considering their application to the phases of an economic cycle – rise, crisis, decline – he tabulates nine different categories for analysis, which must be in turn multiplied by the different aspects of social reality – politics, economics, etc. – resulting in an unwieldy catalogue of possibilities that is really just a tongue-in-cheek dismissal of typological or classificatory rigidities. Or he scrambles Wallerstein's inflexible order, and instead of the core controlling the periphery he makes the suggestion that, in pre-industrial France, it was a case of 'The interior conquered by the periphery'.

The crux of the matter is that Braudel simply does not admit, despite his courteous protestations, the imposition of a grill-like division on history and on the world, or a rigid linear evolution from one European core to one growing world-economy, which eventually culminates in today's almost granite-tough world-system, as Wallerstein would have it, give or take a bump here, a bump there along the road. For Braudel, apart from the fact that history, like life, does not accept ideological constraints, the world economy, his own *économie-monde*, which is basically a large international, usually maritime, network of trade, grew from different European medieval 'world economies' not according to some internal infallible logic leading from dispersion to aggregation, or from core to expansion, but from shifts in the position of the centre resulting from geographical conditions, the accumulation of advantages, favourable and unfavourable political circumstances – Spain, for example, had to bleed itself economically in the Low Countries during the sixteenth century in order to keep civil war away from its frontiers, dixit Braudel – rivalries and warfare, 'in brief', the myriad forms and manifestations of history from which neither caprice nor some degree of hazard were absent. Braudel would not have emphasized the latter, as in the other direction he denied that capitalism was 'rational', but unlike Wallerstein's world-system his own historical approach would not have excluded them either.[158]

The key concept in Braudel's view is not 'unpredictability' but 'complexity', and 'complexity' is something that 'world-system' tried indefatigably to reduce. Other than the process of history, which is full of hitches and contradictions, *économie-monde* has no further meaning for Braudel. Its representation at any one point in time has only a faint resemblance to the all embracing core-periphery pattern than Wallerstein etches on world economic history, which is beyond the facts of history the meaning of history itself.

In this summary telling Braudel's methodology could itself seem schematic – which is not the case, as a reading of the sources will readily reveal – but, even so, it is far less constricting than Wallerstein's. In the end, if Braudel and Wallerstein are at odds, it is because Wallerstein's world-system, when all is taken into account, is basically a restrictive methodological tool. For Braudel, *économie-monde* was just another open-ended instrument of historical analysis, and the core/periphery binomial was a convenient if self-evident metaphoric representation of the way large economies, whether national or international, tend to organize themselves.

The historical studies

Wallerstein's work can be separated into three main component themes: Africa, the history of the world economy, and world-system. Some believe that it also contains a political strategy, which can only be described as a vague thrust towards socialism. All in all, Wallerstein's is the most thorough contemporary exploration and explanation of the origins and perpetuation of international economic inequality from the usual dependency perspective of cultural comparabilities before the onset of European overseas expansionism. We have seen, in general terms, his filiation to the ideological scheme of core-periphery dependence. However, he does not use the ideological category of dependency or economic imperialism, even if his entire approach seems to derive ultimately from a dependency view. Curiously enough, as an Africanist, which Wallerstein mainly was during the 1960s, there is nothing in his work that even vaguely resembles dependency theory, so that from the perspective of his world economy and world-system analyses (which most everyone reads first), the Wallerstein of the 1960s seems almost a stranger to his 1970s and 1980s intellectual persona: the emphasis is always on internal political processes rather than on external dependence – except of the crudest colonial sort, which at any rate is subordinate to his interest in independent Africa – and there is even the hint that he might not have agreed with Rodney's theory of imperialism as the throttling of African potential nationhood.

This changes 'abruptly' with the appearance in 1974 of *The Modern World-System*. This is a subtle, well-argued and elegantly constructed analysis of practically all the major issues on the emergence and almost immediate outward expansion of modern Western capitalism in the sixteenth century, on the growing importance in world capitalist rivalries of politics and the bureaucratic state (after the failure of Spain's attempt to create a world-state within the incipient but already larger world economy), and on the effects of these processes on the European 'peripheries' and 'semi-peripheries'. The basic functional result of the expansion and influence of capitalist forces was the creation of three hierarchical areas with different socio-economic structures and markedly uneven economic and political power: the core, which in effect determined the roles of the others, characterized by wage labour and self-employment; the semi-periphery, where share-cropping predominated and which served to transfer surplus value to the core; and the periphery, in which slavery and 'feudalism' were the dominant forms. Some of the issues Wallerstein raised were the feudal roots of capitalism, the tight meshing of the discovery and settlement of Iberian America with the internal necessities of Western European economies, the causes of the ultimate failure of Spain, the approximate dating of the definitive launching of the world economy, and others. On most of them he superimposed his core/periphery pattern, by which means it was explained how Spain lapsed from being a core area to a semi-periphery and how Poland, through a political failure of nerve, was converted into a periphery functioning as granary for the core.[159]

Six years later, although by then well immersed in what Worsley called 'world-systematics', and so with a lesser impact than his previous volume, Wallerstein published the second volume of *The Modern World-System*, which carried his analysis to 1750. The outlook was the same as before: 'The argument of this work', he explained, 'is that the modern world-system took the form of a capitalist world economy that had its genesis in Europe in the 16th century and that involved the transformation of a particular redistributive or tributary mode of production, that of feudal Europe (Braudel's economic Ancien Régime), into a qualitatively different social system. Since that time, the capitalist world-economy has (a) geographically expanded to cover the entire globe; (b) manifested a cyclical pattern of expansion and contraction. . .and shifting geographical locations of economic roles (the rise and fall of hegemonies, the movements up and down of particular core, peripheral and semi-peripheral zones); and (c) undergone a process of secular transformation, including technological advance, industrialization, proletarianization, and the emergence of structured political resistance to the system itself – a transformation that is still going on today.'

Wallerstein had by then elaborated fully his 'world-system perspective', which was built on the idea of a 'single capitalist world economy' stretching from the sixteenth century to the present. There were, to be sure, individual national entities within it, but their 'different internal socio-economic profiles' and their politics could only be understood by placing them within the system of the world economy, for they were 'parts of a whole reflecting that whole'. To explain the evolution of Wallerstein's analysis through an analogy with his socio-historical categories, if his *World System 1* was the 'periphery' of his own ideological system, *World System*

2 was the 'semi-periphery' in that it showed how the central West European capitalist states (the Netherlands, England and France) warred among each other for supremacy within the world economy and at the same time incorporated into the system in subordinate stations vast areas of the planet. Some of the crucial issues here were the establishment of mercantilism in England and France as a response to Dutch commercial competition, the rise of British naval supremacy compared with France's inward-looking 'gigantism' (a definitely Braudelian conceit), the world-system 'necessity' of 'peripheralizing' India, and the painstaking contortions that were involved in trying to make Sweden, Denmark, Prussia and Austria fit the core/periphery pattern. The most significant change from one volume to the next was that in the second volume the process at the core and the process of the core's action on the periphery and the semi-periphery were given equal treatment, almost with the precision of a time-piece.[160]

The third volume of *The Modern World-System* (1989), which covers the period from 1730 to the 1840s, was as brilliant and as tendentious as the previous ones, and in line with our analogy, it carried the elaboration of his interpretation of modern history one step closer to its culmination, or core, which is today's capitalist world-system. Here again Wallerstein's method consisted in the application of rigid patterns and categories to the events of history with the backing of profuse scholarship and copious quotes. Since his contention has always been the decisive, determinant character of the world economy over and above the processes of individual national entities, he reasoned: (1) that the Industrial Revolution was a misnomer for Britain's strategic and commercial advantage over France, its only rival for world hegemony, because there was no real, verifiable economic superiority of one over the other; (2) that the advantage stemmed from sea-power and was expressed in the Treaty of Paris, which concluded the Seven Years' War; and (3) that the French Revolution was the unavailing French attempt to offset politically Britain's external advantage (although it set the pattern for all future 'anti-systemic' enterprises). In line with his anticipations, he described how Russia and the Ottoman empire were peripheralized and how economic conjunctures determined the course of events in the European American empires, in particular efforts at consolidation and the independence movements.[161]

Wallerstein's amazing erudition cannot disguise the *parti pris* and the selectivity, which are evident from these considerations: (1) all the conclusions are more or less fore-ordained (despite the appearance of inductive reasoning); (2) all analyses follow the same interpretive pattern and fit into standardized conceptual categories; (3) specific issues are always dealt with inside wider categories and there is no evidence of original empirical research. Throughout his historical studies, Wallerstein used broadly Marxist (in the sense of admitting the concepts of MOP and class struggle in a vague, imprecise manner), broadly economic guidelines; in his depiction, the figures of history are indistinct passing shadows easily upstaged by political forces (strong but disincarnate motivations); and as between political and economic forces, the first have the upper hand only when the second either weaken or momentarily drift, although generally they really cannot be distinguished. Capitalism goes everywhere and does anything it wants to, but it must submit to the estimate of the costs of opportunity, so that in the end Wallerstein's analyses resemble nothing better than a theory of historical marginalism.

'World-systematics'

The phase of world-systematics proper, that is, Wallerstein's use of the 'world-system perspective' in a mainly contemporary frame, commenced with his editorship in 1975 of the book *World Inequality*, and includes *The Political Economy of Contemporary Africa* (joint editorship with P. C. W. Gutkind in 1976), *The Capitalist World-Economy* (1979), *Processes of the World-System* (with T. K. Hopkins, 1980), *World Systems Analysis* (with Hopkins, 1982), and *The Politics of the World Economy* (1984). What have these works contributed to the results of the previous historical studies and how have they extended if at all the analytical range of the concept of world-system?

Apart from an essay on the incorporation of Africa into the world economy, Wallerstein's main concerns appear to have been eliciting the implications of his historical researches and their application to contemporary situations. Accordingly, he has tried to hone his repertory of concepts, he has thrown bridges towards and crossed swords with other 'systems' of Third World conceptualization, and he has analysed contemporary political phenomena, in which area he has even dabbled in futurology. 'To peripheralize' has definitely come to mean 'to underdevelop'. 'Peripheral' and 'core-like' economic forms refer to the Marxist categories of 'non-capitalist' or 'pre-capitalist' modes of production, which is an ingenious way of sidestepping the brain-racking problem of 'hybrid' economic formations or of reconciling the coexistence or cohabitation in one economy of 'feudalism' and capitalism. Western development studies took this in stride with the dual-economy model, but it remains a conundrum for the Marxist faithful. Without getting into a tizzy, world-systematics simply states: 'Looking at the world-economy as a whole, some states are clearly "in-between" in the core-periphery structure, in that they house within their borders (in adjacent but often unrelated sectors) both peripheral processes in relation to core states and core-like processes in relation to adjacent peripheral states.' 'Semi-periphery', which Wallerstein introduced to account for the parts of Europe which were 'underdeveloped' historically in relation to the European core, he stretched to cover 'sub-imperialism'. This concept he attributed to A. D. Roberts who, in a 1962 article, noted that 'in the establishment and extension of colonies, an imperialist power often made use of one local group [the Baganda, in this case] to help it rule over other local peoples', but in fact it probably derives from Marini, who had passed it on first to Frank.

In his first confrontation with rival 'systems' on 'world equality' in 1975, Wallerstein lumped development studies and Marxism (mostly of the Soviet variety) into one 'developmental category', which he characterized as unilineal and dogmatic in contrast to his own approach. In a later essay (1982), he modified his own dogmatism and acknowledged 'world-system' debts to development economics (Prebisch and ECLA, Myrdal, and Nurkse, respectively for unequal exchange, 'the principle of circular and cumulative causation', and 'vicious circle of poverty'), and to Marxists such as Baran, Frank, Marini and Emmanuel. But the purpose of this exercise really was to show that they all could be subsumed under the category of world-system analysis, so it really was not a genuine attempt at a synthesis except on his own terms.

In the article in which Wallerstein made these qualified concessions, he gave what is perhaps the final definition of world-system as it enumerated exhaustively all its basic components: division of labour, which encompassed core-periphery, semi-periphery, unequal exchange and capital accumulation; state system, including imperialism, hegemony and the opposition bourgeoisie–proletariat; cyclical rhythms; and secular trends, such as 'commodification' and mechanization. In his forays into political analysis, he has made controversial affirmations such as that the communist nations as a whole form 'a collective capitalist firm' or that they are integrated as a semi-periphery into the world-system, and that movements of national liberation tend to end up in an even lower rank in the system. For these ideas he was roundly criticized by Worsley, who objected to his integrationist core/periphery/semi-periphery model both in its application to the capitalist–communist blocks division (which Worsley accepts as valid) and in its application to the Third World, where Worsely says it underplays the 'non-capitalism dimension' and the 'quite distinctive kinds of capitalism and the phases of development'. Wallerstein's prognostications are of the sort: 'Finally, I expect the world-economy to take a marked upturn once again the 1990s', a self-assurance hardly justified by his assertion in 1975 that 'most conservatives decline to fly the banner openly but hide their conservative ideas under the mantle of liberalism or occasionally even Marxism'.[162]

The one area in which Wallerstein could have made a contribution to dependency different from those of Baran and Frank, who considered the Third World *en bloc* or as manifesting homogenous processual patterns, was in the specific contemporary effects of the world-system on the internal processes of individual countries in the Third World. However, he has in the main limited himself to wide historical research and to general considerations on the formal mechanics and the features of the world-system as a whole, although the books he has edited by himself or in collaboration do contain numerous articles that attempt to relate the particular of national or regional situations to the general of operative world-system forces and needs.

'Schooling by terminology'

The principal motivation of this work has been to elicit from different ideological systems and sources what we call theories on the origins of international economic inequality, as manifested principally in the per capita income differences between the developed and the underdeveloped blocs of nations. To defend these elaborations, which frequently depend on deductions and inferences, we have had to establish often complicated groupings and affinities. In criticizing the resulting formulations we have referred indistinctly to their internal inconsistencies and to historical facts, sometimes by the method of *reductio ad absurdum*. In the case of Wallerstein, we have a triple obligation: we have to prove conclusively his affiliation to the economic imperialism or dependency school, we have to place his specific outlook in a critical light, and we have to deal with his reading of the historical facts, and in addition do all these things at the same time. The ideological criticism shall be undertaken with the proviso that it forms an advance on the special sub-section of the summatory general critique of dependency theory. In the examination of his historical interpretations, which can hardly be avoided in dealing with a fundamentally historical oeuvre (unlike that of most other dependency theorists), we can rightly feel as if we were coming up against a universe of propositions that cannot be dealt with adequately for two reasons: one, the multiplicity of themes and issues involved, and, two, the length of time and space it would take. Therefore, the best that we can expect to achieve in this specific connection is a selective critique of some of the fundamental attitudes and assumptions in his analysis.

With regard to Wallerstein's ideological position, there can hardly subsist any doubts about his allegiance to the transpositional or free-wheeling form of Marxism that we have encountered so often before in our analyses of dependency theory. The use of terms such as 'commodification' and 'surplus transfer' tend clearly in that direction. Wallerstein believes that colonial exploitation contributed crucially to the accumulation of surplus needed for the economic advance of core nations. From his Europe-centred, world-historical analyses, he also perceived accumulation as resulting from the wage-inflation lags periodically affecting European core economies, but this does not alter the role he attributes to colonialism in the general process of capitalist accumulation. Nor has he, any more than other theorists, more than vague statistical surmises on which to base his assertions on the enforced contribution of colonies to European development. Again in the same general line, his world economy (though not Braudel's *économie-monde*) was the result of Western economic expansion whose consequences can be summarized under his concept of 'peripheralization'. In fact, it can be argued that with Wallerstein we have reached the apogee of what could be termed 'schooling by terminology', in this case not from the outside but from the bowels themselves of dependency theory, for it is only in their respective verbalizations that it is possible to distinguish the operations of Wallerstein's world-system from those of other economic-imperialism doctrines. Is his own version, however, any more valid than other dependency formulations? (See Table 4.3.)

Let us take the fundamental concept of periphery. Prebisch used it in the comprehensive sense of non-industrialized economies, and *dependentistas* after him used it to denote the underdeveloped world. Even in these instances there were ambiguities, because Australia and New Zealand, which are not underdeveloped and hence not 'periphery' in dependency usage, certainly could not be considered 'core' in the Prebisch sense. Japan, who could hardly be part of the 'core' after the war, was certainly not 'periphery' even then. Afterwards Japan too became 'core', but 'core' in which sense:

Table 4.3 Schooling by terminology (the forces and process of history according to Frank and Wallerstein).

Frank	– Capitalism as an active historical agent makes decisions in terms of economic motivations. – It imposes exploitative MOPs in Latin America. – It transfers surplus from non-Western lands to the West and it 'underdevelops' the Third World. – Today it 'super-exploits' the Third World and fosters 'sub-imperialism'.
Wallerstein	– The 'world-system' as an active historical agent, whose centres have shifted since the fifteenth century, creates world division of labour (core/semi-periphery/periphery). – It 'peripheralizes' the 'external areas'. – Today it assigns roles and functions in the system and determines or influences processes within the individual units of the system.

in itself as a Far Eastern 'core', or 'core' in being part of the OECD, but not of the EEC? On the other hand, much dependency argumentation derives directly from Lenin, but 'core' does away in one fell swoop with the latter's 'four pillars' formula. Even granting that some of these objections can be explained away easily enough ('core' in our technological era, for instance, has no geographical limitations; not all dependency writers use the concept of 'core'; and so on), the underlying ambiguity of the concept still remains because 'core/periphery' are conceptual archetypes or paradigms, like 'progress', 'inequality', and 'dependence' itself, and they can be employed in any number of unspecific or even inconsistent ways. Wallerstein did try to give them some specificity and in this sense he coined the intermediary link between core and periphery that he called 'semi-periphery'. Even so, he does not dissipate the haze that hugs these concepts as if they were a cerebral bog. 'Periphery' in Prebisch connotes a 'placing' or 'positioning' that can be traced with a pencil on a map (though not evidently isolating it), but in Wallerstein it is essentially a condition of backwardness.

The limits of Wallerstein's world-system (or world economy, another ambiguity he cossets copiously) are defined over the centuries by the expanding frontiers of periphery. Up to the late-nineteenth-century, there was still some room outside that circle and he classified it as 'external area', also of course economically backward, but if periphery is a condition, what distinguishes the 'periphery' from the 'external area'? Certainly not colonialization, because then Latin America would not have been 'periphery' during most of the nineteenth century. Trade with the core, then, on the core's terms? But Europe had been trading actively with Africa since the rounding of Mogador in the fifteenth century, and Wallerstein explicitly considers Africa an 'external area' until the advent of late-nineteenth-century imperialism. A quantum-leap in trade perhaps? But does Wallerstein have the figures to back up this claim? He does not. What he says is that, before 1750, European trade with Africa had been in luxuries and that it was only after Europe, or the world-system (another ambiguity), became interested in African cash-crops, that it gradually incorporated Africa into the core/periphery magic circle. But and but again: were slaves luxuries in the world economy? What were those 'valuable' cash-crops he mentions: yams, millet, peanuts, palm-oil? We suspect that Wallerstein's construct here obeys above all the need to square Britain's opposition to the slave trade, which can not easily be explained on purely economic grounds, with his own Marxist dependency or economic-imperialism outlook. At any rate, the distinction between periphery and external area is by no means as clear as he pretends it is.[163]

Concerning the idea of 'semi-periphery', which again is hard to distinguish from 'periphery' itself, what purpose does it serve? Wallerstein originally 'discovered' it in Spain's decline when the forces of the world economy overwhelmed its inadequately organized political structures. But why not just say that it was 'peripheralized' by the core? Obviously we have here a pure case of reasoning from hindsight. Spain could not be placed on the same footing as the non-European periphery, because it was never underdeveloped in the contemporary sense of the term, so its relatively backward condition had to be given another explanation. Thus was 'semi-periphery' born.

Wallerstein insisted on this concept in *World-System 2*, where he used it to explain the historical ups and downs of Sweden, Prussia and Austria. Yet all these nations developed and have become 'core', and their 'semi-peripheral status' seems to have been either ephemeral or fictitious, which raises the core question of how valid it is to generalize or conceptualize on the basis of conjunctural or transitory historical situations. Even for the origins of the structure of the world-system, the European 'semi-periphery' is a contradiction in terms, because it flaunts Wallerstein's own insistence on one world-system, one process of accumulation, in brief, one unit of historical analysis, to the extent that all of Western Europe, including Wallerstein's 'semi-periphery', as Braudel emphatically contended, participated in the development of Western capitalism. Wallerstein admitted in 1982 that 'semi-periphery' was 'a still rather debatable thesis', but, after making a stab at giving it some kind of contemporary relevance in its assimilation to 'sub-imperialism', he ended by saying rather circularly: 'The argument is that it is a necessary feature (for both economic and political reasons) of a basically triadic world-scale division of labour among, now, core states, semi-peripheral states, and peripheral areas.' But is it clear that this 'triad' was also a 'necessary feature' of pre-nineteenth-century European history?

To close, finally, with the ultimate characterization and justification of Wallerstein's three fundamental socio-historical categories, in terms of the different forms of labour exploitation within them – wage labour at the core, coerced share-cropping in the semi-periphery, slavery and serfdom in the periphery – is this not the feature in his schematization of history that is most resistant to verification and that, therefore, offers the easiest avenue to refutation? On what empirical basis can he place his modern history classification of such countries as Spain and Sweden, Poland and the Ottoman Empire, or even the different parts of the Spanish-American colonial empire? Serfdom in Poland perhaps – though no more than in Russia, which he introduces into the world-system as a semi-periphery – but primarily cash-cropping in Sweden? And where in Spain's semi-peripheral condition would he place the Basque Country and Catalonia, where historically allodial holdings have been the norm?[164]

The question of intentionality

The measure of a true economic-imperialism system of historical analysis resides in the attribution of an impersonal intentionality to the economic currents and forces that, above all other influences and circumstances, shape the interrelated history of nations, or what Marxists themselves, and Wallerstein with them, call 'reification'. Notwithstanding his lofty attitude of impartial scholarship, Wallerstein does precisely that to an extreme that few historians have dared, or at least, few general historians of his eminence. He affirms that the settlement of Spanish America was the result of Europe's hunger for bullion. This was his contribution to the debate on whether it was gold and silver from America that promoted European inflation, or European economic growth that required bullion. Wallerstein, of course, favoured the second thesis. Did he do it, though, on the basis of probatory evidence, or from the necessity to systematize from the assumption of the prevalence of large purposive economic forces in the world economy over, say, the fiscal needs of the Spanish crown? His arguments at any rate consist mainly of quotes from other historians.

Conversely, he claims that mercantilism acquired 'force and coherence' as English (and French) nationalist policy during the economic recession in the seventeenth century to foil the aggressive Dutch commercial hegemony, and he fails to acknowledge Braudel's insistence that mercantilism was more likely born with the modern nation-state; in other words, that it was as much a political as an economic imperative and, as such, it long antedated the mid-seventeenth-century Cromwellian navigation laws.[165] Why the discrepancy between mentor and pupil? We think that it is because the Braudel thesis overturns Wallerstein's neat schema, in which contraction leads to competition, which leads to mercantilism and insinuates the possibility that a tendency to market closures from the sixteenth century could have actually produced contraction and competition later on. Between closure (a political act) and recession (an economic event) as causes, Wallerstein would naturally incline towards the thesis that confirms his belief in the determinative character of historically cohesive economic forces.

But where Wallerstein goes to the limit in his personification of economic forces is in his treatment of the commercial relations between Europe and the rest of the world. In the specific case of India, he accepted the quasi-legendary thesis (originally enunciated by Pliny) of a millennial imbalance of trade between Europe and the East in favour of the latter, which had to be compensated with a constant outflow of bullion. This situation, according to the Wallerstein scenario, obtained until well into the eighteenth century, and signified, in his restrictive definition of peripheralization involving incremental trade or outright colonial annexation, that India was still an external area to the world-economy, one of whose functional norms was that bullion (the ultimate concretion of surplus) had to flow from the periphery to the core and not the other way around. Europe's rapidly advancing industrialization required an expansion of markets abroad and, after 1750, it was 'decided' that India 'would have to be peripheralized', and it was at that time 'that the British began the political conquest of India and its peripheralization'.

Statements like these, in which motivations and purposes are blandly bandied about when and where they are needed to fulfil a preconceived schema, present so many loopholes and dangle so many unanswered propositions that we get the impression that, in spite of the myriad authorities he cites and in spite of the complexity of his intellectual edifices, Wallerstein came no closer than Baran did, in what seem like the remote, somewhat innocent beginnings of the general economic-imperialism hypothesis, to explaining how it was that the West underdeveloped the world.

The nagging question of conscious intentionality, of how world-historical economic forces could act with so much prescience and such unerring rationality, and of how the complexities and contradictions of the contemporary world-system can be explained as a result of such an apparently self-winding and smooth-running mechanism, is not really answered by Wallerstein's casual allegation that 'If things are, in fact, going along the way one wishes, one does not have to intend to do things' (can one separate the rationality of such a system from intentionality?), or his distinction between 'short-run and long-run intentionality', in which the former is what counts in history (was the clockwork-like world-system, then, the product of a long concatenation of 'short-run intentionalities', as if the clock had been put together by a line of perfectly synchronized watchmakers for many generations?).[166] It can be said for Wallerstein that, in exploring so minutely the issues in the history of world capitalism, he at least defined an agenda on which researchers of his persuasion can set to work to their hearts' content, and this was like inaugurating an entirely new era in the history of dependency theory. It may not be the final answer to the problems of economic inequality, but it certainly puts flesh on the bones of Baran's long-view outline.

5 *The overthrow of the orthodoxies and the progress of the West*

The onset of disillusion in development studies

By the late 1960s reality was proving fractious to the implementation of Western developmental techniques and strategies in the Third World. The onset of disillusion in developmentalism can be detected in three directions: the persistence of poverty, the failure of theory to conceal the 'rot', and the proposal of non-reducible practical alternatives. In 1958 the Pakistani development economist, N. Islam, observed that foreign investments from developed countries did not have the same results or produce the same benefits when they were made in India as when they were made in Canada. In Canada the returns, which were marginally less good than those in India, tended to stay in the economy but the profits from investments in India were quickly withdrawn or repatriated.

There were different explanations for this. The one Islam suggested went: 'It has also been seen that political association, no less than socio-cultural similarity between the debtor and the creditor countries, was an important factor in international investment.' It was an understated, eminently objective way of saying that 'blood is thicker than water', or that 'Anglo-Saxons' tend to flock together; and it is probably one of the explanations for the River-Platean economic decadence after the Second World War, when the sources of British capital definitely dried up for Argentina and Uruguay, and American capital thought it saw greener pastures in the Western Pacific, not just Japan, which was virtually obligatory investment market for political reasons, but also in the English-speaking, politically-stable ex-dominions of Australia and New Zealand. It did not matter that the River Plate region had been traditionally very profitable or that India's vast market beckoned: American and British capital, though perhaps more productive there, felt more comfortable elsewhere. Islam's observations went against the soul of *homo economicus*, but they were fairly sound, and as development economics amassed disappointment upon disillusion, the realization that results do not always ensue from rational policies began to seem more and more inevitable. There was the Bauer riposte that *homo economicus* suffers lung paralysis in the presence of a bureaucrat, but in fact Islam's figures covered the period from 'the turn of the present century up to the early 1940s', that is to say, when investors in India did not have to contend with independent upstarts or Soviet emulators such as Mahalanobis.

Equally irrational and incontrovertible were the implications of T. Caplow's question-title of 1971: 'Are rich countries getting richer and poor countries getting poorer?' How could it be that after a quarter century of development policies, development was not taking strong root in the Third World, whereas it had sufficed less than a decade of the Marshall Plan to get Europe on its feet and on the road to prosperity? However dismaying this sounded, the evidence was there, and it was being assembled on the double by development economics itself. In 1969, D. Seers questioned the concept of economic development when he stated flatly that whatever per capita figures expressed, there could be no development with growing poverty, unemployment or inequality.[167]

I. Adelman and C. T. Morris probably established a milestone of sorts in a 1973 monograph in which they said from the outset: 'Indeed it has become clear that economic growth itself not only tends to be accompanied by actual declines in political participation but is one of the prime causes of income inequality.' This was a classic case of hitting two birds with one stone: the standard objectives of economic development and the hopes of modernization theory in so far as these included democratization. These authors were, however, alluding to a problem of redistribution of gains, and it could be countered that growth had occurred, specifically in Brazil, on which country they had based much of their argumentation, and that eventually redistribution would take care of itself, as had been the case in the industrialization of the West. But such was probably not to be expected. C. Elliot and F. de Morsier published in 1975 a related study of Africa, aptly titled *Patterns of Poverty*, in which, as far as it went, all that had transpired after independence and in consequence of development policies was the entrenchment of privilege and of poverty. The rural–urban migration had not lessened the burden of inequality in the countryside, and in the cities, the few privileged, composed of property-owners, the bureaucracy and the full-time employed in services and manufacturing, kept the majority out of jobs rather than producing to create more work. The system, though perhaps more than usually unfair in Africa, was *grosso modo* valid for the rest of the Third World. Here then were neither growth nor prospects for social justice.[168]

H. W. Singer's ever-verdant faith in foreign aid – perhaps also stemming from the fact that he singled out technology as the 'core of the problem' and in one wave brushed away the bristling complexities involved – let some hope shine through in a work he published with J. A. Ansari in 1977, *Rich and Poor Countries*; but M. Todaro's ambitious synthesis in the same year left very little room for illusions about the achievements of development economics, and this despite an exhaustive analysis of its theories and its policies that gave it all conceivable intellectual benefits, even to disciplinary respectability in face of orthodox economics. To start with, Todaro admitted that, given certain distortions easy to maintain and prolong (artificially low agricultural prices, for instance) you could have equilibrium with mass urban unemployment. Theoretically, underdevelopment could last forever. His distinctions between growth and development, with which he virtually jettisoned percentages as a measure of economic performance, meant in effect that social targets displaced industrialization as the main concern of development policy. Todaro's 'retreat' in the name of development economics led him towards two rectifications: a better balance between the rural and the urban sectors, and more emphasis on outward growth. This did not imply that he was joining the *laissez faire* camp, but it was none the less a *mea culpa* coming from so committed a development economist. It also gave succour to the philosophy of 'basic needs', with its emphasis on social rather than strictly economic goals.

By contrast with Todaro's systematic approach, other critiques went for specific targets in the mechanics of development. Aid, on which Singer banked, was dismissed by B. Sutcliffe in 1971 as the transfer of 'some resources from rich countries to poor' ones and as 'a very temporary process'. And, in 1976, Mahbub ul Haq lambasted planning for being 'a numbers game', applying excessive controls, having 'investment illusions', following 'development fashions', remaining divided from implementation, neglecting human resources, and favouring growth without justice.[169] These critiques were not the all-out contempt of a Bauer or a Viner and they came from within development economics itself, although they were no less thorough for all that as they questioned the validity of the original 'four truths' of development economics: statistics, the dual-model, industrialization and planning.

Alternative methods and approaches

'Basic needs' and the 'informal sector'

The 'rot', in the sense of 'unsoundness', could not be dissimulated by some of the general and technical works that were being produced, not in themselves uninstructive or useless by any means – such as Sutcliffe's absolutely deadpan and faultless review of all that had been said and written on *Industry and Development* (1971), or F. Stewart's attempt to salvage the principle of labour-intensive, marginal-choice industrial development in *Technology and Underdevelopment* (1977) – but which were rather nugatory in light of the pronounced limping of development economics overall. Towards the end of the 1970s, in what seemed like a desperate, flung-arms attitude, the World Bank hived off a 'Fourth World' from the bosom of the Third. The countries that by rights, or by misfortune, fell into this category were so poor that they stood beyond the pale of the usual development remedies, which by inference let these stand for the rest of the Third World. They were predominantly agricultural, very-low income countries, for which new small-scale social strategies could be devised. This constituted an effort to impugn the purported unity of the Third World, although it was not totally original as it was implicit in the writings of Kuznets and others, who had cautioned decades earlier against the tendency to consider the Third World as a homogeneous mass. However, the receptivity accorded the idea in the 1980s, which resulted in the convocation of assemblies proclaiming that the 'Fourth World is the world of human scale', had to do with the previous emergence within development studies of alternative methods and approaches to the seemingly endless misery of underdevelopment.[170]

The humblest yet the most trumpeted of those alternatives was baptized 'basic needs'. Arndt traces 'basic needs' to the concern of planners in the Third Word, starting with India in 1962, to provide a 'minimum income for the poor' by channelling a substantial part of growth to the 'bottom decile of income distribution', but these provisions were really part of conventional growth strategies and policy projections. 'Basic needs' as such – a phrase first used in passing by D. Seers in 1969 and M. ul Haq in 1971, according to Arndt – acquired profile in the ILO World Employment Conference in 1975, convened by initiative of L. Emerij. '"Basic needs"', wrote Arndt, 'became the central theme of the conference document, published in 1976 under the title *Employment Growth and Basic Needs*, and in just two or three years this theme was the subject of a very large literature.' In that document, 'basic needs are defined as the minimum standard of living which a society should set for the poorest group of its people' and should cover 'the minimum requirements of a family for personal consumption: food, shelter, clothing', 'access to essential services, such as safe drinking water, sanitation, transport, health and education', and an 'adequately remunerated job for everyone wishing to work'. Exactly what the originality of these objectives was, apart from the insistence on the qualifier 'minimum', is not made clear by Arndt, as it presumably was not by the authors of the report.[171] In truth, the significance of 'basic needs' was not so much in what it put forward in the way of policies as in what it revealed about trends and outlooks within development studies in the 1970s. We would also suggest that, without neglecting the contribution of the ILO, bearing in mind that the phrase 'basic needs' had already been coined and that anyway, like 'development' and 'social justice', it qualifies for the category of conceptual archetype, its roots and its implications are a little more complex. Concerning its origins we should like to refer to E. F. Schumacher, to the fieldwork of K. Hart and to the theoretical work of M. Lipton.

Schumacher, who had been immersed in development issues since the 1930s and who had later been involved with I. Ilyich, one of the co-sponsors of the Fourth World assemblies in the early 1980s, in 1973 wrote the book *Small is Beautiful*, one of the classic social texts of the decade. It reflected the 'back-to-nature' philosophy that had come into vogue during the 1960s, not insignificantly on the back of hippy messianism, and it expressed the increasing fear that industrial civilization was out of control, polluting the environment and bringing depredation with each one of its 'advances'. Another important text from the same 'school' was *The Limits to Growth*, produced by the international organization of intellectuals called the Rome Club. It was attacked by J. Symons and others for underestimating the potential for renovation of capitalism. The pushy free-enterprising 1980s have shouted down much of the clamour for 'smallness', but in its time it contributed to steering development studies away from its lingering tendency to concentrate on industrialization as the one and only answer to the development needs of the Third World.

K. Hart was an anthropologist working in Ghana when he took up and illustrated the idea of 'informal sector' in 1973. It applied to a type of economic activity in underdeveloped societies that thrived among the urban poor and was characterized by 'ease of entry, reliance on indigenous resources, family ownership of enterprises, small-scale of operations, labour-intensive and adapted technology, skills acquired outside the formal school system, and unregulated competitive markets'. Its most common manifestations in the Third World cities were the street-hawkers and the corner stands. The idea of the informal sector was widely adopted, appearing as late as 1985 in Worsley, as a viable instrument for economic improvement among the deprived, complementary to the macro-tactics of development economics, which never seemed to trickle down enough to the masses.[172]

Hart had deliberately restricted his field of vision to one aspect of underdevelopment, that of the make-do struggling of the urban poor. It took an academic viewpoint to raise this modest but fertile descriptive approach to the stature of a theory and methodology. This was in essence what M. Lipton did in his influential 1977 book, *Why Poor People Stay Poor.* He did not take underdevelopment as one large problem requiring one overall solution. He did not, for instance, take up the study of industrialization or of trade strategies, but went into underdevelopment and dismantled piece by piece and from all conceivable angles the dogma that development requires urbanization and the transformation of villages into farm factories. It was not just a question of restoring a balance between rural and urban growth, or of articulating better the two sectors, as some revisionist literature, such as Islam's *Agricultural Policy in Developing Countries* (1974), advocated, but of actually taking things as they were and improving them, of respecting the predominantly rural order in most underdeveloped societies, and protecting and stabilizing it through the conservation of skills, the alleviation of fiscal impositions, the stimulation of production, and the rational adjustment of prices mainly through the market. On behalf of this position, Lipton argued that urbanization had been a fiasco, in fact, 'pseudo-urbanization' because of its impermanence. Underlying the entire edifice was the myth of industrialization schemes based on 'savings' from the countryside. At bottom, his reasoning stemmed from the simple fact of the failure of industrialization and with it the bankruptcy of the conventional wisdom of development economics.[173] At different ends of the rural–urban spectrum, Hart and Lipton coincided in that 'development' was not so much a question of innovating on a large scale, whether through industrialization or through the reformation of 'old ways', as of working with the imperfect clay to hand and shaping humble but serviceable pottery with it. This became one of the the crucial elements in 'basic needs'.

Streeten, a down-to-earth theoretician who had always tended to look for the booby-traps that development theory inadvertently stepped on, but who, nevertheless, as late as 1975 had been wrestling with the paradoxes of Third World industrialization, became one of the most zealous advocates of 'basic needs'. With N. Hicks in a 1979 paper, he rationalized his position by arguing that, since no clear pattern of development emerged from growth and redistributive strategies, the main concern of development economists should be 'the eradication of poverty'. The rest of the article was devoted to an exploration of just what were 'basic needs' and how they were to be met, and to criticizing the so-called 'income approach' to the alleviation of poverty. The measuring rods used were health, education, food, water supply, sanitation and housing, whose supply or availability were largely in the domain of public services, including transfer payments and other redistributive measures. 'In a sense', concluded the authors, 'life expectancy is a kind of weighted "composite" of progress in meeting physiological basic needs.' As to the policy of raising income, which was tantamount to the ultimate goal of standard development strategies, they attacked it, along with such things as disease-spreading 'hydroelectric dams and irrigation or drainage schemes', for either involving more social costs than benefits or for not attending to the satisfaction of real needs, such as when income increases were 'spent on food of lower nutritional value than previously consumed'.

D. Seers, who, like Streeten, was closely associated with the World Bank, was frightened in 1972 by prospects of inequality and poverty into the twenty-first century and envisaged an alternative 'world scenario' with 'strong and more independent nations. . .restricting foreign political and cultural influences, and therefore limiting economic contacts'. It would be a matter, as Lipton also expected, of building development on 'local traditions'. The sort of industries that Seers contemplated would manufacture practical inexpensive goods, such as hoes and bicycles. The concept of development in all this was either infrequently employed or given a meaning alien to the daily literature of development economics. It did not have to do, for example, with trade between the industrialized and the non-industrialized nations, or even with trade exclusively between the latter, but with self-reliance, with making do, like Hart's informal sector, with what you had.[174]

'Basic needs' literature grew for a while during the early 1980s. R. Sandbrook in 1982 stated frankly that rescuing the poor took precedence over economic growth because it was a moral obligation. He was in favour of work-making and communal projects. In a 1984 review of two Streeten books, *First Things First* and *Developmental Perspectives*, Lipton sounded very optimistic about the 'basic needs' approach. Did it work? he asked. 'The answer depends on four main issues. . .First, can basic needs be measured and defined in a way that enables policies to be targeted on the needy? Second, can need be linked to economic demand? Third, can the cost of meeting need, especially the cost to the powerful, be contained? Finally, what is the relationship between meeting needs and achieving growth and development?' The answer to the first question was a definite yes. The answer to the second implied two additional questions: would greater productivity among the very poor (for that was a part of satisfying 'basic needs') be met by insufficient demand, and, if not, would the price of essentials rise? Not 'if poor people supply and demand their own needs, in more or less self-sufficient economic units, from family farms through villages to nations'. The costs of 'basic needs' policies obviously had to come from cash-strapped Third World resource funds, but they were not really very high bearing in mind that those policies often relied on co-operation at the communal level, as in the example he gave from India: 'Translated into *antyodata*, it has meant in India village meetings to identify the five to ten very poorest households – followed by supervised lending to help them buy and manage productive assets: a few goats, a few carpenter's tools, at most simple-fishing equipment or a cycle-rickshaw.' Finally, on the question of growth: 'At the level of the individuals and of nations, there is convincing evidence that better health, nutrition and education are associated not only with greater happiness but with improved economic performance.'[175] How different was this, however, from what Rosenstein-Rodan had written when he preached 'social overhead' in the 1940s? As we said, it really was not the contents that mattered, which after all only reflected what was going on in the Third World, but the angle of vision of development studies, which had been dramatically re-oriented as a consequence of the disillusioning 1960s and 1970s.

'X-efficiency' and the NIEO

There were other alternatives in the 1970s besides 'basic needs' to orthodox development policies. In 1978, H. Leibenstein expounded the notion of 'x-efficiency' as one of the benefits to be gained by a country that accepted the challenge of competing in the world market. The 'gang of four' were doing exactly that from the fringes of far eastern Asia, but their achievements were not yet spectacular enough to overshadow the OPEC 'success story'. The time of export-substitution industrialization would come in the next decade.

In the meantime, other trends were becoming visible in the Third World. The affluence of Third World oil-exporters was virtually financing the cause of the NIEO, even though, according to the predominant opinion in the West, the hardest struck by the successive oil crises of the 1970s were the poorer of the Third World nations, which presumably implied a de facto absence of solidarity within that bloc.[176] Since it had first been adumbrated in the non-aligned conferences of the 1960s, the NIEO had become the main theme at UNCTAD and at international gatherings such as the North–South dialogue held in Paris in 1975 (North–South being a new catchy designation for development–underdevelopment). When all the rhetoric lifts, what remains of the NIEO is the remarkably constant Third World exigence that it be offered 'fair' prices for its commodities, which the First World was not about to do in the 1970s when it was being squeezed without tenderness by even such loyal Third World oil producers as Iran and Saudi Arabia. In any case, the NIEO was not really an alternative to development economics, but a logical projection of state-orchestrated development strategies on international forums. The state in the Third World, which had always been the impresario of developmentalism, was simply making its case heard by brandishing an oil shillelagh. NIEO meant something more than what the formula actually expressed. Like 'informal sector' and 'basic needs', which adverted to a tendency bigger than themselves, it made it very clear that the epicentre of developmentalism, whatever the West did or said, had passed to the countries of the Third World itself. The Third World had had about all the theory it needed from the West and what it wanted now were results, concrete progress towards greater international equality. In the West itself, Singer, Hoogvelt and many others were assiduous propagandizers of the NIEO. Finally, there had been for a long time another alternative to development economics, one that had been proposed both from the West and from the Third World, but it was an alternative one remove away from a complete rebuttal, and it is mainly as a critique of development economics that we meet dependency again in the context of the so-called debate that bears its name.

The dependency debates

Developmentalism and the Marxist dependency critique

What exactly is the dependency debate? When did it start? Is it still going on? To start with, there was not one but various dependency debates. In one sense, it was an ideological struggle against dependency theory by those Marxists who decried its neglect of the concepts of MOP and of class struggle, which they tried to make central to the understanding of underdevelopment and of its origins and future evolution. In another, it was an inevitable face-off between developmentalism and dependency. The first and earlier debate, which was mostly a one-sided critique, is crucial to the course that Marxist theory has taken in the 1980s, but the latter debate, though perhaps less easy to define, has a larger context, a wider audience, and probably greater overall academic implications. Also, it represents, in the context of this work, a culmination in the two parallel intellectual processes of theorization on the issues of international economic inequality that we have been following, and as such we shall give it pride of place. What it was not is easier to say that what it actually was. It was not an organized, ongoing discussion following certain rules of procedure in certain specific venues that started on such-and-such a date. In fact, the only 'places' where it appears to vaguely conform to this model are in the pages of certain books and journals – such as the *Latin American Research Review*, the 1984 edition of Meier's *Leading Issues in Economic Development* and Abel and Lewis's *Latin America: Economic imperialism and the state* – where dependency and anti-dependency opinions are juxtaposed and discussed. In only one case that we know have the opponents actually addressed and refuted each by name on specific issues, and this was in the rather acrimonious confrontation in the pages of the *Latin American Research Review* between D. C. M. Platt and the Steins.

Outside this, the debate was a matter of hither-and-yonder pronouncements, broadsides and snickers from either side. In this sense, it is still going on, with much less fury than it had at its climax, which was probably around the early 1980s. What in this 'debate' leaves no place for ambiguities is that it was, is, and perhaps, in some way or another, will continue being, an issue-less clash between 'Western' and 'Marxist' opinion on how to interpret the origins of underdevelopment and ultimately on how to go about overcoming it. And what the 'debate' or 'debates' actually achieved was to bring together in a sporadic, touch-and-go manner the views and the positions on either side.

It could also, and perhaps more accurately, be interpreted as developmentalism becoming aware of the Marxist dependency critique. The concept of dependency, which, as we have seen, has Marxist credentials going back to Lenin at least, did not figure at all in the early phases of development economics, and this is perfectly understandable since, whereas dependency was a vague archetypal designation for the condition of the weaker nations in the capitalist world economy, development economics involved then a vigorous and promising new approach to the relations, both actual and conceptual, between the developed and the underdeveloped countries, far more interesting and original than the Stalinist nostrums of the early postwar years. Dependency theory gradually acquired its proper contours when it began during the 1960s to shed its *déjà vu* air of political propaganda in a wrapping of dusty theorization in the work of thinkers in the West and in the Third World, especially but not exclusively in Latin America.

The commonplace Western explanation of the rise of dependency theory is that it was a reaction of Latin American intellectuals to the failure of ISI in the late 1960s. According to Seers, 'The realization that import substitution created new, possibly more dangerous, forms of dependence converted the ECLA "structuralists" into "dependency" theorists.'[177] The implication is that formerly committed Latin American development economists suddenly in the 1960s became ranting Marxists. It is shared in essence by O'Brien, Fieldhouse, Streeten, R. Thorp, Arndt and others. However, the facts of the contemporary history of dependency theory simply do not corroborate this explanation. The vast majority of dependency theorists from Baran to Frank and the Latin Americans and on to Wallerstein were Marxists critical from the start of capitalist models of development. The Venezuelan writers from the early 1960s that we alluded to before were Marxist dependency theorists in full, and they certainly entertained few hopes about capitalist development. The same thing can be said of Marini, dos Santos, Hinkelammert and other social critics, and of Halperin-Donghi and Galeano among historians in one way or another affiliated to dependency. None of them was 'convinced' from anything else to dependency, and they did not have to because they had a long tradition in Latin America itself from which they could take a legitimately Marxist definition of dependency. Frank, who was not Latin American, got his own version of dependency, as such defined by him and as such accepted by the majority of commentators, from the 'Monthly Review school', which included a phalanx of adamant anti-capitalists, and Frank himself created a 'dependency school' from his teaching posts in Santiago de Chile, not exactly 'dependent' on ECLA.

The incidence of the failure of ISI on Latin American dependency theorists cannot be denied entirely, but rather than fundamentally motivating, this experience was principally 'more wood for a fire' that had been burning before, with the additional uncertainty that it is not possible to say with precision when it was exactly that ISI had failed. Some of the equivocations around the use of the term 'dependence' come from the resounding 'early' use of it made in works by Cardoso and Faletto and by Sunkel. But Cardoso and Faletto were at least *marxisant* and to complicate matters they were not entirely disabused about the possibilities of capitalist development and therefore can hardly be described as 'motivated' by the failure of ISI. On the other hand, dos Santos, who was decidedly Marxist and anti-developmentalist, is credited by Palma with having presented the 'earliest' and the best (if somewhat circular) version of dependency theory. That leaves Sunkel/Paz, and perhaps others, as the embodiment of ECLA disillusionment with ISI, according to the Western scenario, but they certainly are not considered anywhere as typical dependency writers and their vague invocations of more economic interventionism in underdeveloped economies, like Cardoso and Faletto's carefully modulated endorsement of socially distorting capitalist growth (of the sort denounced by Adelman and Morris), could rightfully be considered an intellectual sideshow in the wider *mise en scène* of dependency theory.

A standing target that hits back

Development economics was a standing target for Marxist dependency theory. Between the two there were no 'grey areas' where issues could be discussed with some hope of consensus, except on the reality of underdevelopment itself. The tries that have been made to somehow 'assimilate' dependency and development studies – notably by Preston, I. Roxborough, Meier, Kitching and Streeten – are not in our opinion too convincing. Preston's intricate categorizations and Streeten's 'litmus-based' teams of 'blues' and 'reds', yield some kind of 'order' in Third World theorization only if one aspect of thinkers such as Frank or Amin is taken out of its wider ideological context.[178] To pretend that they can be lined up in the ranks of Western development research because they favour de-linking underdeveloped economies from the capitalist international economy, which is what relatively orthodox development economists such as Singer, Furtado, Sunkel, Seers and Streeten have sometimes favoured, is to forget that Frank and Amin were always intent on a repudiation of developmentalism lock, stock and barrel. Roxborough and Kitching simply assume that dependency can be studied under 'theories on underdevelopment' without qualifications. But Marxists, if only from the fact that they consider their work 'scientific' and all the rest 'ideological', do not submit to 'assimilation'. And, besides, the awareness of incompatibility is probably mutual.

Development studies took tardy notice of dependency. It was only in the 1984 version of his large compilation on development issues, which first appeared in 1964 but went through editions in 1970 and 1976, that Meier included a section on dependency. By then, in its form as the long-term general theory of economic imperialism, dependency had been around for over two decades at least, and its criticism of development studies had been eliciting ripostes for some years before from the affected, some contemptuous, some hurt, but none too gracious or willing to compromise. This immovable, long-lasting and irreconcilable antagonism between the two sides forms the basis of the debate.

One of the first reactions against dependency by a development economist was uttered by D. Lehman in the 'Introduction' to a collection of essays he edited in 1970 on the crisis within development studies. He turned the tables on the critics from the left and stated flatly: 'The symptoms of crisis should rather be seen in the failure of the self-styled critical, radical and alternative approaches to generate a new theoretical apparatus', and he dismissed the 'thunderous language' of *dependentistas* by diminishing it in comparison with 'Jonathan Levin's classic *Export Economies*, published in 1960'. The truth here, however, is that the Levin book he cited is a static and circular analysis whose pretension to originality lies in the claim that 'No comprehensive picture of export economies' (in itself a misnomer for raw-material exporting economies) existed in 1959. This was to ignore much of the literature of 'orthodox' and 'non-orthodox' development economics. On the part of Lehman it also meant either that he had not read much dependency literature or that, if he had, he had chosen to disregard it.

The famous 1975 P. J. O'Brien essay on dependency, which was descriptive and sympathetic and gave such impetus to the general use of the term, did not, as did his 1985 're-visit' to dependency, confront it with its critics, and in particular he took little notice of the carpings of 'Western' students of development. These were becoming quite sharp by the late 1970s and they did not emanate exclusively from academics in the developed countries. The Indian economist S. Lall, in a 1975 paper, took the idea of dependence to mean underdevelopment, no more and no less, and from that angle went on to argue that since some highly industrialized economies, by definition non-dependent, also were dependent in crucial ways, then either they were not developed or dependence said and explained nothing about underdevelopment except 'to pick off some salient features of modern capitalism as it affects some less developed countries and put them into a distinct category of dependence'.[179]

The Chilean G. Palma's participation in the debate is significant in that he made two attempts, one in 1979 and another in 1981, to define dependency as a method 'to analyze peripheral societies through a "comprehensive social science", which stresses the socio-political nature of the relations of production; in short, the approach is one of political economy, and thus an attempt to revive the nineteenth and twentieth century tradition in this respect'. His praise for 'dependency' research by Laclau, Sunkel and Singer, and his criticism of Frank and dos Santos, were proof of where he stood in the debate, and it also signified that he was trying hard to make a non-Marxist approach to dependent development workable. But he was not anti-Marxist: he accepted in fact dependency's Marxist origins and he even criticized Frank, via Brenner, because of his 'un-Marxist' point of view. His opposition was to Marxist *dependentistas* who did not grasp 'the specificity of the historical process of the penetration of capitalism into the peripheral countries, and only condemn its negative aspects, complementing their analyses with a series of stagnationist theses in an attempt to build a formal theory of underdevelopment. These analyses are mistaken not only because they do not "fit the facts", but because their mechano-formal nature renders them both static and unhistorical.' What he was doing was criticizing the contemporary long-view of economic imperialism, as it was espoused and applied by dependency thinking in Latin America, from the point of view of Marxist sociology with its reliance on changing relations of production through class conflicts, so that his position seemed somewhat ambiguous: on the one hand, he was a developmentalist with Marxist leanings; on the other hand, as Marxist in the same general situation as Cardoso and Faletto and even Sunkel, he associated himself with dependency.[180] Palma by rights belongs in the mode-of-production camp, and if we place him with an equivocal developmentalist stance in the dependency debate, it is because he himself chose that station by defining dependency in a manner that went against the grain of fundamental dependency thinking.

The 1981 Palma essay was part of the Seers-edited *Dependency Theory: A critical reassessment*, and this was clearly and specifically an answer to dependency criticism of development studies, as Seers' 'Introduction' made explicit. In it he said that 'dependency' stemmed from 'structuralism' (the explanation of Latin American inflation as the result of supply inelasticities), in the face of 'widespread political pressures for development'. What brought 'structuralists' and '*dependentistas*' into one fold, or what made '*dependentistas*' out of 'structuralists' (the two possibilities existed in Seers' rendering of the process), was that both points of view held 'that the underdevelopment of Latin America was due to its reliance on exports of primary products, which were subject to terms of trade that both fluctuated in the short-term and deteriorated in the long (the Prebisch-Singer thesis)'. Seers did not endorse, or entirely deny, that possibility. He attributed the little headway that dependency had made in Western developmentalist circles to the view of 'mainstream' economists that it lacked 'rigour'. He himself deplored 'a great deal of writing in the dependency field' for its rather 'low professional quality' and for partaking of the 'shocking habit of ideologically-committed social scientists of all schools, picking out whatever evidence fits one's theories and ignoring the rest'. He shared M. Bienefeld's and D. Evans's contention, expressed in one of the essays in the book, that dependency 'raises the right questions', but Seers put the burden of coming up with the right answers on dependency by pointing out that the example of newly industrializing countries (NICs) such as Singapore, South Korea and Brazil, which could not be treated 'as a temporary, limited exception', flatly contradicted the basic dependency tenet about 'the limits to capitalist development in the periphery'.

NICs was a phrase of wide acceptance, designating a special slot within the concept of underdevelopment. From it would in turn be portioned off today's 'gang of four' or 'four Asian dragons' as the collective designation of the four Asian economies that in the general opinion of economists have definitely broken out of the underdeveloped mould. The surge of these 'dragons' would become in the 1980s one of the main happenings, perhaps the central one, in the field of development studies. It is certainly at the root of the resurgence of the neo-liberal, neo-classical stance that today dominates development economics – if it is still possible to speak of one such, given that the now dominant trend has always in the past denied its relevance – and Seers was certainly right in underlining the issue, although he was not the first to do so, or the only one doing it at the time. The other argument that Seers used to put dependency on the defensive was that, in order for it to be pertinent, it would have to 'embody empirical content'. Here was an unmistakable rejection of dependency in the thick of the debate from the point of view of development studies, and one that seemed fairly final despite Seers use of the distinction between dependency schools, with Palma, Cardoso and Sunkel on one side, and Baran and Frank on the other. The 'de-linking', 'semi-autarchic' model of the latter was definitely in question, entitled to its ideological framework but not deserving of much scientific respect; the former attitude was promising, but it remained under observation.[181]

The 1985 P. J. O'Brien overview of dependency contained a review of the work that was being done in Latin American dependency studies. Most of it was either a refutation of radical dependency or a defence of the anti-imperialist 'liberationist' line. Some of it was of the Marxist sociology school. O'Brien himself had a hard time trying to reconcile the latter approach with dependency, which involved a stinging critique of Cardoso and Faletto.[182] The real dependency answer to development studies could be found in Wallerstein's world-systematics and in the 'discussion papers' (sections of his resolutely anti-capitalist *Crisis* books, with titles such as *Development of Crisis and Crisis of Development* (1979) and *Long Live Transideological Enterprise: The socialist economies in the capitalist international division of labour and West–East–South political economic relations* (1983)) that Frank was putting out from the University of East Anglia, perhaps in response to the output at the Institute of Development Studies at Sussex University, where Seers, Sunkel and others were based. If anything, all this made the divide more manifest and the debate even more hopeless.

A historical debate: D. C. M. Platt v. the Steins

In the historical field D. C. M. Platt, who had taken unto himself the role of number-one dependency-basher, wrote 'an historian's objection' to dependency in a 1980 issue of the *Latin American Research Review*. Unlike Seers, who initially gave dependency the benefit of the doubt on the question of whether or not it was ideological and void of scientific content, Platt took as definitive the definitions of dos Santos and O'Brien to the effect that dependency meant the external conditioning of Latin American economies towards underdevelopment, which is the *ne plus ultra* statement of its ideological stance. He further accepted Stanley and Barbara Stein's *Colonial Heritage of Latin America* as being the best concrete historiographical expression of that definition (which, *obiter dicta*, was not at all warranted, as the Steins were actually stating in summary form, and in English, long-held Latin American opinions). He summarized it thus: 'Latin America, colonial and national, was from the first drawn into the international economy as an exporter of foodstuffs, raw materials and precious metals, and as an importer of capital and manufactured goods.' Platt's answer was to say that Latin America 'stood outside the currents of world trade and finance' and was of no interest and of no concern at all to the capitalist international economy and so could hardly have been forced or even prodded into a situation it considered harmful and did not want. What then prevented Latin America from industrializing and relegated it to the lowly role of supplier of farm produce and raw materials to the powerhouses of capitalism? 'The obstacles to autonomous industrial growth were formidable. Latin America lacked skilled labour. . .suffered from endemic shortage of industrial fuels. . .Domestic markets were small and scattered. . .Exploitable raw materials were in short supply. . .Capital was scarce. . .With handicaps such as these, domestic manufacturing was slow to develop in Latin America with or without the machinations of the metropolis.' In brief, Platt contended that 'Latin American economies in the 19th century were shaped by domestic circumstances' and not by the manipulation of 'planned requirements' from abroad. The origin of production for export was to be found in the 'supply of the home market, and it was on this home market that the whole structure of railways, of public utilities, and of city modernization was built'. The only valid use for him of the dependency cognomen was for the 'banana Republics' and for such cycles as 'the quinine boom in Colombia, Bolivian tin, Amazonian rubber', which hardly mattered to world trade or finance.

The Steins, who had the right of reply in the same issue of the journal, picked at Platt's figures to show that in the period 1820–50 Latin America ranked 'close' to the USA as an importer of British goods. But it was not so much on global statistics that they based their answer to Platt as in the decisive quality of the influence of international trade in shaping the regional, outwardly oriented vocation of Latin American economic activity. Argentina's cattle and raw wool exports were the consequence of a monopsony situation provoked by a combination of the closing of the Bolivian markets, which led to the relocation of ranching in the Buenos Aires region, and of endemic political unrest in the interior. The British were in a position to be the sole buyers of local production, and they made sure that the patterns of production and trade did not change. In the case of Mexico, the Steins showed that the pattern of exports, mainly silver, varied as little, from the colonial situation to independence, as the pattern of imports from Britain, mainly yard goods, which were 'the major factor in the containment of the Mexican artisan and fledgling industrial cotton manufacture'.

This line of argumentation constituted a remarkable illustration of how consistent over nearly a century were the insights and positions of economic-imperialism theory since Hobson had first given it coherent form and included in it the thesis of the de-industrialization of India through the import of cotton wovens. An external arbiter in the dispute could easily have pointed out that whereas Platt's criticism of dependency was statistical, forthright and simple, the Stein's counter-block to it was convoluted and dispersed. It involved complex historical and geographical differentiations, unsuited to polemics over numbers, and they themselves put the finger on the issue: 'It is not primarily the facts that are in dispute in the present controversy', and this too would have seemed perfectly obvious to an impartial observer. For trade and financial dependence to occur – and Platt did not dispute this, but the determining character of the dependence – it was not necessary for the centres of the capitalist system to employ themselves fully: if sufficient interests were involved, they could make it happen and with it economic retardation as well. Latin American economies were no match for Britain's. The means were simply proportionate to the ends, and therefore Platt's statistics did not prove that British capitalism had not contributed to the international economic role of Latin America. Platt's insistence that Latin America was absolutely on its own during the nineteenth century – as he claimed in a further *razzia* into dependency territory in 1985, 'hardly anybody outside Spanish America cared one way or the other for Spanish American politics, trade and finance' – led him to affirm in exasperation that Latin America's underdevelopment was Latin America's own doing (as when, for instance, it utilized foreign capital to finance wars and 'political railways'), and this position, which had to do with fundamental ideological choices on the question of the origins of underdevelopment and economic inequality, was basically what kept 'Western' and dependency historiographies miles apart and made the 'dependency debate' a 'dialogue between the deaf'.[183]

The general critique of dependency

The historical critique

The orthodoxy of development economics was elaborated with specific targets in mind. The acid test of its efficacy was reality itself: how good were its policies and recommendations for achieving economic development in the Third World? It failed the test and turned to the study of the ways and means of alleviating poverty. Its rather circular propositions (public services, redistribution, communal projects) have had no greater impact than they would have had if they had not been formulated. For 'basic needs' there have always been 'basic responses', and exhortations can hardly masquerade as solutions. Dependency, however, can be a rather slippery customer in the context of the world capitalist economy, because it can always retreat into the 'bunker' of saying that its 'revolutionary solutions' have not been adequately tested or have been sabotaged by reactionary capitalist forces. It can still go on denying validity to the Western contention that underdevelopment and economic inequality have endogenous causes, and it can go on proclaiming that both were caused and are being perpetuated by economic imperialism, or whatever other name or phrase is used in its stead, be it dependency, world-system, or simply capitalism.

Dependency, therefore, pretends that it can only be judged as a theory. How well does it function as such? There are two sides or aspects to it: an explanation of the historical expansion of the West and of all that it entailed, in particular both formal and informal colonialism; and a theory on the origins of economic inequality among cultures and nations, in other words, an 'etiology' of capitalist world expansion and a 'pathology' of its consequences.

As a theory on colonialism it probably works better than political and other explanations. As between the notion that British colonialism in India was somehow humanitarian and the charge that it acted on the search for and expectation of profits there is really little to choose. Dependency as a theory on the origins of inequality is another matter. Dependency thinkers agree on one point with other historians and analysts, and they raise two special issues. The point of all-round agreement or consensus is that despite inter-cultural comparabilities before the start of European expansion – in fact, the basis for interpreting inequalities – the seeds of inequality were there to begin with: the West had the upper hand in its dealings with all the other civilizations and cultures. Baran makes it a basic point in his pioneering analysis. Rodney speaks of a gap in development between Europe and Africa. Bagchi even admits that Mughal India was not developing towards capitalism when the British arrived, and he has the backing of no less an authority than Habib. The Steins, and all Latin American dependency historians, uphold the thesis that Latin American independence was not much of an improvement over the previous situation of colonial economic subjection. Needham, the modern historian who comes closest to contesting the superiority of the West, and who is no closer to dependency than a Manchu mandarin to a Hunan peasant, in the end has to find reasons for Chinese stagnation and willy-nilly posits the existence of a Chinese threshold that no culture except the West ever crossed.

Where dependency goes its own way is in pretending that the *ab origine* inequality was not very pronounced and could have been mitigated, or even entirely bridged, if the West had not interfered with and inhibited the spontaneous process towards nationhood and economic development that was *in ovo* in each culture that it affected or subjugated. At the very least, a thinker such as Bagchi affirms that the West retarded the process, and at worse, as in Rodney, that it actually crippled and hand-tied an entire continent. In the case of Latin America, Western capitalism actuated all the levers and exerted all the pressures needed to keep it in a condition of stunted development. Dependency, as well as some non-dependency, historians point to countless signs of cultural achievement and self-reliance as proof that, if it had not been for European colonialism and imperialism, it stands to reason that non-Europeans would have been capable on their own of the same economic achievements, from capitalism down, as Western civilization. For some, the idea that capitalism was a block to progress is profoundly un-Marxist, but since Marx and Engels blew hot and cold on the subject of inter-cultural inequalities, and since their fundamental ethical position was anti-colonialist and egalitarian, dependency theorists and historians are probably justified in thinking that the legitimacy of their Marxist affiliation cannot be gainsaid.

The special issues that their collective works raise are: did the colonialist dependence of non-Western societies actually inhibit a previous economic process of accumulation that was gradually evolving towards capitalism and economic development? And did political subjugation (the throttling of spontaneous nationhood) and informal imperialism prevent any further progress along that road, or, alternatively, would political independence have made any difference in the long run to the creation of the underdeveloped Third World? Since neither capitalism, in the sense of what Braudel calls the world of high-profit commercial enterprise, which involved expansive maritime trade networks from at least the thirteenth century, nor the Industrial Revolution could have happened without the accumulation of surplus, the first question can be broken down into three component parts: Did a surplus exist in non-Western cultures? Was it being put to productive use? And did its expropriation by Europe contribute decisively to its own growth?

From the evidence of commerce all over Asia before and after the arrival of European traders and colonizers, the existence of an exportable surplus can hardly be denied (although this may be questioned in the case of Africa during the seventeenth and eighteenth centuries, when much of the trade going on was in human lives). Serious dependency historians (in India, for example) are not sure that the surplus was going mainly into the circuit of production at the time that Western military and commercial technologies affected other cultures, but all dependency historians agree that after this happens, and after the process of colonialism got seriously under way, the surplus most definitely flowed into the trade circuits of capitalism and eventually into the making of the Industrial Revolution. For them, with or without sufficient statistical proof (most often without it, because it simply does not exist one way or another), the surplus from America, from Asia, and from Africa reappears in increasing Western profits and in Western productivity, which are in fact the proof of its expropriation and transference. In other words, the growth of inequality is the basis of the dependency presumption that inequality was produced by capitalism as part of a continuing historical pattern. The more extreme dependency interpretations even affirm that the industrialization of Europe could not have occurred at all without surplus from non-European lands, and this too is assumed from the size of the development gap that resulted after the eighteenth century.

The trouble with these theories lies in that, if historical reasoning can be reduced to a game of building-blocks of this kind, where what counts are portmanteau concepts, like surplus and accumulation, and large comparisons and generalizations, then history can easily be turned against them. Europe's development, the inception of capitalism itself, began before overseas expansion. Primitive or primary accumulation, a prize Marxist-derived concept to explain the Industrial Revolution, is now thought to have been less significant than it was believed to be in the past. Rather than the result of one 'big push', to which captive colonial muscle gave a decisive shove, industrialization is seen as the product of an accumulation of many individual events and forces over centuries of history, resulting in something akin to the critical mass in a nuclear reactor. The intensification of colonialism, at any rate, did not ensue until after the Industrial Revolution, and even Rodney's dense compilation of African contributions to European development cannot disguise the fact that these contributions were mostly marginal and non-essential. Even slavery, which furnished so much of the labour for European plantation economies in the New World, was defined as a 'luxury' traffic by Wallerstein, a transparent exaggeration that, nevertheless, admits the possibility of debate on the issue of its economic importance to the West. Dependency arguments based on the big concept of surplus are conclusive neither in the sense of explaining the origins or the persistence of inequality, nor in elucidating why and how the Industrial Revolution came about.

If we insist on the statistical proof of dependency arguments that Western expansion contributed crucially to the development of Europe and its industrial breakthrough, we come up to either a dearth of evidence or back again to more surmises, such as those involved in the use of the concept of surplus as an instrument of broad historical interpretation. There are no statistics in Baran, Frank or Wallerstein indicating the amount of surplus extracted by the West from its peripheries, and, therefore, there can be no precise correlation in their works between that surplus and the conjunctures in Europe's process of development. It seems more than likely that silver from the conquest of America fuelled West European economy activity and the commercial and financial rivalries between the advanced capitalist networks of England and Holland. Is it deducible from this that the process leading to England's industrialization was given a necessary impetus, or even that it was accelerated, by the arrival of American bullion at the precise speed that it showed historically? Or would it not have occurred the way it did and when it did even in the absence of colonialist booty? The second question in truth cannot be answered or even explored, because we cannot separate the economic history of the modern world into discrete compartments, but we cannot, in all fairness, go to the other extreme and postulate a necessary seamless relationship between the long history of European capitalism and the shorter history of Europe's gradual, very gradual, absorption of the wide world starting in the mid-fifteenth-century. There is no statistical basis on which to posit such a thing.

The respectable I. Habib provides perhaps the closest approximation to a statistical grounding for the thesis, which he bases on Marx, that the 'drain of wealth from India was essential for the genesis of industrial capitalism', when he argues that 'it might have amounted' (including also that from the West Indies) to 'say 4.8 per cent' of British national income in 1801, and this, in spite of its seemingly small size, 'would still have equalled 70 per cent of the British annual net domestic investment'. This argument, however, apart from the complex assumptions behind it – on the breakdown of that wealth into consumption and investment, on the ultimate destination of the latter, even on the accuracy of its estimations – would seem to indicate, as often in dependency literature, more a programme of academic research than a finished thesis on dependency relations.

Habib remits the opinion of the Marxist M. Dobb, which he does not share, that 'the exploitation of the colonies appears as an element of mercantilist policy rather than as a source of primary accumulation'. Habib's (or Dobb's) distinction is not very clear in that there is no reason to suppose that trade relations could not have been a source of accumulation on the same footing as the direct appropriation of colonial wealth. In any event, the allusion to mercantilist trade policies opens up a residuary distinction on which to put dependency arguments about colonialist surplus on a more plausible foundation. There can be direct appropriation through conquest, and there can also be indirect appropriation through enforced unequal trade relations, and it is to these that Marxist historians in Britain seem to incline in their examination of the relationship between English industrialization and English colonialist policies. C. Hill says explicitly, perhaps conclusively: 'It is difficult to establish any direct connection between wealth amassed in the plunder of India and other colonies and the capital which financed England's industrial revolution', a somewhat ambiguous statement which, however, he had qualified before by saying that 'An essential prerequisite for industrial revolution was large and stable colonial monopoly markets'. And Hobsbawn counterpoints: 'Behind our industrial revolution there lies this concentration on the colonial and "underdeveloped" market overseas, the successful battle to deny them to anyone else.'[184] These much more modest claims are perhaps as far as serious economic-history research would probably allow dependency theory to go in its quest for the proof of its affirmations on the origins of international economic inequality. But they mainly reinforce the assumption that inequality was the pristine condition of the relations between East and West, and they hardly explain the ultimate causes of the economic world hegemony of the West.

The 'blessings' of political independence

If only because the thorniness of the issue is more manipulable, dependency stands on much more solid ground when it claims that Western colonialism and imperialism throttled incipient independent nationhood in Asia and Africa. The historical evidence is also more abundant. Morocco, Egypt and Persia are examples of countries that had enjoyed sovereignty or had short-term potential for modern nationhood before they were occupied as colonies or converted into semi-colonies by European countries. Alternatively, Thailand, Afghanistan and Liberia, on distinctly different levels of cultural evolution, managed to attain the condition of relatively modern nation-states without permanent overt colonialist tutelage. This line of reasoning, however, leads to embarrassing or unanswerable questions such as: Would the East Indies ever have become Indonesia without Dutch rule? Or India what it is without the Raj? The answers would have to be purely contrafactual. Evidently, in the course of time and even if only through what economists call the 'demonstration effect', every non-Western territory in the planet would have become a nation-state, and evidently as well, the resulting colour-scheme in the map of the world would have been different from the one we have now, but, more significantly: Would it have made any difference as far as today's international economic inequality is concerned? Does political independence contribute to development, and does its absence invariably produce underdevelopment? The dependency thesis, which Rodney expressed with more force than anyone else, is that with political independence the colonialized nations of the world would have had a fighting chance, and that therefore if Europe so ruthlessly denied them that chance, it must have been because of the commensurate size of the benefits that it was deriving from them and the fear of losing its hold on those benefits.

Bairoch, in an examination of the 'myths' of colonization and underdevelopment, has honed the issue to fine cliometric sharpness: how have colonialism and independence affected manufacturing production and per capita GNP in the Third World since 1750? His figures, whose sources are not entirely clear and whose reliability he himself admits is 'far from perfect', indicate that in 1750, both in industry and in per capita GNP, the future Third World either level-pegged or surpassed the West, but starting in the following century, manufacturing in the Third World declined to a low of 6.5 per cent of world production in 1953, while per capita GNP remained almost unchanged between the two dates, showing an insignificant 8 per cent gain compared with an increase of 479 per cent in the developed countries. From 1953 to 1980, manufacturing in the Third World increased almost 7 times and per capita GNP went up by 87 per cent from 1950. Clearly, the West does seem to have de-industrialized the Third World and the demise of colonialism seems to have stimulated economic growth.

However, Bairoch's GNP figures for Latin America show that from 1750 to 1860 there was almost no change, from 1860 to 1950 there was an 80 per cent increase (compared with 225 per cent in the West), and from 1950 to 1980 there was another 'hefty' gain of 64 per cent. Bairoch is sceptical about the significance of his figures on the contemporary evolution of the Third World (he thinks they are too optimistic), but even if from the aggregate series we accept the 'logic' that colonialism underdeveloped and independence fostered growth in Asia and Africa, why is that 'logic' so unsatisfactory in the case of Latin America?[185] Why did Latin America not develop after obtaining political independence, if that is all that development required? Rodney's emphasis on the absence of nationhood in Africa certainly cannot apply to a world of independent nations such as Latin America. For Wallerstein, the entry of the Third World into the world-system and its peripheralization (read underdevelopment) occurred by the door of colonialization. So why didn't decolonization lead to de-peripheralization? Within the theoretical rules of his system, that was certainly a possibility, as the economic progress of such 'semi-peripheries' as Austria and Scandinavia demonstrate.

The dependency answer to these objections is that Latin American independence was not real, that it was, in fact, economic dependence, arguably even worse than Spanish colonialist rule. But, one, there are no grounds for claiming that the Latin American republics did not enjoy full political sovereignty after independence, and, two, economic dependence does not necessarily produce underdevelopment, and if anything the contrary: that dependence can lead to development, has all the makings of an even likelier proposition. Argentina and Uruguay developed at the height of the nineteenth-century economic imperialism, and they 'underdeveloped' precisely when imperialism, after the Second World War, was on the wane.

Whatever may be said of Africa and Asia, theorization on Latin American underdevelopment always seems to lead to Latin America itself. Does this then mean that dependency is a valid thesis for parts of the Third World and not for others? That it encompasses the colonialization of Asia and Africa, but not that of Oceania and Australia, or that it stops short even of being fully applicable to Latin America? These possibilities are not contemplated by the theory itself, which is predicated on one capitalism, one world-system, one global set of historical motivations, and one related group of international patterns of action and reaction; and since it cannot make all the facts of history fit these stipulations, then the exceptions leave dependency in tatters, and it cannot reasonably be sustained that there is anything even approaching a fundamental underdeveloping model of dependency. Such being the case, negative implications start invading its theoretical structure. Because economic exploitation per se cannot be denied – for even Western historians admit that it is possible and even likely – it does not follow that imperialist exploitation always operated in a rational, systematic and deliberate way. And if intentionality cannot be proved, than it cannot be said that capitalism set out from its European shores with the aim of 'underdeveloping' the rest of the world and creating inequality for its own benefit. But that it could conquer the world does mean that the inequality was there and that its causes were inside the cultures that had not been able to keep up with the West. It is even likely, although this is also absolutely contrafactual and worthless, that with or without colonialism and dependence the world would have ended up divided, as it is today, into developed and underdeveloped countries. Admittedly, a lot of unnecessary disruption and an incalculable mass of suffering would have been avoided, but then who is to say that the suffering would not have taken place in other ways and through other causes?

Dependency's 'sins of omission'

In sifting the possible from the worthless, it would seem that the most that dependency analysis can yield in exploring the origins of international economic inequality, on the assumption of inter-cultural comparabilities before the onset of European expansion, is that non-Western cultures and nations could perhaps have achieved a greater degree of political and economic development free of Western colonialist and in general commercial domination, although not without the demonstration effect of Western civilization and not very likely to a state of advanced industrialization, and that they contributed marginally, and mainly through unequal trade relations, to the Industrial Revolution. And the complementary claims of dependency that expansive Western capitalism developed internally by underdeveloping its external areas, are not sustainable on its arguments and evidence, although, in the case of the European dependencies in Asia, a valid claim can be made, and has been advanced with varying degrees of plausibility, that Western domination was, on balance, more damaging than constructive. But the latter claim is again strictly contrafactual and seems somewhat exaggerated in the case of Africa. The underdevelopment of Latin America as exclusively a product of European and American economic hegemony (that is, excluding the possibility of crucial endogenous determination), although not contradicted in D. C. M. Platt's argument that Latin America was excentric to British economic interests as a whole, has not been demonstrated either globally or for individual Latin American republics.

This critique of dependency has centred on what the theory argues. But dependency also commits grievous sins of omission, two of which will be briefly indicated here. Frank rejected the psychological implications of modernization theory on what seem like solid reasons based on the assumption of the psychological unity of humanity. But just as the categorization of 'traditional' social attitudes can be carried to suspect extremes, so the denial of cultural influences in economic retardation (which is what Frank's critique implies) can also produce a blind spot. In his Calcutta office, Bagchi pretends to ignore the manacling social effects of caste. Likewise, Latin Americans in their holier-than-thou excoriation of 'Anglo-Saxon' racism neglect to face the implications of their own perhaps more subtle but equally pervasive forms of racial prejudice.

Baran made a perfunctory bow to the environment, perhaps aware of the precedent for that in Marx, but almost no other dependency author considers the environment worthy of even a passing glance. When questioned about Indian agriculture, Habib replied that the Ganges plain was more productive than the temperate climates of Europe because it allowed three harvests of rice a year, which, as arguments go, is as abstract a proposition as a reference to the mountains of surplus agricultural produce in the European Community. After many years of residence in Dar-es-Salaam, Rodney appeared not to be conscious of the enervating effects of the African climate and milieu, to which any medical history of the continent could attest. The dependency distrust of cultural and environmental influences on economic performance is, of course, grounded on its assertion that backwardness can be attributed solely and directly to economic imperialism, but what this attitude reveals is basically a blatant theoretical *parti pris*. Environment and culture alone may not explain underdevelopment and its persistence, but the claims for their socio-historical impact are too cogent to be ignored.

To close the section on dependency, how far did Third World theorization escape from its original Western womb? The long-view economic imperialism model was given shape by Baran, with materials taken from a Marxist tradition stemming from Lenin that went through a Comintern and a Stalinist phase, supplemented by contributions from Western Marxist sources. It incorporated a system of capitalist worldwide exploitation, centred first on Western Europe and then on the United States, governed by purposeful self-regulating mechanisms and by forces embodying rigid unvarying psychological principles and motivations. Withal it had a certain 'aliveness', as if it were being run by an all-powerful intelligence or by a boardroom full of infallible corporate directors, leaving no place for errors or to chance, as in Wallerstein's depiction of the exact historical juncture when Britain 'decided' to 'peripheralize' India, not unlike a company's decision to put a new production unit into operation.

The practice of historiography along these lines is comparable to a mad hatter who fitted all his clients with the same hat-block, yet Third World thinkers mostly accepted it without substantial modification. If changes there were, they tended to emphasize the irresistibility of the centre, the strength of its grip and the inclemency of its purposes, and the vulnerability and powerlessness of the periphery. Efforts to make dependency seem less fateful and less rigid, as Cardoso and Faletto or Palma attempted, have been cast aside by hard-line dependency doctrine, and they themselves never managed to break loose enough from this tendency to really make a moderate dependency outlook workable. There is little leeway therefore to distinguish between 'Western' and Third World dependency theories, and both find themselves at this point in time in a situation where, given the radicalism of their past commitments, they either recant or go on saying over and over that the West underdeveloped the Third World and that capitalist development is a myth. Neither possibility augurs well for the future of dependency.

The *laissez faire* and the Marxist reactions

The attack on the dirigiste state

Perhaps the greatest irony among the many that we have discovered in this conjoint history of the confrontations between Western developmentalism and Marxist economic-dependency theory, is that both tendencies seemed to have very nearly reached the end of their tethers at about the same period, that is, the second half of the 1970s, and both likewise were faced by challenges to their previous predominance from within their own respective camps. Again, both these challenges had actually existed for a long time, and what was happening now was their vigorous re-insertion into the central current of study and debate on underdevelopment as a consequence of changing practical and theoretical circumstances.

In the case of Western developmentalism, what arose to confront the dogmas of development economics was essentially the old neo-liberal, *laissez-faire* critique first formulated during the mainstream phase, which had been given new impetus by, one, the snags in the state-directed development strategies in the Third World, and, two, the confirmation of that critique by the phenomenal growth of the free-enterprise economies of the 'four Asian dragons', all of which had put the Bauer approach back at the top of the agenda with the support of a fresh cohort of fully committed volunteers. Unlike the early development economists, who occasionally indulged themselves in speculation on the far or near causes of underdevelopment, the protagonists of neo-liberal, neo-classical development economics – the title suits them badly and they reject it, but it still applies because their basic interest lies in the means of stimulating growth in the Third World – have turned their backs on this theme and prefer to devote their intellectual energies to the denunciation of the '*dirigiste*' state, as D. Lal calls it, and to the demonstration that the market is the place to go to for economic momentum, even for policy guidance. On general lines, this approach follows two tendencies: that of the theorists of *laissez-faire* as such, among whom are Lal, K. Basu, R. Bideleux, W. Elkan, and Bauer himself, and the strategists of export-substitution industrialization, such as B. Balassa and J. W. Bhagwati. Lest it be thought, however, that the four-dragons example only works for neo-classical development economists, it should be pointed out that the thesis that their development was the result of unadulterated *laissez-faire* liberalism has been criticized to good effect by J. Bergsman and N. Harris.[186]

The MOP, class-struggle alternative

In the Marxist camp, the reaction against dependency was manifest in a strong tendency towards an MOP, class-struggle approach to underdevelopment, and more to the point, towards the study of the development of capitalism in the Third World, which was perhaps better grounded than economic imperialism on the Marx/Engels canon. Frank's iconoclastic and unimpeachably revolutionary exertions thrived, while Latin America and the Third World were agitated by the centrifuges of rapid decolonization, social unrest, revolutionary change, and even by the OPEC disruption of capitalist markets. The fortunes of dependency have ebbed as the Third World has simmered down through exhaustion and economic crisis.

But dependency came under fire from Marxists long before the tide of revolutionary socialism in the Third World had begun to subside. In 1970, E. Mandel wrote that revolution would come first to the imperialist states. The specificity of imperialism lay in that 'it unites the world economy into a single world market, it does not unify society into a homogeneous capitalist milieu'. For Mandel, underdevelopment was the result of the 'universal law of uneven and combined development', a grand pronouncement that allowed for a sneaking sympathy with dependency theses. Other Marxists were less complaisant towards the dependency neglect of the MOP and class-struggle paradigms. The French theoretician C. Palloix attempted in 1971 a Marxist representation of the world economy, which came straight from Luxemburg in that international capital 'required' the existence of national markets. There were in it certain superficial similarities to the world-system that Wallerstein would soon afterwards spring upon the academic world, but all resemblances between the two authors were conclusively confounded when, six years later, Palloix published a treatise devoted to the elaboration of one particular theme in his earlier work: class struggle and capitalism on a world scale.

In the early 1970s, another French Marxist, P. P. Rey, used the concept of articulation of MOPs in order to adapt Marx's dynamic view of socio-historical change to pre-capitalist societies. In his scheme, capitalism first penetrated less developed societies in a subordinate station to the previous MOP, created a different MOP through articulation with it, and eventually would become the dominant MOP. Exactly the same scheme was used by H. Alavi in defining the Indian 'colonial mode of production', except that this author was not as self-assured as Rey in proclaiming that he had discovered a new intermediate mode of production different from capitalism. Since the colonial mode of production was not 'completive' – because it was the 'imperialist bourgeoisie' that modified the previous local MOP, and it was the same bourgeoisie that, in changing Indian society, pocketed the benefits – Alavi wondered whether it should not be considered, rather than a colonial, 'an imperialist MOP that embraces a global unity'. The similarities between these constructs and traditional Marxist interpretations of Latin American reality in terms of dual MOP formations could not be negated by the use of tags such as 'articulation' or 'colonial MOP', and this could be seen in the affinity for MOP analysis of E. Laclau, another orthodox Marxist with a quarrel with dependency. He disdained to engage in disquisitions that altered the original Marxist MOP paradigms and stated forthrightly that, in Latin America as elsewhere, feudalism came before capitalism and that Frank was purblind in not seeing the feudalist character of pre-capitalist Latin American societies.[187]

In his analysis of world capitalism, Palloix had rejected the thesis of the imperialist importance of MNCs, preferring instead the idea of the 'self-expansion of capital on a world scale', and in his 1977 work he relied significantly on the Marxist theory of value, from which he deduced that there was in international capital a 'tendency towards the equalization of conditions of production and of exchange'. This could be interpreted as another refutation of the Emmanuel thesis, and it went considerably further than the Bettelheim critique that exploitation was more intense in industrial societies than in backward economies, in saying that exploitation was the same the world over, or, at least, was quickly heading in that direction. In fact, this went even further than Warren later dared in trying to discredit the statistical evidence of underdevelopment, and the excess of ideology over empirical evidence here showed.

In a merciless but blatantly unfair 1977 criticism of dependency, the American Marxist theoretician R. Brenner cornered Frank's theory into the conclusion that, in emphasizing the unjust relations of exchange between developed and underdeveloped countries, it was in the event a defence of ECLA developmentalism and of third-worldism in general. This was carrying dependency-bashing to unreasonable extremes, since Frank denied developmentalism outright and was always rigorous in advocating radical change directly from underdevelopment to socialism by way of anti-imperialism, a strategy that had impeccable Leninist credentials. In 1979, J. Weeks and E. Dore attempted another refutation of dependency based on the Marxist theory of value, but they mostly kept well within the reasonable limits that their ideological partiality permitted. Their principal argument was that both Emmanuel and Amin, whom they chose as the most respectable spokesmen of the dependency thesis of appropriation-through-exchange, had confused value with exchange value (that is, market prices), and, at precisely the opposite extreme of Emmanuel, they affirmed that unequal exchange was simply inconceivable. They reasoned that in the international market place a mean price was established between products from different conditions of production, which meant that all producers received the same unit price for their goods, but that if some producers received more per labour/time spent on production it was due to their greater efficiency. Weeks and Dore, in a bow to one of dependency's principal concerns, explained that international economic inequality resulted from the interest of 'merchant capital' – which, unlike reproductive capital, was rewarded not according to labour/time but to costs of opportunity – in maintaining and reinforcing pre-capitalist production relations. In the end, however, the authors explained that merchant capital laid the foundations for capitalism and they reiterated the Palloix contention that under the bourgeois mode of production there was a secular trend towards the equalization of the rate of profit, which did not, on the other hand, 'preclude the creation of "blocking" forces which reinforced backwardness'.

Finally, in this review of Marxist dependency critiques, J. G. Taylor justified the introduction of transitional modes of production into Marxist theory with the assertion that Marx had never analysed 'the combination of modes of production', for which reason he wanted to establish a 'new theoretical framework', which would provide 'a basis for analysing economic phenomena, the class structure, and political representation'.[188]

Shared problems and converging criteria

All these theoretical efforts shared a common slew of Marxist problems, apart from the express intent in most of them to prove the deviations of dependency theory from Marxist dogma. They had, first of all, to deal with the hard nut of why capitalism did not seem to be displacing other MOPs in the Third World, which was the equivalent, in dependency and developmentalist terms (for once agreed on something), of why underdevelopment persisted in the Third World. The answer they gave, on the whole, was that the contrary was true; in other words, they avoided the issue, or simply denied it was an issue. In fact, the only MOP theorist who has seriously grappled with it is the British Marxist N. Harris, in whose 1986 model (perhaps the closest anyone has come to a vindication of the much-maligned Warren thesis on imperialism) world capitalism, or simply capitalism, and the Marxist 'laws' on accumulation, on capital flows, on surplus value, and on class exploitation, function to perfection both in the developed world and in the underdeveloped countries. In one audacious swoop, Harris, who used the 'gang of four' as the mainstay of his analysis (with Brazil and Mexico thrown in for good measure), managed to prick the dependency balloon, to debunk orthodox development economics, and to turn the tables on the neo-classic, neo-liberal school of developmentalists. 'In sum', he wrote, 'the process of the dispersal of manufacturing capacity is a general phenomenon, not simply something restricted to the "gang of four". It involved increasingly complex patterns of changing specialisation, interweaving different parts of the world unknowingly in collaborative processes of production. If permitted to continue – and it was quite unclear how it could be stopped – it bid fair to end – or at least render very much more complex – the simple picture of industry in more or less developed countries.' Dependency in his view was transformed into capitalist interdependence, which in turn depends on the capitalist 'laws' of capitalist economic development, not to 'be confused with the conquest of hunger', and not on the will of individual capitalist forces, be they MNCs or entire national entities like the USA itself.[189]

Another of the problems of anti-dependency orthodox-Marxist theoreticians was trying to explain class struggle on a world scale and proletarian solidarity. The stumbling block here is the relatively simple observation that the natural setting for the class struggle is a concrete social situation, specifically society within its national bounds rather than abstract world society. This problem, like the problem of the origins of underdevelopment, was posed deliberately and specifically by dependency theory through its emphasis on international exploitation, and in facing these problems orthodox Marxism was virtually picking up a gauntlet that dependency had flung. On the issue of proletarian world solidarity, MOP theorists did exactly as they had done with regard to the evolution of the backward economies towards the capitalist MOP: they either fudged the issue by claiming without evidence that it was there, or they telescoped it towards a future when all socio-economic tendencies within capitalism would mature; and on the issue of the origins of economic inequality, they likewise tended to look the other way, or fell back on the old chestnut of dual-MOP social systems that inexplicably went on functioning in niches within the capitalist world economy. In fact, on this last issue, it is not easy to distinguish between MOP and dependency theorists.

A curious area of convergence between these two Marxist contentions has to do with the notion of 'merchant capitalism'. We have seen it used in Baran, Frank and Bagchi, among others in the dependency camp, and by Dore and Weeks at least, on the MOP side. What exactly is 'merchant capitalism'? In dependency authors it is simply a means of sidestepping the issue of how it was that 'capitalism' started underdeveloping the non-European nations from the start of European overseas expansion. Since from any Marxist perspective it is highly unlikely that the capitalist MOP could have been fully operative in the sixteenth century, dependency authors (who insist that it was capitalism, and world capitalism to boot, that underdeveloped) had recourse to the idea of a lesser historical form of capitalism, which was precisely 'merchant capitalism'.Dore and Weeks built a theory of underdevelopment specifically on the concept of 'merchant capitalism'. They argue that it is 'merchant capitalism' that prevents the inception of 'industrial capitalism' in backward countries. This would seem to mean, in effect, that capitalism is not one MOP but two, or else, that 'merchant capitalism' or 'merchant capital' is a non-capitalist MOP, and this would seem to imply that it was, for instance, European feudalism that underdeveloped Latin America. In Marx himself, however, 'merchant capital' is mentioned as subservient even in the European pre-capitalist stage, and since this invalidates the creation of the category of 'merchant capitalism', between one absurdity (that pre-capitalist Europe subjugated and underdeveloped the rest of the world) and another absurdity (that capitalism was in some way fully operational when Europe started expanding overseas), we have chosen the lesser of the two, which is to take Baran and Frank at their word when they claim that it was capitalism that underdeveloped. Ironically, the implication of two capitalisms in dependency authors is made fully explicit in Dore and Weeks, and this puts all speculations based on 'merchant capitalism' on an unstable foundation, hardly dissimulated by the ambiguous use of the phrase 'merchant capital' rather than the more forthright 'merchant capitalism'.

Finally, the Yugoslav academic I. Vujacic actually claims that Marx himself made the distinction between these two capitalisms, and that this explains his ambivalent attitude to colonialism: on the one hand, critical when it embodied merchant capitalism, and, on the other, encouraging when it represented the progressive, industrializing capitalist MOP. But this is mostly empathic reasoning, which tries to reconstruct what Marx might have been thinking from hints and fragments in his work.[190]

What, then, is the principal contribution of MOP theory to the issue of the origins of international economic inequality? What Rey – who, according to A. Foster-Carter, is the most brilliant exponent of contemporary MOP theory as applied to less developed countries – actually did was to substitute the dependency scheme, whereby the blocking of development was a formal feature between nations or between cultures, with the idea of the articulation of modes of production, by which means he tried to demonstrate that in the relations between the advanced and the backward countries the necessary analytical references were not 'reified' economic forces, such as those embodied in dependency theses, but modes of production. The substitution of units of analysis does not actually make dependency theses less valid, but it does allow for a process through which eventually capitalism can displace all pre-capitalist MOPs. What seems fairly evident is that, in going back to MOP and class analyses (which is what in effect has been happening, to judge from the appraisals of non-Marxist observers such as Roxborough and Worsley), Marxism in our days has virtually given up on the question of the origins of economic inequality and in this it is back again where Marx, who was not particularly keen on the subject, left things.[191]

In the Third World, MOP and class analyses operate in a context of existing international economic inequality or at least so it seems from the historical perspective assumed by their users, who are mostly unconcerned about the origins of inequality, unlike dependency theorists, one of whose basic contentions is that they can tell when potential equality, in terms of economic and social progress, was cut short and transformed into stagnation or retrogression through unequal inter-cultural and international relations. Neo-Marxists can claim that, since they have never harboured any doubts about the potential equality of humanity, they see no reason to delve into the origins of international economic inequality, and in this they may well be justified, but the assumption of equality does not obviate inequality itself, which for the Third World would seem to be as valid an academic endeavour as the study of the Industrial Revolution for the West. The fact that dependency probably elicits the wrong conclusions might not mean that no other conclusions are valid.

The historical progress of Europe

The short-term and the long-run view

Without deterministic implications, development and underdevelopment can be related as a vertical, mutually reinforcing continuum. This does imply one-sided advantages, and it would not, therefore, be amiss to consider the development of the West for illumination, by way of contrast, on the origins of underdevelopment. The historical fulcrum of Western economic development was, of course, the so-called Industrial Revolution, but there is more than one perspective in which to place it. As with the theory of economic imperialism, there is a short-term and a long-run view of the development of the West. The short-term perspective centres on the origins, the characteristics and the consequences of the Industrial Revolution (M. W. Flinn, P. Mantoux, T. S. Ashton, P. Deane, D. S. Landes, S. Pollard, W. Parker). The long-run view frames the Industrial Revolution in a centuries-long process with a wide political and cultural sweep going back to the Middle Ages (O. C. Cox, J. U. Nef). The historians who assume the latter perspective are in the tradition, started by Marx (adumbrated earlier by Adam Smith) and pursued by Weber, Sombart and Schumpeter, of studies and research into the general development of capitalism. Perhaps the most illustrious and influential contemporary long-run view of Western development was the one presented by F. Braudel. We have referred freely to his ideas in the section on Wallerstein, in order to establish a difference between what we described as a closed ideological system and an open methodology in which there is no attempt to put all of reality under one's belt, so to speak. The aspect that now concerns us is Braudel as philosopher of capitalism and chronicler of the development of the West and of the world economy.

In trying to comprehend capitalism, Braudel does not accept unreservedly or consistently employ the concept of mode of production, and his analyses can be defined as the unschematic search for the forces that within Europe propitiated capitalism and economic progress. For Braudel, when all is said and done, Europe is capitalism, but capitalism also eventually entered into a large, Western historical synthesis. Below capitalism, everything is *économie*, which embraces all productive activity involving interchange. Capitalism was not exclusive to Europe, but it was there that it reached its fullest elevation, and it was from Europe that it spread and absorbed all the other world economies, which were partly capitalist or proto-capitalist but had not managed to achieve the vitality and the assimilative capacity of Europe. In order to explain capitalism, rather than giving a straightforward definition, Braudel finally settled on an analogy to its evolution short of full-fledged industrialism: that of a three-storey building with each floor containing economic activities of increasing degrees of intensity, complexity and latitude. The ground floor is the level of a simple market economy, in which farmers and artisans exchange produce and wares. The floor above is where competition takes place and implies a wider geographic setting, with merchants travelling from market to market. The highest storey or level belongs to long-distance commerce, a risky but extremely profitable activity whose practitioners try to establish arrangements that are a denial of the free and open competition characteristic of the other two levels. It is on the third level that capitalism resides, and it is on this level that the accumulation necessary for industrialism occurs.

In other words, Braudel's view of capitalism is one basically of degree rather than of quality, and his work can legitimately be read as, partly at least, a refutation of Marxist categories and methodologies. Braudel set the emergence and growth of capitalism on a triple foundation, corresponding along general lines to his building analogy. First of all, there must exist an active and expansive market economy, which is a necessary but not sufficient condition for progress. The second requirement is that society must give unqualified sanction to private accumulation and to the search for profits over a long time and at all stages of a capitalist progression. And, finally, there must be commerce on a world scale. The latter is not the be-all and end-all of capitalism, because Braudel at this stage was still considering only its pre-industrial phase, but it is 'the obligatory passage to a higher level of profits'. Europe reached the third storey in Braudel's analogy because it fulfilled those three requirements. What happened elsewhere in the planet?[192]

Runners with tied feet

Concurrently with the history of capitalism in the West, Braudel glances periodically at other cultures, or civilizations, as he prefers to call them. In all of them, the first two stages of *économie* were achieved, sometimes exuberantly and brilliantly, and, in the case of India, there was even a partial, hesitant entry into the third level, but in none of them did society give its total unconditional backing to private accumulation and enterprise as it did in the West. What was even more damaging than withholding this sanction was that the other cultures were dominated and bound up by political despotism, and this was basically what prevented capitalism from becoming an all-encompassing force. Despite its ruthless sway, despotism did not build up adequate defences against external intrusions, and when the West brought to bear on it the brunt of its resources and abilities, it buckled and collapsed, utterly in the case of India.

In Braudel's view, Japan presented the closest parallels with Europe: it only lacked foreign commerce, which the Japanese ruling classes hindered and restricted, in order to keep up with the West. Paradoxically, Japan did allow an 'ancient merchant capitalism' to flourish despite its own despotic tendencies and habits. These views in Braudel which seem to imply that progress requires above all else economic rather than political freedom and also that, historically, despotism is not the thoroughgoing and unvarying monster that Wittfogel portrayed. The most oppressive system of them all, to which Braudel did attribute the worst rigours that Wittfogel described, was that of China, capable of emulating the West in every field, but held back by its own perverse obstinacy in hobbling itself.[193]

Braudel related Europe to the other civilizations through two distinct analytical motions: in one, which is central to his outlook, he described how capitalism virtually made the West into the most powerful of all civilizations or *Hochkulturen*; in the other, he studied and explained the failure of the other societies to attain to full capitalist development. Only subsidiarily did he explore, as dependency historians mainly do, how it was that the West conquered and exploited other cultures. Despite the occasional approval that he gave to dependency arguments, what he presented was basically a disparity in economic vitality between Europe and the rest of the world, and, in the end, probably the safest generalization that can be made from his work on the subject of economic imperialism is that the West did not so much conquer and underdevelop the rest of the world as that it overwhelmed it with the sheer weight of its economic strength. If there is a flaw in all this, if despite the wealth and the brilliance of Braudel's vision we emerge from it still not entirely satisfied that it embraces all that can be said about the inequality between civilizations, it is precisely because Braudel chooses civilizations as the final non-reducible units of his analysis and because he never steps behind his rigorously descriptive method and thus never asks how and why originally his historical units diverged so markedly in their over-arching social self-definition.

Grasping the nettle of the environmental explanation

In the first volume of Braudel's fundamental trilogy on economic history, *Civilization matérielle, économie et capitalisme*, Braudel adverted to certain material disadvantages in non-Western cultures relating to their environments, but he did not develop that idea any further. On the other hand, his assertions on the basic similarities of all higher cultures up to the fifteenth century have a certain gratuitousness about them that is not dispelled by his fulsome descriptions of pre-colonial Indian capitalism or of Arab commercial practices in the lower Middle Ages. He himself admitted that, even in its pre-British heights, capitalism in India left most of society outside its reach and influence.

In order to examine the comparability of cultures before the advent of the Industrial Revolution, the economic historian E. L. Jones decided that he felt 'bound to grasp the nettle of the environmental explanation'. His approach to the task is direct, almost brutal in the way in which it clears the underbrush of lesser issues and goes straight for the big trees. For Jones, by the time that Europe started expanding outwards, there was no question of parity between cultures: Western material advantages were uncontestable and decisive. His explanation for this *ab origine* inequality is twofold: on the one hand, environmental circumstances amply favoured Europe and, on the other hand, despotism terribly handicapped Asia, which contained Europe's only real competitors. Whereas Europe's geography encouraged maritime trade and put it at a relatively safe distance from the depredations of the Central Asian hordes, Asia's 'risk-profile' included periodic catastrophes that stimulated a high rate of reproduction, resulting in overpopulation. The latter argument is crucial in Jones, who wrote: 'This places the explanation of the difference in Asian and European levels of breeding and income squarely in the fertility response to different risk environments.' Whereas in Europe 'fruitful political variety, capital accumulation and trade all seem partly explicable as adjustments to Europe's particular site and endowments', the ultimate geographical disadvantage of Asia was that it was open to invasions from the steppes and these established the despotisms that were so ruinous to its economic evolution.

Jones harps on this theme more than on any other. He calls Asian governments 'imposed, military despotisms', 'regimes of conquest originating from the steppes', 'alien, imposed military despotisms'. Everything else fades in importance by comparison: natural and social disasters, overpopulation, climate, geography and location. Jones did a bit of a throwaway speculation on the possible connection between overpopulation and despotism, but he did not pursue the idea, and this leaves a wide explanatory gap at the heart of his environmental theory on inequality.

The book in which Jones expounds these hypotheses is *The European Miracle* (1981). The 'miracle' that Europe performed was that it managed to avoid despotism and to release its energy and creativity through technological and economic progress. With Montesquieu, Jones apparently believes that despotism is the commonest form of governance because it results from the unbridling of the passions. But these simple inferences leave his environmental ideas a shambles. They explain Europe's natural advantages over Asia, but only cursorily the 'miracle' of Europe's political freedoms and of its states system. And they certainly do not explain the one crucial thing that needs explaining: the genesis and persistence of despotism all over Asia, for it leaves unexplained how it was engendered in the flat expanses of Central Asia where the subjugating hordes originated and how these hordes carried in them so pertinacious a vocation for despotic rule. There is, in addition, the objection to this theory that it does not apply to the origins of Chinese despotism (at least), which was certainly alive and flourishing before the Empire fell under the rule of Mongolian despots.

There are finally serious observable flaws in Jones's analysis. His explanation of Asia's 'overpopulation', if to start with it existed at all (for he offers no conclusive evidence on this score), is prima facie unconvincing. How can catastrophes, which occur only sporadically even in Asia, determine a constant rate of collective fertility? Or, turning the argument around, were not the magnitudes of the demographic disasters he chronicles a consequence rather than a cause of overpopultation? We feel tempted to say that with Jones we are back again with Bernier and Montesquieu and their emphasis on despotism as a cultural manifestation, but this would be unfair because Jones does put his finger firmly on environmental causation with as much scholarship as it is probably possible to muster in our times. He did not simply toy with the concept and he did not bury it under reams of qualifications. And this is important, because if we accept the principles of the psychological unity of humanity, the only valid explanation of inequality has to be environmental.[194]

The trouble with environmental theorizing on the origins of intercultural and international inequality is that ultimately the ground on which it reposes is shaky from the point of view of objective enquiry. We said before that there are two approaches to the study of the development of the West, both centred on the Industrial Revolution, but one short-term, oriented towards the Industrial Revolution itself, and the other long-term, oriented towards the origins and the process of capitalism. There is a third possibility. It can be termed the 'fate' or 'original settlement' hypothesis, and it seeks the origins of inequality in the remote past. Bosschère and Braudel hinted at this. So did A. W. Crosby and perhaps W. McNeill. Jones makes it explicit when he concludes, after discussing Clark and Piggott and McNeill on the ancient origins of medieval farming: 'On this archaeological perspective, therefore, Europeanness lies in the form of the original settlement history.' In other words, the ultimate environmental explanation of inequality would have to go back to the time when the different branches of the human family spread over the Earth and occupied their respective portions of territory, each with its distinctive physical and climatic characteristics. After that, each race followed its own environmentally determined destiny, mingling cautiously on the peripheries but keeping mostly to themselves, until Europeans, who had the pick of the world's environments, sailed out and, as Crosby puts it, started stitching the 'seams of Pangeae'.[195] And therein lies the rub.

One is left with next to nothing on one's hands

The search for environmental causes can lead so far back in time that one could find oneself with next to nothing in one's hands. Jones cites one Ishida, who wrote that 'the lasting character of each people has its roots in the basic culture of the time when the people first came to being'. From this, Ishida explained Asian cereal-eating as a consequence of the graminivorous habits of a family of Australopithecines. Jones wisely refutes: 'At best *Australopithecus* is a doubtful ancestor of *Homo sapiens*.' More to the point, it could be argued, following the bent of environmental theorization, that it gains in force the further back in time the branches of the human family settled the different parts of the Earth, and indeed it is a commonly held paleontological hypothesis that mankind evolved in different places from his wandering ancestor *Homo erectus*, perhaps more than a million years ago, certainly time enough for the environment to have imposed upon each branch any number of physical and socio-cultural exigencies. There is evidence now, however, that *Homo sapiens* might have finally emerged in one place, an African Noah's Ark so to speak, and from there spread to the rest of the globe. But even in this case, we are talking about a time-span of nearly 100,000 years, plenty of time here also for all sorts of migrations, settlements and environmental effects.[196]

If, therefore, the environmental hypothesis on the origins of inequalities does not gain or lose from the scientific research on the origins of man, there is little substance in it to sustain much speculation. Of what conceivable use then can it be? All we can really posit is that, in the absence of scientific proof of genetic racial superiorities, only the environment can explain the modern inequalities between nations, and that these inequalities, from a very long-term perspective, were originally differences that came to be perceived as inequalities owing to certain environmentally determined but transitory advantages in some cultures – the Chinese over the rest of the Far East, Europe over the rest of the world – and that advantages and inequalities will eventually sort themselves out. In this sense, therefore, the idea itself of the origins of inequality is probably unresearchable and can only serve for clarification, comparison and taxonomy, which has in fact been our principal interest all along a work that has taken us on a round, *nihil-novum* trip from the *ab origine* perception of differences and environmental theory to international economic inequality, and back to the likely but nebulous environmental root-cause of human diversity, with culture in the form of despotism thrown in for good measure, the final irony in a journey that has delighted in them.

6 *Conclusions*

What has our search for an explanation of international economic inequality turned up? There have been, we think, three important results: (1) a taxonomy of theories and their historical sources; (2) sufficient material to evaluate from a theoretical perspective the possibility of economic development in the Third World; (3) arguments on the feasibility of the issue itself of the origins of international economic inequality.

The theories analysed through their principal exponents are, basically, the postwar orthodoxy of developmentalism and its denial in the contemporary *laissez-faire*, neo-liberal reaction; and the two main branches of Marxist analysis: the dependency branch, which had its start in a fusion of economic-imperialism theory and Marxist dialectics; and the MOP, class-struggle branch, which claims the mantle of 'orthodox' Marxist socio-economic analysis. This taxonomy in turn has allowed us to categorize explanations of inequality into one pertinent and pertinacious motif, which is environment, and into two general classifications: endogenous and exogenous causations, which in some theorists merge into one combined theoretical outlook (Table 6.1). These explanations proceed on the assumption of the essential unity of

Table 6.1 Basic theories on the origins of international economic inequality and their temporal references.

THEORIES	SOURCES OF INEQUALITY	ORIGINS IN TIME
Developmentalism (e.g. E. L. Jones)	Environmental/ endogenous	Open-ended
Dependency	Environmental/ exogenous	15th to 18th centuries
Braudel	Endogenous/ exogenous	Long 16th century

humanity and consequently of the potential economic equality of nations.

From our own research, can we affirm that economic development is possible in the Third World? The adverse effect of some environments on economic performance cannot be considered an insurmountable cause of continuing underdevelopment. We reject a blanket acceptance of dependency and reduce its usefulness to some marginal academic validity. And, finally, we found nothing in our research to preclude the likely inference that cultural differences in our times will not impede indefinitely the progress of modernization. Ergo, we have to conclude that, theoretically, economic development for the Third World is possible and likely.

This conclusion seems almost irresistible in view of the repeated encounter in our research of the idea of inter-cultural comparabilities before the onset of European world expansionism, which suggests the reasonable possibility that what we perceive today are not so much inequalities as relatively short-term differences of cultural origin that are sorting themselves out. Given the appropriate international circumstances, development and relative equality would then be just a matter of time. What sort of equality, though, is it that we are referring to? To make a potentially interminable disquisition quite brief, we think that it consists for all nations in an acceptable and dignified level of life, access to education for everyone, and the availability of help in times of trouble, be they economic crises or natural disasters.

However, a relatively modest and reasonable definition of development such as the one above raises in turn two fundamental questions: (1) what exactly is the equality that nations are trying to achieve, and (2) what is the point of an enquiry into the origins of inequality?

In the end, probably our most significant conclusion in this respect is that the issue itself of the origins of international economic inequality is of dubious validity. Research on long-term environmental influences, as we saw, is nugatory. In the light of the undeniable weight of cultural forces, the strict exogenous determination of underdevelopment that dependency posits is, to say the least, highly debatable. It is, therefore, virtually impossible to generalize on the theoretical causes of underdevelopment. And since equality itself is a relative proposition, it would seem then that too much can be made of this issue. The feats of nations are relative to cultural and historical conditions, size, and areas of social endeavours. The fact that any absolutist concept of international equality is unrealistic, both in historical terms and as political ambition, need not be considered demeaning. The claims of economic nationalism cannot be denied outright, and need not be trampled gratuitously, but neither should they be made absolute and compulsive. The long and the short of it is that we live in an interdependent world and historical realism compels us to accept the necessity and the conditions of interdependence so long as they do not involve sacrificing the ideals of rational economic progress and of social justice.

Notes

Abbreviations of journals' names

AER	=	American Economic Review
AJS	=	American Journal of Sociology
BJS	=	British Journal of Sociology
CP	=	Comparative Politics
CPS	=	Comparative Political Studies
CR	=	Contemporary Review
DCh	=	Development and Change
EA	=	Economie appliquée
EBLA	=	Economic Bulletin for Latin America
EDCC	=	Economic Development and Cultural Change
EHR	=	Economic History Review
EJ	=	The Economic Journal
EPW	=	Economic and Political Weekly
ER	=	The Economic Record
ES	=	Economy and Society
FP	=	Foreign Policy
HJ	=	Historical Journal
HPE	=	History of Political Economy
HT	=	History and Theory
IA	=	International Affairs
IDR	=	International Development Review
IEJ	=	The Indian Economic Journal
IER	=	The Indian Economic Review
JCA	=	Journal of Contemporary Asia
JCE	=	Journal of Comparative Economics
JDS	=	Journal of Development Studies
JEH	=	Journal of Economic History
JEI	=	Journal of Economic Issues
JMAS	=	Journal of Modern African Studies
JPE	=	Journal of Political Economy
JPS	=	Journal of Peasant Studies
JSAS	=	Journal of Southern African Studies
JSPS	=	The Journal of Social and Political Studies
LAP	=	Latin American Perspectives
LARR	=	Latin American Research Review
MR	=	Monthly Review

MSESS	=	Manchester School of Economics and Social Studies
NGM	=	National Geographic Magazine
NLR	=	New Left Review
OEP	=	Oxford Economic Papers
Or	=	Orbis
PS	=	Politics and Society
QJE	=	Quarterly Journal of Economics
REP	=	Revue d'économie politique
RLS	=	Revista latinoamericana de sociologia
RRPE	=	The Review of Radical Political Economics
SES	=	Social and Economic Studies
SP	=	Sociological Perspectives
SR	=	The Socialist Register
SRs	=	Social Research
SRv	=	Sociological Review
TLS	=	The Times Literary Supplement
TM	=	Tiers monde
WD	=	World Development

Chapter 1

1 C. J. Glacken, *Traces on the Rhodian Shore: Nature and culture in Western thought from ancient times to the end of the 18th century*, California, 1963, pp. 52–8, 82–100, 103–12, 140–1, 265–74, 368–74, 439, 553–9, 562–5, 605–10; Montesquieu, *De l'esprit des lois*, 2 vols, Paris, [1748] 1979, Vol. 1, pp. 187–91, 258–9, 377, 379, 391, 428–31, 468 (compare book XIV, ch. 2, and Glacken, op. cit., pp. 86–7); Adam Smith, *The Wealth of Nations*, London, [1776] 1975, pp. 174–5, 217–19, 319–21; F. Bernier, *Histoire de la dernière révolution des Etats du Grand Mogol*, Paris 1670, and *Suite des mémoires du Sr Bernier sur l'Empire du Grand Mogol*, Paris, 1671; in particular in the first work: 'Lettre a Monseigneur Colbert', Vol. 2, pp. 121–294.

2 S. Zubaida, *Race and Racialism*, London, 1970, pp. 21–2; G. M. Frederickson, *The Arrogance of Race: Historical perspectives on slavery, racism and social inequality*, Wesleyan, 1988; J. Barzun, *Race: A study in superstition*, New York, [1936] 1965, pp. 17–18, 35–9, 51–8, 65, 159–69; L. L. Snyder, *Race: A history of modern ethnic theories*, New York, 1939, pp. 61–72; and *The Idea of Racialism: Its meaning and history*,

New York, 1962, pp. 3, 11; E. Said, *Orientalism*, New York, 1978, pp. 87–8, 133, 147–50, 206–7, 232; G. Lichtheim, *A Short History of Socialism*, London, 1970, p. 180; G. W. Stocking Jr, *Victorian Anthropology*, New York, 1987, pp. 23–4, 47, 58–69, 76, 92–6, 245–73; D. J. Kevles, *In the Name of Eugenics*, New York, 1985; N. Stepan, *The Idea of Race in Science: Great Britain 1800–1960*, Oxford, 1982, pp. 47–66.

3 E. Said, op. cit., p. 162; H. T. Buckle, *History of Civilization in England*, London, [1857–1861] 1878, pp. 39–40, 56–64, 130–4.

4 John Stuart Mill, *On Liberty* [1859], in *Collected Works of J. S. Mill*, Toronto, 1977, Vol. XIX: pp. 224, 401; E. Stokes, *The English Utilitarians and India*, Oxford, 1969, pp. xiii, 31, 42; M. Harris, *The Rise of Anthropological Theory*, London, 1966, pp. 338–9; D. McLellan, *Karl Marx: His life and thought*, London, 1973, pp. 316 ff; M. Molnar, *Marx et Engels et la politique internationale*, Paris, 1975, pp. 189, 252–8; D. Fernbach, 'Introduction' to K. Marx, *Surveys from Exile*, Harmondsworth, 1973, pp. 26–7, 301–25.

5 Molnar, op. cit., pp. 190–221; P. Anderson, *Lineages of the Absolutist State*, London, 1974, pp. 467–72; U. Melotti, *Marx and the Third World*, London, 1972, pp. ix–x; L. Krader, *The Asiatic Mode of Production: Sources, development and critique in the writings of Karl Marx*, Assen, The Netherlands, 1975, pp. 18–19, 62–7.

6 Molnar, op. cit., pp. 234–8; B. O'Leary, *The Asiatic Mode of Production: Oriental despotism, historical materialism and Indian history*, London, 1989, pp. 17–32. F. Braudel calls the AMP an 'explication demodée', in *Le temps du monde*, Paris, 1979, p. 42.

7 I. Habib, 'Classifying pre-Colonial India', *JPS*, January–April 1985, pp. 44–52; E. J. Hobsbawm, 'Introduction' to Karl Marx, *Pre-Capitalist Economic Formations*, London, 1964, p. 50; G. Lichtheim, 'Marx and the "Asiatic Mode of Production"', in S. Avineri (ed.), *Marx's Socialism*, New York, 1972, pp. 193–4, 201–4; Molnar, op. cit., p. 198.

8 Hobsbawm, op. cit., pp. 19–20, 33; Krader, op. cit., pp. 118–75; A. M. Bailey and J. R. Llobera (eds), *The Asiatic Mode of Production: Science and politics*, London, 1981, pp. 23–37.

9 Hobsbawm, op. cit., pp. 11, 19–20, 32–46, 53–63; Molnar, op. cit., 211–21. K. Wittfogel, *Oriental Despotism: A comparative study of total power* New York, [1957] 1981, pp.

xxxv–xxxvi; Melotti, op. cit., pp. 1–7; Anderson, op. cit., pp. 407–17; Molnar, op. cit., pp. 208–10; Braudel, *Les jeux de l'échange*, Paris, 1979, pp. 515 ff; Lichtheim, *A Short History of Socialism*, p. 163.

10 Hobsbawm, op. cit., pp. 50, 58–61. Also, *The Age of Revolution*, London, [1962] 1979, pp. 221–2; Lichtheim, 'Imperialism' (2 parts), *Commentary*, part 1, no. 49, April 1970, p. 63; Anderson, op. cit., pp. 548–9.

11 B. Hindess and P. Q. Hirst, *Pre-Capitalist Modes of Production*, London, 1975, pp. 3, 12; M. Sawer, *Marxism and the Question of the Asiatic Mode of Production*, The Hague, 1977, pp. 233–4; M. Rodinson, *Islam et capitalisme*, Paris, 1966, pp. 74–7; Molnar, op. cit., pp. 221, 247–50; H. Lubasz, 'Marx's concept of the Asiatic mode of production: a genetic analysis', *ES*, November 1984, pp. 456–83; O'Leary, op. cit., pp. 147–50.

12 M. Mehdi, 'A review of the controversy around the Asiatic mode of production', *JCA*, Vol. 18, no. 2, 1988, pp. 207–19; O'Leary, op. cit., pp. 150–1; A. M. Bailey and J. R. Llobera, 'Karl A. Wittfogel and the Asiatic mode of production: a reappraisal', *SRv*, Vol. 27, no. 3, 1979, pp. 541–59.

13 Molnar, op. cit., pp. 377–8; Wittfogel, op. cit., pp. xxi–xlvii, 68–72, 137–57, 528–9.

14 Wittfogel, op. cit., pp. 81–6, 147, 197–200, 389–404, 438–49; Braudel, *Les jeux de l'échange*, Paris, 1979, pp. 525–6; B. McGowan, *Economic Life in Ottoman Europe: Taxation, trade and the struggle for land, 1600–1800*, Cambridge, 1981, pp. 56–8; O'Leary, op. cit., pp. 235–61.

15 Wittfogel, op. cit., pp. 204 ff; Montesquieu, op. cit., Vol. 1, pp. 429–30.

16 Anderson, op. cit., pp. 491, 499–503; O'Leary, op. cit., pp. 307–9.

17 Anderson, op. cit., pp. 420, 429.

18 Molnar, op. cit., p. 261; Anderson, op. cit., pp. 397 ff; Montesquieu, op. cit., Vol. 2, pp. 309 ff; Sawer, op. cit., pp. 228–32.

19 S. P. Dunn, *The Fall and Rise of the Asiatic Mode of Production*, London, 1982, pp. 63–76; Mehdi, op. cit., pp. 216–17; F. Tokei, *Essays on the Asiatic Mode of Production*, Budapest, 1979; Melotti, op. cit., p. 156; Krader, op. cit., pp. 8–9; Lubasz, op. cit., p. 469; Bailey and Llobera, *The Asiatic Mode of Production: Science and politics*, London, 1981, pp. 109–12; Sawer, op. cit., pp. 2–3; O'Leary, op. cit., pp.

139–46, 201–2, 234.

20 Molnar, op. cit., pp. 226, 325; Wittfogel, op. cit., pp. 377–80, 389–400.

21 B. Warren, *Imperialism: Pioneer of capitalism*, London, 1980, pp. 1–7, 48–56, 88–108; C. A. Kiracofe jr, 'Marxist–Leninist theory in the Third World', *JSPS*, Fall 1979, pp. 211–40.

22 I. Habib, 'Marx's perception of India', *The Marxist*, Vol. I, no. 1, 1983, New Delhi, pp. 92–142.

23 Warren, op. cit., pp. 195–203. In one series, he compared the respective per capita GDP growth of selected developed market economies and selected developing market economies, using the year 1970 as a 100-reference for both, from which he obtained two columns with slightly better results for the developing market economies than for the developed. He did not specify the countries involved in the comparison. A superficial analysis of this statistical exercise reveals its uselessness in proving that underdeveloped countries were catching up with the industrialized ones, for it does not take into account the initial development gap between the two groups.

24 A. J. Toynbee, *A Study of History*, a two-volume abridgement by D. C. Somervell, Oxford, 1956: 'The challenge of the environment', pp. 188–225.

25 P. Bairoch, *Le tiers monde dans l'impasse. Le démarrage économique du XVIIIe siècle*, Paris, 1973; Guy Bosschère, *Clefs pour le tiers monde*, Paris, 1973, pp. 9–10; A. K. Biswas, 'Climate, agriculture and economic development', in M. R. and A. K. Biswas (eds), *Food, Climate and Man*, Toronto, 1979, pp. 241–59; A. M. Kamarck, *The Tropics and Economic Development*, Baltimore, 1976, pp. ix–xii, 3–4.

26 P. A. Baran, *The Political Economy of Growth*, New York, 1957, pp. 271–2.

Chapter 2

27 B. Semmel, *Imperialism and Social Reform. English Social Imperialist Thought 1895–1914*, London, 1960, pp. 14, 18–19, 23–31, 35–52; W. J. Mommsen, *Theories of Imperialism*, London, [1977] 1980, pp. 94–100; W. Baumgart, *Imperialism: The idea and reality of British and French colonial expansion*, Oxford, [1975] 1982, pp. 146–55.

28 J. A. Hobson, *Imperialism: A study*, London, 1902, pp. 1–12, 170–206, 242–79, 306–15; R. Owen and B. Sutcliffe

(eds), *Studies in the Theory of Imperialism*, London, 1972, p. 349.

29 Hobson, op. cit., pp. 69–99, 113–15, 135, 180, 229, 327, 329; D. K. Fieldhouse, *The Theory of Capitalist Imperialism*, London, 1967, pp. 1–14.

30 K. E. Knorr, *British Colonial Theories 1570–1854*, Toronto, 1944, pp. 166–74; R. Koebner, 'The concept of economic imperialism', *EHR*, Vol. 11, no. 1, 1949; J. S. Galbraith, 'Myths of the "Little England" era', in A. G. L. Shaw (ed.), *Great Britain and the Colonies*, London, 1970, pp. 27–35.

31 M. W. Doyle, *Empires*, London, 1986, pp. 54–6; Knorr, op. cit., pp. 50–9, 296–300; J. J. Spengler, 'Mercantilist and physiocratic growth theory', in B. F. Hoselitz (ed.), *Theories of Economic Growth*, Glencoe, Ill., 1960, pp. 40–2, 195–204; G. Lichtheim, 'Imperialism', part 1, *Commentary*, no. 49, p. 58; F. List, *The National System of Political Economy*, London, [1841] 1885, pp. 263–70; D. K. Fieldhouse, *Economics and Empire 1830–1914*, London, [1973] 1984, p. 25, and *The Colonial Empires: a comparative survey from the 18th century*, New York, 1966, p. 253; P. Leroy-Beaulieu, *De la colonisation chez les peuples modernes*, Paris, 1874, p. II; E. G. Wakefield, *A View of the Art of Colonization with Reference to the British Empire*, in *The Collected Works of E. G. Wakefield*, Glasgow, 1968, p. 766.

32 J. A. Hobson, 'Free trade and foreign policy', *CR*, August 1898; 'Capitalism and Imperialism in South Africa', *CR*, January 1900, and 'The economic taproot of imperialism', *CR*, August 1902.

33 B. Porter, *Critics of Empire: British radical attitudes to colonialism in Africa 1885–1914*, London, 1968, pp. 44–5, 99–104; Koebner, op. cit., p. 16; N. Etherington, 'Reconsidering theories of imperialism', *HT*, Vol. XXI, 1982.

34 J. A. Hobson, *Imperialism*, London, 1938, pp. 17–20, 33–45, 96–7, (fold-out).

35 H. W. Arndt, *Economic Development: the history of an idea*, Chicago, 1987, p. 18; W. Digby, *'Prosperous' British India*, London, 1901; D. Naoroji, *Poverty and the British Rule in India*, New Delhi [1901] 1962, p. 191; R. C. Dutt, *History of India under Early British Power to the Accession of Queen Victoria in 1837*, London [1906] 1908; T. O. Lloyd, *The British Empire 1558–1983*, Oxford, 1984; M. D. Morris, 'Towards a reinterpretation of nineteenth century Indian economic history', in M. D. Morris (ed.), *Indian Economy*

in the Nineteenth Century: a symposium, Delhi, 1969, pp. 1–15; J. A. Hobson, *Imperialism*, pp. v–xii.

36 Knorr, op. cit., pp. 126–55; D. K. Fieldhouse, *The Colonial Empires*, New York, 1966, pp. 72 ff; Lichtheim, 'Imperialism', part 1, *Commentary*, no. 49, pp. 62–4; Lloyd, op. cit., p. 109.

37 R. Robinson and J. Gallagher, with A. Denny, *Africa and the Victorians: the official mind of imperialism*, London, 1981, pp. 76–121, 160–209, 466; 'The imperialism of free trade', in Shaw, op. cit., pp. 142–63 (originally in *EHR*, Vol. 6, no. 1, 1953).

38 Fieldhouse, *The Colonial Empires*, New York, 1966, p. 209; Baumgart, op. cit., pp. 3–4.

39 Fieldhouse, *The Colonial Empires*, p. 91–4, 147, 179, 363, 373, 382, 393, and *Economics and Empire*, pp. 61, 77, 253–4, 403, 470; Doyle, op. cit., p. 233; V. I. Lenin, *Imperialism: the highest stage of capitalism*, Peking, [1917] 1975, p. 99.

40 Owens and Sutcliffe (eds), *Studies in the Theory of Imperialism*, pp. 331 ff; L. E. Davis and R. A. Huttenback, *Mammon and the Pursuit of Empire: The political economy of British imperialism 1860–1912*, Cambridge, pp. 301–18.

41 Fieldhouse, *The Colonial Empires*, p. 373; D. S. Landes, 'The nature of economic imperialism', *JEH*, December 1961; Doyle, op. cit., pp. 26–30.

42 D. McLellan, *Marxism after Marx*, New York, 1979, pp. 43–5; K. Marx, *Capital: a critique of political economy*, translated by B. Fowkes and introduced by E. Mandel, 3 vols, Harmondsworth, 1976, Vol. 1, pp. 711–24, Vol. 2, pp. 565–98.

43 R. Luxemburg, *The Accumulation of Capital*, [1913], London, 1951, pp. 76–92, 107–38; Marx, *Capital*, Vol. 2, pp. 30–1.

44 Luxemburg, op. cit., pp. 139–54; Marx, *Capital*, Vol. 1, pp. 29–30.

45 Luxemburg, op. cit., pp. 89, 348–67, 419–45.

46 R. Hilferding, *Finance Capital: A study of the latest phase of capitalist development*, London, 1981; McLellan, *Marxism after Marx*, pp. 58–61.

47 Hilferding, op. cit., pp. 301–8, 326–30; McLellan, *Marxism after Marx*, pp. 58–61.

48 Hilferding, op. cit., pp. 311–30.

49 Marx, *Capital*, Vol. 1, pp. 83–6, Vol. 3, pp. 317–79; McLellan, *Marxism after Marx*, pp. 20–38, 97.

50 Lenin, op. cit., pp. 73, 88, 92–3, 98–9, 101.

51 ibid., pp. 105–13, 150.

52 ibid., pp. 69, 125, 128, 130, 148, 150–53. E. Stokes, 'Late-nineteenth-century colonial expansion and the attack on the theory of economic imperialism: a case of mistaken identity', *HJ*, Vol. 12, 1969.

53 J. A. Schumpeter, *Imperialism*, [1919], Oxford, 1951. For an extended discussion of Schumpeter's thesis, see Doyle, op. cit., pp. 155–9.

54 F. Borkenau, *World Communism: a history of the Communist International*, [London, 1938], Ann Arbor, Mich., 1962; I. Deutscher, *Stalin: a political biography*, New York, [1949], 1960, pp. 275–6, 395–8; M. Caballero, 'Latin America and the World Revolution: The Communist International 1918–1943', PhD thesis, London School of Economics, 1985, p. 38.

55 Boersner, *The Bolsheviks and the National and Colonial Question 1917–28*, Geneva, 1957, p. 272.

56 ibid., p. 31; Caballero, op. cit., pp. 115, 126, 129.

57 Caballero, op. cit., p. 48; Boersner, op. cit., pp. 115, 126, 129.

58 Deutscher, op. cit., pp. 294 ff, 402–3; Boersner, op. cit., pp. 179–80. On the ideological repercussions of the Fifth Congress, see G. Kitching, *Development and Underdevelopment in Historical Perspective*, London, 1982, pp. 160–61.

59 Caballero, op. cit., pp. 49–50, 136–42.

60 ibid., p. 272.

Chapter 3

61 L. Wolf-Phillips, 'Why "Third World"?', Third World Foundation Monographs, London, 1980; H. W. Arndt, 'Development economics before 1945', in J. Bhagwati and R. S. Eckaus (eds), *Development and Planning*, London, 1972, and H. W. Arndt, 'Economic development: a semantic history', *EDCC*, April 1981.

62 D. Seers, 'The birth, life and death of development economics', *DCh*, October 1979; G. M. Meier, 'The formative years', in G. M. Meier and D. Seers (eds), *Pioneers in Development*, Oxford, 1984, pp. 3–22; P. Streeten, 'Development dichotomies' in Meier and Seers, op. cit., pp. 337–61; O. Sunkel, with P. Paz, *El subdesarrollo latinoamericano y la teoria del desarrollo*, Mexico, 1970, pp. 344–60; N. S. Subba Rao, *Some Aspects of Economic Planning*, Bangalore, 1935, pp. 178–237; P. Thakurdas *et al.*, *A Brief Memorandum Outlining a Plan of Economic Development for India*, Bombay, 1944; K.

Kurihara, *The Keynesian Theory of Economic Development*, London, 1959; A. Young, 'Increasing returns and economic progress', *EJ*, December 1928.

63 C. Clark, *The Conditions of Economic Progress*, London, 1940, pp. 1–16, and 'Development economics: The early years', in Meier and Seers, op. cit., pp. 59–77.

64 J. H. Boeke, *The Structures of the Netherlands Indian Economy*, New York, 1942, pp. 5–7, 189; Stokes, op. cit., pp. 1–7; P. Anderson, op. cit., p. 421; Luxemburg, op. cit., p. 348; McLellan, *Karl Marx*, pp. 308–9; J. S. Furnivall, *Colonial Policy and Practice: A comparative study of Burma and Netherlands India*, Cambridge, 1948.

65 Our synthesis of Rosenstein-Rodan's ideas is based on a collation of the following articles: 'Problems of industrialisation of Eastern and South-Eastern Europe', *EJ*, June–September 1943; 'The international development of economically backward areas', *IA*, April 1944; 'Notes on the theory of the "big push"', in H. S. Ellis (ed.), *Economic Development for Latin America*, London, 1961; and '*Natura facit saltum*: Analysis of the disequilibrium growth process', in Meier and Seers, op. cit., pp. 205—21.

66 For some of those exhortations, see W. Benson, 'The economic advancement of under-developed areas', in National Peace Council, *The Economic Basis of Peace*, London, 1942; and E. Staley, *World Economic Development: effects on advanced industrial countries*, International Labor Office, Montreal, 1944. Rosenstein-Rodan himself in his 1943 essay cites a pamphlet of the National Planning Association: *International Development Loans*, New York, 1942. In general, see Arndt, 'Development economics before 1945', pp. 24–9. It wasn't principally individuals who were involved either, for the backing for these studies almost invariably came from official and semi-private institutions.

67 Rosenstein-Rodan, 'Programming in theory and in Italian practice', in G. M. Meier, *Leading Issues in Economic Development*, Oxford, 1984, pp. 709–10; T. N. Srinivasam, 'Comment', in Meier and Seers, op. cit., p. 51.

68 K. Mandelbaum, *The Industrialization of Backward Areas*, Oxford, [1945] 1961.

69 D. A. Kay, 'The U.N. and Decolonization', in J. Barros (ed.), *The U.N.: Past, present and future*, New York, 1972, pp. 143–70; R. Townley, *The U.N.: A view from within*, New York, 1968, pp. 217–37.

70 R. Prebisch, *The Economic Development of Latin America and its Principal Problems*, New York, 1950, pp. 8–16, 35–50; 'La moneda y los ciclos económicos en la Argentina' (mimeo), Buenos Aires, 1944; J. L. Love, 'Raul Prebisch and the origins of the doctrine of unequal exchange', *LARR*, Vol. xv, no. 3, 1980.

71 Meier and Seers, op. cit., pp. 189–91.

72 H. W. Singer, 'The terms of trade controversy and the evolution of soft financing: Early years in the U.N.', in Meier and Seers, op. cit., pp. 275–303.

In our survey of development economics we have collected diverse allusions to J. M. Keynes and his theories. What in fact did he and his followers contribute to the discipline? The overwhelming consensus among development economists is that his general theory was virtually inapplicable to underdeveloped economies. The analytical work underwriting this conclusion had been done by the Indian economist V. K. R. V. Rao in 1952. Following Keynes, Rao reasoned that whereas in a developed economy, the marginal propensity to consume decreases with an increase in income and brings down with it the value of the multiplier, thus requiring easier money and higher investment to restore equilibrium with full employment, in an underdeveloped economy 'the marginal propensity to consume is likely to be not far short of unity', which produces a high multiplier 'with the result that comparatively small increments of investment are likely to bring about full employment'. This reading of Keynes led to highly suspect inferences: 'The paradoxical situation, therefore, arises that the poorer the community the greater the ease of obtaining for it a condition of full employment and the smaller the fluctuations in its employment caused by changes in its net investments.' This did not tally with the fact that 'deficit financing and created money' in backward agricultural countries had a minimal multiplier effect on output.

The extremely backward economic structures that were adduced to refute the validity of Keynes for economic development might not have been the only models of underdevelopment available, and there was, besides, the argument that, although it was true that Keynes, undoubtedly influenced in his work by the economic depression of the early 1930s, had aimed at the target of full employment equilibrium at a given level of economic performance, post-Keynesians, and in particular the Briton R. F. Harrod and the American E. Domar, adopted a point of view that contemplated and pretended to explain growth, and this was what development economics was really all about.

H. J. Bruton assumed in a 1955 article that the Harrod/Domar theory was applicable to underdeveloped economies and went about applying it to a relatively simple model of such an economy. He used the formula $\Delta Y = s/k\ Y$, where s is a constant ratio between saving and income and k a constant capital/output ratio. Dividing through by Y, it read $\Delta Y/Y = s/k$. For an increase of, say, 50 to income 1000, the equivalent s was 0.20 and the k was 4. If you looked at the left side of the equation, it showed the growth of income required to absorb new capacity; if on the right, the necessary growth for an increase in income without inflation. The equation modified for an underdeveloped economy appeared thus: $Y/Y = s + b/k$, where b was the balance between debits (M) and credits (X) in current account.

Bruton introduced into his analysis certain unquantifiable variables such as innovations and behavioural trends in consumption. The former would tend to decrease the M/Y ratio and the latter to increase it, but on the whole when income rose in an underdeveloped economy, M would tend to rise also, which would throw b into the red and constrict the growth of Y with resulting unemployment. In any event, Y depended on the sign of b, and b tended to be negative because of technological and behavioural factors in underdeveloped countries. Even if capital flows compensated for a negative balance of trade, Bruton believed that they relieved but did not solve the problem. In sum, analysis had to give way entirely to policy in tackling the problem of growth and employment under conditions of underdevelopment.

R. Nurkse, *Some Aspects of Capital Accumulation in Underdeveloped Countries*, Cairo, 1952, pp. 11, 24–5; V. K. R. V. Rao, 'Investment, income and the multiplier in an underdeveloped economy', *IER*, February 1952; Meier, *Leading Issues in Economic Development*, p. 222; E. Domar, 'Capital expansion, rate of growth and employment', *Econometrica*, April 1946, p. 39; H. J. Bruton, 'Growth models and underdeveloped economies', *JPE*, August 1955; A. P. Thirlwall, *Growth and Development with special reference to developing economies*, London, [1972] 1982, p. 6.

73 In confronting Bairoch and Singer, we are quoting from P. Bairoch, 'Historical roots of underdevelopment: Myths and realities', in W. J. Mommsen and J. Osterhammel (eds), *Imperialism and After: Continuities and discontinuities*, London, 1986, pp. 205–9, and from the Singer article cited in note 72. Although the Bairoch article postdates the Singer article, its arguments and the research for them proceed from work done before both articles.
74 Singer, 'The distribution of gains between investing and borrowing countries', *AER*, May 1950; C. P. Kindelberger, *The Terms of Trade: a European case study*, London, 1956.
75 P. Bairoch, 'Historical roots of underdevelopment', in Mommsen and Osterhammel, op. cit., pp. 205–8.
76 B. Balassa, 'Comment', in Meier and Seers, op. cit., pp. 304–11; J. Spraos, *Inequalizing Trade? A study of the traditional north–south specialisation in the context of terms of trade concepts*, Oxford, 1982, pp. 45–69; Singer, in Meier and Seers, op. cit., pp. 289–91; H. J. Bruton, 'Growth models and underdeveloped economies', *JPE*, August 1955.
77 H. B. Chenery, 'The structuralist approach to development policy', *AER*, May 1975; Preston, *Theories of Development*, London, 1982, pp. 33–7, 101–4, 183–5.
78 Streeten, 'Development dichotomies', in Meier and Seers, op. cit., p. 341; K. Basu, *The Less Developed Economy: A critique of contemporary theory*, London, 1984, p. 4.
79 Arndt, *Economic Development*, pp. 122–6.
80 J. Viner, *International Trade and Economic Development*, Oxford, 1953, [originally lectures delivered in Rio de Janeiro in 1950], pp. 99–100.
81 R. de Oliveira Campos, 'Economic development and inflation with special reference to Latin America', in Meier, *Leading Issues in Economic Development*, pp. 268–73. See also, Seers, 'Inflation and growth: A summary of experience in Latin America', *EBLA*, February 1962, and 'A theory of inflation and growth in underdeveloped economies based on the experience of Latin America', *OEP*, June 1962.
82 Singer, 'Economic progress in underdeveloped countries', *SRs*, March 1949; Nurkse, *Some Aspects of Capital Accumulation in Underdeveloped Countries*, pp. 1–3, 37–43.
83 Meier, *Leading Issues in Economic Development*, p. 284; R. R. Nelson, 'A theory of the low-level equilibrium trap', *AER*, December 1956; H. Leibenstein, *Economic Backwardness and Economic Growth*, New York, 1957, pp. 15–37, 94–110.

84 G. Myrdal, *Economic Theory and Underdeveloped Regions*, London, 1957, pp. 11–22, 26–8; *An International Economy*, London, 1956, pp. 299–335; *The Challenge of World Poverty: A world anti-poverty programme in outline*, Harmondsworth, 1970, pp. 278–9, 280–92; 'International inequality and foreign aid in retrospect', in Meier and Seers, op. cit., pp. 151–65.

85 Nurkse, *Some Aspects of Capital Accumulation in Underdeveloped Countries*, pp. 11–12, 48–9; *Patterns of Trade and Development*, Stockholm, 1959, pp. 36–7; 'Trade theory and development policy', in Meier, *Leading Issues in Economic Development*, pp. 493–7; H. B,. Chenery and A. M. Strout, 'Foreign assistance and economic development', *AER*, September 1966.

86 W. A. Lewis, 'Economic development with unlimited supplies of labour', *MSESS*, May 1954, and 'Development economics in the 1950s', in Meier and Seers, op. cit., pp. 119–37; J. C. H. Fei and G. Ranis, *Development of the Labour Surplus Economy: Theory and policy*, Homewood, Ill., 1964, p. 26; 'Economic development in historical perspective', *AER*, May 1969; Ranis and Fei, 'A theory of economic development', *AER*, September 1961; Meier, *Leading Issues in Economic Development*, pp. 162–7.

87 W. A. Lewis, *The Principle of Economic Planning*, London, [1949] 1963, p. 3; and *The Theory of Economic Growth*, London, 1957; J. Tinbergen, *The Design of Development*, Baltimore, 1958, and 'Development modelling: The state of the art', in Meier, *Leading Issues in Economic Development*, pp. 129–32; P. Mahalanobis, 'Some observations on the process of growth of national income', *Sankhya*, Vol. 12, part 4, 1953. On Mahalanobis's influence on policy, see A. H. Hanson, 'Power shifts and regional balances', in *The Crisis of Indian Planning: economic planning in the 1960s*, London, 1968, p. 43.

88 Meier, *Leading Issues in Economic Development*, pp. 119, 376; Nurkse, *Some Aspects of Capital Accumulation in Underdeveloped Countries*, p. 25–7; C. Peter Timmer, 'Food prices and food policy analysis in LDCs', in Meier, op. cit., pp. 476–83; Chenery, 'Development policy in underdeveloped countries: The role of industrialization in development programs', *AER*, May 1955; Leibenstein, op. cit., pp. 94–110.

89 Myrdal, *Against the Stream: Critical essays in economics*, London, 1974, [originally Stockholm, 1973] pp. 4, 434; *The Challenge of World Poverty*, pp. 49, 64, 71–2, 211–13, 227–42;

and *Asian Drama: An enquiry into the poverty of nations*, 3 vols, Harmondsworth, 1968, pp. 60, 676–81, 861, 2121–38.

90 T. Parsons, *The Social System*, London, 1952, pp. 180–200; D. Lehman (ed.), *Development Theory: Four critical studies*, London, 1970, p. 4; D. McLelland, *The Achieving Society*, Princeton, NJ, 1961; E. Hagen, *On the Theory of Social Change: How economic growth begins*, Homewood, Ill., 1962; B. Higgins, *Economic Development: Principles, problems and policies*, New York, 1959, pp. 304–7; B. F. Hoselitz, *Non-Economic Aspects of Economic Growth*, Glencoe, Ill., 1960, pp. 28–42; D. Lerner, *The Passing of Traditional Society: Modernizing the Middle East*, New York, 1958; A. Foster-Carter, *The Sociology of Development*, Ormskirk, Lancs, 1985.

91 P. W. Preston, *New Trends in Development Theory*, London, 1985, pp. 14, 17–20; A. G. Frank, 'The sociology of development and the underdevelopment of sociology', in *Latin America: Underdevelopment of revolution. Essays on the development of underdevelopment and the principal enemy*, New York, 1969, pp. 21–78. See also, I. Oxaal, T. Barnett and D. Booth (eds), *Beyond the Sociology of Development*, London, 1975.

92 W. W. Rostow, 'Development: The political economy of the Marshallian long period', in Meier and Seers, op. cit., pp. 227–61, and *The Stages of Economic Growth: A non-communist manifesto*, Cambridge, 1960, Chapter 4; Thirlwall, op. cit., pp. 42–7.

93 A. Fishlow, 'Empty economic stages?', *EJ*, March 1965; S. Kuznets, 'Notes on stages of economic growth', in A. Eckstein (ed.), *Comparisons of Economic Systems*, Berkeley, Calif., pp. 254–7.

94 Ranis and Fei, 'A theory of economic development', *AER*, September 1961, p. 557.

95 The mainstream phase ended with attempts at synthesis, denoting the maturity attained by development economics, or, at least, the considerable ground covered till then. See G. M. Meier and R. E. Baldwin, *Economic Development* (1957); C. P. Kindleberger, *Economic Development* (1958); B. Higgins, op. cit. (1959).

96 N. Kaldor, 'Taxation for economic development', *JMAS*, Vol. 1, no. 1, 1963.

97 Meier, *Leading Issues in Economic Development*, p. 106; Kuznets, *Economic Change*, New York, 1953, pp. 246–52.

98 A. O. Hirschman, *The Strategy of Economic Development*, New Haven, Conn., 1958, pp. 6–7, 62, 98–116, 120, 156–70;

'A Dissenter's confession: "The strategy of economic development" reconsidered', in Meier and Seers, op. cit., pp. 87–111; *Journey Towards Progress*, New York, 1963, pp. 5–7.

99 P. T. Bauer and B. S. Yamey, *The Economics of Underdeveloped Countries*, Cambridge, 1957, pp. 103, 249–55; Bauer, *Dissent on Development: Studies and debates in development economics*, London, 1971, pp. 17–28; J. Wood, 'Do ideas matter? Peter Bauer's polemical problems', *Encounter*, December 1984; H. Myint, 'An interpretation of economic backwardness', *OEP*, January 1954, and 'The "classical theory" of international trade and the underdeveloped countries', *EJ*, June 1958; Meier, *Leading Issues in Economic Development*, pp. 430–1.

100 T. W. Schultz, 'Capital formation by education', *JPE*, December 1960; 'Investment in human capital', *AER*, March 1961; 'Reflections on investment in man', *JPE*, October 1962; *Transforming Traditional Agriculture*, New Haven, Conn., 1964, pp. 53–4, 63–70; and *Economic Growth and Agriculture*, New York, 1968; D. W. Jorgenson, 'The development of a dual economy', *EJ*, June 1961; H. M. Southworth and B. F. Johnston, *Agricultural Development and Economic Growth*, Ithaca, NY, 1967, p. vii; M. Lipton, 'Strategy for agriculture: Urban bias and rural planning', in *The Crisis of Indian Planning*, pp. 83–147.

101 J. Freyssinet, *Le concept de sous-développement*, Paris, 1966, pp. 31–44, 69–74, 122–3, 148–9, 177–97, 209–10, 251–75, 300–9; C. Furtado, *Desarollo y subdesarrollo*, Buenos Aires, 1961, pp. 76–8, 118–19, 150–5, 162–8, 171–7, 212, and *Subdesarrollo y estancamiento en America Latina*, Buenos Aires, 1964, pp. 11, 64–6.

102 P. Streeten, 'The frontiers of development studies: some issues of development policy', *JDS*, October 1967; 'Industralization in a unified development strategy', in Meier, *Leading Issues in Economic Development*, p. 37; 'Development ideas in historical perspective', ibid., p. 111; Seers, 'The meaning of development, *IDR*, December 1969. See also, Arndt, *Economic Development*, p. 91.

Chapter 4

103 *New Times*, Moscow, nos. 12, 20, 1946; nos. 24, 27, 48, 1947; no. 51, 1948; nos. 3, 7, 19, 21, 39, 43, 47, 1949;

nos. 6, 12, 22, 1950; no. 11, 1951. See also, J. Gregory Oswald, 'Contemporary Soviet research on Latin America', in L. Hanke (ed.), *History of Latin American Civilization*, 2 vols, London, 1967.

104 *New Times*, no. 21, 1951.

105 H. Magdoff, 'The achievement of Paul Baran', *MR*, March 1965, pp. 63–80; R. B. Sutcliffe, introduction to P. Baran, *The Political Economy of Growth*, [New York, 1957], Harmondsworth, 1978, pp, 60–1; G. Palma, 'Dependency: A formal theory of underdevelopment or a methodology for the analysis of concrete situations of underdevelopment?' in Meier, *Leading Issues in Economic Development*, p. 139; A. M. Hoogvelt, *The Third World in Global Development*, London, 1982, pp. 165–6; T. K. Hopkins and I. Wallerstein, *World Systems Analysis: Theory and methodology*, Beverly Hills, Calif., 1982, p. 46.

106 P. Baran, 'Economic development of backward areas', *MR*, August 1951.

107 Baran, 'On the political economy of backwardness', *MSESS*, Vol. xx, 1952.

108 J. J. Sebreli, *Tercer mundo: mito burgués*, Buenos Aires, 1975, pp. 33–4; P. Worsley, *The Third World*, London, 1964, pp. 50–1, 232, 245, and *The Three Worlds: Culture and world development*, London, 1984, pp. 297–306, 323; G. de Bosschère, *Clefs pour le tiers monde*, pp. 210–24; I. L. Horowitz, *Three Worlds of Development: The theory and practice of international stratification*, New York, 1966; G. Dalton, *Economic Systems and Society: Capitalism, communism and third world*, Harmondsworth, 1974; N. Harris, *The End of the Third World: NICs and the Decline of an Ideology*, London, 1986, pp. 11–29; C. Rangel, *El tercermundismo*, Caracas, 1982, pp. 53–84; A. Angelopoulos, *Le tiers monde face au pays riches: perspectives pour l'an 2000*, Paris, 1972; Y. Lacoste, *Unité et diversité du tiers monde*, Paris, 1980.

109 *Guia del Tercer Mundo*, Lisbon, 1983, pp. 368–9.

110 S. Amin, 'Les effets structurels de l'intégration internationale des économies précapitalistes. Une étude théorique du mécanisme qui a engendré les économies dites sous-développés', PhD thesis, Université de Paris, 1957, pp. 1–19, 37, 52–6, 175–6, 207–55, 301–9, 319–20, 358–70, 380, 485, 536–7, 612.

111 ibid., pp. 39, 82–3, 95, 607, 615–16, 625–6.

112 Marx, *Capital*, Vol. 1, pp. 872–940, 781–94; Lenin, *Imperialism*, pp. 112–13, 144; J. Nun, 'Superpoblacion relativa, ejército industrial de reserva y masa marginal', *RLS*, Vol.

4, no. 2, 1969.

113 Baran, *The Political Economy of Growth*, New York, 1957, pp. 22–4, 44, 60–2, 85, 108–9, 118–19.

114 Baran, *The Political Economy of Growth*, New York, 1957, pp. 140–3.

115 ibid., pp. 147–8.

116 ibid., pp. 11–12, 111, 150, 236–7; Baran, *The Political Economy of Growth*, Harmondsworth, 1978, p. 120.

117 P. Jalée, *Le pillage du tiers monde*, Paris, [1965] 1982, pp. 152–3; K. Nkrumah, *Neo-Colonialism: The last stage of imperialism*, London, [1965] 1974, p. ix.

118 Jalée, op. cit., pp. 150–2; E. Ruiz Garcia, *El tercer mundo*, Madrid, 1967; P. Moussa, *Les nations prolétaires*, Paris, 1959; G. de Bosschère, *Autopsie de la colonisation*, Paris, 1967, p. 10.

119 P. A. Baran and P. M. Sweezy, 'Notes on the theory of imperialism', in *Problems of Economic Dynamics and Planning. Essays in Honour of Michael Kalecki*, Warsaw, 1966; P. M. Sweezy, 'Obstacles to economic development', in C. H. Feinstein (ed.), *Socialism, Capitalism and Economic Growth*, Cambridge, 1967; T. Kemp, *Theories of Imperialism*, London, 1967; Mommsen, op. cit., pp. 122–4; H. Magdoff, 'Economic aspects of U.S. Imperialism', *MR*, November 1966, 'The age of imperialism' (part 2), *MR*, October 1968, pp. 18–64, and 'Is imperialism really necessary?' *MR*, October–November 1970. For further studies on the imperialism of MNCs, see J. K. Galbraith, *The New Industrial State*, New York, 1967 and *Economics and the Public Purpose*, Boston, 1973, and R. J. Barnet, *The Lean Years: Politics in the age of scarcity*, New York, 1980.

120 J. C. Mariategui, *Siete ensayos de interpretación de la realidad peruana*, Lima, 1928; D. A. Rangel, *La Venezuela agraria*, Caracas, 1969; D. F. Maza Zabala, *Venezuela: una economía dependiente*, Caracas, 1974; and *Los mecanismos de la dependencia*, Caracas, 1973; A. Cordoba and H. Silva Michelena, *Aspectos teóricos del subdesarrollo*, Caracas, 1967. For a full bibliography on these theorists, see *Libros al día*, Caracas, Vol. 1 no. 19, 15–30 May, 1976, *MR*, March 1965, p. 74, and *MR*, November 1962 and January 1963; Anderson, op. cit., p. 401; Hobsbawm, 'Introduction' to Karl Marx, *Pre-Capitalist Economic Formations*, p. 63.

121 F. Fanon, *The Wretched of the Earth*, New York, 1968 [originally Paris, 1963], pp. 99, 102–3, 128–9, 150, 175; P. Freire,

Pedagogía del oprimido, Montevideo, 1968. For a Marxist critique of Debray's thesis, see 'Regis Debray and the Latin American Revolution', *MR*, July–August 1968.

122 On the failure of the Alliance for Progress, see A. F. Lowenthal, 'US Policy towards Latin America; Liberal, radical, and burocratic perspectives', *LARR*, no. 3, 1973.

123 C. Abel and C. Lewis (eds), *Latin America: Economic imperialism and the state*, London, 1984, pp. 16, 40, 397–404.

124 R. A. Packenham, 'Plus ça change,. . .: The English edition of Cardoso and Faletto's *Dependencia y desarrollo en America Latina', LARR*, Vol. xvii, no. 3, 1982.

125 F. H. Cardoso and E. Faletto, *Dependency and Development in Latin America*, London, 1979, pp. xi–xii, xxii–xxiv, 172–6, 213; Cardoso, *Ideologias dela Burguesia Industrial en Sociedades Dependientes (Argentina y Brasil)*, Mexico, 1971.

126 Cardoso and Faletto, op. cit., pp. ix, xx, 5–7.

127 ibid., pp. xv–xix, 66–73.

128 Abel and Lewis, op. cit., pp. 70–91. On Gramsci, see E. J. Hobsbawm, 'The great Gramsci', *The New York Review of Books*, 4 April 1974.

129 Apart from the Marxist current, Latin American intellectuals had few explanations for the origins of economic retardation, although they had been conscious of socio-economic backwardness since the onset of independence. On the whole, the shackles on progress were identified by both intellectuals and politicians as ignorance, social inconformity and rebelliousness. This diagnosis was usually accompanied by internalized Eurocentric attitudes, not devoid of frankly racist overtones.

Some choice texts exhibiting internalized Eurocentrism (and in some cases racism itself) are L. Vallenilla Lanz, *Cesarismo democrático*, Caracas, [1909] 1952; J. E. Rodo, *Ariel*, Montevideo, 1805, on which see the interesting article by E. Rodriguez Monegal, 'Las metamorfosis de Caliban', in *Caliban*, Casa de la cultura latinoamericana, London, no. 2, n.d; and F. Garcia Calderon, *Les démocraties d'Amérique latine*, Paris, 1912.

130 In our opinion the most brilliant and lucid presentation of the specific moderate Latin American version of dependency, one that is admirably exempt from ideological cant of any sort, is contained in the closing pages (pp. 306–80) of Sunkel, op. cit. (See note 62). It is not a Marxist or an anti-capitalist work, yet it demolishes from within ECLA doctrines on

economic development.

131 T. dos Santos, *Dependencia y cambio social*, Caracas, 1974, pp. 5–8; R. M. Marini, *Subdesarrollo y revolución*, Mexico, 1969, pp. 122–35, and 'Brazilian "independence" and imperialist integration', *MR*, December 1965.

132 A. G. Frank, *Dependent Accumulation and Underdevelopment*, New York, 1978, pp. xi–xvii; 'Not feudalism – capitalism', *MR*, December 1963; and *Critique and Anti-Critique: Essays in dependence and reformism*, London, 1984, p. viii; T. Halperin-Donghi, '"Dependency theory" and Latin American historiography', *LARR*, Vol. xvii, no. 3, 1982, p. 131.

133 Frank, *Capitalism and Underdevelopment in Latin America: Historical Studies of Chile and Brazil*, London, 1969, pp. 10, 19, 46–55, 67–99, 115–20, 148–50, 152–9, 162–7, 168–80, 201–18.

134 Frank, 'The development of underdevelopment', *MR*, September 1966.

135 Frank, *Lumpenbourgeoisie, Lumpendevelopment. Dependence, class and politics in Latin America*, New York, 1972, pp. 17–25; *World Accumulation, 1492–1789*, New York, 1978, pp. 11–24.

136 Abel and Lewis, op. cit., p. 57.

137 Frank, *Capitalism and Underdevelopment in Latin America*, pp. xi–xvii.

138 Frank, *Dependent Accumulation and Underdevelopment*, pp. xi–xvii; WA, pp. 11–23.

139 ibid., pp. 239–45.

140 ibid., pp. 241–57.

141 Frank, *La crisis mundial*, Vol. 1: *El tercer mundo*, Madrid, 1980, pp. 8–10, 23–9, 95–6, 119–20, 231–6, 275–9, 325–35, 346–353. For Frank's (and Amin's) apocalyptic vision of the crisis of capitalism, see Frank, *Reflections on the World Economic Crisis*, New York, 1981, pp. 143–61.

142 'The misery of being exploited by capitalists is insignificant compared to the misery of not being exploited.' J. Robinson, quoted in J. K. Galbraith, *The Nature of Mass Poverty*, Cambridge, Mass., 1979.

'Capital created underdevelopment not because it exploited the underdeveloped world, but because it did not exploit enough.' G. Kay, *Development and Underdevelopment. A Marxist analysis*, London 1975, p. x.

143 Consistent with these extreme anti-capitalist views, the alternative political paradigm that served as compass to much if not all of the radical dependency criticism of development

theory (as development studies were usually called in Latin America, especially their economic branch) was 'socialist development'. F. Hinkelammert offers as good as example as any of this attitude in Latin America. His *El subdesarrollo latinoamericano* (Caracas, 1975) listed all the obstacles to capitalist development in Latin America and concluded in pious exasperation by bringing out the *deus ex machina* of socialism.

144 Sir J. Sarkar, *Economics of British India*, Calcutta, 1909; P. Spear, *The Oxford History of Modern India*, Oxford, 1965, pp. 286–94. A constructive passion for modernization is present also, to be extremely selective, in such works as *Stern Reckoning: A survey of the events leading to and following the Partition of India* (New Delhi, 1948), by G. D. Khosla, and in *Social Background to Indian Nationalism* (Bombay, 1948), by A. R. Desai.

145 Nkrumah came to Marxism from anticolonialism. Other writers who followed a similar trajectory were A. Césaire, A. Cabral and A. Memmi. See Césaire, *Discourse of Colonialism*, New York, 1972 [originally in French, 1955], a work very close in spirit to Fanon; and Cabral, *Revolution in Guinea. An African people's struggle*, London, 1969.

146 S. Amin, *Accumulation on a World Scale: A critique of the theory of underdevelopment*, New York, 1974, pp. 2–3, 14–25, 35, 507–26.

147 Amin, *Unequal Development: an essay on the social formation of peripheral capitalism*, Sussex, 1973, pp. 51–8, 73–7, 174–5, 183–96, 283–5; J. G. Gurley, 'Economic development: a Marxist view', in Meier, *Leading Issues in Economic Development*, pp. 133–9.

148 Amin, *Unequal Development*, pp. 138–44; A. Emmanuel, *Unequal Exchange: a study of the imperialism of trade*, London, 1972 [originally Paris, 1969], pp. 80–91, 263–70, 299–307: C. Bettelheim, 'Economic inequalities between nations and international solidarity', *MR*, January 1970.

149 W. Rodney, *How Europe Underdeveloped Africa*, London, [1973] 1983, pp. 46–8, 57–80, 85–7, 95–9, 127, 160.

150 ibid., pp. 125–46, 166, 179–80, 186–90, 212, 219–20, 225, 250, 273, 280.

151 In a personal interview with the author, Bagchi described Frank as a 'pamphleteer' and rejected the formula 'the development of underdevelopment'. A. K. Bagchi, *The Political Economy of Underdevelopment*, Cambridge, 1982, pp. 4–5, 13–15, 33–4, 39, 48–68, 149, 179.

152 ibid., pp. 3, 187–97, 249; Bagchi, 'Towards a correct reading of Lenin's theory of imperialism', *EPW*, July 1983.
153 Kitching, op. cit., pp. 55–6, 163, 174–6.
154 Owen and Sutcliffe, op. cit., pp. 331–78; M. B. Brown, *After Imperialism*, London, 1962; M. B. Brown (ed.), *The Anatomy of Underdevelopment: Documents on economic policy in the Third World*, Nottingham, 1974; and *The Economics of Imperialism*, Harmondsworth, 1974, pp. 17–29.
155 A. Brewer, *Marxist Theories of Imperialism*, London, 1980, pp. 16–17.
156 I. Wallerstein, *The Modern World System*. Vol. 1: *Capitalist Agriculture and the Origins of the European World Economy in the 16th Century*, New York, 1974, p. xi.
157 F. Braudel, *Le temps du monde*, Paris, 1979, pp. 12–15, 28, 39, 42, 44, 380.
158 ibid., pp. 55, 61, 30, 518.
159 Wallerstein, *Africa: The politics of independence*, New York, 1961, and *The Road to Independence: Ghana and the Ivory Coast*, Paris, 1964, pp. 75–6; *The Modern World System*, Vol. 1, pp. 36–8, 51, 63, 70–91, 103, 112, 132–6, 162, 210, 256–7, 290–1, 304, 309, 315, 336, 349.
160 Wallerstein, *The Modern World-System*. Vol. 2: *Mercantilism and the consolidation of the European world economy, 1600–1750*, New York, 1980, pp. 8, 37, 44, 51–2, 57, 62–3, 70–1, 103–4; *World Inequality, Origins and Perspectives of the World-System*, Nottingham, 1975, p. 16.
161 Wallerstein, *The Modern World-System*. Vol. 3: *The second era of great expansion of the capitalist world-economy, 1730–1840s*, San Diego, Calif., 1989.
162 T. K. Hopkins and I. Wallerstein (eds), *World Systems Analysis*, pp. 45–57; Wallerstein *World Inequality*, (ed.), pp. 13–15; Hopkins and Wallerstein, *Processes of the World-System*, Beverly Hills, Calif., 1980, p. 179; P. Worsley, 'One world or three? A critique of the world-system theory of Immanuel Wallerstein', *SR*, 1980, pp. 299–325.
163 Wallerstein, 'The three stages of African involvement in the world-economy', in P. W. Gutkind and I. Wallerstein (eds), *The Political Economy of Contemporary Africa*, Beverly Hills, Calif., 1976, pp. 30–57.
164 Wallerstein, *The Modern World System*, Vol. 1, pp. 87, 91, 178–91; *The Modern World System*, Vol. 2, pp. 203–21, 225–41, 315; Hopkins and Wallerstein, *World Systems Analysis*, p. 47.

165 Wallerstein, *The Modern World System*, Vol. 1, pp. 51, 70–91, 336; *The Modern World System*, Vol. 2, pp. 75–6, 109; Braudel, *Les jeux de l'échange*, Paris, 1979, pp. 483–9.

166 Hopkins and Wallerstein, *World Systems Analysis*, p. 94; Wallerstein, *The Modern World System*, Vol. 2, pp. 97–8. On the secular imbalance in gold flow between East and West, see C. V.Wedgwood, *The Spoils of Time: A short history of the world*, Vol. 1: *From Earliest Times to the 16th Century*, London, 1984, p. 336.

Chapter 5

167 N. Islam, *Foreign Capital and Economic Development: Japan, India and Canada*, Tokyo, 1960 [originally Dacca, 1958], pp. 125, 230; T. Caplow, 'Are rich countries getting richer and poor countries getting poorer?', *FP*, no. 3, 1971; Arndt, *Economic Development*, pp. 89, 91; R. Cortes Conde, 'Some notes on the industrial development of Argentina and Canada in the 1920s' , in D. C. M. Platt and G. di Tella (eds), *Argentina, Australia and Canada: Studies in comparative development 1870–1965*, London, 1985.

168 I. Adelman and C. T. Morris, *Economic Growth and Social Equity in Developing Countries*, Stanford, Calif., 1973, pp. 1–2; C. Elliott and F. de Morsier, *Patterns of Poverty: A study of social and economic stratification*, New York, 1975.

169 M. Todaro, *Economics for a Developing World. An introduction to principles, problems and policies for development*, London, 1977, pp. 215–26; R. B. Sutcliffe, *Industry and Underdevelopment*, London, 1971, p. 287; M. ul Haq, *The Poverty Curtain: Choices for the Third World*, New York, 1976, pp. 12–26.

170 The case for development economics as a whole was presented in M. McQueen, *The Economics of Development: Problems and policies* (London, 1973), which was also a succinct effort at intellectual synthesis.

F. Stewart, *Technology and Underdevelopment*, London, 1977; Arndt, *Economic Development*, pp. 100–6; World Bank, *World Development Report 1979*, pp. 6–7.

The so-called Fourth Assembly of the Fourth World was convoked in May 1985 by the Gandhi Peace Foundation based in New Delhi. Despite an initial flurry of publicity, however, the impact of the 'Fourth World' has been relatively minor.

171 Arndt, *Economic Development*, pp. 101–6.

172 K. Hart, 'Informal income opportunities and urban unemployment in Ghana', *JMAS*, March 1973; Worsley, *The Three Worlds*, pp. 175, 210–13; Meier, *Leading Issues in Economic Development*, pp. 183–4, 189.

173 M. Lipton, *Why Poor People Stay Poor: A study of urban bias in world development*, London, 1977, pp. 223–9. An analogous effort, but dealing with the means to alleviate the plight of the urban poor, was undertaken in A. Gilbert and J. Gugler, *Cities, Poverty and Development*, Oxford, 1982.

174 N. Hicks and P. Streeten, 'Indicators of development: The search for a basic needs yardstick', *WD*, Vol. 7, 1979; Streeten, *First Things First*, Oxford, 1981; 'Industrialization in a unified development strategy', *WD*, January 1975; D. Seers, 'Alternative scenarios for "developing" countries: the fundamental issues' (mimeo), Brighton, 1977.

175 R. Sandbrook, *The Politics of Basic Needs – Urban aspects of assaulting poverty in Africa*, London, 1982, pp. 1, 243; Lipton, 'The absolutely deprived', *TLS*, 31 August 1984, p. 972.

176 Meier, *Leading Issues in Economic Development*, p. 395; C. Ramirez-Faria, 'La leyenda negra de la OPEP', *Politica Internacional* (Caracas), July–September 1986.

177 Seers (ed), *Dependency Theory: A critical reassessment*, London, 1981, p. 14; Arndt, *Economic Development*, pp. 120–2.

178 Seers, *Dependency Theory*, pp. 350–1.

179 Lehman, op. cit., pp. 3–6; S. Lall, 'Is dependence a useful concept in analysing underdevelopment?', *WD*, Vol. 2., no. 11, 1975.

180 G. Palma, 'Dependency and development: A critical overview', in Seers, *Dependency Theory*, pp. 63–9.

181 Seers, *Dependency Theory*, pp. 13–19.

182 P. J. O'Brien, 'Dependency revisited', in Abel and Lewis, op. cit., pp. 62–5.

183 D. C. M. Platt, 'Dependency in 19th century Latin America', *LARR*, Vol. XV, no. 1, 1980, and 'Dependency and the historian: further objections', in Abel and Lewis, op. cit., p. 36; S. J. and B. H. Stein, 'Comment', *LARR*, Vol. XV, no. 1, 1980.

184 Habib, 'Marx's perception of India', *The Marxist*, Vol. 1, 1983, pp. 123–4; Braudel, *Les jeux de l'échange*, Paris, 1979, p. 503; C. Hill, *Reformation and the Industrial Revolution: A social and economic history of Britain, 1530–1780*, London, 1967, pp. 191–5; E. J. Hobsbawm, *Industry and Empire: An economic history of Britain since 1756*, London, 1968, pp. 36–8.

185 Bairoch, 'Historical roots of underdevelopment' (see n. 73), pp. 197–200, 202–5.
186 D. Lal, *The Poverty of 'Development Economics'*, London, 1984; R. Bideleux, *Communism and Development*, London, 1985; B. Balassa, *The Newly Industrializing Countries in the World Economy*, New York, 1981; J. Bergsman, in Meier, *Leading Issues in Economic Development*, pp. 56–61; N. Harris, *The End of the Third World*, London, 1986, pp. 31–45; J. Bhagwati, *Dependence and Interdependence*, Oxford, 1985.
187 E. Mandel, 'The laws of uneven development', *NLR*, January–February 1970; C. Palloix, *L'économie mondiale*, 2 vols, Paris, 1971, and 'The self-expansion of capital on a world scale', *RRPE*, Summer 1977; P.-P.Rey, *Colonialisme, neocolonialisme et transition au capitalisme. Exemple de la 'Comilog' au Congo-Brazzaville*, Paris, 1971; H. Alavi, 'India and the colonial MOP', *SR*, 1975; E. Laclau, 'Feudalism and capitalism in Latin America', *NLR*, Vol. 67, 1977.
188 R. Brenner, 'The origins of capitalist development: A critique of neo-Smithian Marxism', *NLR*, July–August 1977; J. Weeks and E. Dore, 'International exchange and the causes of backwardness', *LAP*, Spring 1979; J. G. Taylor, *From Modernization to Modes of Production: A critique of the sociologies of development and underdevelopment*, London, 1979, pp. ix–xxii.
189 N. Harris, *The End of the Third World*, London, 1986, pp. 69, 78, 116–17, 137–9, 187, 200.
190 I. Vujacic, 'Marx and Engels on Development and underdevelopment: the restoration of a certain coherence', *HPE*, Spring 1988.
191 A. Foster-Carter, 'The mode of production controversy', *NLR*, January–February 1978; I. Roxborough, *Theories of Underdevelopment*, London, 1979, pp, 42–90, 159–63; Worsley, *The Three Worlds*, pp. 41, 189, 204, 302; C. A. Barone, *Marxist Thought on Imperialism: Survey and critique*, London, 1985.
192 Braudel, *Capitalism and Material Life, 1400–1800*, New York, 1973 [originally Paris, 1967]; *Les jeux de l'échange*, Paris, 1979, pp. 7–9, 36, 79, 113, 197–200, 327, 329, 403, 413, 463, 494, 507, 535–6; *Le temps du monde*, Paris, 1979, pp. 74, 105, 118, 145–6, 221, 332, 472, 480, 511–13, 528–9, 538–9.
193 Braudel, *Les jeux de l'échange*, pp. 102, 111, 498–9, 503, 519–34, 540; *Le temps du monde*, pp. 428–61.

194 Braudel, *Capitalism and Material Life*, pp. 18–20; E. L. Jones, *The European Miracle: Environments, economies and geopolitics in the history of Europe and Asia*, Cambridge, 1981, pp. 5, 8, 18–41, 57, 69, 73, 84, 93, 102–3, 108, 117, 159–71, 181, 226–38. Jones had already advanced some of his ideas on despotism in 'The historic role of agrarian change in economic development', in E. L. Jones and S. J. Woolf (eds), *Agrarian Change and Economic Development*, London, 1969.

195 A. W. Crosby, *Ecological Imperialism: The biological expansion of Europe, 900–1900*, Cambridge, 1986, p. 21; Jones, *The European Miracle*, p. 13; Bosschère, *Clefs pour le tiers monde*, Paris, 1973, pp. 12–17.

196 J. J. Putnam, 'The search for modern humans', *NGM*, October 1988, pp. 438–77; *The Economist*, 13 August 1988, pp. 77–80.

Further reading

R. T. Anstey, *The Atlantic Slave Trade and the British Abolition 1760–1810*, London, 1975.

G. Arrighi, *La geometria dell'imperialismo*, Milan, 1978.

F. Braudel, *On History*, Chicago, 1980.

J. B. Bury, *The Idea of Progress: An inquiry into its origins and growth*, London, 1920.

R. H. Chilcote and J. C. Edelstein (eds), *Latin America: The struggle with dependency and beyond*, New York, 1974.

S. Clarkson, *The Soviet Theory of Development: India and the TW in Marxist-Leninist scholarship*, Toronto, 1978.

P. D. Curtin (ed.), *Imperialism*, New York, 1971.

C. Dewey and A. G. Hopkins (eds), *The Imperial Impact: Studies in the economic history of Africa and India*, London, 1978.

E. D. Genovese, *The Political Economy of Slavery: Studies in the economy and society of the slave South*, New York, 1961.

A. Gerschenkron, *Economic Backwardness in Historical Perspective*, Cambridge, Mass., 1952.

J. A. Gobineau, *Essai sur l'inégalité des races humaines*, 4 vols, Paris, 1853–55.

I. Habib, 'Potentialities of capitalist development in the economy of Mughal India', *JEH*, March 1969.

M. Harris, *Cannibals and Kings: The origins of cultures*, London, 1978.

R. L. Heilbroner, *The Nature and Logic of Capitalism*, New York, 1985.

R. Hilton, *The Transition from Feudalism to Capitalism*, London, 1976.

R. F. Holland, *European Decolonization 1918–1981*, London, 1985.

R. Jenkins, *Exploitation: The world power structure and the inequality of nations*, London, 1970.

V. G. Kiernan, *The Lords of Human Kind*, London, 1969.

D. Lach, *Asia in the Making of Europe*, Vol. I: *The Century of Discovery*, Chicago, 1965.

D. S. Landes, *The Unbound Prometheus: Technological change and industrial development in Western Europe from 1750 to the present*, London, 1969.

I. Lewis (ed.), *History and Social Anthropology*, London, 1968.
T. H. von Laue, *The World Revolution of Modernization. The twentieth century in global perspective*, New York, 1987.
S. B. Liss, *Marxist Thought in Latin America*, Berkeley, Calif., 1984.
J. Lynch, *Spain under the Habsburgs*, Vol. I: *Empire and Absolutism. 1516–1598*, Oxford, 1964.
J. Lynch, *The Spanish–American Revolutions 1808–1826*, New York, 1973.
E. Mandel, *Long Waves of Capitalist Development*, Cambridge, 1980
E. Mandel, 'L'accumulation primitive et l'industrialisation du tiers monde', in V. Fay (ed.), *En partant du 'Capital'*, Paris, 1968.
R. Minami, *The Economic Development of Japan: A quantitative study*, London, 1986.
R. Minami, *The Turning Point in Economic Development: Japan's experience*, Tokyo, 1973.
B. Moore jr., *Injustice: The social bases of obedience and revolt*, New York, 1978.
B. Moore jr., *Social Origins of Dicatatorship and Democracy. Lord and peasant in the making of the modern world*, Boston, 1966.
M. Morner, *Race Mixture in the History of Latin America*, Boston, 1967.
J. Morris, *Pax Britannica. The climax of an empire*, London, 1968.
K. M. Panikkar, *Asia and Western Dominance. A survey of the Vasco da Gama epoch of Asian history 1498–1945*, London, 1953.
G. Parker, *The Military Revolution: Military innovation and the rise of the West, 1500–1800*, Cambridge, 1988.
J. Petras (ed), *Latin America: From dependence to revolution*, New York, 1973.
J. R. S. Phillips, *The Medieval Expansion of Europe*, Oxford, 1988.
H. Pirenne, *Histoire économique et sociale du moyen âge*, Paris, 11963.
D. C. M. Platt, *Finance, Trade, and Politics in British Foreign Policy 1815–1914*, Oxford, 1986.
R. Prebisch, *Nueva politica comercial para el desarrollo*, Mexico, 1964.
P. Ramet and F. Lopez–Alves, 'Moscow and the revolutionary left in Latin America', *Orbis*, Summer 1984.
O. Ransford, *'Bid the sickness cease': Disease in the history of Black Africa*, London, 1983.
L. G. Reynolds, *Economic Growth in the Third World, 1850–1980*, New Haven, Conn., 1985.
M. Sagrega, *Los racismos en America 'Latina'*, Buenos Aires, 1974.

A. Sauvy, *Théorie générale de la population*, 2 vols, Paris, 1952.
J. R. Seeley, *The Expansion of England*, London 1882.
E. Churchill Semple, *Influences of Geographic Environment on the Basis of Ratzel's System of Anthropo-Geography*, London, 1911.
N. Smith, *Uneven Development: Nature, capital and the production of space*, London, 1984.
S. J. and B. H. Stein, *The Colonial Heritage of Latin America: Essays in economic dependence in perspective*, New York, 1970.
S. J. Stern, 'Feudalism, capitalism and the world-system in the perspective of Latin America and the Caribbean', *American Historical Review*, October 1988.
T. R. Trautman, *Lewis Henry Morgan and the Invention of Kinship*, University of California, 1987.
R. W. Tucker, *The Inequality of Nations*, New York, 1977.
B. Warren, 'Imperialism and capitalist industrialization', *NLR*, September–October 1973.
H. Wolpe (ed.), *The Articulation of Modes of Production. Essays from 'Economy and Society'*, London, 1980.

Index